Inward Being and Outward Identity: The Orthodox Churches in the 21st Century

Special Issue Editor
John A. Jillions

MDPI • Basel • Beijing • Wuhan • Barcelona • Belgrade

MDPI

Special Issue Editor
John A. Jillions
St Vladimir's Orthodox Theological Seminary
USA

Editorial Office
MDPI AG
St. Alban-Anlage 66
Basel, Switzerland

This edition is a reprint of the Special Issue published online in the open access journal *Religions* (ISSN 2077-1444) from 2016–2018 (available at: http://www.mdpi.com/journal/religions/special_issues/orthodox_churches).

For citation purposes, cite each article independently as indicated on the article page online and as indicated below:

Lastname, F.M.; Lastname, F.M. Article title. *Journal Name* **Year**, *Article number*, page range.

First Editon 2018

ISBN 978-3-03842-697-4 (Pbk)
ISBN 978-3-03842-698-1 (PDF)

Table of Contents

About the Special Issue Editor

John A. Jillions is Chancellor of the Orthodox Church in America and Associate Professor of Religion and Culture at St Vladimir's Orthodox Theological Seminary in Yonkers, New York. He was a founding director of the Institute for Orthodox Christian Studies in Cambridge, UK and served as its first Principal from 1997 to 2002. In 2003–2011 he taught at the Sheptytsky Institute for Eastern Christian Studies and Saint Paul University (Ottawa). He was educated at McGill University (Montreal, BA Economics), St Vladimir's Orthodox Theological Seminary (MDiv, DMin) and Aristotle University of Thessalonica in Greece (PhD, New Testament.) His publishing, research and teaching have been in the areas of New Testament, 20th century Orthodox thought, ecumenism, and pastoral theology. As an Orthodox priest he has served communities in the USA, Australia, Greece, England and Canada.

religions

MDPI

Editorial

Introduction: "Inward Being and Outward Identity: The Orthodox Churches in the 21st Century"

John A. Jillions

Saint Vladimir's Orthodox Theological Seminary, 575 Scarsdale Road, Yonkers, NY 10707, USA;
jjillions@svots.edu

Received: 19 October 2017; Accepted: 23 October 2017; Published: 24 October 2017

As the title indicates, taken together the fourteen papers in this Special Issue of *Religions* give a broad view of what might be called the inner and outer life of the Orthodox Church, with each of the papers focusing on a particular area of research and reflection.

In recent decades, there has been an explosion of books and articles on the Orthodox Churches, both Eastern Orthodox and Oriental Orthodox (the articles in this issue focus on the former.) There is widespread interest in the spiritual life of the Orthodox Church: prayer, worship, theology, saints, art, music, ascetic practices and ways of living, monasticism, and how its self-understanding as a repository of ancient Christian tradition is interwoven and evolving in what Charles Taylor calls the cross-pressures of the secular age.

At the same time, the quarter-century following the collapse of the Soviet Union has seen the Orthodox Church emerge from persecution and martyrdom to rebuild the infrastructure of churches, monasteries and Christian social services decimated by the Communist years. In that process the Orthodox Churches have also become powerful public, political, nationalist and cultural forces in Russia and Eastern Europe. They are now frequently perceived as closely aligned with restrictive government policies, suspicious of democracy, freedom, human rights and minorities. In contrast, Orthodox Christians in the Middle East live a tenuous existence—often shared with Muslims—in the face of war, sectarian violence and official and unofficial duress and persecution. Meanwhile, in areas of emigration and mission in Western Europe, the Americas, Australia, parts of sub-Saharan Africa and other regions outside its traditional homelands Orthodox Christianity is also taking hold as a self-consciously distinct minority religion that is attracting a steady stream of converts while struggling for its identity in a secular environment increasingly hostile to traditional Christianity.

In the midst of these competing global forces, and an Orthodox world dominated by Old World Churches, the leaders of the disparate and often quarrelsome branches of Eastern Orthodoxy, led by Patriarch Bartholomew of Constantinople as "first among equals," have been attempting to bring a measure of unity as they seek to remain true to the "faith which was once for all delivered to the saints" (Jude 1:3) while also confronting the challenges of the 21st century.

An important step in that direction was taken at "The Holy and Great Council" of the Eastern Orthodox Churches which took place on Crete in June 2016 during the week of Pentecost (https://www.holycouncil.org). Patriarch Bartholomew presided, and although the Council's status and authority are disputed by several of the Orthodox Churches which did not send delegations (Antioch, Russia, Georgia, Bulgaria) the fact remains that this council was decades in preparation and was the largest and most diverse council of Eastern Orthodox bishops in many centuries. The agenda was modest and did not attempt to address some of the most pressing issues facing the Orthodox Churches, but it provoked some valuable discussion (see for example Nathanael Symeonides 2016.) At the very least it demonstrated awareness of questions that the Orthodox must consider and act upon.

> The Holy and Great Council has **opened our horizon** towards the contemporary diverse and multifarious world. It has emphasised our responsibility in place and in time, ever

with the perspective of eternity. The Orthodox Church, preserving intact her Sacramental and Soteriological character, is sensitive to the pain, the distress and the cry for justice and peace of the peoples of the world. She "proclaims day after day the good tidings of His salvation, announcing His glory among the nations and His wonders among all peoples" (Psalm 95). (Holy and Great Council 2016, Message 12)

How well are Orthodox Churches listening and responding to the changing cultures they are living in? And in these new conditions what does it mean to be faithful to the inner life of the Church, while being engaged "for the life of the world"? These are the main underlying questions the papers here are attempting to address.

One of the particular aims of this collection has been to give readers unfamiliar with Orthodox Christianity a set of articles that are at once both academically rigorous and also convey the inner dimension of the Church. This means that a number of these scholars are participants in as well as observers of Orthodox life, and can therefore attempt to translate for outsiders that mysterious personal dimension that is at the heart of any religion, and without which descriptions are incomplete. As Andrew Louth has written, Christian theology is not simply a matter of learning, "it is tested and manifested in a life that lives close to the mystery of God in Christ...and, so far as it is discerned, awakens in the heart a sense of wondering awe which is the light in which we see light" (Louth 1983, p. 147.)

The articles collected here address a range of theoretical issues and contemporary cases that illustrate them.

In "Orthodoxy in Engagement with the 'Outer' World: The Dynamic of the 'Inward-Outward' Cycle" **Razvan Porumb** looks at the forces that drive Orthodox inner life and its engagement with the secular and ecumenical worlds. **Rico Monge** explores secularization theory and its relation to Russia in "'Neither Victim nor Executioner': Essential Insights from Secularization Theory for the Revitalization of the Russian Orthodox Church in the Contemporary World." The increasing influence of religion on filmmaking in "post-secular" Russia is the subject of "Knocking on a Saint's Door, or a Quest for Holiness in a Post-Secular Society" by **Natalia Naydenova and Yulia Ebzeeva**.

Two articles look specifically at Orthodox thinking (and action) in relation to other religions and other Christian bodies. **Paul Ladouceur** gives a comprehensive overview and analysis in "Religious Diversity in Modern Orthodox Thought." In "Ecumenism: Rapprochement Through Co-working to Reconciliation" **Cyril Hovorun** reconsiders the methods of ecumenism and looks at the example of co-working by Christians from different churches during the Ukrainian Maidan (the revolution of 2014) as signaling a more fruitful methodology.

Dumitru Staniloae (1903–1993) was the foremost Romanian theologian of the 20th century. He argued that Orthodox emphasis on liturgy needs to be balanced with service to people. **Ionut Untea** considers this in "Service and Pro-Existence in the Thought of Romanian Theologian Dumitru Staniloae: A Path for the Orthodox Church Facing the Challenge of Globalization."

Two articles address specific contemporary issues: ecology and sexuality. **Elizabeth Theokritoff** surveys Orthodox thinking on the environment in "Green Patriarch, Green Patristics: Reclaiming the Deep Ecology of Christian Tradition." Orthodox writers are increasingly going deep into the sources of Orthodox thought and practice to consider the spiritual significance of the material universe and the place of human beings within it. **Joseph William Black**, who teaches theology in Kenya, analyzes the results of a survey of some 500 Kenyan youth in "Sex, Abortion, Domestic Violence and Other Unmentionables: Orthodox Christian Youth in Kenya and Windows into Their Attitudes about Sex."

Two of the contributions bring a more personal dimension to the collection, which is entirely appropriate for an issue dealing with "inward being." **Mary Ford's** essay, "Reflections on Reading the Scriptures as an Orthodox Christian," argues that while historical criticism is valuable in an Orthodox context (she teaches New Testament and hermeneutics in an Orthodox seminary), the ultimate purpose of reading Scripture is to become holy, and this "is achieved primarily through living the gospel." **Kyriacos C. Markides** reflects on thirty years of field research as a sociologist in "The

Healing Spirituality of Eastern Orthodoxy: A Personal Journey of Discovery." He argues that the spiritual practices of the Christian East may contribute to "the cultivation of the intuitive, spiritual side of human beings that has been repressed over the centuries because of the dominance of rationalism and scientific materialism."

Liturgy is at the heart of Orthodox life. **Christina M. Gschwandtner** examines its philosophical underpinnings in "Mimesis or Metamorphosis? Eastern Orthodox Liturgical Practice and Its Philosophical Background." She explores how liturgy negotiates imitation and transformation, inner and outer, heavenly and earthly. **Nicholas Denysenko's** "Death and Dying in Orthodox Liturgy" looks at the ways liturgy shapes the inner and outer lives of worshippers as rehearsal of dying and rising to new life. **Boris Knorre**, of the National Research University Higher School of Economics in Moscow, looks at Alexander Schmemann's ecclesiology in light of experience in contemporary Russia, in "The Problem of the Church's Defensiveness and Reductionism in Fr. Alexander Schmemann's Ecclesiology (Based on His Journals)."

Alexander Schmemann (1921–1983) was one of the leading Orthodox theologians of the 20th century, and his thought was grounded in the Orthodox experience of liturgy. To bring this volume to a close, **Michael Plekon** reviews and critically assesses Schmemann's life, work and continuing significance in "The Liturgy of Life: Alexander Schmemann."

Conflicts of Interest: The author declares no conflict of interest.

References

Holy and Great Council. 2016. Message of the Holy and Great Council of the Orthodox Church. Available online: https://www.holycouncil.org/-/message (accessed on 18 October 2017).

Louth, Andrew. 1983. *Discerning the Mystery: An Essay on the Nature of Theology.* Oxford: Clarendon Press.

Archimandrite Nathanael Symeonides, ed. 2016. *Toward the Holy and Great Council: Theological Reflections.* New York: Greek Orthodox Archdiocese of America.

religions

MDPI

Article

Orthodoxy in Engagement with the 'Outer' World. The Dynamic of the 'Inward-Outward' Cycle

Razvan Porumb

Institute for Orthodox Christian Studies, The Cambridge Theological Federation, 25–27 High Street Chesterton, Cambridge CB4 1NQ, UK; grp29@cam.ac.uk

Received: 24 May 2017; Accepted: 20 July 2017; Published: 25 July 2017

Abstract: This study explores the tension between the centripetal and centrifugal forces informing the activity of the Orthodox Church—both with regard to its interaction with the secular world and the wider ecumenical scene. The Church is called to look inwardly as an essential connection with its intimate sacramental life. This contraction must be followed organically by a movement of expansion—a continuing sacramental interaction with the secular local context and the wider Christian world. This cyclical movement (inward-outward) informs all Christian life in a mutually perpetuating rotation. Although the reaction to any engagement with the 'outer' dimensions is often one of rejection, it is nevertheless crucial as it brings fullness and fulfils the vocation and identity of the Orthodox Church.

Keywords: practical theology; ecumenism; Orthodoxy

1. Introduction

An attempt to construe both practical theology and ecumenism from an Orthodox point of view—in conjunction—was first occasioned, in my case, some fourteen years ago, while studying for an Master of Arts in Pastoral Theology in Cambridge. Not only was I—a lay Romanian student—to gauge and examine my own involvement within the pastoral component of my native Orthodox context, but I was challenged to do so in the uniquely ecumenical context of learning in the Cambridge Theological Federation. What started, however, as a thankless, overwhelmingly intricate task, gave rise to some significant realisations that inspired much of my subsequent understanding of theology. Having also been involved for quite some time in a number of ecumenical milieus and blessed with having acquired a number of inspiring friendships across the world, not far into my research I came to the understanding that ecumenism deals primarily with the inter-relationship between people. That, despite being generally perceived as having a 'wider' global, international, inter-denominational orientation, ecumenism starts at the personal level of every Christian. Ecumenism does not seek unity for the sake of unity alone, or as the goal of an established programme or agenda, but it seeks the communion in friendship and love of the Triune God, for sharing the mystery of the one Body of Christ. Ecumenism also springs out of love and concern for our fellow human beings' salvation and wellbeing. In its essence—I came to realise—the ecumenical vector is akin to pastoral care, it is a ministry, a type of pastoral care that attempts to reach beyond the parish, the diocese, the denomination, and into the wider *oikumene*. 'Ecumenical' equals 'pastoral' in a wider-reaching sense.

As we will see in the following section, one of the assumptions of Orthodox theology is that all theology is in fact 'pastoral' or 'practical'. An initial mention should be made that the term 'pastoral theology' is not used here in its customary Orthodox understanding, which would place it in immediate correlation with the work of the ministers of the Church (priests or bishops). 'Pastoral' is used here in its traditionally Protestant British understanding where it refers to practices that 'bear upon or form a concern for the Christian community' (Woodward and Stephen 2000, p. 6). This communitarian, society-oriented focus is of particular usefulness to this study—as is the implicit connection between pastoral and practical theology. Indeed, in the British context, the terms 'practical theology' and 'pastoral theology' are interdependent to such a degree that they are often used interchangeably or as a twin concept. While being a branch of practical theology, pastoral theology is arguably its most vital and relevant form of expression as it addresses the immediate and stringent necessities of society. Again, this communitarian focus is of particular relevance in the context of this study, given its specific aim, and so the terms 'practical' and 'pastoral' will be used here in close association.

If all theology is presumed thus to be 'pastoral' or 'practical', by the same token it can also be said that all theology has an ecumenical imperative—as will be shown in the second part of this study. Both for practical theology and for ecumenism, there is an emphasis on contextuality, praxis (the practice of theology as opposed to its theoretical approach), and action. To be ecumenical is understood to imply common action, social involvement, a contextual approach (both to groups and individuals), which are also the very goals of pastoral/practical theology/care. A distinctive element in the case of ecumenism is the search for unity, for the catholicity of the Church of Christ, but this is a calling to all theology, irrespective of its focus. Thus, simply doing theology—in its original plenary 'holistic' understanding, as participatory endeavor—means implicitly to be at the same time pastoral and ecumenical.

However, Orthodox theology presents baffling internal tensions in both its practical and ecumenical dimensions. When doing practical theology, the Orthodox waver between the calling to personal intimate prayer, between prayer within the context of the local liturgical congregation and the outer involvement within the wider Church community and society at large. This is not only demonstrated by what seems to be an insistence on liturgical and spiritual life, but also by the rather more diffident unstructured approach the Orthodox seem to have towards social involvement. The Orthodox Church has received a degree of criticism for being overly 'other-worldly', with a 'tendency to look inwards and "above" the affairs of this world, thus not focusing on direct missionary action or social service' (Molokotos-Liederman 2010)[1]. Its 'established reputation', according to John Meyendorff, 'consists in its purported detachment from historical realities, its concern with mysticism, its one-sided dedication to liturgical contemplation of eternal truths, and its forgetfulness of the concrete needs of human society, as such' (Meyendorff 1979, p. 118). This is something that influential Orthodox theologian Georges Florovsky also mentioned when referring to the Russian Orthodox context where, in his view, 'there was no important movement of social Christianity' (Belopopsky 2003)[2].

As regards the Orthodox Church's relation to ecumenism, this is widely regarded as a 'problem' or predicament. The dilemma and associated Orthodox rationale revolves around the strong Orthodox belief that the Orthodox Church is the 'one, holy and catholic' Church. This simple algorithm follows a clear-cut logic: the Orthodox Church is the one, true Church of Christ, and, since there can be only one Church of Christ (not several 'churches' of Christ), the churches that are not Orthodox are simply outside the one true Church. Reunion of Christians would implicitly mean for the non-Orthodox re-joining the one true Church—the Orthodox Church. Ecumenism, as a move towards the reunion of Christians, can therefore only mean the re-joining of and reunion with the Orthodox Church.

A small—though not fringe or insignificant—and certainly very vocal contingent of Orthodox anti-ecumenists view the mere participation of the Orthodox in ecumenical meetings as a betrayal of their identity and of the truth of faith. In general lines, they accuse Orthodox participants in ecumenical circles of conceding too easily to the dominant Protestant ethos. They argue that this has led to a 'diluted' expression of genuine Orthodox ecclesiology, and to the presentation of two contradictory views: on the one hand to an affirmation of the Orthodox Church as the One, True Church, but on the other,

---

[1] An article based on research commissioned by the International Orthodox Christian Charities (IOCC) between 2008 and 2009.
[2] Paper initially presented (in an earlier version) at the Cambridge Institute for Orthodox Christian Studies, Cambridge, UK, 2003.

to an acceptance of a 'plurality' of Churches as part of the Christian world. It is often implied that such contradictions may lead to a rupture or schism within the Orthodox Church or may compromise its integrity. As for the non-Orthodox, these are often described by the anti-ecumenical groups as perilous 'heretics', who attempt somehow to corrupt the purity of the Church. They are 'enemies' or devious adversaries, no longer viewed as our neighbours or fellow Christians.

Again we see here an instinctual reaction of rejection of any outward movement towards the reality situated outside of what are perceived to be ecclesiological borders of the Orthodox Church. The focus tends to be 'inwards', whereas the outward vector is viewed with suspicion and uncertainty. The outside world is once again shut out as a foregone peril and a risky commitment that ought to be avoided. The ensuing problem here—as this study suggests—is not simply an incomplete or insufficient participation of the Orthodox in societal action or ecumenical exchange, however regrettable such shortcomings may be.

The issue is that, in both cases of social and catholicity-bound orientation, failure to engage 'outwards' represents a betrayal of true Orthodox theological commitment and neglect of the original calling of Orthodoxy, which seeks not only to safeguard and internalise the truth of faith, but also to share it with the world in the spirit of love, courage and hope. As we will see below, even when seen as inheritance of 'pure' Christianity and cherished treasure and gift from Christ, Orthodoxy was nonetheless granted to the Orthodox to share and witness with the whole world, with the entire humanity—both closer-by in the societies they live in, but also farther apart in the more distant human quarters. This is not an optional or redundant vector, and failure to understand and follow this calling equates with a major identity crisis for the Orthodox. The inward focus must be followed by an outward movement—in a continuous pulsation—which is what this study will attempt to demonstrate.

2. Inwards and Outwards in Orthodox Practical Theology

When addressing practical theology—as well as pretty much every other theological theme—the Orthodox will often start by talking about their life in the Church or about praying for each other. Orthodox scholar John Jillions identifies two essential aspects of Orthodox pastoral theology: 'liturgical life ('where two or three are gathered', Mt. 18:20) and the inner life ('go into your room and shut the door', Mt. 6:6)' (Jillions 2003, p. 164). Each of these aspects, in Jillions' view, reinforces the other (Jillions 2003, p. 164.). For a non-Orthodox this approach may hardly seem convincing, as attendance of Church services and praying for one another does little in practical terms for helping our brothers and sisters in need. After all, 'practical' or 'pastoral' implies an interaction with the others, something that happens outside of oneself, something to do with reaching out to the others. And yet the Orthodox tend to start from inner life, from a withdrawal within. This approach reveals a fundamental tension in Orthodox theology between gathering within the protective space of the Church and engaging with the world, between withdrawal and engagement, between contemplation and praxis. It points to an apparently paradoxical polarity: withdrawal from society, or even rejection of the secular world, but, at the same time, the conscience that the 'outside' secular world needs also be embraced. While these two directions may seem mutually exclusive, they work together as a complementary pair. Mention should be made at this point that this is not, by any means, a tension present only in the Orthodox tradition—as it is bound to underline all Christian thought, irrespective of tradition. Nor is it a novel angle in the field of theology. This study aims to explore how this polarity interplays with the areas of practical/pastoral theology and ecumenism—from an Orthodox vantage point.

This contradictory approach could bring about a certain apathy among Orthodox faithful with regard to their practical social involvement—and we saw earlier that a number of Orthodox theologians think this to be the case. However, in its proper understanding, liturgical life is pastoral *par excellence*, as the Eucharistic liturgy should shape a particular type of community, cultivating in each member of the Church an attitude of self-giving to the other members of the community. As for prayer, this is not properly seen as passive contemplation and individual exercise, but as an inner state generating action. In an ideal world, prayer should breed and inform both the liturgical life of the faithful and their inner life.

One cannot emphasize enough the centrality of the Liturgy in the Orthodox tradition—seen primarily as a sacramental space, a transfigured universe centred around the mystery of the Eucharist. In the words of Father Georges Florovsky: 'Christianity is a liturgical religion. The Church is first of all a worshipping community. Worship comes first, doctrine and discipline second' (Ware 1964, p. 271). 'Orthodoxy sees human beings above all else as liturgical creatures', also wrote celebrated author Kallistos Ware, 'who are most truly themselves when they glorify God, and who find their perfection and self-fulfilment in worship' (Ware 1964, p. 272). The Eucharistic Liturgy is not to be seen as self-centred service and action, but as a service for the building of the one Body of Christ. In theory at least, the liturgical assembly is the Father's House, where the invitation to the banquet of the heavenly bread is constantly voiced and addressed not only to the members of the Church, but also to strangers and to the whole world. This banquet is meant to transport the liturgical community beyond this reality into the life of the Triune God. It is a foretaste of the Kingdom of Heaven, a journey from our world into the reality of God and back. It is the main channel of communion and communication with God. If we are to recognize the face of Christ in the face of our neighbour, and if we are to show Christ's responsibility and love to our neighbours, we must be in communion of love with God and always be seeking to deepen still further this life-giving communion. For indeed, 'this is the nature of love: the more we depart from the centre and do not love God, the more we depart from the neighbour' (Dorotheus of Gaza and Ciobotea 2001). The spiritual life of the faithful and their individual prayer should be both a preparation for the participation in the Liturgy and, at the same time, a continuation of the prayerful state achieved during the Eucharistic event. In prayer the human being 'converses with God, he/she enters, through grace, into communion with Him, and lives in God' (Theophan the Recluse 1966).

Undistinguishable from prayer in the Orthodox tradition is the practice of withdrawn self-examination or *hesychast* life. Hesychasm (from the Greek ἡσυχία, *esychia*, meaning 'silence' or 'stillness') refers to the Eastern tradition of contemplation, as practiced mostly in monastic communities or by hermits, but which remains an injunction for all lay society as well. It is based primarily on Christ's instruction in Matthew 6:6: 'But when you pray, go into your room and shut the door and pray to your Father who is in secret; and your Father who sees in secret will reward you'.

Shutting the world out temporarily in quiet and secluded prayer and focusing intently on their 'secret' dialogue with God, on their inner spiritual state constitutes for the Orthodox the starting point of all life within the Church. Of course, lay people cannot be *hesychasts* in the same way that monastics can. Too literal an interpretation and application of *hesychasm* could ultimately lead to a dysfunctional life within society. But the community of the Church can use the *hesychast* model of silent still prayer as a paradigm inspiring their spiritual lives. Jillions emphasizes that 'the invisible but transformed inner life leads to visibly transformed action. [...] Far from abandoning the world, the transfiguration of the world—society, economics, politics, art, music—becomes possible through Christian praying, living, and acting from within this transfigured inner life' (Jillions 2003, p. 166). And, referring to the *hesychast* paradigm, Metropolitan Hierotheos of Nafpaktos, also notes that: 'this activity takes on, at the same time, social character, for when the human person is treated, he/she becomes at once the most sociable of persons' (Hierotheos 1994, p. 12). Transfiguration through prayer is seen here as a healing process which prepares the Christian for a loving, responsible interaction with his/her neighbours. This, in turn—it is understood—can prompt a gradual change of the entire society.

A significant tension or polarity becomes evident—between the rejection and the embracing of the secular world, between withdrawal from society and its sanctification by bringing Christ's presence in the midst of the secular world. And the most emphatic model for this tension in the Orthodox world is the polarity between monasticism and life in society. Monasticism represents total and complete devotion to a life in prayer, to a life revolving around the mysteries of the Church. But it is also seen in the Orthodox context as a rejection of the secular world, world which is inherently bound to a downward spiral and follows a life different from the life in Christ. Can then Christians be expected to engage with the traitorous secular society in which they live? Is that not, in fact, what Christians are called to do according to the communitarian model they are supposed to follow in their everyday life?

Addressing these two diverging views of the world that Orthodox communities hold, withdrawal and involvement, Orthodox American theologian Stanley Harakas brings a very revealing vision, which addresses not only the monastic universe, but the entire Orthodox society:

> One [tendency] is a radical rejection of the world. In this vision only the 'people of God' are holy, while the world by definition finds itself in full submission to the demonic. [...] The other tendency is contrasted to this essential denigration and rejection of the world in what might be called the incarnational vision of the world. Here, the Church sees itself as obligated to reach out to the world, to be somehow a vehicle for injecting at least some measure of the divine in an environment which has rejected it, but which cannot find its own purpose and fulfilment without it. Christian evangelisation seeks to convert it; philanthropy to correct its worst effects upon the lives of people; and social concern to modify its structures for the sake of fairness and justice. (Harakas 1988, pp. 13–14)

It is then in this incarnational vision of the world wherein the Orthodox practical and pastoral theological process takes place, the space in which philanthropy and social concern constitute vehicles for inoculating God's presence into the world. These two contrasting tendencies are held together in an 'unresolved, yet mutually influential paradox' (Harakas 1988, p. 14). Human persons seem to travel tirelessly back and forth between contemplative isolation and immersion in the perilous societal reality, bringing Christ's divine peace and love to the society, while at the same time carrying the community back with them into the solitude of prayer. While in seclusion, they can only find fullness by relating to the community that speaks of and connects them with God's triune society. When in the world, they feel like foreigners in an inauspicious secular land, seen as inherently rejecting the truths of faith. In this theological vision, they are rotating incessantly between the two realities and finding sense and strength only in the element of communion—communion with God through the sacraments, as well as the parallel communion with society through a prayerful ministry to the others.

A reconciliation of this apparent contradiction is resolved in the Orthodox world through the special dynamic that exists between monastic communities and the secular world. Monasteries are not closed off to society, their withdrawal does not mean a 'breaking off' from the Church community in the city. They are seen as simply drawing to one side to pray, while society is invited outside of its comfort zone to explore such spaces where they can encounter a different paradigm of Christian life. Monasteries do interact with society, sometimes very directly, by organising projects to help the poor, the sick, and the suffering, according to the model of the ancient Basiliades, which were essentially hospitals run by monastic communities. Certainly there is a great deal of spiritual counselling taking place in monastic communities, and people from the secular world often use them as alternatives to secular therapy programmes. Monasticism is not a paradigm whereby a group of people try to save themselves, but it represents a structure that tries to save the world by withdrawing from the world. While this may not always be mirrored by the reality on the ground, this nevertheless constitutes the theological vision that underlies monastic reality in the Orthodox world.

The Orthodox model of pastoral or practical involvement is then not annulled by this tension between the 'inner'-'outer' vectors as a irreconcilable contradiction, but in fact rests on it as a positive constructive complementarity. Orthodox pastoral theology—indeed all theology—is seen as a continuous inward-outward motion, without ever breaking up into its elements. There is not an 'inward' without an 'outward'; there is never any rest or status quo but always a dynamic ceaseless pulsation. A model for such a dynamic model was proposed by Dyonisius the Areopagite (5th–6th century AD) in a helpfully visual description:

> And the soul hath (1) a circular movement—viz. an introversion from things without and the unified concentration of its spiritual powers—which gives it a kind of fixed revolution,

and, turning it from the multiplicity without, draws it together first into itself. (2) And the soul moves with a spiral motion whensoever (according to its capacity) it is enlightened with truths of Divine Knowledge [. . .]. (3) And it moves straight forward when it does not enter into itself to feel the stirrings of its spiritual unity (for this, as I said, is the circular motion), but goes forth unto the things around it and feels an influence coming even from the outward world, as from a rich abundance of cunning tokens, drawing it unto the simple unity of contemplative acts. (Rolt 2007, pp. 98–99)

This three-stage movement is in fact characteristic for any Orthodox approach to theology: the movement within; the movement within is pulled upwards; the circular motion, freed of its inward centripetal drive, turns longitudinally towards the external world. This is repeated in a cycle that characterises the fundamental dynamic of Christian life: 'retreat to engage', an individual growth in Christ that is shared with and 'transferred' to one's community. Humans move inward so that they can move outward. Although Dyonisius mentions the outward motion as focusing on 'a rich abundance of tokens', the internal logic of Orthodox theology implicitly connects this outward movement with human society. There cannot be theologically any action in isolation, but only within the community of the Church, according to the Trinitarian model of God, in the image of whom we humans function—as one multi-hypostatic being.

This possible Orthodox model of practical theology, of societal commitment and ministry focuses first on one's centripetal movement of inner exploration, on one's intimate dialogue with Christ in the Trinity. The faithful are thus 'replenished' with God's gift of love, their thoughts and feelings re-calibrated and tuned according to the pattern of the Triune love. The second stage is that of the journey of *theosis*, when the faithful join the communion of the Trinity as the ultimate fulfilment and plenitude of life. This communitarian transcendence takes practitioners to the third stage, when rotation becomes centrifugal and embraces the world and society. This third stage brings completion and gives meaning to the theological act, and is best encapsulated in the liturgical gathering centred around the Eucharist and the sacraments, both inside, within the walls of the church, but also outside the church, in people's homes and in the squares of the city.[3]

Thus the sacramental life of the Church has two joined dimensions: the 'sacrament of the altar' and the 'sacrament of the neighbour'. The liturgical life and the societal involvement of the faithful are brought into an inseparable complementarity. The Orthodox regard any activity within the Church community—including the pastoral or social one—as implausible, should this not be related or connected to the spiritual, liturgical and sacramental life of the Church. The 'sacrament of the brother'—the starting point of any pastoral/societal process in the Orthodox context—has its roots in the Eucharistic Liturgy, which it continues and completes. By seeking and achieving deification, by entering into communion with the head of the Church which is Christ, the faithful are implicitly entering into a special and genuine communion with one another. The Church thus becomes a communion of deification, whence union with God starts in communion with the other humans.

Therefore, what may initially seem as a contradiction, becomes the very internal logic of Orthodox pastoral theology. Yes, Orthodox practical theology does start with a 'self-centred' movement 'within', of prayer and introspection, but only in order to then move 'without', towards a selfless communion with the Church community and with the entire society—starting at the local level and advancing in expanding concentric circles to humanity at large, as we will also see next. Like in a breathing movement, the inner vector is to be followed by an outer vector, and then back inwards—ad infinitum. The inner-outer dialectic is not a contradiction but a rotation.

---

3   A more detailed description of this proposed model can be found in "An Orthodox Model of Practical/Pastoral Theology" (Porumb 2017, pp. 127–54).

3. Inwards and Outwards in the Orthodox Rapport to Ecumenism

When attempting to define the concept of 'Orthodoxy', Orthodox theologians seem to approach it from two main viewpoints: Orthodoxy is seen as a concept antinomic to non-Orthodoxy or heterodoxy; and Orthodoxy is seen as inheritance of and connection to the past, more exactly the Apostolic age and the early centuries of the Church. It is also true that Orthodox scholars are at the same time eager to point out that Orthodoxy is not defined merely as the right alternative to 'heterodoxies', but is a concept preceding the appearance of heresies, having its own internal logic and dynamics. In the words of Orthodox writers: 'Orthodoxy is a living condition, the ceaseless life of the Church' (Botsis 1980, p. 8); or 'the true path of faith which has always been carefully preserved in the history of the Church, from of old was called straight, right, [...] that is, "Orthodoxy"' (Pomazansky 1994, pp. 23–24). The Orthodox are also keen to emphasize that tradition is not only an inheritance and a connection with the past, but a continuous, dynamic reality inspired by the constant work of the Holy Spirit inside the Church—as we will see below.

It is, however, fair to say that the Orthodox habitually define themselves as defenders of the Apostolic inheritance in the face of erroneous groups. This connection with the legacy of the past is well-known, as the Orthodox see a central importance in the writings of the Fathers of the Church, as well as in the wider and more complex inheritance of the Church—which embraces everything from the importance of the first seven Ecumenical Councils with the role attributed to the Lady Theotokos, to the veneration of the Saints, the Liturgical universe, and all associated rituals, the use of relics and icons, monasticism, fasting, etc.

More importantly, however, the Orthodox Church sees its role in the Christian world as 'special' and prophetic, as it alone—it claims—has remained the faithful carrier and witness of the truth of faith, precisely to ultimately call back all stranded Christian groups back to the one original Church. In the words of Georges Florovsky: 'By her inner consciousness the Orthodox Church is bound to claim an exceptional position in divided Christendom. She is also bound to claim for herself an exceptional and peculiar task in all endeavours to overcome the present sore disunity of Christians and to recover that Christian unity which has been given once and has been lost' (Florovsky 1989, pp. 140–41). Or as Orthodox academic Ioan Sauca put it: 'The Orthodox Church, by her inner conviction and consciousness, has a special and exceptional position in divided Christendom, as the bearer of and the witness to the tradition of the ancient undivided Church from which all existing denominations stem, by way of reduction and separation' (Sauca 2004, p. 212).

What then, is the Orthodox Church's relationship with the 'divided Christendom'? The Orthodox Church often tends to see other Christians as outside the One Church, their 'Christian' character being 'incomplete'—at best—or even absent, according to some interpretations. The Orthodox Church sees itself as the One Church. Not merely as a continuator of the primal Church, a faithful retainer of its doctrine and ethos, or an inheritor and guardian of the fullness of faith, but *the* Church of the Apostolic age, in all its fullness, unchanged, unbroken and undented. The fact that it now represents only a proportion of the Christian world does not and cannot influence this plenitude, as the fullness of Christ's faith and truth are more, so to speak, a matter of 'quality' rather than 'quantity'.

When it comes to unity, then, the Orthodox Church does not see it as anything else but the reconstitution of the One Orthodox Church. The only sense it sees in ecumenism is the healing of the schisms that have separated the Christians in the first place. While the Orthodox Church seems to be prepared to accept cultural diversity—which indeed already characterizes the Orthodox universe, made up, as it is, of a multitude of local or national Churches, each with its own characteristic tradition and ethos—it struggles however in accepting a diversity and plurality of churches. 'The Orthodox cannot accept the idea of a "parity of denominations"', stated the Orthodox participants following the New Delhi General Assembly of the World Council of Churches in 1961. 'The Orthodox Church is not a confession, one of many, one among the many' (World Council of Churches 1999). For the Orthodox, the reunion of Christians means the re-joining of the one true Orthodox Church. The purpose of the

Orthodox participating in ecumenical meetings can only be to try and bring the other denomination back to Orthodoxy.

Yet, this return to Orthodoxy, this 'conversion' is not to be seen as submission to some centre of influence: 'it must not be thought that Orthodox demand the submission of other Christians to a particular centre of power and jurisdiction', writes Metropolitan Kallistos Ware. 'Orthodoxy desires their reconciliation not their absorption' (Ware 1964, p. 317). The other Christians are called essentially to be converted to a way of life—lived according to the doctrines and in the purity of faith of the early Church. This calling to rediscover the purity of Orthodoxy is addressed not only to the non-Orthodox but also to the Orthodox themselves. In the words of Dumitru Staniloae, a major Romanian theologian: 'Orthodoxy proposes to all Christians a treasure belonging to all and which can serve as a basis for the renewal of all even in the midst of the communities they may belong to. Even the members of the Orthodox Church need to rediscover Orthodoxy' (De Beauregard and Staniloae 2000, p. 41)[4].

Orthodoxy, it is believed, has not safeguarded the truth of Christ's Church *from* the other Christians who are seen as having departed from it and chosen less perfect ways, but, in a sense, *for* them. As a matter of self-identity, Orthodoxy believes it contains within itself, alongside the salvific truth, the structure and model of Church's unity, which awaits the return of its separated elements, thus re-accomplishing the quintessential Christ-centred unity and oneness of the Church. 'Structure' here refers both to 'external' aspects of the organisation of the Orthodox Church—like episcopal structure, hierarchy, conciliar decision-making etc.—and 'internal' aspects—like liturgical structure, spiritual practices, teaching etc.[5] Sadly this unifying structure and model of the Orthodox Church(es) works less effectively in practice than in theory, as the Orthodox have some difficulty in gathering together as one Church (see the failed attempt of the Council of Crete, revisited later in this study). However, the truth of faith, Christ himself, cannot bring witness to the world by ignoring the wound and tragedy of division, but struggles continuously to heal and unite. Thus the Orthodox Church should not seek to justify divisions and separate Christians into 'those who are called' and 'those who are no longer called'. Orthodoxy, as the way of life in Christ, by its inherent inner drive and structure, seeks to make itself known in the world, and to unite the world in Christ, according to the model of the Holy Trinity—the supreme structure of unity. Orthodoxy cannot remain detached or indifferent in front of divisions, but it should call for active participation towards unity, as part of its far-reaching aspiration towards renewal and transfiguration of humanity. It ought to address the call to unity not simply to 'others' but mainly to itself as the 'main actor' in God's plan of saving humanity.

This is the fundamental tension that becomes evident in the vision that the Orthodox tend to have of Orthodoxy in its relations with ecumenism or with the other Christian traditions: On the one hand, the Orthodox have a tendency to focus on the community of the one true Church, which they perceive to be the Orthodox Church. From this perspective they can hardly summon up any interest towards what is to be found 'outside' the Church itself, and lamentably feel little—if any—responsibility towards the various traditions which, despite sharing to a degree the same apostolic tradition, are seen to have veered away from the Church. The 'ethos' of these 'outside' traditions feels different now, and so do their liturgical and sacramental life in the Church. Thus the responsibility both for the separation and for the efforts invested in a 'return' to the former unity of the Church seems to be transferred exclusively—and unjustly—onto the non-Orthodox groups.

On the other hand, Orthodoxy has kept and guarded in fullness the tradition of the early Church in all its complexity—unchanged, it is believed—not only for its own sake, but also—perhaps mostly—for the benefit of the entire humanity, and in particular, it can be argued, for the benefit of its separated

---

[4]   My translation. My Italics.
[5]   The Russian document 'Basic Principles of the Attitude of the Russian Orthodox Church toward the Other Christian Confessions' states that 'the Orthodox Church asserts that genuine unity is possible only in the bosom of the One, Holy, Catholic and Apostolic Church (The Russian Orthodox Church 2000). All other "models" of unity seem to us to be unacceptable.' Orthodoxy appears thus, in a sense, as the only viable 'model' for unity.

brothers and sisters who, though once 'Orthodox', have chosen to be (as the Orthodox often see it), or simply found themselves outside the Church. Ultimately the Orthodox divorce from and the implicit 'excommunication' of the departing groups happened not as a definitive condemnation, 'break up', or definitive dissociation from the outside Christian world. This gesture ultimately had a 'pedagogical' purpose.[6] Whether justified or not, this punitive dismissal was not entirely devoid of love, but aimed at making the 'offending' groups become aware of their mistake, repent, and eventually return to the true faith that they had previously rejected. It was by contrast to the 'erroneous' groups, tha the Church proclaimed itself 'Orthodox', that is plainly rejecting the error, but also reminding the offenders and everyone else where the truth had remained safely kept.

On the one hand, then, the Orthodox believe they were granted the crucial mission and responsibility to keep the structure and tradition of the original true Church of Christ. They were entrusted with this invaluable treasure as a salvific platform for the Church, and for the entire humankind. Safeguarding this inheritance as a matter of identity meant that, if human groups or trends were ever to venture, be pushed or 'lured' away from the core of faith, the Church was to remain steadfast to its unchangeable truth, as a beacon forever calling humanity back to the essential core of Christian faith. That is the enormous responsibility that the Orthodox see as entrusted to themselves and it represents nothing less than what they essentially see themselves to be.

On the other hand, the Orthodox are faced again and again with the difficult reality that the former Christian world is now separated and fragmented and that—according to their own understanding of 'Church'—certain Christian groups no longer share in the same unified Eucharistic, sacramental and liturgical universe, and thus appear to be placed in an uncertain dimension which the Orthodox cannot always perceive and acknowledge as 'Church'. While the Orthodox were prepared to exclude from Orthodoxy a great chunk of the former larger Church, they have never managed to ascribe a precise place, role or status for these 'outside' groups. What seems to remain a common perception is that the non-Orthodox have 'voluntarily' placed themselves outside the Church of Christ, which represents essentially the only *locum* and *praxis* and structure for salvation. Moreover, these departing groups have been associated with various heresies of old, having been actively opposed—once, but perhaps now still—to the accepted Orthodox mainstream doctrine of the Church. This could bring an element of risk or a downright threat to those Orthodox Christians brave (or 'foolish') enough to venture outside the secure walls of the Orthodox Church, as it is often claimed by anti-ecumenical advocates. Even the more moderate Orthodox faithful will sometimes fail to see how anything outside the organic body of the one true Church—always the same, never changed or diminished—can have any real relevance for them, particularly as this vision of Orthodoxy as a society 'chosen' to live the life of Christ comes tinted in the rosy glow of a special prophetic calling reserved for the Orthodox alone.[7]

How is the Orthodox faithful or theologian to desire the return of the break-away communities to the former Orthodoxy, when the Church itself does not seem to need or pursue this return? 'The Orthodox Church […] is full; it lacks not' (Fr. John Reeves 1996). At the same time, he/she is called to proclaim the right path to all those who have veered outside the Orthodox way. This outlines an antinomy or an existential dilemma between the calling to focus inwardly, on an ever-tightening communion of the Orthodox Church, within the safety of its own ecclesiological borders, of its own sacramental universe—on the one hand. On the other hand, there is the calling—just like in the case of practical theology—to external engagement with the others, not as compromise done in the name of Christian brotherhood and harmony, but as the very identity and purpose of Orthodoxy. Or, to employ the words of Catholic ecumenist Paul D. Murray, when he referred more generally to the Church's drive towards catholicity, this resembles a wavering 'between the centripetal and the centrifugal

---

[6] According to the Russian Orthodox Church document 'Basic Principles of Attitude to the Non-Orthodox': 'Even while excommunicating one of her members, sealed by her on the day of his baptism, the Church hopes for his return. She considers excommunication itself to be a means of spiritual rebirth for such person.' (The Russian Orthodox Church 2000).

[7] These ideas are developed more fully in Orthodoxy and ecumenism: Towards active metanoia (Porumb 2008).

forces of the Spirit's activity in the world; between constant gathering in communion and continual evangelical dispersal and engagement throughout the world' (Murray 2008, p. 18).

It can be argued that this internal tension mirrors to a degree the fundamental tension within Orthodoxy between tradition(s) and Tradition. The tension here is between the inheritance of the tradition(s) of the past, and the current ongoing experiencing of this inheritance in the life of the Orthodox community. Tradition may be an essential characteristic of the Church which connects it with the past, but it is also to be seen as a 'dynamic' reality. According to Greek academic Panagiotis Bratsiotis, 'in the Orthodox Church, tradition is not regarded as a static factor—as many non-Orthodox people think—but as a dynamic one. Loyalty to tradition does not simply mean slavish attachment to the past and to external authority, but a living connection with the entire past experience of the Church' (Bratsiotis 1964, p. 24).

Orthodox theologians needed to reaffirm tradition in a capitalized form, as Tradition (a relatively modern device in Orthodox theology)—a living reality, which, although connecting them with the past, is essentially and eternally 'contemporary', since it concerns the ongoing life of the Church as informed by the Holy Spirit. As put by Patriarch Daniel of Romania, 'the Church is inevitably Tradition, that is to say a dynamic process of continuity and renewal in the Holy Spirit, who bears witness to the crucified and risen Christ, throughout the ages, involving the human and historical dimension as partner in communion with the eternal Trinity' (Ciobotea 2001, p. 157).

The tension here has been resolved by defining Tradition as a dynamic reality, a vision different from tradition as inheritance or hereditary truth. By accepting both concepts operating in parallel, Orthodox theology has embraced this polarity as a fruitful complementary insight. Just like in the case of practical theology addressed in the first part of this study, the reflexive 'internal' approach focusing on a 'household' matrix of spiritual self-analysis has been complemented by a dynamic whirl (energised by the Holy Spirit) which transfigures self-contemplation into an outward ceaseless motion of regeneration and engagement in communion with the Church and the wider world.

No effective resolution however has yet been reached in the case of the internal tension within Orthodoxy between its outreach vector of witness in love to the world and its defensive drive focusing exclusively within, onto its ecclesiologically protected universe. What may have seemed like a solution to many Orthodox has been an unfortunate brutal amputation of the outward communitarian vector, replacing it with vehement condemnations of any ecumenical attempt and denouncing as perilous and traitorous any Orthodox engagement with other Christian communities. Thus, 'all non-Orthodox are heretics' according—among many others—to recently-canonized Orthodox writer, Father Justin Popović. 'What fellowship hath righteousness with unrighteousness?', he adds (Popović 1975). According to Orthodox scholar Constantine Cavarnos, ecumenical dialogue weakens the 'spiritual immune system', which leads to 'spiritual AIDS' where the sufferer 'becomes completely insensitive to doctrinal differences that distinguish Orthodoxy or true belief, from heresy or false belief' (Cavarnos 1996, p. 54). The internet is crowded with anathemas and condemnations of ecumenism as 'heresy of heresies', 'ecclesiological heresy', 'panheresy', etc.—most of which denunciations come from the Orthodox.

It can be argued that this same reflex against the outward communitarian vector is so embedded in the mind-set of certain Orthodox groups, that it even makes the organisation of an international Orthodox council a strenuous task. The recent long-anticipated attempt to hold a Pan-Orthodox Council in Crete in 2016 (according to the model of the seven ancient Ecumenical Councils, the last of which took place in 787 AD!), was achieved in a rather anticlimactic fashion after being boycotted by the Churches of Russia, Bulgaria, Georgia and Antioch, triggering extraneous denunciations from factions all across the Orthodox world and casting embarrassment on the Orthodo—particularly in light of their oft-affirmed claim that they are 'bearers of, and witnesses to the tradition of the ancient undivided Church' (World Council of Churches 1999). It also cast serious doubt on how well the Orthodox themselves understand their own inner structure and communion. Incidentally, the Council in Crete reaffirmed the Orthodox commitment to ecumenism and condemned those who oppose ecumenical engagement—which further alienated some of the dissenting Churches. It is true that the way ecumenical processes are conducted today is not without irritating quirks and disappointments, and the ecumenical movement is clearly in need of a reboot, perhaps in a different ethos and following different structures and principles.[8] However, barring the Orthodox faithful—as a matter of jaundiced principle—from any openness towards the other Christians is not only wrong, but in contradiction of what Orthodoxy in its very essence stands for. Even an Orthodoxy defined primarily by opposition to external 'heterodoxies' is still supposed to engage with these as a 'correctional' force—not to shut itself in in spiteful isolation. Moreover, subscribed within an eminently Trinitarian vision, the Orthodox Church believes the lives of its faithful are to mirror the dynamics of the Triune God, a model which 'spurs us on to grow and think continuously in spirit, and helps us both pass continually beyond any level we may have already reached in our personal communion with God and among ourselves' (Staniloae 2005, p. 247).

The catholicity of the Church—as fundamental foundational principle—should mimic the perfect catholicity in love of the Trinity and, despite external human factors being often an obstruction, the Christian drive towards catholicity and communion in love is to remain intact. This energy needs to remain inexorable, ultimately bound to overcome any borders—cultural, ecclesiological or otherwise—just as the scope of each of the Persons of the Trinity is ever-outbound and ever-persistent in loving *perichoresis*. Thus, ceasing all communication and interaction with what is perceived to be a treacherous and dangerous 'heterodox' universe cannot resolve the intrinsic tension between the Orthodoxy's centrifugal and centripetal drives. It can only serve—at most—as temporary suspension of the predicament.

What this study proposes is that here too, the antinomy between the 'inward' and 'outward' tendencies can in fact operate in complementary rotation. The ecumenical process can clearly be circumscribed within the practical dimension of theology, but this dynamic should not remain an external initiative, a 'diplomatic' or 'political' endeavour. This paradigm needs to be replaced with a vision of unity resting on Christ's sacraments and fuelled by Trinitarian love. After all, the urge towards the catholicity of the Church effectuated through an attempt to reach the unity of all Christians comes for the Orthodox from their very eucharistic Liturgy, when the congregation chants: 'For the peace of the whole world, for the welfare of the holy Churches of God, and for the union of all, let us pray to the Lord' (Lash 1995, p. 3). The call to unity around the Eucharist is addressed to the whole humankind. According to Staniloae, ecumenism should be seen as 'a state, a reality in which the Holy Spirit urges the Churches to love each other, as their separation was not only an open conflict but also a lack of love' (Ciobotea 2001, p. 244).

Thus, ecumenism originates and occurs on a personal and inter-personal level, so to speak only of a programmatic, institutional ecumenism, and thus to 'depersonalize' it to a degree may lead to an incomplete understanding of the concept. In exercising its vocation of action and engagement, ecumenism does not break away from theology as an independent 'specialist' approach, but should remain an integral part of theology. According to this vision, this kind of 'spiritual ecumenism' remains inextricably linked to the spiritual components of Christian life—prayer, liturgy, transformation (*metanoia*). These dimensions inform a spiritual dynamic engagement which leads to a gradual and continuous transformation of the human being. This perspective also points to the fact that ecumenism, as 'mainstream' theology, is a calling and a vocation addressed to all, and not only to a specialized few.

For renowned Catholic scholar Yves Congar, 'ecumenism, presupposes a movement or conversion and reform co-extensive with the whole life of the community.' For Congar, ecumenism requires 'a profound moral and even religious conversion' in oneself, in the process of which one becomes 'a different person' (Avis 2012, p. 424)—a vision of ecumenism closely connected to the concept of *metanoia*, transformation. Romanian ecumenist Ion Bria's concept of 'the Liturgy after the Liturgy'

---

8   See first chapter (Evans 1996); also, (Aram 1995; Dulles 2007).

reveals the fact that the Orthodox might be interested in placing the ecumenical endeavour within the reality of the 'second Liturgy'—that of concrete action inspired from and nourished by common and individual prayer, constantly anchored in the communion with Christ, and, through him, with the others. In fact, for Bria, 'the Liturgy after the Liturgy' model is seen as 'an inspiration and impulse for reconstructing the Church in history after the Eucharistic model and vision' (Bria 1996, p. 87).

This approach, therefore, implies for the Orthodox a re-deepening and re-discovering of their own faith and identity. Any outward ecumenical process should certainly not imply disregarding or relativizing the Orthodox truth of faith or acting independently from it, but, on the contrary, acting as inspired by the sacramental life of the Church. As so aptly expressed by Murray, the ecumenical process should not be about reaching the lowest common denominator, but 'about becoming more deeply, more richly, more fully Catholic (more fully Methodist, more fully Anglican, etc.)' (Murray 2008, p. 16). Murray's vision gravitates around the twin notions of Receptive Ecumenism and Catholic Learning, where a 'transformational receptivity' maintains a constant spirit of openness to learn and receive from the others—with a view to become gradually and constantly transformed, ever-closer to the plenitude of the life in Christ. Thus becoming more Anglican, Orthodox, Catholic etc. does not mean stubbornly clinging to one's particular distinctive tenets but, on the contrary, to allow oneself to grow and be enhanced continually through learning from others, to become ever more fully Christian in one's own particular context. This process of conversion does not imply 'a loss, nor a diminishment but a finding, a freeing, an intensification, and an enrichment' (Murray 2008, p. 16). Thus, Christians are to become 'more fully, more richly, what we already are' (Murray 2008, p. 6).

When one enters into ecumenical activities and encounters, one must be aware that he/she needs to commit to this reality not only on a programmatic level, but also on a deeply spiritual level. Moreover, although an eminently participatory endeavour, ecumenism remains firmly anchored in the realm of theology and in close connexion with its spiritual components: prayer, liturgy, inner transformation. This means that ecumenical participation is as much about prayer as it is about dialogue and sharing and this type of spiritually-grounded ecumenism could constitute the beginning of a new paradigm, more suited for the twenty-first century: an ecumenism of faith and commitment.

There is a risk involved here, of course, and participants like the ones coming from Orthodox contexts would have to struggle greatly with their fear of losing their identity or betraying their inheritance. This would be however, an ecumenism linked and paired with the life of Church communities and with their sacramental life. It is an ecumenism that concerns every single member of the parish, and not a selected specialised class of theologians, whose work remains clouded in the 'external' sphere of diplomatic dialogue. Trust would thus rest on a different set of parameters which would sanction it to a different degree. While the idea of plunging into an ecumenical endeavour head-on, abandoning all suspicions and fears overnight, and relying solely on faith may be a feasible idea for many, this would have to be, however, a very gradual process, involving a careful and steady process of awareness-building in all the communities of the faithful around the world.

4. Conclusions

Thus, to sum up the findings of our reflection, if tension has a logic in practical/pastoral theology, as a complementary movement between the two 'inner' and 'outer' vectors—so too it is true about ecumenical engagement. The polarity here between isolation (or inward focus) and outreach must not necessarily be seen as a destructive contradiction, but as a constructive constant movement between the two poles. The two extremes might be in fact necessary for the practical ecumenical process to work.

The 'centrifugal' orientation is necessary not as an 'isolation' or 'dissociation', but as a deeper understanding of what Orthodoxy is—as a more intimate connection with the sacramental life of the Church. A true ecumenical engagement would aim not to distil or dilute what Orthodoxy is, but to allow the faithful to become more fully Orthodox, in their life within their Church community but also vis-à-vis the outer Christian world—thus fulfilling the missionary and communitarian requirement intrinsic to their own faith. If this movement within is followed by an outward vector of witness and engagement, this should be seen only as a complementary aspect making up a continuous rotation, a revolving dialectic of the ecumenical endeavour, just like the case of practical theology.

Any contraction must be followed organically by a movement of expansion—a continuing sacramental interaction with the secular local context of the faithful and the wider Christian world. This inward-outward movement informs all Christian life in a mutually perpetuating rotation or pulsation. Although the reaction to any engagement with the 'outer' dimension is often one of rejection, this engagement is nevertheless crucial as it brings fullness, and fulfils the vocation and identity of the Orthodox Church, informed by an ever-increasing catholicity according to the structure of the Holy Trinity.

Conflicts of Interest: The author declares no conflict of interest.

References

Aram, I. 1995. The ecumenical movement at a crossroads. *The Ecumenical Review* 47: 472–78.

Avis, Paul. 2012. 'Unreal worlds meeting'? Realism and illusion in ecumenical dialogue. *Theology* 115: 420–26. [CrossRef]

Belopopsky, Alexander. 2003. Orthodox Diakonia: An Introduction. Available online: www.iocc.org/orthodoxdiakonia/content/alexanderbelopopsky.pdf (accessed on 17 January 2017).

Botsis, Peter A. 1980. *What Is Orthodoxy*. Athens: Peter A. Botsis.

Bratsiotis, Panagiotis I. 1964. The fundamental principles and main characteristics of the Orthodox Church. In *The Orthodox Ethos*. Edited by Angelos J. Philippou. Oxford: Holywell Press.

Bria, Ion. 1996. *The Liturgy after the Liturgy. Mission and Witness from an Orthodox Perspective*. Geneva: WCC Publications.

Cavarnos, Constantine. 1996. *Ecumenism Examined*. Belmont: Institute for Byzantine and Modern Greek Studies.

Ciobotea, Daniel (Metropolitan). 2001. *Confessing the Truth in Love. Orthodox Perceptions of Life, Mission and Unity*. Iasi: Trinitas.

De Beauregard, Marc-Antoine Costa, and Dumitru Staniloae. 2000. *Mica Dogmatica Vorbita. Dialoguri la Cernica (Short Spoken Dogmatics. Dialogues at Cernica)*. Sibiu: Deisis.

Dorotheus of Gaza, and Daniel (Metropolitan) Ciobotea. 2001. *Confessing the Truth in Love. Orthodox Perceptions of Life, Mission and Unity*. Iasi: Trinitas.

Dulles, Cardinal Avery. 2007. Saving Ecumenism from Itself. *First Things*. December. Available online: https://www.firstthings.com/article/2007/12/saving-ecumenism-from-itself (accessed on 22 July 2017).

Gillian R. Evans, ed. 1996. The Winter of Ecumenism? In *Method in Ecumenical Theology: The Lessons so Far*. Cambridge: Cambridge University Press, pp. 19–40.

Florovsky, Georges. 1989. *Ecumenism I. A Doctrinal Approach*. Vaduz: Buchervertriebsanstalt, pp. 140–41.

Harakas, Stanley S. 1988. Orthodoxy in America: Continuity, Discontinuity, Newness. In *Orthodox Perspectives on Pastoral Praxis. Papers of the Intra-Orthodox Conference on Pastoral Praxis (24–25 September 1986)*. Edited by Theodore Stylianopoulos. Brookline: Holy Cross Orthodox Press.

Hierotheos, Nafpaktos (Metropolitan). 1994. *Orthodox Spirituality. A Brief Introduction*. Translated by Vlachos Hierotheos. Levadia: Birth of the Theotokos Monastery.

Jillions, John A. 2003. Pastoral Theology: Reflections from an Orthodox Perspective. *British Journal of Theological Education* 13: 161–74. [CrossRef]

Lash, Ephrem. 1995. *The Divine Liturgy of St John Chrysostom*. Oxford: Oxford University Press.

Meyendorff, John. 1979. The Christian Gospel and Social Responsibility: The Eastern Orthodox Tradition in History. In *Continuity and Discontinuity in Church History, Studies in the History of Christian Thought 14*. Edited by F. Forrester Church and Timothy George. Leiden: Brill Publishers.

Molokotos-Liederman, Lina. 2010. Orthodox Social Service and the Role of the Orthodox Church in the Greek Economic Crisis. Available online: http://www.faithineurope.org.uk/lina.pdf (accessed on 7 February 2017).

Murray, Paul D. 2008. Receptive ecumenism and Catholic learning—Establishing the agenda. In *Receptive Ecumenism and the Call to Catholic Learning. Exploring a Way for Contemporary Ecumenism*. Edited by Paul D. Murray. Oxford: Oxford University Press, pp. 5–26.

Pomazansky, Michael. 1994. *Orthodox Dogmatic. A Concise Exposition*. Platina: Saint Herman of Alaska Brotherhood.

Porumb, Razvan. 2008. Orthodoxy and Ecumenism: Towards Active Metanoia. Ph.D. dissertation, Anglia Ruskin University, Cambridge, UK. Available online: anglia.ac.uk/582334 (accessed on 25 July 2017).

Porumb, Razvan. 2017. An Orthodox Model of Practical/Pastoral Theology. *International Journal of Practical Theology* 21: 127–54. [CrossRef]

Fr. John Reeves. 1996. The Price of Ecumenism. How Ecumenism Has Hurt the Orthodox Church. *Orthodoxy Christian Information Centre*. Available online: http://Orthodoxinfo.com/ecumenism/tca_priceofecumenism.aspx (accessed on 1 April 2017).

Rolt, Clarence Edwin. 2007. *Dionysius the Areopagite: On the Divine Names and the Mystical Theology*. New York: Cosimo Classics.

Sauca, Ioan. 2004. The Church beyond our boundaries. The ecumenical vocation of Orthodoxy. *The Ecumenical Review* 56: 211–25. [CrossRef]

Staniloae, Dumitru. 2005. *Orthodox Dogmatic Theology: The Experience of God, Vol. 1: Revelation and knowledge of the Triune God*. Brookline: Holy Cross Orthodox Press.

Theophan the Recluse. 1966. What is Prayer? In *The Art of Prayer. An Orthodox Anthology*. Edited by Chariton of Valamo Igumen. London: Faber and Faber, p. 21.

The Russian Orthodox Church. 2000. Basic Principles of Attitude to the Non-Orthodox. Available online: https://mospat.ru/en/documents/attitude-to-the-non-orthodox (accessed on 2 March 2017).

Popović, Justin (Archimandrite). 1975. 'Orthodoxy and Ecumenism. An Orthodox Appraisal and Testimony'. Available online: http://www.synodinresistance.org/Theology_en/E3a4012Popovic.pdf (accessed on 1 June 2009).

Ware, Timothy (Kallistos). 1964. *The Orthodox Church*. Baltimore: Penguin Books.

Woodward James, and Pattison Stephen, eds. 2000. *The Blackwell Reader in Pastoral and Practical Theology*. Oxford: Blackwell.

World Council of Churches. 1999. Orthodox contribution to New Delhi Assembly (Section Report on Unity, New Delhi, India, 1961). *World Council of Churches*, December 1. Available online: www.oikoumene.org/en/resources/documents/wcc-programmes/ecumenical-movement-in-the-21st-century/member-churches/special-commission-on-participation-of-orthodox-churches/first-plenary-meeting-documents-december-1999/orthodox-contribution-to-new-delhi-assembly (accessed on 1 May 2017).

religions

MDPI

Article

'Neither Victim nor Executioner': Essential Insights from Secularization Theory for the Revitalization of the Russian Orthodox Church in the Contemporary World

Rico G. Monge

College of Arts and Sciences, University of San Diego, San Diego, CA 92110, USA; rmonge@sandiego.edu

Received: 22 June 2017; Accepted: 16 August 2017; Published: 28 August 2017

Abstract: This essay explores two recent expressions of hostility towards secularization by Russian Orthodox officials (one from the Holy Synod of ROCOR and the other from Metropolitan Archbishop Hilarion Alfeyev), and evaluates the likely consequences of this hostility. Drawing from secularization theorists including Peter Berger, Jose Casanova, and Charles Taylor, as well as the thought of Albert Camus, this essay argues that the long-term health of the Russian Orthodox Church will benefit from embracing insights from secularization theorists rather than attempting to "desecularize" Russian society with state support.

Keywords: Christian; Orthodox; spirituality; theology; state; identity; human rights; Russia; persecution; secularism

1. Introduction

In a 2014 address to the Pontifical Theological Faculty of Southern Italy, Metropolitan Hilarion Alfeyev of the Moscow Patriarchate of the Russian Orthodox Church (hereafter ROC) asserted, "no matter what researchers say about church-state relations in Byzantium and Rus, at her very heart the Church has remained free, irrespective of the external political circumstance" (Alfeyev 2014). This lofty theological statement stands outside the reach of empirical scrutiny, as it is impossible for "researchers" to examine the inward "heart" of the Church and thus verify or falsify Alfeyev's claim. However, what can be examined is, first, that which is at stake in making such claims, and second, what quality of fruit such claims potentially bear. In the larger context of the address, which will be analyzed at length below, it becomes clear that Alfeyev wishes to neutralize any concerns about potential negative effects that might arise from increasing collaboration between the ROC and the secular nation-state known as the Russian Federation. Rather, he wishes to celebrate the dawn of a new era of freedom for Russian Orthodox Christianity, and the immense positive possibilities this era has opened up, by drawing parallels between present church-state relations in Russia and those of the Roman Empire after the Edict of Milan in 313 CE. Moreover, Alfeyev wishes to present church-state relations in Russia as a powerful antidote to Western European and North American secularization.

Following the lead of Alfeyev's address, this essay aims not to empirically analyze what is currently happening in Russia and Russian Orthodoxy. Such is the work of sociologists and historians and lies outside of my expertise[1]. Rather, I aim to evaluate philosophically and theologically the

---

[1] A number of quality monographs written from these perspectives have recently appeared and are well-worth consulting. For insight into the Russian Orthodox Church's impact on Russian culture and society, see Zoe Knox's *Russian Society and the Russian Church* (Knox 2005). For an analysis of the effects of Russia's "forced secularization" on its contemporary religious revival, see Christopher Marsh's *Religion and the State in Russia and China* (Marsh 2011). Finally, for an in depth look at how

potential benefit and harm that may come to the ROC if its leadership continues to embrace the notion that a "symphony" of church and state is possible, let alone desirable. I derive the primary hermeneutics employed in this evaluation from the work of prominent secularization theorists including Peter L. Berger, Jose Casanova, Talal Asad and Charles Taylor. In doing so, I will validate many Russian criticisms of Western constructions of secularity and its concomitant consumer culture, while also identifying how and why the current models for combatting "secularization" are overly defensive reactions against the West, reactions which will likely do the ROC incalculable harm. The goal here is neither to celebrate Russia's "re-Christianization" nor to denigrate the contemporary Russian Orthodox Church as a re-imperialized pseudo-state religion. Rather, my approach mirrors that of Nicholas Berdyaev on socialism and capitalism:

> A real reconciliation of East and West is impossible and inconceivable on the basis of a materialistic Communism, or of a materialistic Capitalism, or indeed of a materialistic Socialism. The third way will neither be "anti-Communist" nor "anti-Capitalist". It will recognize the truth in liberal democracy, and it will equally recognize the truth in Communism. A critique of Communism and Marxism does not entail an enmity towards Soviet Russia, just as a critique of liberal democracy does not entail enmity towards the west (Berdyaev 1949, p. 80).

Just as Berdyaev looks for an affirmative third way that avoids reactionary dualistic constructions, I seek to employ insights from secularization theorists to illuminate a dialectic of victim mentality and triumphalism present in two contemporary Russian Orthodox statements, one from the aforementioned Metropolitan Hilarion Alfeyev and another from the governing synod of the Russian Orthodox Church Outside Russia (hereafter ROCOR). What I aim to suggest is that the Russian Orthodox Church as a whole will best achieve the freedom and flourishing it seeks by embracing more nuanced understandings of secularization rather than fleeing from what it perceives to be secularization as such. To accomplish this end, this essay will proceed in four distinct sections: the first section will set forth a working definition of the terms "secular" and "secularization"; the second section will analyze and evaluate ROCOR's recent official statement on the Russian Revolution of 1917 and its implicit rejection of all secularization; the third section will engage with Alfeyev's critique of Western secularism in which he favorably compares the era of the Edict of Milan to the present state of affairs in Russia, arguing that both together represent a superior model for church-state interaction than that of Western secularization; and the fourth section will glean insights from secularization theorists in order to not only shed light on valid Russian Orthodox concerns about "the West," but also to demonstrate how current ROC and ROCOR attitudes towards church-state relations are likely to harm the health of Russian Orthodoxy in the long term. The essay will conclude by proposing the mentality the Church must adopt towards all state relations if it is to fulfill its prophetic mission to the world.

2. Defining "Secular" and "Secularization"

Like any term, the words "secular" and "secularization" have a range of meanings and any attempt to claim, "this is what this word *really* means" is linguistically naïve. Indeed, defining "the secular" has proven so contentious that some have advocated abandoning use of the term altogether (Berger 1990, p. 106). Such approaches are not helpful; rather, careful examination of the way these terms have been historically used can play an invaluable role in illuminating what is at stake for individuals and communities when they take stances in for or against what they understand these terms to signify. Furthermore, by setting forth a working definition one can gain hermeneutic tools that facilitate productive ways in which to interpret complex phenomena. For these reasons, I employ

---

the Russian Orthodox Church has affected public policy and legislation, see Irina Papkova's *The Orthodox Church and Russian Politics* (Papkova 2011).

the definitions laid down by one of the foundational figures of secularization theory, Peter L. Berger for this article.

In his landmark work, *The Sacred Canopy*, Berger observes that these terms were first used in a morally neutral mode in Western Europe to describe both intra-ecclesial realities and also the transfer of property away from church authority. In the former case, regular clergy designated those who followed a monastic rule (*regula*), whereas secular clergy were those who operated in "the world" outside of the confines of a monastery and outside of a monastic rule of obedience. In the latter case, "secularization" referred to the byproduct of Protestant–Catholic warfare, in which lands under ecclesial authority were transferred to state authorities or private citizens. Over time, however, the terms have come to take on "highly charged" moral valences depending on whether those using these words are sympathetic or hostile to religion. As Berger puts it, "in anti-clerical and 'progressive' circles it has come to stand for the liberation of modern man from religious tutelage, while in circles connected with the traditional churches it has been attacked as 'de-Christianization,' 'paganization,' and the like" (Berger 1990, p. 106). As we shall see below, much Russian Orthodox discourse defines secularization in precisely these ways. It is thus used both to denigrate the hegemony of Western Enlightenment liberal democracy and its perceived freedom from the shackles of religion[2], while also equating secularism with anti-Christian hostility and moral libertinism. On the flip side, there are Christian thinkers in Europe and America who have championed secularization (and by this they mean secular humanism) as the evidence that Euro-American culture has positively appropriated Christian values in a way that no longer requires acceptance of institutional Christianity, let alone belief in God. Harvey Cox, Gabriel Vahanian, and Thomas J.J. Altizer have each in their own way hailed secular humanism as Christianity's natural triumphant enculturation (Cox 2013; Vahanian 2008; Altizer 2002)[3].

Berger's working definition of secularization, however, eschews moral valuations in order to describe the phenomenon itself and to identify and elucidate the mechanisms by which secularization progresses. Thus he defines secularization as "the process by which sectors of society and culture are removed from the domination of religious institutions and symbols" (Berger 1990, p. 107). Careful attention to Berger's language is key. He does not assert that religious institutions and symbols no longer have any place in a secularized society; rather, he indicates that a secular society is one in which religion is *a* voice in the public sphere, but no longer *the* voice in the public sphere. Or, as Jeffrey Stout has put it, discourse in the public sphere is no longer framed by "a single theological perspective ... shared by all ... interlocutors" (Stout 2004, p. 97). A hallmark of this removal of domination is the separation of church and state, which, again, does not mean that religious voices are to be excluded from political discourse. Instead, they no longer control the discourse nor do they unilaterally dictate policy-making. Beyond the political sphere, secularization "affects the totality of cultural life and of ideation, and may be observed in the decline of religious contents in the arts, in philosophy, in literature and, most important of all, in the rise of science as an autonomous, thoroughly secular perspective on the world" (Berger 1990, p. 107). As with politics, this does not mean that religion is excluded from the realms of art, philosophy, literature and science. Instead, art no longer is compelled to focus on religious themes in order to be considered valid, philosophy no longer is constrained to develop systems of thought that reinforce the dominant religious ideology, literature is no longer merely a conduit for expressing religious values in poetic forms, and science is no longer pressured to keep its findings in line with religious narratives concerning the cosmos. Nevertheless, in

---

2 Cf. the Enlightenment-based political ideals of Immanuel Kant, David Hume, John Locke, Jean-Jacques Rousseau, and Thomas Hobbes, among others (Kant 2016; Hume 1990, 2016; Locke 1988; Rousseau 2009; Hobbes 1996).
3 Cox, Vahanian and Altizer are all influenced by Friedrich Nietzsche's overall philosophy and critique of culture, including the proclamation of the "death of God." Their positive valuation of the secular rests in their essential agreement with Nietzsche's statement that "if they [secular atheist humanists of England] consequently think they no longer have need of Christianity as a guarantee of morality; that is merely the consequence of the ascendancy of Christian evaluation and an expression of the strength and depth of this ascendancy" (Nietzsche 1990, p. 81).

a secular society (according to Berger's definition), religion may continue to have a "seat at the table" in inspiring the arts and literature and in guiding philosophical and scientific inquiry. It simply is no longer allowed to *control* them.

3. Resentment and Triumphalism in ROCOR's Epistle on the Bolshevik Revolution

While the majority of Russian Orthodox clerics were strikingly silent on the 100th anniversary of the Bolshevik Revolution, the semi-autonomous governing synod of ROCOR spoke out emphatically in its "Epistle of the Synod of Bishops of the Russian Orthodox Church Outside of Russia on the 100th Anniversary of the Tragic Revolution in Russia and Beginning of the Godless Persecutions"[4]. ROCOR's epistle is unsurprisingly vitriolic in its tone given this ecclesial jurisdiction's tumultuous history. After 1927, ROCOR broke communion with the ROC due to the latter's agreement to submit to the demands of the Soviet government. Communion between the two churches was not restored until 2007. Thus, unlike the ROC, ROCOR never came to accept any legitimacy to the Soviet state and, moreover, preserves to this day a sensibility that stands firmly against even Berger's aforementioned morally neutral definition of secularization. As we shall see, ROCOR's epistle not only rejects the separation of church and state, it argues that Russian Orthodoxy ought to wield power over Russian culture by eradicating all cultural symbols of Russia's Soviet cultural past. The point here is not to condemn these attitudes; indeed, they are completely understandable responses to the atrocities of Vladimir Lenin and Josef Stalin. Hence, the epistle calls on the Russian people to "rid Red Square of the remains of the main persecutor and executioner of the 20th century [Lenin]," and to destroy the monuments to him as "symbols of catastrophe, tragedy, and of the destruction of our God-given Sovereignty" (Synod of Bishops 2017). Given Lenin's role as a principal architect of the mass killings known as the "Red Terror," ROCOR's request is quite compelling[5].

ROCOR's demand that Lenin's tomb and monuments be destroyed, however, becomes more problematic when one considers the rationale given for doing so[6]. Instead of invoking concepts like "human rights," "war crimes," or "political genocide,"—concepts that have cross-cultural and interreligious/irreligious currency—ROCOR argues that the Russian state *must* do this in order to repent of its "rejection of the Divinely-ordained [Tsarist] government" and thereby enact a "symbol of reconciliation of the Russian nation with the Lord." This theological imperative also requires returning the names of all cities, oblasts (provinces), and streets to their "historic" Christian names. Ultimately, ROCOR concludes that nothing less than a total rejection of secularization will suffice, arguing that "every Russian person" should "come to the conclusion that in his God-preserved nation, there is no place for the symbols of the godless state and the names of militant atheists" (Synod of Bishops 2017). ROCOR's theo-political vision thus reveals two significant difficulties: first, a belief that the Russian state must again become Christianized to the degree that there is no room for activist dissent, and second, an unexamined assumption that a state can genuinely be anything but godless. Put differently, ROCOR asserts an unaltered faith in the Byzantine model of *symphonia* between church and state as the only proper way for the Orthodox Church to function[7].

Why is *symphonia* necessary on a practical level for ROCOR? While the reasons are too numerous to recount here, the Epistle itself reveals one key geopolitical component—a deep resentment towards

---

[4] Since 2007, ROCOR is "semi-autonomous" in that it is officially a part of the Moscow Patriarchate, but holds ecclesiastical jurisdiction over the majority of Russian Orthodox Churches in Western Europe, the United States, Canada, Latin America, Australia and New Zealand. Its headquarters are in New York City.

[5] For a detailed account of the ideology and atrocities of the "Red Terror," see *Lenin's Terror* (Ryan 2012).

[6] See activist and lawyer Lena Zezulin's critique of ROCOR's Epistle for a brief but similar appraisal to the one I offer here (Zezulin 2017).

[7] *Symphonia* is the Byzantine political theory that church and state can and should operate in harmony with each other, with neither side dominating the other. After the fall of Constantinople (aka 2nd Rome) and its Caesars, Russians came to understand Moscow as 3rd Rome, and the rulers of the Russian Empire took over the title of Caesar (Tsar), thus continuing the ideal of *symphonia*. See *An Examination of Church-State Relations in the Byzantine and Russian Empires With an Emphasis on Ideology and Models of Interaction*, (Gvosdev 2001).

Western imperialism and Western secularization. There is a deeply rooted belief that only if the Russian Church and Russian State speak as one can they stand up against these oppressive external powers effectively. Again, it should be stressed that this resentment does have a certain degree of legitimacy, and is shared by many Russians who are of different faith traditions than Eastern Orthodox Christianity[8]. No doubt referring to the increasing hostilities the United States and its NATO allies are currently fomenting against Russia, ROCOR states, "it is important to note that the constant denigration of Russia on the part of 'Western civilization' we see today existed a hundred years ago and, in fact, much earlier. The world despised the Russian Empire, the heir to Holy Orthodox Rus" (Synod of Bishops 2017). This resentment towards the hypocrisy and abusiveness of the United States and NATO is, quite arguably, well founded. Ironically, this very hypocrisy and abusiveness has been documented extensively by a number of American secular humanist intellectuals[9].

For ROCOR, *symphonia* is also deeply practical, because the Russian Revolution and all of its accompanying horrors stem directly from the rejection of *symphonia*. Widespread poverty, corruption in the royal family, Tsar Nicholas II's debilitation of Russia through the Russo-Japanese War (1904–1905), and the failures of the ROC and the Russian Imperial State to address these and other pressing issues are rejected categorically as non-contributing factors lest culpability fall upon anyone but the revolutionaries themselves. "We must not," continues the Epistle, "under any circumstances justify the actions of those responsible for the deadly revolution." The blame instead rests firmly on the shoulders of those who "neglect[ed] faith in Christ" and who rejected "the Divinely-ordained government." Quoting St. Markary Nevsky, ROCOR makes clear their belief that the primary (perhaps sole) problem was "blasphemy against God and plots against his anointed one [the Tsar]" (Synod of Bishops 2017). Given that "anointed one" is the equivalent of the Hebrew term "Messiah" (and its corresponding Greek term "Christos"), such assertions can sound like wantonly blasphemous attributions of "messianicity" to the Emperor. However problematic this doctrine may be, these statements can be fully understood only if one understands that Byzantine *symphonia* maintained that the Church's role was to manifest the Priesthood of Christ in the world, while the anointed Emperor was to manifest the Kingship of Christ. According to Eusebius, monarchy and not democracy was God's approved political system, and thus the Christian Emperor was the "friend of God" who possessed a "sacred kingship," was God's conqueror of the enemies of the faith through "usages of war," and was the "interpreter of the Word of God" (Eusebius 2005). While Eusebius's ideas clearly were novel (Christianity thrived for its first 300 years without an emperor), and although his ideas were never dogmatized, they became ingrained in Byzantine culture and its Russian inheritors. Understood contextually, while ROCOR's position has no firm theological grounding, it is nevertheless true that they are adhering faithfully to a 1700 year-old trajectory of Orthodox political thought.

This faithful adherence to *symphonia* in turn creates two major problems that will be revisited below in light of contemporary secularization theory. First, ROCOR has consistently conflated political martyrdom with martyrdom for the faith, which is directly related to their conflation of church and state. Accordingly, they assert that the Revolution brought about the "martyric death of the Tsar himself and his most August family." But how, one might ask, were their deaths "martyric"? They were not

---

8   Indeed, at the same meeting with Putin in which Patriarch Kirill, primate of the ROC, referred to Putin's rule as "a miracle of God," two prominent Muslim leaders in Russia also expressed their support. Mufti Ravil Gainutdin told Putin, "Muslims know you, Muslims trust you, Muslims are wishing you success," while Mufti Ismail Berdiyev explained further, "You are the only person who has shown the United States its place" (Bryanski 2012).

9   Consider, for example, how the United States and its allies relentlessly have criticized Russian legislation against "promotion of homosexuality," to the point of even entertaining the idea of boycotting the Sochi Winter Olympics of 2014, while, at the same time, turning a blind eye to Middle-Eastern allies such as Saudi Arabia where homosexuality is punishable by death. Also relevant is the blatant hypocrisy of American accusations against Russia for "hacking" the 2016 American Presidential election, when the United States has a record of meddling in countless democratic elections across the world since the end of World War II. See, for example, *On Western Terrorism* (Chomsky and Vltcheck 2013), *Hegemony or Survival* (Chomsky 2003), *Empire's Workshop* (Grandin 2007), *Exposing the Lies of Empire* (Vltcheck 2015) and *The Shock Doctrine: The Rise of Disaster Capitalism* (Klein 2008).

killed for their faith. They were not told to renounce Jesus Christ or be executed, as the early Christian martyrs prior to the Edict of Milan were. They were killed for their social class, their crimes (real or perceived) against the Russian people, and their politics[10]. Referring to the majority of the Romanov family as Christian martyrs makes sense only if one interprets the death of Tsar Nicholas II (and the royal family) as the assassination of the "friend of God" and "sacred king." Crucial here, is that deeming Nicholas II's death as martyric, vitiates the power of the canonization of Grand Duchess Elizabeth Romanov (St. Elizabeth the New Martyr). Elizabeth forgave the revolutionary who murdered her husband (and pleaded for his life to be spared), then renounced her wealth and royal status and became a nun, and worked tirelessly for the next 13 years of her life to alleviate the sufferings of the poor and oppressed. The implications of the sharp differences between Grand Duchess Elizabeth and Tsar Nicholas II will become all the more significant in light of the insights of secularization theory.

The second major problem created by ROCOR's absolutist insistence on *symphonia* revolves around its accusation that "the educated classes in Russia, raised in so-called "Westernizing" traditions, pushed Russia with almost suicidal relentlessness into the abyss, pushing the Russian people in every way possible to reject their faith, their Tsar and their Fatherland" (Synod of Bishops 2017). Again we see that ROCOR sees Orthodox Christianity, the Tsar, and the Russian State as inextricably linked, which in turn inhibits thoughtful reflection on *why* these things happened. While ROCOR's description here is largely accurate, it fails to ask crucial questions that secularization theory will help illuminate. Why did the educated classes come to reject these concepts? And what do we make of the countless Russian Orthodox theologians, philosophers, writers, and artists who remained committed to the Orthodox faith but rejected Tsarism and statist nationalism[11]?

4. Freedom, Anti-Secularization and Metropolitan Hilarion Alfeyev

Unlike ROCOR's epistle, Metropolitan Hilarion Alfeyev's address to the Pontifical Theological Faculty avoids both triumphalism and overt nostalgia for Russia's tsarist heritage. Instead, Alfeyev's address consists of three major (and interrelated) claims worthy of analysis and evaluation: (1) a critique of the West and its apotheosis of "liberal democracy"; (2) a defense of the concept of "symphonia"; and (3) a reading of Constantine's Edict of Milan as parallel to the contemporary situation in Russia under the governance of Vladimir Putin. As we will see below, secularization theory will validate important aspects of Alfeyev's critique of the West, while also providing important crucial warnings concerning the likely outcomes that will result from a wholesale embrace of *symphonia* and the Edict of Milan which ushered in this era in ancient Christianity.

Alfeyev's critique of the West itself consists of two main assertions, which, at first glance seem to contradict each other. On the one hand, Alfeyev is concerned that Western liberal democracies are themselves becoming increasingly totalitarian, while, on the other, he believes that they are decaying into an ethos of libertine amorality. Close attention to his argument, however, reveals a cohesive (if not entirely persuasive) thesis. In short, Alfeyev maintains that Western liberal democracies are increasingly limiting the freedom of their own populaces and exerting dominance over non-Western countries and cultures, while concealing this dominance through the ideal of a freedom that constitutes little more than freedom from all forms of traditional morality. In this regard, Alfeyev's concerns are not far from Charles DeGaulle's, who was deeply concerned about "the American will to power cloaked in idealism." Alfeyev links the present situation in Europe and America to the pre-Constantinian

---

[10] During the "Red Terror," for example, religion played little to no role in determining who should be executed. Martin Latsis, high ranking official of the Bolshevik police (the Cheka) instructed his subordinates, "Do not look in materials you have gathered for evidence that a suspect acted or spoke against the Soviet authorities. The first question you should ask him is what class he belongs to, what is his origin, education, profession. These questions should determine his fate. This is the essence of the Red Terror" (Tolczyk 1999, p. 19).

[11] I have here in mind Fyodor Dostoevsky, Vladimir Soloviev, Wassily Kandinsky, Nicholas Berdyaev, Alexei Khomiakov, Maria Skobtsova (St. Maria of Paris) and, although he ultimately charted his own path outside the official confines of the Orthodox Church, Leo Tolstoy.

Roman Empire, arguing that what "is happening today in the West is the gradual restoration of the Pax Romana, of global international hegemony." Secularization is thus, for Alfeyev, the liberation of the modern liberal democratic state from the checks to its power that Christianity has to offer, for the removal of state power from religious influence "has in reality released ... the European super-state, which is the cultural heir of the Roman Empire, a colossal energy of subjugation to authority." His most forceful assertion along these lines, which resonates strongly with the concerns of Western intellectuals from Noam Chomsky to Glenn Greenwald, is based on the ever-growing power of the security state and its burgeoning surveillance apparatus[12]. He describes the "burning energy" of the security state thus:

> This burning energy today aims to break completely with Christianity which has restrained its totalitarian impulses for seventeen centuries. As a result this energy unconsciously strives towards the establishment of an absolute dictatorship, which will demand the establishment of complete control over every member of society. Is this not where we are heading for 'in the interests of security' in agreeing to the obligatory introduction of electronic passports, of universal fingerprinting and the ubiquitous presence of closed-circuit television cameras? After all, this can be used for other purposes which can also be ascribed to 'strengthening security measures (Alfeyev 2014).

While Alfeyev's claim that post-Constantinian Christianity restrained the totalitarian impulses of nation-states is beyond dubious, we shall see below that his core concern that Christianity bears within it the potential to resist totalitarianism resonates heavily with the thesis of Jose Casanova regarding the place of religion in today's public sphere.

The second part of Alfeyev's claim, that the only freedom guaranteed in modern Western nation states is freedom from morality, begins to reveal that Alfeyev's ideal model for church-state interaction is itself a restoration of *symphonia*, which has been historically far more totalitarian than Alfeyev wishes to admit. Further developing his linkage of the pre-Constantinian Roman Empire with Western liberal democracies, Alfeyev ultimately makes the highly unsubstantiated claim that the latter are worse than the former. Accordingly, he contends that the Roman Empire was largely indifferent towards immorality, while modern democracies are concerned with *promoting* immorality as normative. Alfeyev's primary problem with both the Romans and the modern democratic state is that religion is reduced to a tool that bolsters state power. As he puts it,

> The modern-day democratic state is even viewed by some as the role of guarantor of the legal status of immorality, for it protects citizens from the encroachments of 'religious sanctimoniousness.' The role of religion, as in Rome, is seen in an exclusively utilitarian light—it is the servant of the state without any claims to truth, the 'personal affair of each individual.' And yet the state must be recognized unconditionally and we must obey its laws, including those that undermine its foundations (Alfeyev 2014).

According to Alfeyev, therefore, the pre-Constantinian Roman Empire and the modern liberal democratic state each desire absolute power, protecting their citizens only from having to be subject to religiously defined moral norms. For this reason, Alfeyev sees the great contribution of Constantine to be the creation of a new space in which symphonia between Church and state "allowed the Church fully to reveal herself in her ministry to thousands of people, to realize her gracious gifts in history, to exert an influence on the formation of many cultures and traditions" (Alfeyev 2014). It is this "greatest merit of Constantine" that Alfeyev argues is being reduplicated in Vladimir Putin's Russia.

Alfeyev's endorsement of symphonia ultimately reveals that he defines ecclesiastical freedom primarily in terms of the Church's freedom to exert influence over the state. Furthermore, the

---

[12] In addition to the aforementioned works of Chomsky, Vltchek, and Grandin, see Greenwald's *No Place to Hide: Edward Snowden, the NSA, and the U.S. Surveillance State* (Greenwald 2014).

"secularization" that he opposes is not the official separation of powers (as in Berger's definition), but any situation in which the state increases its power and wields this power over the Church. Hence, he does not romanticize the entire Tsarist era of Russian Orthodoxy, noting that "with the abolition of the Patriarchate [under Tsar Peter the Great] and the setting up in 1721 of the Holy Ruling Synod ... there began the period of secularization and the subjugation of the Church to the state" (Alfeyev 2014). For Alfeyev, the Church must neither merge with the state, nor become subject to it, nor serve the state in a utilitarian way that increases state power. Rather, the Church must be free to exert a transformative influence over state and society.

As already noted, Alfeyev takes the perfect model for this interaction to be the post-Constantinian era ushered in by the Edict of Milan, and he claims that this is again the current model for interaction in Russia. The Edict of Milan ushered in "a golden age of Christianity" during which, according to Alfeyev's selective narrative, "influenced the renewal of all of society's institutions, gave a new integral foundation to family relationships and the attitude towards women, and ensured the gradual eradication of the institution of slavery in the empire" (Alfeyev 2014). Focusing only on these arguably positive influences, Alfeyev contends that ecclesial power "upon entering the structure of state power, did not merge with it," but was the primary catalyst for the positive transformation of European society. These developments are so thoroughly sacrosanct in Alfeyev's understanding, that the rejection of *symphonia* "would spell the death of civilization for our continent." Fortunately, this has not yet become the case, for "today the Church and state in Russia, as well as in some countries in the post-Soviet expanse, are able to speak with a single voice and express a united position," while at the same time the "principle of mutual non-interference of Church and state in the internal affairs of each other must be preserved and is being preserved" (Alfeyev 2014). In short, a new "golden age of Christianity" is being reborn in Russia and other post-Soviet states, because the spirit of the Edict of Milan has itself been reborn in these nation states[13].

5. The Edict of Milan: Edict of Toleration or Edict Increasing State Power?

In light of these bold claims, we must ask whether Alfeyev's interpretation of the Edict of Milan (and its long-term social and political consequences) is compelling or even tenable. In Alfeyev's reading, the Edict of Milan "in essence recognized the fact that the Church is not some marginal sect that corrupted the traditional pillars of society. On the contrary, the document's authors were convinced that Christians were capable of directing the mercy of God to all the people." In other words, the Edict was a recognition by Constantine (and the other officials who drafted it) of the value of Christianity and its ability to bring transformative grace to all of Roman society, revitalizing its morality. Through this peculiarly idealistic lens, Alfeyev asserts, "it is precisely this moral potential, rooted within the free human person, that the emperor Constantine saw in Christianity when he allowed this powerful positive creative energy to be released and act upon all of society." Because of his emphasis on the "free human person," Alfeyev is careful to differentiate Constantine's Edict of Milan from Theodosius I's Edict of Thessalonica (380 CE), "which proclaimed Christianity to be a state religion and placed the traditional pagan religion in effect outside of the law." The Edict of Milan thus represents a "golden age" because it preserves the freedom of the individual person, while also opening up the space through which Roman society was permanently transformed and morally improved. Moreover,

---

13 Hence Alfeyev explicitly states, "Something similar to what happened in the Roman Empire in 313 took place twenty six years ago within the then Soviet Union. We were witnesses to how the Church in our country, after many trails and bloody victims, suddenly came out of the ghetto, rose up from her knees and began her triumphant march through the cities and villages. A significant part of society again discovered its Christian identity." Reinforcing the idea that these developments are unequivocally positive, he goes on to state that "certain events in the Church's history cannot be explained other than as a divine miracle. Such a miracle was the era following the Edict of Milan in 313. No less a miracle happened in our country at the end of the 1980s. Could people, who only a few years before this risked their welfare for their faith, and in some instances their lives too, evaluate the freedom that had unexpectedly fallen on their heads as anything other than a divine miracle?" (Alfeyev 2014).

it is the Edict of Milan that "opened a new page in the life of the Roman Empire: it determined the paradigm of the development of church-state relations in the countries that came into being after its collapse or under its cultural influence" (Alfeyev 2014).

There are three main problems with Alfeyev's triumphalistic interpretation of the Edict of Milan. First, the text of the Edict of Milan itself reveals that its aims were to increase state power and potentially resurrect the Pax Romana, not bring about the transformation of the Roman society and its morals. Second, the "golden age of Christianity" to which Alfeyev refers is not possible to ascribe to the era of the Edict of Milan in a way that remains separable from the Edict of Thessalonica, the sixth-century code of Justinian, and the fusion of Church-state power that occurred in Medieval Western Europe. Finally, Alfeyev's complaints against the contemporary West reveal that he yearns not for the era of the Edict of Milan and its tolerance, but rather for the post-Theodosian and post-Justinian eras of extensive Christian hegemony over all aspects of social life.

In order to understand how the Edict of Milan was intended to increase state power, it is necessary to recall the main reasons given for the persecution of Christians in the first place. According to Tertullian (c. 155–c. 240 CE), Christians were frequently scapegoated by the Romans for not submitting to the imperial cult and thus becoming "the cause of every public defeat and every misfortune of the people. If the Tiber rises to the city walls, if the Nile does not rise to the fields, if the sky stays the same, if the earth moves, if there is a famine, a plague, straightaway the cry is heard, 'The Christians to the lions!'" (Tertullian *Apologeticum 40*, *ANF* 3:47). Tertullian's claim makes sense only if one understands that from the reign of Augustus (27 BCE-14 CE), the Roman imperial religion had come to consist of "religious festivals [which] proclaimed the 'good news' (*euangelion*) of the deified emperor, who, as savior or son of God, had brought peace, faith, and justice into the world. Assuming the highest priestly office, that of *pontifex maximus*, the emperor himself became a divine being in Roman imperial religion" (Chidester 2000, p. 5). Because Christians refused to participate in these festivals and to offer incense to the deified emperor, their refusals were seen not only as subversive to the values of the state and of Roman society, but also as potentially awakening the ire of the very gods that protected the Roman Empire. Accordingly, "Christian rejection of the gods registered as an attack on the city. In these terms, Christians were charged with committing crimes not only against the gods, but also against society" (Chidester 2000, p. 75). Christians were dangerous "atheists," who were weakening the state by causing both natural and supernatural dissention.

If the Edict of Milan were merely about promoting "tolerance" of these dangerous Christian dissidents, it would have been an unnecessary proclamation, for the Edict of Toleration by Emperor Galerius in 311 CE had already made Christianity a legal religion and ended the persecution of Christians throughout the Empire. Mere toleration, however, is not the same as affirmation, or, *a fortiori* appropriation. Hence, two years later the Edict of Milan was promulgated by Constantine with language that indicates a clear intent to increase state power and reclaim the Pax Romana, which had disintegrated nearly a century earlier. The text of the Edict thus clearly states that "we ... grant to the Christians and others full authority to observe that religion which each preferred; whence any Divinity whatsoever in the seat of the heavens may be propitious and kindly disposed to us and all who are placed under our rule" (Edict of Milan 313). Christians were no longer merely to be tolerated as harmless pseudo-subversives; they were to receive full inclusion so that their God might too become one of the protectors of the Empire, who "may show in all things His usual favor and benevolence." Finally, the Edict makes clear that other religions have previously been granted full inclusion "for the sake of the peace of our times," and that extending this full inclusion to Christians will create a more powerful, stable state that is more fully equipped to resurrect some semblance of the Pax Romana. Ironic, then, are Alfeyev's claims that it is only Western liberal democracies that wish to increase their power and enforce a new Pax Romana, when the very text of the Edict of Milan indicates that it was promulgated in order to achieve these same aims[14].

Even more problematic than Alfeyev's misreading of the purpose of the Edict of Milan, however, is the manner in which he claims that the era that it ushered in was the "golden age of Christianity." Whether intentional or not, by making this claim, Alfeyev subtly elides the era of the Edict of Milan (313–379 CE) with Theodosius's Edict of Thessalonica (making Christianity the official religion of the Roman Empire), and the Code of Justinian (compiled between 528–529 CE). For if Alfeyev truly means to focus only on the period between 313 and 379, six of the seven Ecumenical Councils of the Orthodox Churches would be excluded. Moreover, the great cultural achievements he extols in the arts, politics, and culture all come after Theodosius and Justinian. Byzantine iconography and music, the architectural marvels of the Hagia Sophia, and the encoding of Christian morality in civil law, all of which are implied by Alfeyev's phrase "golden age" occur long after Christianity achieves mere acceptance within the Empire.

The stakes are high in this subtle elision of eras, for Alfeyev has also stated that this is the new era of Russian church-state interaction. For in the codes of Theodosius and Justinian we find that the formerly persecuted have become the persecutors. In the Theodosian laws of the late 4th century, for example, we find, enshrined in law, instructions for the punishment of those deemed to be Christian heretics (including heavy fines), orders to close all pagan temples and to execute those who continue to practice pagan temple sacrifices, the abrogation of property rights for those who convert from Christianity to paganism, and protocols for fining and publicly shaming those who profess the Manichaean religion (Theodosius 1997). Under Justinian, such regulations were intensified. Justinian closed the Academy of Plato and Aristotle, and left only one religion, Judaism, with legal status besides non-heretical Christianity. However, Judaism itself was subject to standards set forth by Justinian's laws. Jews were allowed to gather and read their "Sacred Scriptures" in Hebrew, but could do so only if Greek or Latin were also used so that the average citizen could understand and scrutinize what was being read and taught. This was to ensure that "there shall be no opportunity for their interpreters, who make use only of the Hebrew, to corrupt it in any way they like, since the ignorance of the public conceals their depravity." Reading of the Mishnah was prohibited entirely, and Jewish congregations were only considered valid if they taught that there was a resurrection of the dead. Put differently, the Byzantine state made itself the arbiter of what constituted "true Judaism" both in terms of orthodoxy and orthopraxy (Justinian 1998).

Is too much being made here of Alfeyev's elision of the era of Milan with that which came later through the use of the term "golden age"? It seems that one could charitably grant that perhaps he was simply using sloppy or imprecise language. However, his complaints against what he perceives to be the menace of secularization demonstrate otherwise. Pro-LGBT billboards in England, an "all is permitted attitude" he alleges to be characteristic of the West, and the infamous Pussy Riot incident at Christ the Savior Cathedral in Moscow, are all evidence of a rising "totalitarian freedom." This "totalitarian freedom, based on human passions," threatens to "return us to the times of the pagans" and "instead of respect for the feelings of other people, it preaches an all-is-permitted attitude, ignoring the beliefs and values of the majority" (Alfeyev 2014)[15]. Yet in each of these cases, Western security states teetering towards totalitarianism are not enforcing libertinism and suppressing dissent; rather, private citizens are voicing their opinions in the public sphere with differing levels of intensity. However intensely private citizens may be voicing their opinions, one is left wondering

---

[14] For an excellent collection of recent essays on the legacy of Constantine's Edict, see *Christianity, Democracy, and the Shadow of Constantine* (Demacopoulos and Papanikolaou 2016).

[15] The "Pussy Riot Incident" is a particularly complex issue as it was, on the one hand, an act of protest against government and ecclesiastical corruption, and, on the other hand, an act of trespass in private sacred space that was deemed highly offensive by much of the Russian populace. For nuanced and competing assessments of what was at stake in Pussy Riot's act of protest see both "An Appeal to Mary: An Analysis of Pussy Riot's Punk Performance in Moscow" (Denysenko 2013), and "Women on the Fault Lines of Faith: Pussy Riot and the Insider/Outsider Challenge to Post-Soviet Orthodoxy" (Shevzov 2014).

how Alfeyev can logically equate such free expression with totalitarianism and oppression. Ironically, it is Alfeyev who appears to be countenancing state suppression of dissenting minority voices that offend the sensibilities of the majority. Accordingly, one can only conclude that Alfeyev believes Russia's legislation suppressing the kinds of billboards he laments seeing in England is "freedom," while allowing private citizens to fund such billboards is totalitarianism.

6. Validation and Admonition from Secularization Theorists

"Historically speaking, Christianity has been its own gravedigger" (Berger 1990, p. 129). Berger's socio-historical reworking of Nietzsche's proclamation that "God is dead, and we have killed him," is no less ominous nor is it any less insightful than the philosopher's earth-shaking assessment of Euro-American culture. Of crucial importance here is that the core issues identified above in ROCOR's epistle and Alfeyev's address bear within themselves all of the elements through which Christianity dug its own grave. The danger, in short, is that a resurgent Russian Orthodoxy appears poised to become its own gravedigger. Perhaps of even greater importance is that the concerns of ROCOR and Alfeyev also miss the elements Jose Casanova has identified as central to the revitalization of Christianity in the contemporary context.

Let us recapitulate five essential points drawn from the ROCOR epistle and the Alfeyev address. First, ROCOR has consistently conflated political martyrdom with martyrdom for the faith, which is directly related to their conflation of church and state. Second, ROCOR's absolutist insistence on *symphonia* revolves around its accusation that "the educated classes in Russia, raised in so-called 'Westernizing' traditions, pushed Russia with almost suicidal relentlessness into the abyss." Third, Alfeyev's positions indicate that increase in state power is positive so long as it corresponds with an increase in the power of the Church to enforce its morality as socially normative. Fourth, Alfeyev's stance inherently privileges the feelings of the majority within a given population, thereby implicitly endorsing the suppression and marginalization of dissenting or minority voices. Fifth, both ROCOR and Alfeyev express significant concern about the hegemony Western liberal democracies hold and the aggressiveness by which they impose their will both on their own populaces and on other cultures.

Of these five points, the first four all illustrate characteristics of how Christianity became its "own gravedigger." While Berger identifies a number of complex factors that fuel secularization in a way that renders religion increasingly irrelevant, the most pertinent ones to explore here are the unintended consequences that result from Christianity's conception of history as linear and, moreover, as a story of progress (Berger 1990, pp. 117–19). That is, Christianity gave the world a set of ethics and values, along with a conception of history that presupposes progress towards greater and greater actualization of these ethics and values. For example, the Christian Scriptures preach universal and unconditional love (e.g., 1 Cor 13), a duty to care for the poor (e.g., James 2–5), and a radically egalitarian message of the equality of all before God (e.g., Galatians 3). Because of its cultural ascendancy it transformed the values of Roman Empire and thus the European culture descended from it. Once these values are taken as "self-evident" within a culture, what then happens to the various churches when they no longer promote progress in these areas, and indeed often become obstacles to such progress? What happens when Christendom begins to stand in the way of universal and unconditional love? What happens when it merges with political and economic powers that ignore or even villainize the poor? What happens when Christianity manifests itself as deeply hierarchical and patriarchal instead of radically egalitarian?

The answer, to repeat the phrase again, is that through these instances "Christianity becomes its own gravedigger." As Berger puts it, the result is that the "consciousness of Western man" is thrown into a crisis that inaugurates "an age of revolution" (Berger 1990, p. 79). More specifically, to quote Albert Camus, humanity "launches the essential undertaking of rebellion, which is that of replacing the reign of grace with the reign of justice" (Camus 1956, p. 56). The secular revolutionary, who has internalized the values laid down by Christianity, begins to oppose the Church for standing in the way of progress in love, in care for the poor, in promoting egalitarianism, etc. Put differently, because Christianity made promises that it now refuses to keep, it appears instead as institutionalized injustice—an agent of hate, a defender of the rich and legitimizer of wealth accumulation, and an upholder of oppressive hierarchical systems. In doing so, Christians largely become guardians of the status quo and "traditional values," especially sexual norms, while secular humanists paradoxically become those most passionately committed to social progress that actualizes the core proclamations of the Gospel. When such a state of affairs has developed, the bulk of Christianity renders itself largely irrelevant at best, and an enemy to be opposed and overthrown at its worst[16].

If we consult the work of Charles Taylor and Mikhail Epstein, we find evidence these processes may already be beginning to occur in Russia, in ways far more subtle than the "Pussy Riot Incident" or organized protests against both the ROC and the Putin government. Taylor, following Epstein, argues that secularization in Russia is most prevalent not in such overtly rebellious movements, but in the large number of Russian people who are embracing "minimal religion" instead of devout practice of Russian Orthodox Christianity. "Minimal religion" correlates rather well to the growing number of people in Western Europe and North America who identify as "spiritual but not religious" (Taylor 2007, p. 535). Elaborating on Epstein's groundbreaking study, Taylor states, "'Minimal religion' is a spirituality lived in one's immediate circle, with family and friends, rather than in churches, one especially aware of the particular, both in individual human beings, and in the places and things which surround us. In response to the universalist concern for the "distant one" stressed in Marxist communism, it seeks to honor the 'image and likeness of God' in the particular people who share our lives" (Taylor 2007, p. 534). In other words, a significant portion of the Russian populace is recognizing the common cultural values that were shared both by their Russian Orthodox Church and by the Marxist Soviet government. At the same time, they retain a certain independence and individualism because they recognize both of these institutions as having ultimately betrayed their own ideals. In sum, if Taylor and Epstein are correct about the rising prevalence of "minimal religion" in Russia, it would appear that the Berger (and Camus) thesis is unfolding in contemporary Russia as significant portions of the populace have accepted the key values of Christianity and Marxism, while becoming suspicious of both the ROC and the Russian state's interest in embodying these values[17].

Is there then any way for the Russian Orthodox Church and other organized religious institutions to remain relevant and even flourish in the contemporary world? Jose Casanova's landmark *Public Religions in the Modern World* argues that the answer, "on the basis of . . . empirical evidence," is "an unconditional yes" (Casanova 1994, p. 38). In Casanova's reading, because Western liberal democracies themselves grew out of Enlightenment appropriation of the core Christian values mentioned above, especially egalitarianism, they are representative of the kind of secularizing revolution for which Berger's theories account. However, Casanova also agrees with fellow secularization theorist Talal Asad[18], as well as with ROCOR and Alfeyev, that Western liberal democracies have in turn betrayed these same ideals in deeply imperialistic and hegemonic ways. As Casanova incisively puts it, "the two dynamos of modernity, the capitalist market and the administrative state, continue their self-propelled march toward a world system, wrecking and challenging every pre-modern tradition and life form that stands in their way" (Casanova 1994, p. 234). According to Casanova, this development has opened up a renewed space for religious vitality in

---

[16] Nevertheless, it is important not to confuse Christian defense of traditional values, with "fundamentalism" or "extremism." For an illuminating exploration of the differences between these positions, and, moreover, how they are playing out in contemporary Russia, see "Postsecular Conflicts and the Global Struggle for Traditional Values" (Stoeckl 2016).

[17] Hard statistics on what Epstein and Taylor describe as "minimal religion" and its affinities with both Russian Orthodox Christianity and Soviet Communism are difficult to ascertain. A number of recent Pew research studies appear to support their assertions, however. See, for example, Epstein's "Minimal Religion" and "Post-Atheism: From Apophatic Theology to 'Minimal Religion'" in *Russian Postmodernism* (Epstein 1999), and compare with two Pew surveys and the conclusions drawn from them (Diamant 2017; Masci 2017).

[18] See, for example, Asad's *Formations of the Secular* (Asad 2003) for a similar line of argumentation that critiques on Western liberal democracies and their attempts to unilaterally enforce Western constructions of secularity on predominantly Islamic cultures.

a modern, secular context that does not attempt to "undo" secularization and return to a merger of religious and state institutions.

The dialectical mechanism that Casanova identifies as opening up this renewed space for religious vitality is both complex and straightforward. He explains:

> A mutually reinforcing dynamic of recognition and rapprochement between religion and modernity has taken place, bringing to a close the conflictive cycles opened up by the Enlightenment critique of religion. On the one hand, the critical recognition of the dialectics of enlightenment and the postmodern self-limitation placed upon the rationalist project of secular redemption have led to a rediscovery of the validity claims of religion and to a recognition of the positive role of the Catholic church in setting limits to the absolutist tendencies of the modern state, whether in its Polish communist variant or in its Latin American "national security" variant (Casanova 1994, p. 62).

As proof of this thesis, Casanova engages in five case studies, three of which focus on how in Spain, Poland, and Brazil, the Roman Catholic Church transitioned away from state-sponsorship and participation in national oligarchical structures to supporting instead egalitarian movements, labor movements, and economic justice movements. That is, in each case, the Roman Catholic Church divested itself of formal power and began to take a stance against corporate and state power on behalf of those who were oppressed, suffering, or disenfranchised. In a nutshell, the Catholic Church began to actively promote the very values that the state was (ideally) supposed to uphold and yet had betrayed. What was the result? In each case, the Roman Catholic Church experienced a significant resurgence in the respect of the populace at large (amongst both Catholics and non-Catholics), as well as an increase in regular attendance at religious services (Casanova 1994, pp. 75–134). The great irony is that "it was this voluntary 'disestablishment' of Catholicism, this change of self-identity, which permitted the Catholic church to play an active role in processes of democratization from Spain to Poland, from Brazil to the Philippines" (Casanova 1994, p. 62). As the saying goes, "turnabout is fair play." When and where nation-states based on Enlightenment ideology were democratizing forces that broke down oppressive power structures, they gained greater credibility than religious institutions. Now that liberal nation-states and their collusion with oligarchic corporate forces have become increasingly oppressive, religious movements that stand against these powers as democratizing forces regain their credibility against the state.

Let us return now to the first four points gleaned from ROCOR's epistle and Alfeyev's address and analyze why, if Berger and Casanova are correct, the ROC may be unwittingly digging its own grave. As noted, ROCOR has conflated political martyrdom with martyrdom for the faith. If Tsar Nicholas (Romanov) II's death is martyric in the same fashion that St. Elizabeth Romanov's is, a perfect opportunity for the ROC to champion the Church as defender of the poor and oppressed is lost. St. Elizabeth divested herself from her noble status and worked tirelessly amongst the poor—and yet was killed by the Bolsheviks anyway. She is a powerful and enduring symbol of how a person living out the Gospel can actualize human liberation more effectively than either a Tsarist state or a Marxist one. By elevating Tsar Nicholas to the same status, this symbol is all but neutralized, and the ROC is re-enshrined as the church of the powerful and the elite.

Furthermore, ROCOR blames the revolution on the apostasy of "the educated classes in Russia, raised in so-called 'Westernizing' traditions." But why did they apostatize in the first place? Was it not for the very reasons that Berger and Casanova identify, namely, that the ROC had arguably betrayed the Gospel through its failure to oppose an oppressive state that the Bolsheviks arose as a this-worldly "messianism" bent on actualizing the promises of the Gospel in this world and not deferring it to an afterlife? Third, Alfeyev's endorsement of using state power to combat Western sexual libertinism, while remaining silent on the state's duty to promote equality and uplift the destitute, likewise suggests a bleak future for the vitality of the ROC in Russian culture. Finally, Alfeyev's stance privileges the feelings of the majority within a given population, and endorses the suppression and marginalization of dissenting or minority voices. Such a posture may "play well" in the short run, but is virtually guaranteed to replicate the "apostasy of the educated classes," which, in turn, will have a trickle-down effect to Russian society more broadly.

7. Conclusion: Or, How Not to Dig Our Own Graves

What, then, is the best path forward? In my opinion, as both a philosopher of religion and Eastern Orthodox theologian (and minister), I believe the answer lies in the title of this present collection of essays, *Inward Being and Outward Identity*. Only if the ROC, and the Orthodox Churches strive to come to a place where our inward ideals (the Gospel itself) and outward manifestations are one and the same will we flourish and remain vibrant in a secular world. Only if the Church promotes Christ's unconditional love and takes a consistent stand for the oppressed and marginalized in the face of increasing state power, whether this be in Western liberal democracies or in Russia and the former Soviet-bloc countries, will it overflow with the culturally transformative power of the Gospel. For this reason, I have not yet discussed the fifth point stressed by both ROCOR and Alfeyev, namely, their desire to resist the hegemony Western liberal democracies currently possess and the aggressiveness by which they impose their collective will both on their own populaces and on other cultures.

This final point sheds light on at least one reason why the ROC and the Russian government currently have high approval ratings with the Russian populace. As secularization theorists like Berger and Talal Asad note, "While secularization may be viewed as a global phenomenon of modern societies, it is not uniformly distributed within them" (Berger 1990, p. 108)[19]. For both Berger and Asad, secularization and its manifestations will differ greatly depending on whether they occur in a Protestant, Catholic, Orthodox, Sunni, Shia, Hindu, or Buddhist context, as the secular as such will always retain many of the religious and cultural values even after these values no longer exert official dominance over state institutions and popular culture. Accordingly, when, for example, French post-Catholic understandings of "the secular" are imposed on a largely Muslim populace in Algeria, any resulting backlash is not against secularization itself, but against the oppression that results from colonizing another culture with an alien construction of what counts as genuinely "modern" and "secular." In this regard, the ROC's resistance to "Westernization" can be read as a way in which the ROC is functioning as a democratizing force in a manner that would fall under the umbrella of what Casanova describes. The crucial issue, then, is that this does not become the sole manner in which the ROC enacts resistance to oppression and promotes human freedom.

Curiously enough, the broader answer lies embedded within Alfeyev's address, although it is unfortunately left undeveloped, unexplored, and, ultimately, contradicted by the rest of Alfeyev's conclusions. For Alfeyev contends that more than any other religion or ideology, Christianity possesses a "reverential attitude towards freedom" that has the power to resist "totalitarian" and "despotic" states. Thus he quotes "the great Russian philosopher Nikolai Berdyaev [who] said that 'freedom, above all freedom, is the soul of Christian philosophy and this is what cannot be granted by any other abstract and rationalistic philosophy'" (Alfeyev 2014). Alfeyev thus agrees with Berdyaev on the level of "inward being" but remains, wittingly or unwittingly, an opponent of Berdyaev in terms of "outward identity." This is because Berdyaev, while he endorsed "theocracy," did so as an avowed anarchist, not as a believer in Tsarism, monarchy, democracy, or any other state power. As Berdyaev himself states:

> If a religious rebirth be possible, only then on this soil will there be the revealing of the religious meaning of secular culture and earthly liberation, the revealing of the truth about mankind. For the new religious consciousness the declaration of the will of God is together with this a declaration of the rights of man, a revealing of the Divine within mankind ... This will be the victory of the true theocracy, whether over a false democratism—the apotheosis of the quantitative collectivity of human wills, or so also over

---

[19] See also *Formations of the Secular* (Asad 2003, pp. 1–20, 181–204).

the false theocraticism—all that apotheosis of the human will within Caesaropapism or Papocaesarism. Christ cannot have human vicarage in the person of the tsar or high-priest. He—is Himself the Tsar and High-Priest, and He will reign in the world. 'Thy Kingdom come, Thy Will be done on earth, as it is in Heaven" (Berdyaev 1907).

Berdyaev believed strongly in the transformation of culture through the message of the Gospel, but because the message of the Gospel is about human freedom and divine indwelling of the human being, state coercion has no role to play in it, whether it be the coercion of the masses in a "liberal democratic" state, or a coercion by a monarch in an imperial or dictatorial state. For Berdyaev, Christianity is a community of people freely living in solidarity with each other and the will of God, and accordingly the state literally has no role to play in promotion of the Gospel. Berdyaev's views also align seamlessly with Casanova's. The key to Christianity's rebirth lies not in having "toleration" or "*symphonia*" from a governmental power, but in being the force that is defending and manifesting "the rights of man."

Understood this way, the "golden age" of Christianity, if we are going to audaciously label any age as such, ought to be understood as its first three centuries, when Christians freely associated and influenced society by their genuine love of each other and willingness to be persecuted unto death to bear witness to what Berdyaev calls "the declaration of the rights of man." The martyrs did not "buy" a later golden age with their blood as Alfeyev asserts; theirs was the age in which Christians were most free to reenact the life, the teachings, and the death of Jesus. Christianity is a free association of human community. Nations are not. As the American historian Howard Zinn put it:

> Nations are not communities and never have been. The history of any country, presented as the history of a family, conceals fierce conflicts of interest (sometimes exploding, most often repressed) between conquerors and conquered, masters and slaves, capitalists and workers, dominators and dominated in race and sex. And in such a world of conflict, a world of victims and executioners, it is the job of thinking people, as Albert Camus suggested, not to be on the side of the executioners (Zinn 2009, p. 10).

If one agrees with Zinn, we might reformulate this phrase (again in a way that Casanova would approve of) to state, "it is the unequivocal duty of Christians not to be on the side of the executioners." If we turn to the original Camus quote that Zinn has paraphrased, we will find a fitting conclusion to this essay, for Camus's exact words are that if we think in a manner "free of fear as well as pretension, we may be able to help create the conditions for a just philosophy and for a provisional accord among those of us unwilling to be either victims or executioners" (Camus 2006, p. 261). It is fear that drives religious figures to again and again seek the support of the state or *symphonia* with it. But no one who reads the lives of St. Stephen, St. Ignatius of Antioch, St. Perpetua, St. Polycarp, St. Elizabeth the New Martyr, and the like will find fearful victims. Rather, it is the martyrs who again and again assert that it is they who hold true power and freedom, while their executioners are the actual victims of the state's directives. If Orthodoxy seeks not to become "its own gravedigger," all of us in the Church would do well to stand with the martyrs and with Camus, unwilling to be either victim or executioner.

Conflicts of Interest: The author declares no conflict of interest.

References

Alfeyev, Hilarion (Metropolitan Hilarion). 2014. The Theology of Freedom: Christianity and Secular Power from the Edict of Milan to the Present. Available online: https://mospat.ru/en/2014/10/18/news109757/ (accessed on 3 May 2017).

Altizer, Thomas J. J. 2002. *The New Gospel of Christian Atheism*. Aurora: Davies Group.

Asad, Talal. 2003. *Formations of the Secular: Christianity, Islam, Modernity*. Stanford: Stanford University Press.

Berdyaev, Nicholas (Nikolai). 1907. Nihilism on a Religious Soil. Translated by Fr. S. Janos. *Berdyaev Online Library*, May 6. Available online: http://www.berdyaev.com/berdiaev/berd_lib/1907_135_4.html (accessed on 3 May 2017).

Berdyaev, Nicholas (Nikolai). 1949. Political Testament. Translated by E. Lampert. *World Review* Spring: 32–37, 80.

Berger, Peter. 1990. *The Sacred Canopy: Elements of a Sociological Theory of Religion*. New York: Anchor Books.

Bryanski, Gleb. 2012. Russian Patriarch Calls Putin Era "Miracle of God." *Reuters*, February 9. Available online: http://uk.reuters.com/article/uk-russia-putin-religion-idUKTRE81722Y20120208 (accessed on 3 May 2017).

Camus, Albert. 1956. *The Rebel*. New York: Vintage Books.

Camus, Albert. 2006. Neither Victims nor Executioners. In *Camus at Combat: Writing 1944–1947*. Translated by Arthur Goldhammer. Princeton: Princeton University Press, pp. 256–76.

Casanova, Jose. 1994. *Public Religions in the Modern World*. Chicago: University of Chicago Press.

Chidester, David. 2000. *Christianity: A Global History*. New York: HarperCollins.

Chomsky, Noam. 2003. *Hegemony or Survival: America's Quest for Global Dominance (American Empire Project)*. New York: Henry Holt.

Chomsky, Noam, and Andre Vltcheck. 2013. *On Western Terrorism: From Hiroshima to Drone Warfare*. New York: Palgrave MacMillan.

Cox, Harvey. 2013. *The Secular City: Secularization and Urbanization in Theological Perspective*. Princeton: Princeton University Press.

Demacopoulos George E., and Aristotle Papanikolaou, eds. 2016. *Christianity, Democracy, and the Shadow of Constantine*. New York: Fordham University Press.

Denysenko, Nicholas. 2013. An Appeal to Mary: An Analysis of Pussy Riot's Punk Performance in Moscow. *Journal of the American Academy of Religion* 81: 1061–92. [CrossRef]

Diamant, Jeff. 2017. Orthodox Christians in Central and Eastern Europe favor strong role for Russia in geopolitics, religion. *Pew Research Center*, May 11. Available online: http://www.pewresearch.org/fact-tank/2017/05/11/orthodox-christians-in-central-and-eastern-europe-favor-strong-role-for-russia-in-geopolitics-religion/ (accessed on 1 August 2017).

Edict of Milan. 313. Galerius and Constantine: Edicts of Toleration 311/313. Translated by University of Pennsylvania Department of History. Available online: http://sourcebooks.fordham.edu/halsall/source/edict-milan.asp (accessed on 3 May 2017).

Epstein, Mikhail. 1999. "Minimal Religion", and "Post-Atheism: From Apophatic Theology to 'Minimal Religion.'". In *Russian Postmodernism: New Perspectives in Post-Soviet Culture*. Edited by Mikhaïl Epstein, Alexander Genis and Slobodanka Vladiv-Glover. New York and Oxford: Berghahn Books.

Eusebius. 2005. Orations in Praise of Constantine. Available online: http://www.ccel.org/ccel/schaff/npnf201.iv.viii.iii.html (accessed on 3 May 2017).

Grandin, Greg. 2007. *Empire's Workshop: Latin America, the United States, and the Rise of the New Imperialism*. New York: Henry Holt.

Greenwald, Glenn. 2014. *No Place to Hide: Edward Snowden, the NSA, and the U.S. Surveillance State*. New York: Henry Holt.

Gvosdev, Nikolas K. 2001. *An Examination of Church-State Relations in the Byzantine and Russian Empires with an Emphasis on Ideology and Models of Interaction*. Lewiston: Edwin Mellen.

Hobbes, Thomas. 1996. *Leviathan*. Cambridge: Cambridge University Press.

Hume, David. 1990. *Dialogues Concerning Natural Religion*. New York: Penguin Books.

Hume, David. 2016. *Of the Original Contract*. Baltimore: Laissez Faire Books.

Justinian, I. 1998. Medieval Sourcebook: Justinian: Novella 146: On Jews. Available online: http://sourcebooks.fordham.edu/Halsall/source/novel146.asp (accessed on 3 May 2017).

Kant, Immanuel. 2016. *Kant: Political Writings*. Edited by H. S. Reiss. Translated by H. B. Nisbet. Cambridge: Cambridge University Press.

Klein, Naomi. 2008. *The Shock Doctrine: The Rise of Disaster Capitalism*. New York: Henry Holt.

Knox, Zoe. 2005. *Russian Society and the Russian Church: Religion in Russia after Communism*. New York: Routledge.

Locke, John. 1988. *Two Treatises of Government*. Cambridge: Cambridge University Press.

Marsh, Christopher. 2011. *Religion and the State in Russia and China: Suppression, Survival, and Revival*. London: Bloomsbury Academic.

Masci, David. 2017. In Russia, Nostalgia for Soviet Union and Positive Feelings about Stalin. *Pew Research Center*. June 29. Available online: http://www.pewresearch.org/fact-tank/2017/06/29/in-russia-nostalgia-for-soviet-union-and-positive-feelings-about-stalin/ (accessed on 1 August 2017).

Nietzsche, Friedrich. 1990. *Twilight of the Idols and the Antichrist*. Translated by R. J. Hollingdale. New York: Penguin.

Papkova, Irina. 2011. *The Orthodox Church and Russian Politics*. Oxford: Oxford University Press.

Rousseau, Jean-Jacques. 2009. *Discourse on the Origin and Basis of Inequality among Men*. Oxford: Oxford University Press.

Ryan, James. 2012. *Lenin's Terror: The Ideological Origins of Early Soviet State Violence*. London: Routledge.

Shevzov, Vera. 2014. Women on the Fault Lines of Faith: Pussy Riot and the Insider/Outsider Challenge to Post-Soviet Orthodoxy. *Religion and Gender* 4: 121–44. [CrossRef]

Stoeckl, Kristina. 2016. Postsecular Conflicts and the Global Struggle for Traditional Values. *State, Religion, Church* 3: 102–16.

Stout, Jeffrey. 2004. *Democracy and Tradition*. Princeton: Princeton University Press.

Synod of Bishops. 2017. Epistle of the Synod of Bishops of the Russian Orthodox Church Outside of Russia on the 100th Anniversary of the Tragic Revolution in Russia and Beginning of the Godless Persecutions. Available online: http://www.pravoslavie.ru/english/101826.htm (accessed on 3 May 2017).

Taylor, Charles. 2007. *A Secular Age*. Cambridge: Harvard University Press.

Theodosius, I. 1997. Medieval Sourcebook: Banning of Other Religions: Theodosian Code XVI.i.2. Available online: https://sourcebooks.fordham.edu/source/theodcodeXVI.html (accessed on 3 May 2017).

Tolczyk, Dariusz. 1999. *See No Evil: Literary Cover-ups and Discoveries of the Soviet Camp Experience*. New Haven: Yale University Press.

Vahanian, Gabriel. 2008. *Praise of the Secular*. Charlottesville: University of Virginia Press.

Vltchek, Andre. 2015. *Exposing Lies of the Empire*. Jakarta: PT Badak Merah Semesta.

Zezulin, Lena. 2017. ROCOR Commentary on the February Revolution: Blame the West and Link Putin to the Tsars. *Public Orthodoxy*. April 20. Available online: https://publicorthodoxy.org/2017/04/20/rocor-february-revolution/ (accessed on 1 August 2017).

Zinn, Howard. 2009. *A People's History of the United States*. New York: HarperCollins.

religions

Article

Knocking on a Saint's Door, or a Quest for Holiness in a Post-Secular Society

Natalia Naydenova * and Yulia Ebzeeva

Philological Department, Peoples' Friendship University of Russia, 10 Miklukho-Maklay Street,
Moscow 117198, Russia; julia_eb@list.ru
* Correspondence: nns1306@mail.ru

Academic Editor: John A Jillions
Received: 23 March 2017; Accepted: 3 May 2017; Published: 17 May 2017

Abstract: The article examines *Successors* (*Nasledniki*, 2015) directed by Vladimir Khotinenko, illustrating a recent trend in the Russian film-making industry, namely, a rising interest in religious topics. While the Orthodox faith is widely seen by Russian political leaders as a basic aspect of national identity, the Church is also becoming more and more visible in the life of society, with religious holidays and events now receiving a higher profile in the public domain. The article analyzes how these trends shape the public consciousness and are reflected in the cinema production of recent years. *Successors*, a one location movie focusing on the debate over the role of Saint Sergius of Radonezh in the history of Russia, demonstrates that this 14th-century monk is very much present in the lives and minds of people 700 years later. In turn, this suggests that, under a layer of cynicism and consumerism, there is a growing hunger for holiness in a post-secular society.

Keywords: religious cinema; Russian cinema; Russian Orthodox Church; post-secular society; Saint Sergius of Radonezh; Khotinenko

1. Introduction

"It is not at all fortuitous that today's society is called post-secular", said the Patriarch of Moscow and All Rus, Kirill, in an interview (Patriarch of Moscow and All Russia Kirill 2009). The term 'post-secular', popularized by Jürgen Habermas, is used to describe a society where "religion maintains a public influence and relevance, while the secularistic certainty that religion will disappear worldwide in the course of modernization is losing ground" (Habermas 2008, p. 21). After 70 years of official atheism, Russia has experienced "a change in consciousness" (Habermas 2008, p. 20), with the resurgence of the Orthodox Church at the end of the 20th century. With civil components of the national identity providing little of sustenance (Sinelina 2013, p. 14), it is religious and ethnic aspects that have come to the forefront. Today's proliferation of religious discourses, on a national level in connection with value-laden civil issues and controversies (Habermas 2008, p. 20), suggests not only an intense public interest in religion, but also a belief that it can help in providing a more secure sense of collective and individual national identities (Rousselet and Agadjanian 2010).

In January 2016, the Synaxis of the Primates of the Orthodox Churches in Geneva adopted the draft document, entitled *The Mission of the Orthodox Church in Today's World*, wherein clause 13 expresses major concern over a growing "secularization in the face of a spiritual crisis", hence "a pressing need to highlight the importance of holiness" (Synaxis of the Primates of the Orthodox Churches 2016, p. 36). In the contemporary mediated world, these are first and foremost media texts that reflect, reinforce and shape systems of beliefs (Silverblatt et al. 2015, p. 3). Films remain a significant medium for the circulation of discourses in the Foucauldian sense; namely, in producing meaning and forming the objects of which they speak (Foucault 1972, p. 54). In this regard, as Joseph Kickasola puts it, "deploying and engaging with religious tropes is certainly not the same as assent to their foundational meanings, but it does imply a dialogue with those traditions, at the very least" (Kickasola 2016).

As Costica Bradatan points out, the relationship between cinema and religion is not only of a 'representational' nature, such that film becomes more than a mere vehicle for religious topics, notions, or symbols 'illustrating' them in a mechanical fashion. Beyond this, as Bradatan goes on, "Films and religion share a set of more fundamental, ontological suppositions" in that, "from its inception, film became intrinsically linked to the sacred" (Bradatan 2014, p. 2). Suffice it to remember André Bazin's *pacte de croyance* between the film and the viewer (Bazin 1975, p. 372). S. Brent Plate goes even further, drawing structural parallels between the altar and the screen (Plate 2008, p. vii). The latter comparison is reminiscent of the ideological mechanism of the Soviet atheist campaign, where cinemas were housed in former church buildings and elements of religious discourse were appropriated and re-invented to promote new values. Nikolay Berdyaev, in fact, recognized that "Communism [...] wants to be a religion itself, to take the place of Christianity. It professes to answer the religious questions of the human soul and to give a meaning to life" (Berdyaev 1960, p. 158). Cinema was certainly the most efficient propaganda mechanism in the heyday of anti-religious campaigns in the USSR. Likewise, the enhancement of the Russian Orthodox Church's position in the late 2000s triggered a growing number of feature films with a religious component, such as *The Island* (*Ostrov*, 2006) by Pavel Lungin, focusing on repentance, *The Priest* (*Pop*, 2009) by Vladimir Khotinenko, about the Church during the Second World War, and Andrey Zvyagintsev's controversial *Leviathan* (*Leviafan*, 2014).

Religious motifs were also found in TV series and cartoons. Thus, the events of the action mini-series, *Save Yourself, Brother* (*Spasajsja, Brat*, 2015), take place in a monastery. *The Wonderworker* (*Chudotvorica*), a television show consisting of 12 episodes, also released in 2015, is based on the hagiography of Saint Matrona of Moscow, one of the most popular Orthodox saints of the 20th century. *Serafima's Extraordinary Journey* (*Neobyknovennoe Puteshestvie Serafimy*, 2015), the first animated fantasy promoting Orthodox ideas through an adventure story, attracted a large audience. It tells the story of an 11-year-old girl, a daughter of a priest executed during the great terror of the 1930s. Supported by her patron saint, Serafima manages to overcome all hardships, maintains her faith and at last is reunited with her mother. Finally, the recent success of Kirill Serebrennikov's *The Disciple* (*Uchenik*) at Cannes 2016, featuring the story of a student obsessed with religion, shows that, to paraphrase Bazin, 'the cinema is still interested in God" (Bazin 2002, p. 61).

Moreover, beyond the cinema, state authorities, in the face of the threat of disintegration, have placed their own faith in religious holidays and events. This is the case, with the public holiday known as the National Unity Day, which takes place on 4 November. It was reinstated in 2005 to replace the 'Day of the Great October Socialist Revolution', celebrated under the Communist regime on 7 November. The National Unity Day commemorates the popular uprising which expelled Polish occupation forces from Moscow in 1612, thus ending the Time of Troubles, and also coincides with the feast day of Russia's most famous icon—Our Lady of Kazan.

Another recent example, dating back to 2014, is the commemoration of the 700th anniversary of Saint Sergius of Radonezh, the founder of Russian spiritual mysticism in the 14th century. He is also considered to be the peace-maker who united the feuding Russian princes, thus laying the foundations of uniting the Russian lands under the leadership of Moscow. The celebrations were financed by the Ministry of Culture at a cost of 6.5 billion roubles (Ministry of Culture of the Russian Federation 2014). On 17 July 2014, Patriarch Kirill delivered a speech at the Holy Trinity-Saint Sergius Lavra, the most important Russian monastery, situated in Sergiev Posad, claiming that holiness has always been intrinsic to "the Russian national idea" (Patriarch of Moscow and All Russia Kirill 2014, pp. 17–18). His speech was followed by Vladimir Putin's address to the heads of the delegations of the Orthodox Churches, where the President expressed his hope for their "moral and spiritual support in promoting the values we serve together" (Patriarch of Moscow and All Russia Kirill 2014, p. 19). The events commemorating the anniversary of one of the most venerated Russian saints included exhibitions, and, most importantly, television programs and films. The latter includes *Successors*, a feature film that will be the focus of the rest of this article.

2. A Room with a Saint

Successors was produced and directed by Vladimir Khotinenko, a famous Russian director known for such films as *A Moslem* (*Musulmanin*, 1995), *72 Metres* (*72 Metra*, 2003), and *The Priest* (*Pop*, 2009). The film did not have a robust budget. Therefore, the shooting lasted only 19 days. What strikes one first about the film is the originality of its setting: the events take place in a TV studio, where a talk show is being filmed. We can recall only two examples of the one location movies in the Soviet cinema: *Bonus* (*Premija*, 1974) by Sergey Mikaelyan and *Garage* (*Garazh*, 1979) by Eldar Ryazanov. As the journalist Dmitry Anokhin states, both films became classics of the Russian cinema a long time ago (Anokhin 2015, p. 76). As for the most recent period in the country's history, the only example, prior to Khotinenko's *Successors*, was Nikita Mikhalkov's *12* (2007). It should be remembered that Khotinenko hosted a talk show on Russian TV, which might have helped him. However, the director of 25 films confesses that *Successors* is "the most capricious and least predictable of his children". He does not expect the message of the film to reach society as a whole but to touch the souls of people individually. As he puts it, "If something moves in the spectator's soul, I can consider my objective achieved" (Anokhin 2015, p. 76).

The events of *Successors* take place in the summer of 2014, in a studio, where a talk show hosted by Gleb Tregubov is being filmed. Six guests have been invited to share their opinions on Saint Sergius: a successful political expert affiliated with the government authorities, German Zvonarevsky (played by actor Anatoly Bely), his former classmate and also now a professional historian, Dmitry Osipov (Alexander Korotkov), a former colonel and a neophyte politician, Vladimir Skvortsov nicknamed the 'patriot' (Alexander Baluev), a famous pop singer, Angelina Nevedina (Agrippina Steklova), a monk of Saint Sergius Lavra Father Cyprian (Sergey Kachanov) and, finally, a pediatrician from Sergiev Posad Ekaterina Kuznetsova (Alla Yuganova). They are not just seen through the eyes of the audience but also through the eyes of the technical staff of the talk show: we thus see images transmitted from the multi-camera setup, from studio monitors on the director's desk, and on the general producer's laptop. The spectator is also given a sneak view of how the show is prepared: a crowd of extras at the entrance are instructed to switch off their cell phones and, at the assistant's signal, to rehearse their applause. Among the extras there are two young men, Pasha and Stas, who use the talk show as an alibi after having taken part in the brutal beating of a migrant from Central Asia. Stas is one of the attackers while Pasha is the head of the gang.

The speakers' opinions on Saint Sergius and his role in the history of Russia reflect the current debate over national identity and the current situation in Ukraine. The saint is seen as having a variety of roles: as a humble monk, a perspicacious politician, and even as a dissident. We see how history can be manipulated in support of one's own stance. Thus, for the politician, Saint Sergius is the one who stopped the feud among local princes and united the country, which is certainly in line with the official rhetoric of the State and the Church. He also suggests omitting or paraphrasing some parts of the saint's life to make it more suitable for promulgating his own message. In contrast, for the 'patriot', the saint embodies 'Holy Rus' as a transcendental concept of a unifying national force and inter-confessional dialogue based on common moral and spiritual values. Both of these opinions, though, are vigorously contested by the historian, who argues that the Russian nation barely existed in the times of Saint Sergius.

The format of the show is used to introduce catechetical elements, consisting first and foremost of a description of Saint Sergius' life turning the film to a certain extent into a 'catechism-in-pictures' (Bazin 2002). A detailed account of the saint's life is given in special introductory videos, which are set alongside flash interviews conducted in the street. According to Khotinenko, the passers-by who participated in the interviews were not aware of taking part in a feature film: "Initially, we wanted to make a documentary. It was only afterwards that we got an order from the Ministry of Culture and changed our plans" (Anokhin 2015, p. 75).

Apart from Baluev, the film does not boast the participation of any stars, but it does contain cameo appearances by real members of show-business; namely, Olga Shelest, Alexander Oleshko and Alexander Gordon. It is the latter who informs Gleb, in a friendly chat during the break, that the show is about to be closed. This makes him take the drastic decision to abandon the script and to start live streaming the talk show over the internet. When Gleb starts live streaming the show, he orders to fill the studio with thick smoke from a previous program about the Apocalypse.

The talk show resumes with a blunt question: "Isn't it time to recognize that the baptizing of Rus was a mistake, that this poisoned Byzantine root is at the origin of all our troubles?" This marks a turning point in the plot. The participants of the talk show accept the challenge and begin to show their true colors. In a private conversation with his former classmate, Zvonarevsky repents his preference for making easy money over conducting disinterested science. The doctor is unhappy in her marriage, while the historian has no family of his own and is involved in an endless quest for historical truth. The pop diva turns out not to be as silly and frivolous as she appears. Finally, the colonel, the so-called 'patriot', is taken away in an ambulance after having received a call from his son who is a drug addict.

Once the show finishes, Pasha wants Stas to follow him, but after talking to Father Cyprian the boy declines his offer. The gang leader pretends not to be offended at all. He gives Stas a hug, saying, "Don't forget me" and "It's OK—we'll settle up one day". However, at the very last moment, and when he least expects it, Pasha gives Stas a sneaky punch. When Stas falls on the ground, the gang leader spits on him. This scene constitutes a brief preview of the standoff with the evil the young man will have to face after the closing credits of the film.

However, the quintessence of the film is expressed in an eloquent scene that appears on the official poster of the film. It shows Father Cyprian sitting alone in the studio next to the dummy of a tyrannosaur, which has been prepared for the following night's show, *World Without People*. This grotesque episode can be interpreted in various ways. For example, the lonely figure of the monk could represent a silent witness to the apocalyptic times that the people will have to endure. Likewise, the monster could presage future powers equivalent to the tyrant from the Book of Revelation. Finally, the scene might allegorically suggest humanity's eventual self-extermination.

3. *Successors*: A Family Portrait of Russian Society

The talk show participants provide a vivid portrait of contemporary Russian society and the opinions that they voice are certainly those at the heart of today's debates. As Anokhin points out, the major question that arises for the spectator is how a shifty and ambitious political expert, a loser scientist, a silly pop diva, and an audience that applauds on command, can be the successors to a saint. The conversation during the talk show reveals the guests' disdain for contemporary Russian society, showing how easily manipulated and overfed the public are by the mass media, being capable of clichéd thinking only.

Paradoxically, the most enigmatic character in the film turns out to be the pop singer, who, at first glance, seems the most stereotypical and therefore predictable. Her superficial and banal comments during the first part of the show form a stark contrast with the thoughts she shares in private with the doctor, in the second part:

> They keep arguing over why Sergius left [the monastery he founded]. I think it's like in a family: if you have it, there's no need to prove anything to anyone. And if not ... There's no point in it.

When astounded Ekaterina asks her to voice this opinion in public, Angelina refuses: "I haven't come here to say smart things. There are specially trained people for this purpose."

During the show, Angelina is more than once publicly ridiculed for her songs. However, when asked to sing, she performs arias from operas by Puccini and Borodin, demonstrating that she has the vigorous and beautiful voice of a professional, talented singer. Aside from this, she seems to be the only one who knows how to address a priest. At the beginning of the film, Gleb uses an erroneous term and is corrected by his assistant, who previously looked it up on the internet. When the colonel has a heart attack, it is Angelina who lets Father Cyprian in, saying: "Please, come in, *batyushka*" [diminutive for "Father," an affectionate term of respect for a priest].

The audience is given an insight into Angelina's character through a biblical allusion, used initially by the 'patriot', who exclaims that the showman is worse than the prima donna because "he knows what he is doing". Later, at the end of the talk show, this passage from Saint Luke (23:33–4) is echoed by Angelina when, with a defenseless smile, she declares that she does not know what she is doing. Although her words refer to a quite mundane situation (she cannot get back home because she has let her driver go), after everything the participants have been through during the show, they seem to have deeper implications. This is also alluded to in Angelina's last name—Nevedina—which literally means 'the one who does not know'.

The Church is represented in the film by Father Cyprian, who is the last-minute replacement for another clergyman. Unlike his colleague, whose absence is lamented by the talk show host, Father Cyprian is not experienced in appearing on TV. He looks at the surrounding environment with a mixture of curiosity, sorrow, and pain. He speaks little, and, when he does, his words sound simple and even naive.

When talking to the other talk show participants, Father Cyprian answers the list of most frequently asked questions of neophyte believers and refutes many of the current stereotypes held by people. For instance, when Angelina shares her excitement about fasting ("I adore fasting! Prawns, rocket salad"), the monk gently disagrees: "Why should you push yourself to such extremes? As an elder said, you can even eat meat, the main idea is not to eat each other." Father Cyprian speaks with subtle humor, avoiding any moralizing or preaching. At the same time, he does not pretend to have a monopoly on the truth. When Stas desperately asks him what to do about his family situation, Father Cyprian looks at him in sorrow and confesses, "I don't know".

Father Cyprian answers mundane queries with passages from religious texts. For instance, when the showman exclaims that Russians will soon be banned from visiting foreign countries, the monk quotes a sentence from the prayer composed by the elders of the Optina Monastery at the end of the 19th century: "Grant unto me, O Lord, that with peace of mind I may face all that this new day is to bring" (the translations of the prayers in this article are from http://www.ocf.org.), adding: "There are no exceptions mentioned there about everyday hardships or not travelling abroad on holidays".

It should be noted that there seems to be no lay believer among the talk show guests, whereas, in the traditional Soviet propaganda, such figure was usually embodied by an old woman, an obscurant church goer, frequently, and pejoratively, called *babka* (old crone). At first glance, this typical character appears to be physically absent from *Successors*, but she turns out to be behind the scene. When the guests are asked to provide a word which they associate with Saint Sergius, the doctor says 'grandma' (*babushka*) provoking laughter among the audience. The laughter seems to arise because her response strikes them as irrelevant, bewildering the studio viewers. It is only towards the end of the film that the doctor tells them all that her grandmother secretly kept Saint Sergius' head when his relics were confiscated after the revolution of 1917. Thus, a gloomy, ignorant *babka* from Soviet propaganda turns into a kind *babushka*; that is, a keeper of family and even national, spiritual values.

If *babushka* represents one pole of moral values, though, Pasha represents the other, epitomizing a nonchalant, self-confident evil. His appearance speaks for itself: he is dressed almost entirely in black leather, with a T-shirt imprinted with a wolf baring his teeth—one of the Orthodox prayers to be read before the Holy Communion pleads for delivering from becoming "the prey of the wolf of souls", a metaphorical designation of evil thoughts—and on his iPhone screen he has a huge crown.

When speaking to his friends about Stas, Pasha says: "He's a normal guy. He's one of our kind. He's just a newbie, but that'll come with time. Okay, he'll have his baptism of fire tomorrow." Pasha's words might bring to mind those of Pyotr Verkhovensky, a revolutionary character from

Dostoyevsky's *Demons*, where the chapter describing the meeting of an insurrectionist cell is titled *Among our Own* (Dostoyevsky 2008). It should also be mentioned that Khotinenko recently directed a mini-series on Dostoyevsky's *Demons*. The use of that possessive pronoun, 'our', suggests that Stas faces a dramatic choice: whether to maintain his independence or be manipulated by Pasha, who, like Verkhovensky, cements the bonds among his gang members by the "baptismal rite" of terrorizing and even murdering Asian migrants. In fact, Stas was wounded earlier in the day as a result of his involvement in the collective beating of a market seller. His resultant scar confronts him like a Christian stigmata, reminding him of the past he is about to reject, but which will cling to him tenaciously.

Successors does not simply mirror the most typical traits of contemporary Russian characters, but suggests that they are more complex and, most importantly, capable of change. The key message of the film is that conversion (*metanoia* in Orthodox ascetics) is an option open to everyone, although, as represented by the film's creators, it is only possible by engaging with Christianity. Philosopher and theologian Bernard Lonergan distinguishes three interrelated forms of conversion: intellectual, moral and religious. Intellectual conversion involves the discovery of a "truth attained by cognitional self-transcendence" (Lonergan 1973, pp. 239–40), whereas moral conversion requires "a change in the criterion of one's decisions and choices from satisfactions to values" (Lonergan 1973, p. 240). Both of these forms are 'sublated' by religious conversion, which involves the "fated acceptance of a vocation to holiness" (Lonergan 1973, p. 240).

This film draws most centrally on a narrative of moral conversion, which is securely underpinned by a religious moment. Thus Stas' change of heart is triggered by the words of Father Cyprian about Saint Sergius. Stas then confesses to the monk, "I wanted to kill [my father], but I listened to you and felt such an anguish". Therefore, it is implied that it is the synergy of the saint and his disciple that make the young man change the vector of his life. Stas' desire to kill his biological father, an alcoholic who beats his mother, is replaced by a longing to come closer to his Heavenly Father, albeit, it is recognized, this will not be an easy task. In the words of Saint Matthew (7: 13–14), Stas clearly chooses 'the narrow gate', as evidenced in his final exchange with Father Cyprian:

> Stas: "I want to do it in a human way, like people do! If that one . . . Sergius . . . could do it . . . it means that it is possible?"
>
> Father Cyprian: "It is necessary. But it's not easy."

The issue of choice is also raised in connection with Gleb Tregubov, the show's presenter: "You seem to have made your choice today", the monk surprises him by asking, after the show is over. For, following his last appearance on air, Gleb intends to leave not only Moscow but show business itself. However, once he has made this decision, he is immediately tempted by his boss (who is also his lover). She offers him the chance of hosting a new, "anti-corruption" talk show. It remains unclear what he will choose, but the banner in the final episode, advertising the new TV show, contains the words, "It's up to you!" When asked about the highlights of the open finale, Khotinenko says: "For me, it's [Stas'] smile. It's the process that started in his soul. Let God grant it to all of us . . . " (Anokhin 2015, p. 76).

4. A Long Path to *Metanoia*

In Russian culture, Saint Sergius is represented as dynamic and versatile, opening up an endless road to the future. The description of his life contains numerous examples of his pilgrimages across Russia, during which he founded monasteries and acquired new disciples. One of the talk show participants picks up on this, saying, "Father Superior walked across the vast Russian land on his own feet". Historian Vasily Klyuchevsky noted that the spiritual influence of Saint Sergius "outlasted his earthly life and transformed his name . . . into an eternally active moral engine" (Klyuchevsky 2014, p. 78—translation from http://russia-ic.com/people/Historical_Figures%20//757). This notion of Saint Sergius as a human dynamo runs like a thread through the film, invisibly connecting him to his successors.

It is surely significant, then, that the opening theme of the talk show features a train travelling through history. "Everyone has his own path: from a person to a nation as a whole", declares the monk at one point in the show. The climax of the film is reached when Ekaterina tells the family story about the rescue of Saint Sergius' head after his relics were desecrated by the Bolsheviks. The doctor, in turn, speaks over the background noise of the train. Her story grabs the audience's attention. It is based on real events and features Father Pavel Florensky, a famous mathematician and theologian, who rescued the saint's head, and Father Pavel Golubtsov, who took it out of the monastery to its new hiding place. Yet again, the monologue about the saint's relics is driven by the idea of permanent movement. Father Pavel Golubtsov carried the saint's head along the Kazanskaya railroad for a long time. Ekaterina emphasizes that even when the priest was on the train, he never sat down, nor did he put the precious thing he carried on the seat, owing to his veneration of the sacred relics. He kept walking back and forth through the train cars for the entire trip:

> You see, nobody watched him. And even had he sat down, I'm sure no one would have reproached him. Sometimes I ask myself: and I, do I have anything in my life for the sake of which I would walk like this? Something I would keep like this? Be ready to give my life for? Well, family . . . but . . . something else?

This passage homes in on one of the key questions raised by the creators of the film. For there seems to be an unconscious desire amongst modern people to find something beyond the mundane happiness and values celebrated by today's "society of consumption". As Gleb declares bitterly, after hearing the story of Pavel Florensky's refusal to leave Russia and his voluntary martyrdom for the Orthodox faith: "I don't understand what is so bad about saving your life?! Bring up your children, go abroad, start from scratch? Why do you always have to go to extremes?" This rhetorical question already contains the answer, as a response Gleb makes elsewhere—"Just to live well."—is shown to be an inadequate basis for a fulfilled life. A comfortable lifestyle, however much it is advertised as the ideal, leaves people empty in the long run. There is always the hunger of the soul for something beyond.

This idea is crystallized in the closing scene of the film, which shows a message written on a bridge wall, signed by someone nicknamed 'Wizard': "This is the clue—it is the future of postmodernism. I invented you". This graffito, along with its spelling mistakes, almost literally constitutes the 'writing on the wall', being a warning to postmodern society, where the souls of those seduced by simulacra are endlessly reinvented by some invisible 'wizard', obscuring the real values by the smokescreen of relentless consumerist propaganda.

At the end of the film, Stas is shown leaving his gloomy residential area and crossing the bridge along the railroad. In the background, as the wheels of the train sound, he leaves behind the walls defaced by graffiti, looks at the new district of Moscow, called *Moskva-City*, with its skyscrapers, then pauses for a while before noticing a billboard announcing Gleb Tregubov's new talk show. The show is called *Emergency Brake* and its slogan is: "Stop! I'm getting off". This closing episode encapsulates the main idea of the film: that is, it is never too late to pull the handle of the emergency brake and embark upon a new path.

The choice evoked in the film—between truth and lie, good and evil—can best be captured in Dostoyevsky's famous quotation about the field of life: that "God and the devil are fighting there and the battlefield is the heart of man" (Dostoyevsky 1929, p. 130). Thus the doctor asks, "What does good mean for you?", while evoking the professional burnout experienced by her colleague working at a hospice. To which Father Cyprian's words might provide a suitable reply: "Maybe Saint Sergius' story is about making your choice . . . between the truth for me, the truth for the people and the truth for God".

5. Conclusions

When reflecting on Saint John Chrysostom's homily on Acts, Father John Jillions says that "we are safest when in the company of the saints". Saint John Chrysostom does not mean the saints of ancient days. He urges his listeners to seek out the holy people of today, visiting them and inviting them into our homes. Thus they will absorb how to be peaceful and safe even in the midst of storms (Jillions 2015).

In the 21st century, characterized by the atomization of society and the evident helplessness of individuals in the face of globalization, people seem to be more desperate to connect with the metaphysical side of life; that is, somewhere that they try to find responses to the questions which cannot be answered from a materialistic point of view. Father Cyprian tries to capture this insight when he states: "What is important about Sergius is that he existed. And most importantly that he is with us now. He is above time".

The reception of the film by the critics was predominantly positive. It was called a litmus paper, a portrait, or even a diagnosis of the Russian society (Vasilieva 2015; Anisimova 2015; Kolensky 2015). The reviewers were almost unanimous in praising the narrative structure of the film, compared to Bakhtin's polyphony, which allowed "to tell the story full of gaps, contradictions, different interpretations of the same events" (Zabaluev 2015; Ostashevsky 2015). But among this multitude of voices it is the quiet voice of Saint Sergius that sounds loud symbolizing 'miracle and hope' for the film creator: "He could stand between the most implacable enemies and peacefully speak about the soul" (Ostashevsky 2015).

Successors is not the only Russian film featuring a saint as the key character. In *Serafima's Extraordinary Journey*, an animated film mentioned at the beginning of this article, Saint Serafim plays a crucial role. He is Serafima's friend, whose intercession helps her become reunited with her family, both spiritually and physically. It is easy for Serafima, a child "pure at heart" (Matthew 5:8), to take the saint by the hand and trustingly follow him. For a grown-up person living in the contemporary world, full of "the lust of the flesh, the lust of the eyes, and the pride of life" (John 2:15–17), it is a lot more difficult, if not nigh on impossible. Therefore, Saint Sergius, also being one of the characters of the film, is invisibly present in the studio, giving answers to the desperate questions emanating from people's souls, although not everyone is yet ready to understand them or, most importantly, to accept them.

Author Contributions: The research was designed by Natalia Naydenova. The analysis was carried out by Natalia Naydenova and Yulia Ebzeeva and they wrote the paper together.

Conflicts of Interest: The authors declare no conflict of interest.

References

Anisimova, Lyudmila. 2015. Fil'm Khotinenko "Nasledniki"—Portret sovremennoj Rossii. October 5. Available online: http://press.lv/post/film-hotinenko-nasledniki-portret-sovremennoj-rossii/ (accessed on 8 March 2017).
Anokhin, Dmitry. 2015. Zerkalo dlja kameo. *Zhurnal Moskovskoj Patriarhii* 11: 74–76.
Bazin, André. 1975. *Qu'est-ce que le cinéma*. Paris: Cerf.
Bazin, André. 2002. Cinema and Theology: The Case of *Heaven over the Marshes*. *Journal of Religion and Film* 2: 15. Available online: http://digitalcommons.unomaha.edu/cgi/viewcontent.cgi?article=1763&context=jrf (accessed on 8 March 2017).
Berdyaev, Nikolay. 1960. *The Origin of Russian Communism*. Ann Arbor: University of Michigan Press.
Bradatan, Costica. 2014. Introduction: Dealing (Visibly) in Things not Seen. In *Religion in Contemporary European Cinema: The Postsecular Constellation*. Edited by Costica Bradatan and Camil Ungureanu. New York: Routledge, pp. 1–10.
Dostoyevsky, Fyodor. 1929. *The Brothers Karamazov*. Translated by Constance Garnett. New York: Modern Library.
Dostoyevsky, Fyodor. 2008. *Demons*. Translated by Robert A. Maguire. London: Penguin Classics.

Foucault, Michel. 1972. *The Archaeology of Knowledge*. New York: Pantheon Books.

Habermas, Jurgen. 2008. Notes on Post-Secular Society. *New Perspectives Quarterly* 25: 17–29. [CrossRef]

Jillions, John A. 2015. Acts 27:1–44 Safe in the Company of the Saints. June 23. Available online: https://oca.org/reflections/fr.-john-jillions/june-23--2015 (accessed on 8 March 2017).

Kickasola, Joseph. 2016. Tracking the Fallen Apple: Ineffability, Religious Tropes, and Existential Despair in Nuri Bilge Ceylan's Once Upon a Time in Anatolia. *Journal of Religion & Film* 20: 13. Available online: http://digitalcommons.unomaha.edu/jrf/vol20/iss1/13 (accessed on 8 March 2017).

Klyuchevsky, Vasily. 2014. Znachenie Prepodobnogo Sergija Radonezhskogo dlja russkogo naroda i gosudarstva. *Razvitie Lichnosti* 4: 60–80.

Kolensky, Alexey. 2015. Vladimir Khotinenko: "Ne ozhidal, chto televizionshhikam moja kartina pokazhetsja obidnoj". October 27. Available online: http://portal-kultura.ru/articles/person/123811-vladimir-khotinenko-ne-ozhidal-chto-televizionshchikam-moya-kartina-pokazhetsya-obidnoy/ (accessed on 8 March 2017).

Lonergan, Bernard. 1973. *Method in Theology*. New York: Herder and Herder.

Ministry of Culture of the Russian Federation. 2014. Rossija gotovitsja otprazdnovat' 700-letie so dnja rozhdenija prepodobnogo Sergija Radonezhskogo. April 30. Available online: http://mkrf.ru/press-center/news/ministerstvo/rossiya-gotovitsya-otprazdnovat-700-letie-so-dnya-rozhdeniya-prepodobnogo-sergiya (accessed on 8 March 2017).

Ostashevsky, Dmitry. 2015. Recenzija: "Nasledniki" Vladimira Khotinenko. June 29. Available online: http://thr.ru/cinema/recenzia-nasledniki-vladimira-hotinenko/ (accessed on 8 March 2017).

Patriarch of Moscow and All Russia Kirill. 2009. Cerkovnaja zhizn' dolzhna byt' sluzheniem. *Izvestija*. Available online: http://izvestia.ru/news/348393 (accessed on 8 March 2017).

Patriarch of Moscow and All Russia Kirill. 2014. Igumen zemli Russkoj. *Zhurnal Moskovskoj Patriarhii* 8: 14–19.

Plate, S. Brent. 2008. *Religion and Film. Cinema and the Re-creation of the World*. London: Wallflower.

Rousselet, Kathy, and Alexander Agadjanian. 2010. Individual and Collective Identities in Russian Orthodoxy. In *Eastern Christians in Anthropological Perspective*. Edited by Chris Hann and Hermann Goltz. Oakland: University of California Press, pp. 265–79.

Silverblatt, Art, Jane Ferry, and Barbara Finan. 2015. *Approaches to Media Literacy: A Handbook*. London: New York: Routledge.

Sinelina, Yulia. 2013. Religija v sovremennom mire. *Expert* 1: 14–20.

Synaxis of the Primates of the Orthodox Churches. 2016. Missija Pravoslavnoj Cerkvi v sovremennom mire. *Zhurnal Moskovskoj Patriarhii* 4: 31–36.

Vasilieva, Yulia. 2015. Vladimir Khotinenko: "Nasledniki—lakmusovaja bumazhka Rossii.". December 2. Available online: http://sobesednik.ru/kultura-i-tv/20151202-vladimir-hotinenko-nasledniki-lakmusovaya-bumazhka-rossii (accessed on 8 March 2017).

Zabaluev, Yaroslav. 2015. Dym russkogo apokalipsisa. June 25. Available online: https://www.gazeta.ru/culture/2015/06/25/a_6854185.shtml (accessed on 8 March 2017).

religions

MDPI

Article

Religious Diversity in Modern Orthodox Thought

Paul Ladouceur [1,2]

[1] Orthodox School of Theology at Trinity College, Faculty of Divinity, University of Toronto, Toronto, ON M5S 1H8, Canada; 123thabor@gmail.com

[2] Faculté de théologie et de sciences religieuses, Université Laval, Québec, QC G1V 0A6, Canada

Academic Editor: John Jillions

Received: 4 January 2017; Accepted: 2 April 2017; Published: 27 April 2017

Abstract: This essay explores different approaches to non-Christian religions in Orthodox thought, from the early Fathers to the present day. Among modern Orthodox theologians, Georges Khodr and Anastasios Yannoulatos inherit an *inclusivist* or tolerant attitude to religious diversity from Justin Martyr and other early Fathers, while Seraphim Rose represents an *exclusivist* or intolerant position, characteristic of Tertullian. Philip Sherrard's thinking on non-Christian religions can be described as *religious pluralism*, while that of Lev Gillet is close to *comparative theology*. Despite the absence of formal Orthodox declarations concerning religious diversity, Orthodox thought on the subject since World War II converges around the notions of inclusivism and comparative theology, considering that non-Christian religions are mysteriously "included" in the missions of Christ and the Holy Spirit in the world and that their adherents can achieve salvation as understood in Christianity.

Keywords: religious diversity; Christianity; non-Christian religions; Orthodoxy; Justin Martyr; Georges Khodr; Anastasios Yannoulatos; exclusivism; inclusivism; religious pluralism

1. The Early Fathers and Non-Christian Religions

Early Christian thinking on non-Christian religions was conditioned by the pagan polytheism of the Roman Empire, religious aspects of Greek philosophy and links between Christianity and Judaism; including the incorporation, not without some hesitation, of the Jewish sacred books into the Christian Bible. Some early Christian thinkers, especially St Justin Martyr (c.100–c.165) had a cautiously positive view concerning the existence of elements of truth among pagan philosophers and Jewish sages, while Tertullian (c.155–c.240) represented a less tolerant view, which became more dominant in later Christian thinking. Later in history, Orthodoxy had extensive historical experience, not entirely negative, of life as a religious and cultural minority under non-Christian regimes in Persia, the Arabic Middle East and the Ottoman Empire. For long centuries Christian communities were in a 'survival mode' under Muslim rule in these areas, which made theological reflection on the meaning of religious diversity in God's plan for salvation difficult. Only in recent times have Orthodox theologians begun to reflect more systematically on the theological significance of non-Christian religions, especially as Orthodoxy is increasingly confronted with this reality both in countries of Orthodox immigration in Western Europe and North America, and increasingly in countries of Orthodox tradition. Contemporary Orthodox attitudes towards religious diversity are often linked with thinking on secularism, human rights and the religious policy of the State.

Several notions concerning non-Christian religions which have come down to us from the ancient Fathers are still relevant. The most important is no doubt from Justin Martyr, who applies the Hellenistic notion of the "seeds of the Logos" (*logos spermatikos*) in a Christian sense. Although there is some question of what exactly Justin meant by the term, his writings suggest that he was referring to those aspects of Christian truth present in the philosophers. Michel Fédou defines Justin's doctrine of the *logos spermatikos* as "a universal divine communication in the world of the nations, in the

expectation of the full revelation of the Logos of God at the moment of the Incarnation (Fédou 2009)."
Justin recognizes that pagan philosophers, especially Socrates and Plato, had a degree of knowledge of truth, but that the fullness of truth resides only in Christian revelation. He even goes so far as to refer to certain Greek philosophers and various Jewish figures as Christians:

> We have been taught that Christ is the First-born of God, and we have suggested...that he is the *logos* of whom every race of men and women were partakers. And they who lived with the *logos* are Christians, even though they have been thought atheists; as, among the Greeks, Socrates and Heraclitus, and people like them; and among the barbarians[1], Abraham, and Ananias, and Asarias, and Misael, and Elias (Justin Martyr 1997, *First Apology*, 1.46).

> For whatever either lawgivers or philosophers uttered well, they elaborated according to their share of *logos* by invention and contemplation. But since they did not know all that concerns *logos*, who is Christ, they often contradicted themselves (Justin Martyr 1997, *Second Apology*, 1.10).

In his polemical treatise *Against the Heathen*, St Athanasius of Alexandria (c.296–373) recognizes, like Justin before him, the possibility that pagans can rise to knowledge of truth. Possessing a rational soul and free will, pagans can abandon idolatry and return to the true God:

> Just as they turned away from God with their mind and invented gods from nonexistent entities, so they can rise towards God with the mind of their soul and again turn back towards him. They can turn back if they cast off the stain of all desire which they have put on, and wash themselves until they have eliminated every addition foreign to the soul and show it unadulterated, as it was made, in order that in this way they may be able to contemplate therewith the Word of the Father, in whose image they were made in the beginning (Athanasius 1971, 1.34).

Other early Christian thinkers who recognized the existence of goodness and elements of truth in pagan religions, and especially in the philosophers, include Clement of Alexandria (c.150–c.215), Origen (c.184–c.253), Basil the Great (329–379), Gregory Nazianzus (329–390) and Augustine (354–430)[2].

But a critical evaluation of other religions also found support in early Christianity, inheriting the negative attitude towards pagan idolatry in both the Old Testament and the New Testament. Tertullian represents the more conservative strain of early Christian thought, seeing in other religions only the work of demons, and more specifically considering that pagan gods are demons. In his *Apology*, Tertullian sets out to demonstrate to his pagan addressee that the pagan gods and demons are the same beings under different appellations, "that the nature (*qualitas*) of both terms is the same (Tertullian 1950, 1.23.4)."

Tertullian suggests that if a Christian were to interrogate a person possessed by an evil spirit and a person considered to be under the influence of a god (for instance, a priestess of Cybele), both would confess that they are inhabited by a devil (Tertullian 1950, ll. 23.4–6). To him this clearly proves the falsity of the demons' pretension to divine status, since even if the spirits' admission is a lie it shows that "your [i.e., pagan] divinity has become subject to the Christians" and, therefore, is not a true divinity (Tertullian 1950, 1.23.8). If pagan ideas about the divine were true the demons would never usurp it, nor would the gods deny it when questioned by a Christian (Tertullian 1950, 1.23.10). Tertullian concludes that, since he has proven that the beings whom pagans worship are not gods, his interlocutor must confess them to be devils (Tertullian 1950, 1.23.).

---

[1]   Justin is writing between 155 and 157 to the Emperor Antoninus (ruled 138 to 161). The "barbarians" here are the Jews.
[2]   For an overview of early Christian thinking on other religions and philosophies, see (Giannoulatos 1971, pp. 13–31; Sherrard 1998, pp. 55–61).

Tertullian acknowledges that some philosophers openly attack pagan superstitions and have the same teachings on morality and virtue as Christians. Yet he criticizes the philosophers, such as Socrates, for corrupting truth by offering sacrifices to false gods and by ranking demons next to gods. These corruptions of the truth, according to Tertullian, ensure that the philosophers are tolerated in the Roman Empire, while Christians—who uphold the truth in all respects—suffer persecution (Tertullian 1950, 1.46).

Byzantine thinking on non-Christian religions was strongly influenced by shifting attitudes toward Judaism and, later, towards Islam. From the more tolerant and open early approaches of Justin, Clement and others, subsequent writings on non-Christian religions moved to more a more hostile and intolerant approach. Islam was first seen as a Christian heresy because of its rejection of the divinity of Christ, notably by St. John of Damascus (676–749)[3]. But subsequent Byzantine attitudes varied from anti-Jewish and anti-Islamic polemics to attempts at theological dialogue, such as in the writing of St. Gregory Palamas (1296–1359) during his captivity by the Turks in 1354–1355 before he was finally released for a ransom[4].

The two positions can be summarized thus: that non-Christian religions contain elements of truth and can somehow be assimilated to Christianity; and that they are false doctrines, works of demons intended to lead Christians astray, or more broadly, have no merit for salvation. These two strands of ancient Christian thinking about non-Christian religions, and especially Greek philosophy, have come down to modern times.

2. Modern Orthodox Thought on Religious Diversity

The relationship between Orthodoxy and non-Christian religions has not featured highly on the modern Orthodox theological agenda. Major twentieth-century theologians such as Sergius Bulgakov, Vladimir Lossky, Georges Florovsky and John Zizioulas have not addressed the question directly. Some leading figures of the Russian religious renaissance of the late nineteenth and early twentieth centuries, notably Vladimir Soloviev, Pavel Florensky and Sergius Bulgakov, reflected on the thorny issue of Jewish-Christian relations, but these writings do not lead to a coherent theology of religious diversity. On the other hand, certain features of the Christologies and ecclesiologies of these theologians are relevant to a theology of religious diversity. Bulgakov writes, for example, in his major work on the Church *The Bride of the Lamb* (1945):

> The doctrine of the Church as the body of Christ, as the temple of the Holy Spirit, has, first of all, an anthropological significance. This doctrine affirms a certain pan-christism and pan-pneumatism, to which no limits are set. In this aspect this doctrine contains the idea that, after the Incarnation and the Pentecost, Christ is the head of humankind and therefore lives in all humankind. The same thing is affirmed concerning the Holy Spirit.

> The limits of the Church mystically or ontologically coincide with the limits of the power of the Incarnation and the Pentecost; but these limits *do not exist at all*. "And the Word was made flesh" (Jn 1:14); the incarnation of the Lord as the divine-human person of Christ consisted in the assumption of the whole Adam, "perfect" humanity. There are no limits to this assumption, either external or internal. Christ's humanity is the inner human condition of every human being . . . All human beings belong to Christ's humanity. And if this human condition is the Church as the body of Christ, then, in this sense, all humanity belongs to the Church (Bulgakov [1945] 2002, pp. 261, 266).

---

[3] Islam features as "Heresy 101" under the title "Against the Ishmaelites" in *Against Heresies*, a contested work attributed to John of Damascus. Another work by the Damascene is "Disputation between a Christian and a Saracen." For the Greek text of the former and selections from the latter, with English translations, see (Janosik 2016). See also earlier references in (Giannoulatos 1971, n.54, p. 34)

[4] On this episode and the resulting writings of Palamas, see (Arnakis 1951) and (Sloboda 2017).

Bulgakov's Christological, Pneumatological and ecclesiological universalism as reflected here can be interpreted to suggest that Christ and the Holy Spirit act beyond the visible limits of Christianity and that non-Christian religions are somehow "included" in the mystery of the Church. This is of course speculative since Bulgakov did not explicitly extend his thinking to non-Christian religions[5].

Orthodox ecclesiology since the mid-nineteenth century has devoted considerable attention to Orthodoxy in relation to other Christian churches and confessions, but very little on non-Christian religions. Nonetheless, several theologians have written significantly on the question. We shall focus here on the main lines of thought of Orthodox figures who represent a broad range of approaches to religious diversity. Their writings on non-Christian religions are not extensive, consisting mainly of articles, essays and chapters in books, but nonetheless sketch out basic elements of Orthodox thinking, both positive and negative, on non-Christian religions.

One of the earliest modern presentations of an Orthodox position on non-Christian religions was an address by Metropolitan Georges Khodr of Mount Lebanon (b. 1923) at the Central Committee of the World Council of Churches in Addis Ababa in 1971, under the title "Christianity in a Pluralistic World—The Economy of the Holy Spirit (Khodre 1971a; Khodre 1971b; Kinnamon and Cope 1997)." Khodr, a leading Orthodox ecumenist and promoter of dialogue between Christianity and Islam, argues for a vision of the Church as "the instrument of the mystery of the salvation of the nations" by appeals to the Noahic covenant, divine freedom and kenosis, the universality of the economy of Christ and especially the Resurrection, and the mysterious, unbounded presence of the Holy Spirit. "The Church's task is to perceive...even in the world of the religions," writes Khodr, "the God who is hidden within it, in anticipation of the final concrete manifestation of the Mystery (Khodre 1971a, p. 197)." Khodr's bold thinking culminates in a universal and eschatological vision of world religions:

> Christ is hidden everywhere in the mystery of his self-abasement. Any reading of religions is a reading in Christ. It is Christ alone who is received as light when grace visits a Brahmin, a Buddhist or a Moslem reading his scriptures. [...] All who are visited by the Spirit are the people of God. The Church represents the first-fruits of all humanity called to salvation. [...] The main task is to identify all the Christic values in other religions, to show Christ as their bond and his love as their fulfillment (Khodre 1971a, pp. 198, 200, 202).

But Khodr does perhaps get carried away with himself in one statement: "Every martyr for truth, every man persecuted for what he believes to be justice, dies in union with Christ (Khodre 1971a, p. 198)." This sweeping hypothesis requires a deeper exploration, since extremists of all sorts may be persecuted and die for what they believe to be right.

Together with Georges Khodr, Archbishop Anastasios Yannoulatos (b. 1929) is another leading figure in Orthodox thought concerning religious diversity. Yannoulatos studied theology and world religions in Athens and in Germany and served as Acting Archbishop in East Africa from 1981 to 1991, becoming primate of the Orthodox Church of Albania in 1992. In 1971 he published a survey of the evolution of Christian thinking on non-Christian religions from the early Church to the Second Vatican Council, including patristic, Byzantine, Protestant and Roman Catholic approaches over the centuries (Giannoulatos 1971). In a 1974 essay, Anastasios Yannoulatos grounds an Orthodox approach to non-Christian religions in the theology of the human person and the need for humans to exist in communion with other persons, a "communion [*koinonia*] of love," which takes as its point of departure and model the communion among the divine Persons of the Holy Trinity. Yannoulatos has no hesitation in showing his colors: "The universality of the Church does not mean exclusivity; it means all-inclusiveness (Yannoulatos 2003, p. 29)." And later in the same essay he writes: "People who have different beliefs never lose the basic attributes of their spiritual identity: they never cease to be 'children of God,' created in 'in God's image,' and hence our brothers and sisters. God is the Father of

---

5   This line of speculation can be read into other Orthodox thinkers whose ecclesiology is also universalist, for example Vladimir Soloviev (Soloviev 1948), especially pp. 99–102.

us all (Yannoulatos 2003, p. 43)." While this approach reiterates the ontological equality of all humans regardless of religion or even non-religion, it does not, as Yannoulatos recognizes, deal with the more specific issue of a theological understanding of non-Christian religions: "An analysis of Christian theories on how to understand other religions will not be undertaken here. I believe that a satisfactory solution to this problem has not yet been found. We are still looking (Yannoulatos 2003, p. 43)."

In a 1989 paper Yannoulatos tackles head-on the issue of the theological significance of non-Christian religions. After a brief historical survey of Christian attitudes towards other religions from the earliest times, Yannoulatos classifies Christian theories and attitudes towards other religions into six categories, covering the full gamut from Tertullian's view that non-Christian religions are the work of the devil, to relativism and syncretism (Yannoulatos 1989, pp. 132–35). Building on his earlier Trinitarian foundation of human relations, he postulates three key concepts for an Orthodox theology of religions. First, the "universal radiance of God's glory": there is but one God, even if people have widely-diverging conceptions about God; hence, "God's glory pervades all of heaven and earth and every shape and form of life (Yannoulatos 1989, pp. 139–40)." The second principle is founded on the ontological equality of all humans, who thus have a common origin and destiny, extended to include universal divine revelation: "The universal character of divine revelation to humanity is related to our innate religious sense." (Yannoulatos 1989, p. 141). Yannoulatos' third principle is universal divine providence. God constantly provides for creation and humanity: "God has never stopped caring for the whole world that he created." (Yannoulatos 1989, p. 141). Yannoulatos refers to God's covenants with Adam and Eve (Gn 2:16–17) and with Noah (Gn 9:8–17). Like Khodr before him, Yannoulatos considers that the Noahic covenant is universal, permanent and all-pervasive, not only between God and Noah, but to all Noah's descendents, "all flesh that is on the earth" (Gn 9:16). "All human beings," he concludes, "are in a relationship with God through some previous covenant to which he himself set his own seal." (Yannoulatos 1989, pp. 141–42).

These fundamental principles serve as the underpinning of a Christological basis of an Orthodox understanding of other religions, not in an exclusivist sense of barring those who do not know or acknowledge Christ from salvation, but to affirm, with Justin Martyr and other early Christian writers, that Christ, the Logos of God, is "the true Light which gives light to every man coming into the world" (Jn 1:8). But Yannoulatos also ventures into more perilous territory by affirming that it is the constant activity of the Holy Spirit which assures "the manifestation of the Trinitarian God's presence—everywhere in the world, throughout time and for all eternity," and "continues to act for the salvation of every person and the fulfillment and completion of the entire world (Yannoulatos 1989, p. 149)." Yannoulatos appears to subscribe here to the theory of a twofold divine economy, attributed to Vladimir Lossky, whereby Christ is active primarily among Christians and the Holy Spirit among non-Christians. In his book *The Mystical Theology of the Eastern Church* (1944), Lossky devotes a chapter to "The Economy of the Son" and another to "The Economy of the Holy Spirit." This suggests a real distinction in the economies of the Second and Third Persons of the Holy Trinity, assumed to be respectively within Christianity and beyond the boundaries of Christianity. Although Lossky does not actually assert distinct "economies" of the Son and the Holy Spirit in the world, he is criticized for implying this[6].

While Yannoulatos does not really clarify the respective roles of Christ and Holy Spirit in world religions, he does affirm that "the criterion by which Christians evaluate and accept different religious ideas and principles is Jesus Christ, the Word of God and incarnation of God's love." (Yannoulatos 1989, p. 152).

Philip Sherrard (1922–1995) was an English scholar, author and translator who contributed greatly to increasing awareness of Modern Greek culture and literature, especially poetry. Sherrard also wrote

---

[6] For criticisms of Lossky's *The Mystical Theology of the Eastern Church*, see (Zizioulas 1994; Florovsky 1958; Verkhovsky 1958; Vassiliadis 1991).

on a wide range of philosophical and theological themes. In his book *Christianity: Lineaments of a Sacred Tradition* (1998), he presents one of the most open views of religious diversity of any Orthodox writer. From a call for the Church to renounce "the claim that the Christian revelation constitutes the sole and universal revelation of the universal Truth" (Sherrard 1998, p. 53), Sherrard goes on to enunciate an inclusivist position following on Georges Khodr: "Any deep reading of another religion is a reading of the Logos, of Christ. It is the Logos who is received in the spiritual illumination of a Brahmin, a Buddhist, or a Moslem." (Sherrard 1998, p. 62). But he goes much further, expounding a doctrine of religious pluralism (in the technical sense): "Sacred traditions other than their own [Christians'] are divinely-instituted ways of spiritual realization... There may be as many ways to God as there are individual human beings [...] Since God is infinite, there is nothing to prevent him from choosing to reveal himself in an infinite number of limited forms, all of which he himself, in his non-manifest nature, infinitely transcends." (Sherrard 1998, pp. 63, 70).

The foundation of Sherrard's position is a conviction of a unity of truth, "an underlying metaphysical order, a series of timeless and universal principles from which all derives and on which all depends... the essential unity of the unchanging, non-manifest, and timeless principles themselves." (Sherrard 1998, pp. 62, 63). Sherrard is expressing here the central teaching of the "traditionalist" or "perennialist" school of thought. This school, following its principal modern architects the philosophers René Guénon (1886–1951) and Aldous Huxley (1894–1963), emphasizes the existence of primordial and universal truths upon which all major world religions draw as their prime source. "There is the Truth," writes Sherrard, "as it is 'laid up in heaven' in its preformal and purely metaphysical state; and there is this Truth as it is when translated into the various doctrines and symbolic languages of the human race." (Sherrard 1998, p. 64). Sherrard leaves open the possibility that one religious tradition may more fully express the metaphysical Truth than others. "Certain forms" in which God reveals himself may "enshrine his reality more fully than others"; one religious tradition rooted in true revelation may "express God's wisdom and knowledge more fully than others." (Sherrard 1998, pp. 70, 73–74). But Sherrard stops short of claiming that Christianity, let alone Orthodoxy, is precisely the tradition that most fully and accurately reflects divine reality or the transcendent Truth of which he speaks.

Nicholas Arseniev (1888–1977) taught Orthodox theology in Russia until 1920, then in Königsburg and Warsaw until 1939 and after World War II at St Vladimir's Seminary in New York. In his book *Revelation of Life Eternal* (1960), Arseniev sketches an outline of a Christian attitude towards the religious quests and beliefs of humanity beyond Judeo-Christian revelation, based on the premise "that there is a certain knowledge of God or a yearning and craving and searching after him given to all." (Arseniev 1982, p. 41). Arseniev explores this theme from the perspective of the simultaneous existence in religious traditions of both "a higher conception or rather a higher experience of God" and "the rubbish and trash of often morally repulsive and even ludicrous polytheistic and polydemonistic conceptions." (Arseniev 1982, p. 47). But even in animistic religions dominated by the latter, there may occur a *"breaking through"* of a higher conception of divinity, such as the notion of a "merciful Supreme Father." Arseniev gives a number of examples, from the Bushmen of South Africa, the Hinayâna Buddhist notion of nirvana, the Aztecs of Mexico and the Pygmies of Africa. He challenges a long-held view that there has been an evolution in the history of religion from lower to higher forms. Citing examples from anthropological studies of religious beliefs and practices in pre-modern societies, Arseniev argues that "in many cases [there] seems to be an *evolution of descent, of religious deterioration.*" (Arseniev 1982, pp. 47–51, 53–58). Arseniev's perspective on non-Christian religions is decidedly committed: the values represented in the Judeo-Christian tradition are the standard against which he measures other religious traditions and practices.

Fr. Lev Gillet (1893–1980) was engaged in interreligious dialogue long before any formal interreligious movement. Gillet, better known under his pen-name "A Monk of the Eastern Church," was a French Catholic priest and monk who joined the Orthodox Church in Paris in 1928[7]. In 1938 he moved to England, where he was closely associated with the Fellowship of Saint Alban and Saint Sergius. Engaged in Jewish-Christian relations, in his first years in England he was chaplain for a hostel occupied by young Jews and Jewish Christian refugees from Germany and Austria until the British authorities interned its occupants as "enemy aliens" in early 1940. The Religious Society of Friends (Quakers) then provided Gillet a fellowship to study Jewish theology and Jewish-Christian relations, the result of which was a remarkable and pioneering book, *Communion in the Messiah*, published in 1942 at the height of World War II (Gillet [1942] [2003] 2013). Going beyond advocating Christian solidarity with persecuted Jews in Hitler's Europe, Gillet sets out to identify points of convergence between Jewish and Christian theology, spirituality and religious practices. He focuses, as the title of book indicates, on the notion of the Messiah, and also other common theological insights such as the Jewish *shekinah*, the divine Presence or indwelling[8].

After the war, Gillet worked for many years for the Union for the Study of Great Religions based in London, preparing "book lists" for the Union's journal—in effect, reviews of publications relevant to interreligious understanding. Gillet was also Secretary of the World Congress of Faiths devoted to interreligious dialogue for five years (1961–1965). One of his responsibilities was to prepare meetings of the Congress, including acting as resource person for interfaith services—no small challenge. Gillet never wrote explicitly about his interreligious experience, but it is likely out of these activities that he published a unique series of meditations focused on the notion of Supreme Being as "limitless love[9]." (Gillet 1971).

A sharp contrast with the Orthodox personalities that we have considered so far, Fr. Seraphim Rose (1934–1982), an American convert to Orthodoxy, inherits the Tertullian strand of early Christian thought concerning non-Christian religions. Rose's main concern in his book *Orthodoxy and the Religion of the Future* (1975) is to expose and denounce forms of religious and quasi-religious beliefs and spirituality which became widespread in the United States after World War II, including Islam, Hinduism, yoga, zen, transcendental meditation, Hare Krishna, Maharaj-ji, the charismatic revival, the New Age, personal sects typified by the Jonestown Massacre of 1978, and Unidentified Flying Objects (UFOs)—the components, one surmises, of "the religion of the future." Rose's objective is to warn Orthodox believers about the dangers of straying from the Orthodox faith inherent in these movements, but the book suffers from categorical language and weak theological justification for affirmations and critiques. Rose goes on to condemn Orthodox participation in the ecumenical movement and in inter-religious dialogue, casting the entire book in an anti-ecumenical, denunciatory, conspiratorial and apocalyptic vision of exotic religious movements threatening Orthodoxy.

Rose writes that dialogue with non-Christian religions is the product "of a diabolical 'suggestion' that can capture only those who have already departed so far from Christianity as to be virtual pagans: worshippers of the *god of this world*, Satan (2 Cor 4:4), and followers of whatever intellectual fashion this powerful god is capable of inspiring." (Rose 1975, p. xxix). His main Orthodox target here is none other than Georges Khodr, severely taken to task for his January 1971 address to the Central Committee of the World Council of Churches. Rose accuses Khodr of leading "the avant-garde of Orthodox apostates" who "speak of the 'spiritual riches' and 'authentic spiritual life' of the non-Christian religions." (Rose 1975, pp. xxix–xxx). Rose raises several serious theological objections to Khodr, including Khodr's "projections" of Christ into non-Christian religions, the problem of Khodr's statement about martyrs for truth dying in communion with Christ, and Khodr's apparent separation of the economy of the Holy Spirit from the economy of Christ (Rose 1975, pp. xxx–xxxi). Rose misrepresents the last point as: "It is the 'Holy Spirit,' conceived as totally independent of Christ and his Church, that is really the

---

[7] See Élisabeth Behr-Sigel's masterly biography (Behr-Sigel 1993), English version (Behr-Sigel 1999). The subtitle of the French is missing in the English.
[8] On the Shekinah, see (Gillet [1942] [2003] 2013, pp. 80–87, 138, 228–29).
[9] See the discussion in (Behr-Sigel 1993, pp. 515–19, 556–68).

common denominator of all the world's religions." (Rose 1975, p. xxxi). For Rose, this is then a heresy because it "denies the very nature of the Holy Trinity" with "no aim but to undermine and destroy the whole idea and reality of the Church of Christ." (Rose 1975, p. xxxi). Stripping away the impetuous language, Rose raises but does not resolve the major theological issue concerning the respective roles of Christ and the Holy Spirit beyond the visible boundaries of the Church, especially in non-Christian religions, and indeed in people of good faith without religious belief.

3. Orthodoxy and Theologies of Religious Diversity

The thinking of ancient Fathers and of modern Orthodox theologians on non-Christian religions can be considered in the light of typologies of interreligious theology. In 1983, the Anglican theologian Alan Race (b. 1951) put forward a three-fold typology of Christian attitudes to non-Christian religions based on the possibility of salvation outside Christianity (Race 1993). An *exclusivist* position is grounded on the imperative and universal finality of divine revelation in Christ. It considers that non-Christian religions are globally "excluded" from the history of salvation, as summarized by Marianne Moyaert expressing the exclusivist position: "The divine incarnation in Christ is... *ontologically* constitutive for salvation. But not all are redeemed: only those who recognize Jesus Christ as their personal Savior sent by God can be redeemed." (Moyaert 2012, p. 27). Christians are those who are called to salvation in Christ; non-Christian religions cannot offer salvation, leaving non-Christians beyond salvation. As we saw above, among the ancient Fathers Tertullian is considered the pre-eminent exponent of exclusivism. The *inclusivist* position considers that non-Christian religions carry certain truths and values of Christianity, despite their errors, and can thus be considered as somehow "included" in the mystery of Christ and the mission of the Holy Spirit among the nations: "Salvation is still Christological, but in an ontological rather than epistemological sense: one can be saved even without knowing Christ at all." (Moyaert 2012, p. 30). Justin Martyr, Clement and Origen reflect this inclusivism. *Religious pluralism* goes further than inclusivism by considering that all great religious traditions are of divine origin and are equally valid paths to God and to salvation. Religious traditions, Christianity included, "constitute different ways of experiencing, conceiving and living in relation to a transcendent divine Reality which transcends all our varied visions of it." (Hick [1989] 2004, pp. 235–36).

Both exclusivism and inclusivism are essentially faith-based theologies which agree on the universality of Christ and Christian revelation. Religious pluralism, while not incompatible with Christianity, takes a more restrictive view of the significance of Christ and Christianity by considering Christianity as one religion among many, all legitimate paths to God. In contrast, the ancient Fathers did not consider Christianity to be simply one path to God among others, but inherently superior because of its divine origin and divine Founder and Head. Eminent modern representatives of these three theologies of religious diversity are often considered to be the Protestant theologian Karl Barth (1886–1968) (exclusivism); the Catholic theologian Karl Rahner (1904–1984) (inclusivism); and the Anglo-American philosopher of religion and theologian John Hick (1922–2012) (religious pluralism)[10].

In addition to this typology of Christian attitudes towards non-Christian religions, a slightly different polarity is based on the extent of Christian claims in the face of other religions. *Absolutism* considers that only Christianity is absolute or universal, in that Christianity alone has the fullness of truth and thus the universal claims of other religions are false. Both exclusivism and inclusivism are forms of absolutism or universalism. At the opposite pole, *relativism* accords the same value to all religions. Christianity is seen as one religion among others, with no stronger claim to truth than other religions, or to no religion for that matter. A form of relativism lies at the theoretical base of religious pluralism and of the modern, secular, religiously-neutral state—even if the state itself incorporates certain Christian notions.

---

[10] Foundational writings include notably (Brunner and Barth 1946; Rahner 1966, pp. 115–34; Hick 1973).

Pushed to an extreme, exclusivism and absolutism can lead to religious *fundamentalism*, typically characterized by intolerance, even to hostility and violence against other religions and their followers. At the other end of the spectrum, religious pluralism, carried to its limits, can open the door to *syncretism*: attempts to associate in one religious vision beliefs and practices from different traditions which may or may not be inherently irreconcilable, such as attempts to incorporate reincarnation into Christianity (Ladouceur 2006, p. 214).

Although Race's three-fold typology became commonplace in interreligious studies, it has been under increasing criticism since the late 1990s and has undergone a process of refinement, with sub-categories of each basic approach identified[11]. The main critique is that it is based on Christian soteriology—who can be saved in terms of Christ's salvific mission—and thus does not allow non-Christian religions to be themselves as human responses to the fundamental questions of the existence of the world and the meaning of life.

Other models have come forward in response to critiques of soteriological typology. Against a Christian soteriological view of world religions is *particularism*, which emphasizes distinctiveness and differences among world religions. Particularism, founded on a cultural-linguistic outlook, argues that "religions are thought of primarily as different idioms for construing reality, expressing experience and ordering life," according to leading advocate George Lindbeck (b. 1923), an American Lutheran theologian (Lindbeck 1984, p. 47). This approach proposes no common framework for comparing religions, but rather, in contrast with universal claims of religions and notions of perennial philosophy, emphasizes irreducible differences among religions "that cannot be traced back to a common ground or universal structure." (Moyaert 2012, p. 35). Different religions "may have incommensurable notions of truth, of experience and of categorical adequacy, and therefore also of what it would mean for something to be most important (i.e., 'God')." (Lindbeck 1984, p. 49). Apart from widely varying ideas concerning the nature of a Supreme Being, such irreconcilable differences could include notions such as karma and reincarnation, versus redemption and a single life, and nirvana versus heaven, the Kingdom of God or even the Orthodox conception of theosis.

The *comparative theology* approach also seeks to understand religions in themselves, but goes beyond this to identify points of congruence and divergence among religions. Like particularism, comparative theology discards a priori interpretative schemes (such as Christian soteriology) and "a global meta-perspective on religion," but instead "sets out to understanding the meaning of the Christian tradition by exploring it in the light of the teachings of other religious traditions." (Moyaert 2012). Comparative theology allows religions to speak for themselves—there is considerable emphasis on the study of primary sacred texts—but at the same time examines them from a Christian standpoint, not as a neutral bystander. It aims at bringing views of different religious traditions "into dialogue and even argument," writes the American Jesuit Francis Clooney (b. 1950), a leading advocate of comparative theology, "and thus promote a new, more integral conversation wherein traditions can remain distinct although their theologies are no longer separable. A religion may be unique, but its theology is not." (Clooney 2001, p. 8).

In comparison with the diversity and maturity of modern Orthodox thinking on the Church, and indeed on ecumenical theology, Orthodox theological reflection on religious diversity is still in its formative stages. Metropolitan Georges Khodr and Archbishop Anastasios Yannoulatos are pioneers in the field, despite the small number of their writings devoted to the subject. In the soteriological model of religious diversity, Khodr and Yannoulatos represent *inclusivist* theological positions concerning non-Christian religions, with a cautiously positive outlook on religious diversity, while upholding the universality of Orthodoxy's claims. Nicholas Arseniev also represents an inclusivist approach with perhaps some elements of comparative theology, but without hesitating to critique cruder

---

[11] For overviews of critiques of the soteriological typology, see (Moyaert 2012; D'Costa 2009, pp. 1–54).

aspects of non-Christian religious practices such as human sacrifice, which he assimilates to lower religious manifestations[12].

Fr. Seraphim Rose, highly critical of both Orthodox involvement in ecumenism and interreligious dialogue, represents an Orthodox *exclusivist* position, spilling into fundamentalism (but not to the point of advocating physical violence against non-conformists). Opponents of an inclusivist approach to religious pluralism typically make no attempt to reconcile an entirely negative view of other religions with divine goodness and providence; a theology of the universal import of Christ's salvific mission; or divine goodness with the creation of a large portion of humanity with no opportunity to accede to Christianity and hence, according to exclusivist theology, beyond salvation. The question of religious diversity has not featured on the agenda of Orthodox neo-traditionalists or fundamentalists, other than Seraphim Rose. They have largely focused their energies on attacking ecumenism and Orthodox believers engaged in ecumenical endeavors. Nonetheless the logic of the neo-traditionalist approach to non-Orthodox Christians suggests that the neo-traditionalists would rally to the exclusivist camp—if their theology excludes non-Orthodox Christians from the Church and salvation, to be consistent they would also exclude non-Christians as well.

Philip Sherrard could be identified with *religious pluralism* as defined above. Although Sherrard vacillates between inclusivism and religious pluralism, many statements in his book *Christianity: Lineaments of Sacred Tradition* point in the latter direction. Religious pluralism in the strict sense is unlikely to appeal to many Orthodox theologians since it appears to entail a surrender of the universal claims of Christian revelation and the missions of Christ and the Holy Spirit in favor of a relativistic approach to religious diversity. In contrast, the main line of Orthodox thought would see Christ as the perennial philosophy who shines forth, however obscurely at times, in non-Christian religions: "I am the Way and the Truth and the Life" (Jn 14:6).

Fr. Lev Gillet's approach to Judaism in his book *Communion in the Messiah* and, as far as we are aware, his work for the Union for the Study of Great Religions and the World Congress of Faiths, make him an Orthodox pioneer in *comparative theology*. Parallel with his commitment to building bridges between Orthodox and other Christians, Gillet sought to highlight what religious traditions share in common rather than focus on fundamental differences. Yet he certainly never lost or diluted his commitment to Orthodoxy. Unfortunately, he never wrote a reflective piece on his approach to religious diversity, and even Élisabeth Behr-Sigel says little about this aspect of his life in her biography of Fr. Lev.

The Holy and Great Council of the Orthodox Church held in Crete in June 2016 did not pronounce itself on religious diversity as such, but several Council documents contain positive statements on religious diversity. The document "The Mission of the Orthodox Church in Today's World" endorses Orthodox involvement in promoting inter-religious harmony: "The various local Orthodox Churches can contribute to inter-religious understanding and co-operation for the peaceful co-existence and harmonious living together in society, without this involving any religious syncretism." (Holy and Great Council 2016c, §A.3). The Council's Encyclical and the Message state that "Honest interfaith dialogue contributes to the development of mutual trust and to the promotion of peace and reconciliation." The only other reference in the Council's decisions to non-Christians is a restatement of the long-standing Orthodox practice of refusing marriages between Orthodox and non-Christians: "Marriage between Orthodox and non-Christians is categorically forbidden in accordance with canonical *akribeia*." (Holy and Great Council 2016a, §II, 5, iii.; Holy and Great Council 2016b, §17).

Ecumenical Patriarchs Athenagoras I (Kokkinakis) (1886–1972; patriarch 1948–1972) and Bartholomew I (Archontonis) (b. 1940; patriarch since 1991) manifest an open yet discerning attitude towards non-Christian religions. In conversations with the French theologian Olivier Clément,

---

12   Other Orthodox who endorse an inclusivist approach include (Karmiris 1980); (Constantelos 1992), also in (Swidler and Mojzes 1990); and (Papademetriou n.d.).

Athenagoras I refers to similarities between Orthodox and Islamic practices of the invocation of the Name of God and the practice of "fools for God" and to the important place that Jesus occupies in Islam. He is confident that "the old suspicions [between Muslims and Christians] are subsiding and will continue to subside" (Clément 1969, p. 176)—this was in 1968, before the rise of Islamic radicalism. In a similar vein, Bartholomew I makes positive remarks about Judaism, Islam, Hinduism and Buddhism—and even the New Age movement—as partial reflections, even if distorted, of the Logos of God (Clément 1997, pp. 197–226). Bartholomew I sees points of convergence between Orthodox and Jewish theology in such areas as primacy of the person, divine energies and divine presence in creation, wisdom, divine kenosis and aspects of spirituality. At the same time he is realistic in recognizing that there are also fundamental divergences and even contradictions on essential questions among major religions, as in his critique of the absence of a notion of a subsisting human person in Hinduism and Buddhism (Clément 1997, pp. 222–24), and in his address to the Conference on Interreligious Dialogue held in Istanbul in March 1998 (Bartholomew I. 1998, Second Period, 5, I, pp. 103–7; Metropolitan Emmanuel of France 2010).

In this admittedly limited survey of modern Orthodox theologians, religious inclusivism emerges as the preferred Orthodox theology of religious diversity, with Georges Khodr and Anastasios Yannoulatos as leading representatives together with Ecumenical Patriarchs Athenagoras I and Bartholomew I. Although the principal representatives of the Russian religious renaissance did not elaborate a formal theology of religions, the universalist ecclesiology of Sergius Bulgakov for one is also consistent with inclusivism. In authors such as Nicholas Arseniev and Lev Gillet, upholding the universal claims of Christianity opens to a comparative theological approach to world religions. This places Orthodox inclusivists in a comparable attitude towards non-Christian religions and philosophies as Justin Martyr, Clement and other early Fathers of the Church, extending Christ's salvific mission to non-Christians (to the extent that it is valid to project the modern soteriological typology unto the ancient Fathers). Seraphim Rose inherits the exclusivist theology of Tertullian, while Philip Sherrard seems to advocate a theology of religious pluralism based on perennialist philosophy. There are no representatives of the particularist approach in our survey—in fact, few Orthodox theologians are scholars of non-Christian religions, with Georges Khodr (Islam) and Lev Gillet (Judaism) as exceptions. With his book *Communion in the Messiah* (1942), Gillet can be considered a forerunner of comparative theology. Comparative theology lends itself to interreligious contact and dialogue, in which both Khodr and Gillet were engaged.

Despite an Orthodox preference for inclusivist and comparative theology approaches to non-Christian religions, there are still major unresolved questions. These include the extent of Christ's salvific mission beyond the limits of Christianity, divine inspiration in other religious traditions and their sacred writings, non-Christian religions as valid paths to God and salvation, the relationship of Christ and the Holy Spirit in world religions, and the status of non-Christians with respect to the Church. The arrival of large numbers of non-Christian migrants and refugees from the Middle East, Africa and Asia in Western Europe and North America, and, to a more limited extent, in countries of Orthodox tradition, should stimulate greater attention to the development of a robust Orthodox theology of religious diversity.

Conflicts of Interest: The author declares no conflict of interest.

References

Arnakis, G. Georgiades. 1951. Gregory Palamas among the Turks and Documents of His Captivity as Historical Sources. *Speculum* 26: 104–18. [CrossRef]

Arseniev, Nicholas. 1982. *Revelation of Life Eternal: An Introduction to the Christian Message*. Yonkers: St Vladimir's Seminary Press.

Athanasius. 1971. Against the Heathen. In *Contra Gentes and De Incarnatione*. Oxford: Clarendon Press.

Bartholomew I. 1998. Greeting. (Conference on Interreligious Dialogue [Istanbul, March 7, 1998]). *Orthodoxia* (January–March): 103–7.

Behr-Sigel, Élisabeth. 1993. *Un Moine de l'Église d'Orient, le père Lev Gillet: Un libre croyant universaliste, évangélique et mystique*. Paris: Le Cerf.

Behr-Sigel, Elisabeth. 1999. *A Monk of the Eastern Church, Fr. Lev Gillet*. London: Fellowship of Saint Alban and Saint Sergius.

Brunner, Emil, and Karl Barth. 1946. *Natural Theology*. London: Geoffrey Bles/Centenary Press.

Bulgakov, Sergius. [1945] 2002. *The Bride of the Lamb*. Translated by Boris Jakim. Grand Rapids, Eerdmans and Edinburgh: T&T Clark.

Clément, Olivier. 1969. *Dialogues Avec le Patriarche Athénagoras*. Paris: Fayard.

Clément, Olivier. 1997. *Conversations with Ecumenical Patriarch Bartholomew I*. Crestwood: St Vladimir's Seminary Press.

Clooney, Francis. 2001. *Hindu God, Christian God: How Reason Helps Break Down the Boundaries between Religions*. New York: Oxford University Press.

Constantelos, Demetrios J. 1992. *The Attitude of Orthodox Christians toward Non-Christians*. Brookline: Holy Cross Orthodox Press.

D'Costa, Gavin. 2009. *Christianity and World Religions: Disputed Questions in the Theology of Religions*. Chichester: Wiley-Blackwell, pp. 1–54.

Fédou, Michel. 2009. La doctrine du Logos chez Justin: Enjeux philosophiques et théologiques. *Kentron* 25: 145–58.

Florovsky, Georges. 1958. Review of the English translation of Vladimir Lossky's *The Mystical Theology*. *The Journal of Religion* 38: 207–8. [CrossRef]

Giannoulatos [Yannoulatos], Anastasios. 1971. *Various Christian Approaches to Other Religions (A Historical Outline)*. Athens: Poreuthentes.

Gillet, Lev. [1942] [2003] 2013. *Communion in the Messiah: Studies in the Relationship between Judaism and Christianity*. London: Lutterworth; Clarke, James, Eugene: Wipf & Stock.

Gillet, Lev. 1971. Un Moine de l'Église d'Orient. In *L'Amour Sans Limites*. Chevetogne: Éditions de Chevetogne. Translation in Gillet, Lev. 1977. *In Thy Presence*. London: Mowbray, Crestwood: St. Vladimir's Seminary Press.

Hick, John. 1973. *God and the Universe of Faiths*. London: Macmillan.

Hick, John. [1989] 2004. *An Interpretation of Religion: Human Responses to the Transcendent*. New Haven and London: Yale University Press.

Holy and Great Council. 2016a. The Sacrament of Marriage and Its Impediments. Available online: https://www.holycouncil.org/-/marriage (accessed on 23 December 2016).

Holy and Great Council. 2016b. Encyclical of the Holy and Great Council of the Orthodox Church. Available online: https://www.holycouncil.org/-/encyclical-holy-council (accessed on 23 December 2016).

Holy and Great Council. 2016c. The Mission of the Orthodox Church in Today's World. Available online: https://www.holycouncil.org/-/mission-orthodox-church-todays-world (accessed on 23 December 2016).

Janosik, Daniel J. 2016. *John of Damascus, First Apologist to the Muslims*. Eugene: Pickwick Publications.

Justin Martyr. 1997. *The First and Second Apologies*. New York: Paulist Press.

Karmiris, Ioannis. 1980. The Universality of Salvation in Christ. *Theologia* 51: 645–91. (*Theologia* 52: 14–45 [in Greek]).

Khodre, Georges. 1971a. Le Christianisme dans un monde pluraliste: L'économie du Saint-Esprit. *Irénikon* 44: 191–202.

Khodr, Georges. 1971b. Christianity in a Pluralistic World: The Economy of the Holy Spirit. *The Ecumenical Review* 23: 118–28. Reprinted in *Sobornost* (Summer 1971); *Sourozh* 53 (August 1993): 9–18.

Michael Kinnamon, and Brian Cope, eds. 1997. *The Ecumenical Movement: An Anthology of Key Texts and Voices*. Geneva: WCC Publications.

Ladouceur, Paul. 2006. Christianisme et réincarnation. *Contacts, Revue Française D'orthodoxie* 58: 238–56.

Lindbeck, George. 1984. *The Nature of Doctrine: Religion and Theology in a Postliberal Age*. London: SPCK.

Metropolitan Emmanuel of France. 2010. Keynote Address. International Council of Christians and Jews. June. Available online: www.ccjr.us/dialogika-resources/documents-and-statements/e-orthodox/1013-emmanuel2010june22 (accessed on 28 December 2016).

Moyaert, Marianne. 2012. Recent Developments in the Theology of Interreligious Dialogue: From Soteriological Openness to Hermeneutical Openness. *Modern Theology* 28: 25–52. [CrossRef]

Papademetriou, George. n.d. An Orthodox Christian View of Non-Christian Religions. Available online: www.goarch.org/ourfaith/ourfaith8089 (accessed on 28 October 2016).

Race, Alan. 1993. *Christians and Religious Pluralism: Patterns in the Christian Theology of Religions*. London: SCM Press.

Rahner, Karl. 1966. Christianity and the Non-Christian Religions. In *Theological Investigations*. London: Darton, Longman Todd, vol. 5, pp. 115–34.

Rose, Seraphim. 1975. Introduction. In *Orthodoxy and the Religion of the Future*. Platina: St. Herman of Alaska Brotherhood.

Sherrard, Philip. 1998. *Christianity: Lineaments of a Sacred Tradition*. Brookline: Holy Crosss Orthodox Press.

Sloboda, Nazar. 2017. The Conversations of Gregory Palamas during His Ottoman Captivity. Available online: http://www.academia.edu/12253003/THE_CONVERSATIONS_OF_GREGORY_PALAMAS_DURING_HIS_OTTOMAN_CAPTIVITY_1354-1355_ (accessed on 3 March 2017).

Soloviev, Vladimir. 1948. *Russia and the Universal Church (1889)*. London: Geoffrey Bles/Centenary Press.

Leonard Swidler, and Paul Mojzes, eds. 1990. *Attitudes of Religions and Ideologies toward the Outsider*. Lewiston: Edward Melon.

Tertullian. 1950. Apology. In *Apologetical Works and Minucius Felix Octavius*. Washington: Catholic University of America Press.

Vassiliadis, Petros. 1991. Greek Theology in the Making, Trends and Facts in the 80s—Vision for the 90s. *St Vladimir's Theological Quarterly* 35: 33–52.

Verkhovsky, Serge. 1958. Review of Vladimir Lossky *The Mystical Theology of the Orthodox Church*. *St Vladimir's Theological Quarterly* 2: 52–54.

Yannoulatos, Anastasios. 1989. *A Theological Approach to Understanding Other Religions*. London: Facing the World.

Yannoulatos, Anastasios. 2003. Toward a Global Community: Resources and Responsibilities (1974). In *Facing the World: Orthodox Christian Essays on Global Concerns*. Crestwood: WCC/St. Vladimir's Seminary Press, pp. 15–47.

Zizioulas, John. 1994. The Church as Communion: A Presentation on the World Conference Theme. In *On the Way to Fuller Koinonia: Official Report of the Fifth World Conference on Faith and Order*. Edited by Thomas F. Best and Günther Gassmann. Geneva: World Council of Churches Publications.

religions

MDPI

Article

Ecumenism: Rapprochement Through Co-working to Reconciliation

Cyril Hovorun

Huffington Ecumenical Institute, Loyola Marymount University, 1 LMU Drive, Los Angeles, CA 90045, USA;
hei@lmu.edu

Academic Editor: John A. Jillions
Received: 6 February 2017; Accepted: 7 April 2017; Published: 27 April 2017

Abstract: This paper explores some forms of interaction between the Catholic and Orthodox churches in different contexts. Some of these forms are helpful, but not always efficient, and some are not helpful. Theological dialogues belong to the former category of interactions: they are helpful, but not efficient. Alliances on an ideological basis, for instance on the basis of "traditional values," are unhelpful, because they polarise the churches internally. This article instead proposes a collaboration in the public domain as an alternative way of rapprochement between the two churches. The Ukrainian Maidan (the revolution of 2014) exemplifies a co-working space, which proved to be efficient for restoring trust between Orthodox and Greek Catholics.

Keywords: ecumenical dialogues; culture wars; ideology; public domain; maidan

---

What has been called the Great Schism between eastern and western Christianity was not a one-day event. It was not even a one-year event, although the formal year of their separation is believed to be 1054, when the delegation of the Roman See to Constantinople placed on the altar in Hagia Sophia the bull of excommunication of the patriarch Michael Keroularios, and was excommunicated in return. The process of separation began long before that date and was finalised long after (Louth 2007). It lasted for centuries and was complicated; it comprised currents on different levels and was delayed by many setbacks. Similarly, when the restoration of unity happens, it will not be a one-day or even a one-year event. It will last long decades, maybe even centuries. As a matter of fact, this process is already happening. Less time has passed since reconciliation began than it had taken for the process of separation. As regards complexity, the process of reconciliation mirrors the complexity of the separation at the turn of the second millennium. It features multi-layer currents and multiple setbacks.

In what follows, we will consider these three forms of the rapprochement between the Catholic and Orthodox churches: theological dialogue, "ideological ecumenism," and co-working in the public square. Each of these forms has its advantages and disadvantages. Some of them are healthier and more authentic, and others are less so.

At the top of the process of reconciliation, there is the official international Orthodox-Catholic dialogue (Savvatos 2014, pp. 487–89). It is conducted by a commission, whose official name is "The Joint International Commission for Theological Dialogue Between the Catholic Church and the Orthodox Church." This commission held its first session in 1980, a year after a formal decision to have such a dialogue was taken by Pope John Paul II and Patriarch Demitrios of Constantinople. The initial momentum for this dialogue was the first meeting since the Middle Ages between the Pope of Rome, Paul VI, and the Patriarch of Constantinople, Athenagoras, in January of 1964 in Jerusalem. The follow-up of that meeting was the lifting of the anathemas from 1054. This was a rather symbolic act, which signified a turning point from the pattern of confrontation to the pattern of dialogue in the relations between the two churches.

The logic of any theological dialogue, including the one between the Orthodox and Catholic churches, can be schematised in the following way. It is commonly believed that all major splits in the church were caused by theological disagreements or, to be precise, by theological formulas. In the case of the Orthodox-Catholic relationship, it was the insertion of *Filioque* to the Nicean creed. After the church hierarchs disagreed on these formulas, they decided to cease communion with each other. The restoration of unity, therefore, has to follow a reversed path: the hierarchs should agree on common theological formulas and then could resume communion with each other. Theological dialogues, thus, struggle to work out common theological formulas as an instrument of the restoration of unity.

This logic, however, has a couple of faults. First, it is based on the belief in the "magic" power, as it were, of theological formulas. This belief goes back to the era of scholasticism. This era began not in Western Europe in the Middle Ages, but in Asia Minor in the Late Antiquity. Scholasticism emerged in the fourth century and turned into a main theological method in the second part of the fifth century, approximately during the generation of the disciples of Cyril of Alexandria.[1] Cyril, who was the most important theological figure in that period, concluded the era when the meaning of theological formulas mattered more than their wording. That is why he was not consistent in the use of theological language, as for instance in the case of the Christological formula, "one nature of the incarnated God Word."[2] This was not yet a formula, but a part of a theological narrative. The disciples of Cyril, however, turned this dictum to a formula, and disagreed on its interpretation.

Some of them synthesised a new Christological *formula* on the basis of the languages of Cyril and Pope Leo. This formula, "one hypostasis of Jesus Christ in two natures," was adopted by the council of Chalcedon (Hovorun 2015a, p. 451). Another group of Cyril's disciples, under the leadership of the patriarch of Alexandria Dioskoros and the patriarch of Antioch Severos, opposed the Chalcedon and insisted that the words of the Alexandrian archbishop should be taken literally. Both parties departed from Cyril's flexible attitude toward theological language and arrived at a scholastic perception of it.

As mentioned above, this early Byzantine scholasticism featured a belief in the almost magical power of theological formulas. This attitude to theological formulas, as if they were "spells," became one of the reasons for the divisions between the churches in the fifth–sixth centuries. One group refused to accept *one* nature in Jesus, while for the other, *two* natures was unacceptable. Their insistence on a particular wording was different from the Arian controversy a century earlier. Unlike the terms "one" and "two natures," the terms *homoousios* (consubstantial), *homoiousios* (of a similar substance), and *homios* (a similar) were not synonyms, but signified completely different relationships between the Father and the Son in the Trinity. This difference in attitude to theological formulas explains why, in contrast to the Nicean theologians in the fourth century, the so-called neo-Chalcedonian theologians, who followed the council of Chalcedon and synthesised its language with the language of Cyril (Hovorun 2015b, pp. 106–24), in the sixth century accepted the language of the anti-Chalcedonians and agreed that the formula "one nature" can be used together with "two natures." Unfortunately, it was already too late to heal the division between Chalcedonians and anti-Chalcedonians, which had already happened and had become institutionalised in parallel ecclesial structures. Thus, it is not a coincidence that the first great schism between the churches in the fifth century; Rome and Constantinople on the one side, and Alexandria and Antioch on the other, happened in the period of the rise of early Byzantine scholasticism. A century before that, when an even more serious theological issue of Arianism erupted, it did not cause the same sort of schism between Arians and Niceans. This was partially because, in the fourth century, theologians could still go around formulas and accepted different interpretations of the words.

---

[1] I argue about this in my presentation "Cyril of Alexandria: a phenomenological theologian?" (Hovorun 2015a, pp. 378–444).
[2] "Μί α φύσισ τοῦ Θεοῦ Λόγου σεσαρκωμένου." *Quod unus sit Christus*, in (Durand 1964, p. 378).

When, in the modern era, theologians put into theological formulas the same faith as in the fifth century, they act anachronistically. In the era of abundance of hermeneutical methods, theological formulas became disenchanted. By invoking them, theologians can no longer change the reality of the church life—something they were able to do in the period of Late Antiquity and the Middle Ages. On the one hand, unity of the church cannot happen without agreeing on theological formulas. On the other hand, even when churches agree on common theological formulas, these formulas do not have the power to restore communion between churches anymore.

A second misleading assumption regarding theological formulas, as they are being discussed in the dialogues, is that they are exclusively about theology. In the era of Late Antiquity, there were not many semantic instruments to express people's cultural and political concerns. Theology instead offered the most elaborated language to talk about non-theological issues. That is why theological formulas were underpinned by various political and social agendas; they were not just about theology. For instance, Arianism, with its stress on the monarchy of the Father in the Trinity, effectively enhanced the monarchy of the Christian emperors.[3] Later theological movements, such as Severianism, Monothelitism, and Iconoclasm, also contributed to the consolidation of imperial authority.

With the passage of time, theological formulas often turned into identities. Large groups of people, which today would be called nations, adopted them as their distinct characteristics. For instance, the emergence of Coptic ethnicity was facilitated by the rejection of the council of Chalcedon by many Egyptian Christians. Armenians and Georgians also became polarised by their attitude to the Chalcedon. Theological formulas turned into cultural phenomena and thus lost, to a great extent, their original theological meaning. This means, for instance, that pro- and anti-Chalcedonian identities of different Christian groups in the Middle East today do not imply that those groups understand or give any significance to the Chalcedon as a theological phenomenon. Chalcedon now matters as a cultural phenomenon only. Most people are not aware of the theological differences that had led to the separation between the Eastern and Oriental churches in the fifth century. Nevertheless, they would protect these differences as their identity against anyone who would try to undermine them. If theologians and bishops would tell them that there are no theological differences anymore, this can be perceived by the people on the both sides of the Chalcedonian divide as an existential threat to who they are.

All these cultural connotations that theological formulas absorbed during their historic journey make them an insufficient instrument for the restoration of Christian unity in our days. When the official dialogues try to arrive at a common formula, they usually disregard its cultural connotations. As a result, the method of theological formulas alone, unfortunately, cannot secure the restoration of unity. What the theological formulas did in the past cannot be undone in the same way—by casting their spell on the divide.

The dialogue between the Eastern and Oriental churches has demonstrated this persuasively. This is the earliest of the bilateral dialogues (since 1964) and is the only one that has been completed successfully.[4] The dialogue resulted in two theological statements: one was adopted in 1989 in the Anba Bishoy monastery in Egypt, and the other, a more elaborated version of the previous one, was adopted in 1990 in Chambésy, Switzerland.[5] The Chambésy statement contains theological formulas based on the Christological language of Cyril of Alexandria. It repeats the wording elaborated in the framework of Neo-Chalcedonianism. The articles of the Chambésy statement were drafted jointly by the Chalcedonian and non-Chalcedonian theologians, and were eventually received by most members

---

[3] This discussion was initiated by Erik Peterson in *Der Monotheismus als politisches Problem; ein Beitrag zur Geschichte der politischen Theologie im Imperium Romanum* (Peterson 1935).

[4] This is a common Eastern and Oriental understanding of the results of this dialogue. What followed the completion of the theological phase of the dialogue, was called a "pastoral" phase, which began in 1993 and was to solve practical issues, such as commemoration of common Saints. See (Ovidiu 2014, pp. 508–28).

[5] All the statements of the dialogue are available at (Orthodox Unity n.d.).

of the dialogue. This was celebrated as a big success, which, however, was not acknowledged by all churches officially. The reasons for this had to do not with theology, but with the role of theological formulas as cultural denominators and people's identities, as described above. It turned out that theological matters do not matter for most Christians in the East any more, at least not to the extent they used to matter when their churches departed from each other. Theology has turned into people's identity, and this identity cannot be changed just by theological formulas. As a result, both Eastern and Oriental churches hesitate to implement the theological results of the dialogue and do not proceed to the restoration of communion.

The same will probably happen to the Orthodox-Catholic dialogue, if one day it will produce a common theological formula, which would resolve the differences between the two traditions. Most likely, such a formula will not lead to the restoration of unity, at least not automatically. This means that, in addition to theology, other issues should be tackled in the framework of the dialogue, including people's identities and culture. In other words, the dialogue should also deal with these questions: what does it mean to be a Catholic or an Orthodox, and how are these identities perceived by the followers of both traditions? These questions make the dialogue more complicated. However, without addressing them, the dialogue will most probable stumble on the same obstacles that the Eastern-Oriental dialogue has stumbled upon.

Dialogue is not a traditional way of solving theological issues. In the Byzantine past, such issues were solved at councils, by the exchange of letters and delegations, and through the mediation of emperors. Dialogue, as a form of conflict-resolution, is a product of modern times and was invented to tackle political problems. This does not, however, make dialogue something alien to the church. Moreover, it has effectively substituted other, more traditional, forms of rapprochement. Now it constitutes the commonest instrument of rapprochement between the churches.

There are also other forms of interaction between the divided churches which can be borrowed from political life. These forms can be both productive and counter-productive.

One of them employs ideological platforms and follows the pattern of the culture wars. The largest clashing political platforms of our time are two ideologies, which can be called "liberal" and "conservative." Their names and polarity reflect mostly the American political system, and as such they should not be applied too generally. Nevertheless, schematic distinction between "liberalism" and "conservatism" can be useful in explaining different ideological currents in the churches, as well as their attitudes to other Christians and to ecumenism.

The divide between "liberal" and "conservative" approaches seems to be stronger than many other divides, including theological ones. Many churches experience internal divisions along this ideological line. Conservative wings in these churches feel closer to each other than to the liberal wings in their own churches. The same applies to the liberal wings. This creates a precondition for what can be called "ideological ecumenism"—a rapprochement between the churches not on a theological basis, but on an ideological one. In this ecumenism, theology is substituted by ideology.

In some sense, this substitution can be effective, because theology does not touch many people in the churches anymore. Only a limited number of enthusiasts can follow theological arguments and make them relevant to their lives and communities. Ideologies, in contrast, are capable of enchanting many more people in the churches, especially when they are rendered in theological languages. As a result, they have more power than theology to mobilise different groups in the churches.

Ideologies, however, do more harm than benefit to the churches. First, unlike theology, which bridges this world with the divine, ideologies keep people confined to the agendas of this world. They emerged in the period of the Enlightenment as a product of secularisation of Christian societies.[6] As a result, they cannot elevate the human mind and spirit to God. Second, "ideological ecumenism" disintegrates communities from within: it alienates "liberal" and "conservative" members of the

---

[6] I analyse in detail the origins of ideologies in the modern era in "Ideology and Religion" (Hovorun 2016).

churches and communities from each other. Third, ideologies cannot secure sustainable alliances between followers of the same ideology from different churches.

The history of the American "fundamentalism" during the twentieth century clearly illustrates these shortcomings of the "ideological ecumenism." Soon after "fundamentalist" groups emerged in the 1920s in different Protestant churches in the United States, they began approaching each other. Simultaneously they distanced themselves from more "liberal" groups and thus caused schisms within their own churches. For example, the Northern Presbyterians and Northern Baptists became divided almost equally (Marsden 1980, pp. 164–65). The "fundamentalists" could not reconcile themselves with those whom they called "liberals," because they considered the latter to believe in almost a different religion. Characteristic in this regard is a statement by J. Gresham Machen (1881–1937) from the Princeton Theological Seminary:

> In the sphere of religion, in particular, the present time is a time of conflict; the great redemptive religion which has always been known as Christianity is battling against a totally diverse type of religious belief, which is only the more destructive of the Christian faith because it makes use of traditional Christian terminology. This modern non-redemptive religion is called "modernism" or "liberalism." (Machen 1923, p. 2)

At the same time, the "fundamentalists" perceived other "fundamentalists" as belonging to their own religion, even though they belonged to other churches. Thus, "fundamentalist" alliances began developing (Harris 1998, p. 28). One of the earliest of these was the World Christian Fundamentals Association (WCFA). In such alliances, ideological conservatism became more important than the doctrinal differences between denominations. Most of these attempts, however, failed to sustain themselves for a long time or to foster productive cooperation between the churches.

Ideological alliances occurred not only on the basis of conservative ideology. Liberal ideology also sometimes tried to substitute for theology in the ecumenical movements. The largest ecumenical organisation in the world, the World Council of Churches (WCC), which was constructed on theological principles, from time to time fell into the trap of ideological bias, mostly of a leftward tilt. This was, for instance, when the Orthodox churches from the Soviet Block tried to promote through the WCC the ideological agendas of the Communist regimes behind them. These agendas resonated with many "liberal" Christians in the global ecumenical movement.

Moreover, antagonism between pro-ecumenical and anti-ecumenical movements within different churches can be also interpreted as an extrapolation of ideology-based cultural wars. For many anti-ecumenical groups, which exist in most churches, their dissatisfaction with the ecumenical movement is a way to promote their conservative agenda. For instance, radical anti-ecumenists in the Orthodox world, such as groups of the so-called "True Orthodox Christians" or "Old-calendarists," are radical conservatives with clear ideological and political agendas. In a similar way, many groups in the churches who promote the ecumenical agenda are also liberal. Ecumenism for many is a way of expressing and practicing their open liberal views. This does not, however, necessarily undermine their desire for Christian unity.

A recent example of "ideological ecumenism" is an attempt to establish an alliance between the Russian Orthodox and Roman Catholic churches. This initiative was suggested by the Russian church. The logic of such an offer from Moscow is explained by the following. Soon after Patriarch Kirill was elected as the new primate of the Russian Orthodox Church in 2010, he led the church in a strictly conservative direction. "Liberals" were libelled as not-quite-Orthodox, and conservatism was proclaimed a standard of Orthodoxy. At that time, the pope of Rome was a conservative, Benedict XVI. The coincidence of two primates who promoted a similar conservative agenda urged some to promote an alliance between the two churches on the basis of this agenda. Fortunately, this initiative was not picked up by Rome. It is unlikely that such an alliance would have survived under the more liberal Pope Francis.

The political framework offers to the churches not only temptations, but also healthy opportunities for rapprochement. This is particularly the case when the churches work together for the same causes of justice and solidarity. These causes are not ideological. Unlike ideologies, which project political programs onto religion and thus reduce the theological scope of the church, causes of justice and solidarity project the principles of Christian faith onto the public domain. These causes do not reduce or constrain the nature and purpose of the church, but implement its theological vision through social action. Therefore, this sort of social activity of the church does not incur the same sort of reductions that ideologies do. It does not divide churches according to ideological criteria, but actually bridges different ideological platforms. When churches struggle together for the same causes of justice and solidarity, they grow closer to each other. This can be illustrated by the following scheme (Figure 1):

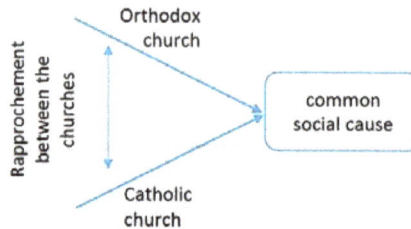

Figure 1. Rapprochement between the churches in the public square.

There are good examples that illustrate how ecumenically effective the struggle of different churches for the same social causes can be. One was the campaign against apartheid, which consolidated the South African churches, particularly in the framework of the South African Council of Churches (SACC). This ecumenical organisation became an inter-denominational and non-ideological platform for overthrowing apartheid, especially under the leadership of the Anglican Archbishop of Cape Town, Desmond Tutu. After the apartheid was officially abandoned and condemned, the churches continued working together in restoring justice and integrity to the society in South Africa, through the Truth and Reconciliation Commission. Similar commissions in other countries, which had been torn by political abuses and totalitarianisms, have also been supported by different churches. Through participation in these commissions, the churches contributed to the restoration of justice and solidarity in their societies. This participation also helped them become closer to each other and contributed to genuine ecumenism.

Another example is more recent: the so-called "Revolution of dignity" in Ukraine. This happened during the winter 2013–14, when hundreds of thousand Ukrainians came to the central square of the country's capital Kyiv, the Maidan, to protest against the injustice and authoritarianism imposed by former President Viktor Yanukovych. His regime tried to forcefully dissipate the originally and purposely peaceful protests, which caused clashes that led to around one hundred casualties. Protesters fell from the fire of snipers and police, which led to the ousting of President Yanukovych, who fled to Russia.

During all three months of the protests, the Ukrainian churches were together with the people at the Maidan, each church to a different extent. The protesters prayed together, regardless of their ecclesial affiliations, and were encouraged by clergy of different churches. The Ukrainian churches, before the manifestations at the Maidan, felt quite hostile to each other. The confrontation was particularly severe between the Orthodox churches of the Moscow and Kyiv Patriarchate, as well as between the Moscow Patriarchate and the Ukrainian Greek Catholic Church. When the Maidan happened, however, even the priests (though not the bishops) of the Moscow Patriarchate came there together. They prayed on the central stage of the protests, despite their differences and hostilities in the past. The Maidan, thus, became an important ecumenical event and spurred on momentum for rapprochement between the churches, especially on the level of lay people and clergy (Hovorun 2014). It brought together the churches, which were previously not able even to begin a dialogue with each other. In this way the Maidancreated a space that enabled the churches to achieve more than any dialogue managed to do.

Unfortunately, after the victory of the "Revolution of dignity," some churches withdrew from the common public space and locked themselves up in their usual rhetoric of exclusion and condemnation of others. In particular, this happened to the Ukrainian Orthodox Church of the Moscow Patriarchate. The momentum towards rapprochement, which was created by the Maidan, was quenched. This occurred mostly because of the Russian aggression against Ukraine that followed. Russian propaganda flooded Ukraine with "post-truth" filled with the messages of hatred and division. The Moscow Patriarchate in Ukraine appeared most vulnerable to the effects of this propaganda.

Nevertheless, the Maidan showed the Ukrainian churches a pattern towards reconciliation, which can parallel more traditional dialogues. Particularly interesting is how the Orthodox and Greek Catholic churches came along. At the public square of the Maidan, their faithful and priests stood next to each other. The Maidan, thus, showed that the Orthodox and Greek Catholic church can be best friends and not necessarily antagonists. This can serve as an example for the Orthodox and Catholic churches. Pursuing common good in the public domain can help them continue moving closer to each other. This does not mean that the co-working of the churches in the public square should be a substitute dialogue and other ways of rapprochement. It only means that such work can and should be done in parallel to theological conversations.

Acknowledgments: This article is published as a part of fellowship at the Huffington Ecumenical Institute at Loyola Marymount University in Los Angeles.

Conflicts of Interest: The author declares no conflict of interest.

References

de Durand, G. M. 1964. Cyrille d'Alexandrie. Deux dialogues christologiques. *L'antiquité classique* 33: 508–11.

Harris, Harriet A. 1998. *Fundamentalism and Evangelicals*. Oxford and New York: Oxford University Press.

Hovorun, Cyril. 2014. Christians in Ukraine: Ecumenism in the Trenches. Available online: http://www.catholicworldreport.com/Item/2970/christians_in_ukraine_ecumenism_in_the_trenches.aspx#.Uzt2Rq1dVWg (accessed on 13 April 2017).

Hovorun, Cyril. 2015a. Cyril of Alexandria: A phenomenological theologian? Paper presented at the XVII International Conference on Patristic Studies, Oxford, UK, August 10–14.

Hovorun, Cyril. 2015b. Maximus, a Cautious Neo-Chalcedonian. In *The Oxford Handbook of Maximus the Confessor*. Edited by Pauline Allen and Bronwen Neil. Oxford: Oxford University Press.

Hovorun, Cyril. 2016. Ideology and Religion. *Kyiv-Mohyla Humanities Journal* 3: 23–35. [CrossRef]

Louth, Andrew. 2007. *Greek East and Latin West: the Church, AD 681–1071*. Crestwood: St. Vladimir's Seminary Press.

Machen, J. Gresham. 1923. *Christianity and Liberalism*. New York: Macmillan.

Marsden, George M. 1980. *Fundamentalism and American Culture: The Shaping of Twentieth Century Evangelicalism, 1870–1925*. New York: Oxford University Press.

Orthodox Unity. Various Documents Concerning Eastern Orthodox and Oriental Orthodox Joint Commission and Unity: Official Statements. Available online: https://orthodoxjointcommission.wordpress.com/category/official-statements (accessed on 4 February 2017).

Ovidiu, Ioan. 2014. Eastern Orthodox—Oriental Orthodox Dialogue—A Historical and Theological Survey. In *Orthodox Handbook on Ecumenism: Resources for Theological Education*. Edited by Panteles Kalaitzides, Thomas E. FitzGerald, Cyril Hovorun, Aikaterini Pekridou, Nikolaos Asproulis, Dietrich Werner and Guy Liagre. Oxford: Regnum, pp. 508–28.

Peterson, Erik. 1935. *Der Monotheismus als politisches Problem; ein Beitrag zur Geschichte der politischen Theologie im Imperium Romanum*. Leipzig: Hegner.

Savvatos, Chrysostomos. 2014. Orthodox Dialogue with the Roman Catholic Church. In *Orthodox Handbook on Ecumenism: Resources for Theological Education*. Edited by Panteles Kalaitzides, Thomas E. FitzGerald, Cyril Hovorun, Aikaterini Pekridou, Nikolaos Asproulis, Dietrich Werner and Guy Liagre. Oxford: Regnum.

MDPI

Article

Mimesis or Metamorphosis? Eastern Orthodox Liturgical Practice and Its Philosophical Background

Christina M. Gschwandtner

Philosophy Department, Fordham University, 441 E. Fordham Rd., Bronx, NY 10458, USA; gschwandtner@fordham.edu

Academic Editor: John Jillions
Received: 12 April 2017; Accepted: 27 April 2017; Published: 12 May 2017

Abstract: What does Eastern Orthodox liturgy do? Is it a mimetic remembrance of Christ's acts or about a transformation of the believers who come to worship? This paper explores the larger philosophical worldview within which patristic liturgy emerged in order to negotiate this tension between mimetic and transformative aspects of liturgical practice. It suggests that ancient philosophical conceptions of the cosmos and of soul and body underlie and can hence elucidate what Byzantine liturgy does. Liturgy tries to unify soul and body, heaven and earth, in a particular way. Liturgy seeks to transform the human person and the cosmos in such a manner that they come to image and match each other. The introduction to the paper briefly examines some contemporary accounts to show the stakes of the question about what liturgy "does" and the role mimesis and metamorphosis play in this debate. The main part of the paper explores the shared philosophical heritage regarding imitation and transformation, inner and outer, heavenly and earthly in order to understand more fully the background for how liturgy negotiates these dimensions. The conclusion to the paper draws out the implications of this patristic heritage for making sense of what contemporary liturgy does in a broader sense.

Keywords: liturgy; mimesis; transformation; cosmos; philosophy; Maximus

---

"What does liturgy do?" wonders Robert Taft in an article that goes on to list 16 theses about what happens in liturgy and what it is supposed to accomplish (Taft 1992). He concludes that liturgy is about encounter with Christ and the "spiritual formation of the Church" (Taft 1992, p. 211).[1] Liturgy celebrates the activity of Christ, expresses the faith of the Church, and transforms us.[2] Alexander Rentel grapples with a similar question about what liturgy is and does (Rentel 2015). Like Taft, he argues that liturgy must be centered on Christ and that it is a revelation of God's love, but acknowledges that this leaves unanswered why we do it in precisely this way and how exactly particular liturgical practices accomplish this.[3] He argues that liturgy has to be more fully understood in order for it to lead to "a constant transformation of the mind"; this "requires work, training, and discipline" (Rentel 2015, pp. 226, 229). Throughout the article he stresses both the mimetic function of liturgy as revealing Christ's mystery and its intent to work transformatively in our lives.

---

[1] The summaries in the next sentence refer to claims he makes on pp. 207, 203, and 201, respectively.

[2] In a more recent book he asks what the Byzantines might have experienced in church. Here no claims are made about how liturgy might transform the worshipper, but his account is primarily descriptive (who was there? where did people stand? what did they see? what happened?) (Taft 2006).

[3] "In the mysteries, Christ is revealed and comes and dwells amongst the faithful. In their celebration, Christ unites himself to his people and grows into one with them, stifling sin and enlivening the faithful with his own life and grating them a share in his victory" (Rentel 2015, p. 221). But "a fundamental understanding of what happens in liturgy does not come easily even to those who have dedicated themselves to theological study" (Rentel 2015, p. 222) and often there is "a tragic feeling of disconnection between the Orthodox liturgy and [a] person's life" (Rentel 2015, p. 223).

This question about mimesis and metamorphosis, about whether liturgy images or represents something or whether it instead is meant to "do" something, to transform us in some way, often hovers uneasily in the background and at times moves explicitly into the foreground of many contemporary reflections on liturgy, both Eastern and Western. At times this is presented as an either/or option. Either liturgy is primarily about remembering Christ and his salvific actions on our behalf, in which case liturgy is primarily mimetic, representing his life and action in some fashion to enable the act of anamnesis as the primary function of liturgy. Or liturgy is primarily about transforming its participants in some way, having some significant impact on their lives, shaping them in some fashion. Such transformation is often read in an eschatological way: somehow liturgy makes "real" what will be and enables us to begin to enter into the coming kingdom. At times these tensions are compounded by distinctions between an "inner" and an "outer" reality; the ways in which "physical" or material dimensions interact with (or possibly hinder) the supposedly more "spiritual" aspects of liturgy.

In some way this dilemma goes back to the patristic mystagogies. Germanos of Constantinople and Nicholas Cabasilas, for example, strongly stress the mimetic function (Cabasilas 1960; Germanos of Constantinople 1984). Each aspect of liturgy is supposed to show or represent some aspect of Christ's life, from his conception leading up to his crucifixion and resurrection. Indeed, the liturgical year itself in its cycle of feasts seems to have such a mimetic function. Liturgy, on this account, is primarily about helping us remember and celebrate Christ's salvific action. Other thinkers, such as Maximus the Confessor, whose vision has gained tremendous popularity in the twentieth century, conceive of liturgy in more transformative and eschatological terms (Maximus the Confessor 1985). Here liturgy is meant to unite and transform the whole cosmos; it is an eschatological anticipation of what will be.

Many contemporary accounts try to hold these two dimensions together, but it is not always very clear how they interact with each other or how the tension between them can be resolved. At times, mimesis is taken as the precondition for metamorphosis, that is to say, somehow imaging Christ's actions mimetically within liturgy (the Sunday liturgy or the annual festal cycle) enables participants in liturgy to become more like him. This paper will seek to show that we can better understand the "how" of the possible interactions and relationships of these dimensions of liturgy (and therefore the question of how liturgy functions or what liturgy is supposed to "do"), if we pay more careful attention to the larger philosophical worldview within which liturgy emerged.[4] This may also suggest upon closer examination that the connection might function in reverse of what is often supposed: maybe it is not just mimesis that leads to metamorphosis, but metamorphosis is required in order for mimesis to be accomplished. The introduction to the paper will briefly examine some contemporary accounts that negotiate this tension in different ways to show the stakes of the question about what liturgy "does" and the role mimesis and metamorphosis play in this debate. The main part of the paper will then turn to an exploration of the shared philosophical heritage regarding imitation and transformation, inner and outer, heavenly and earthly in order to understand more fully the background of how liturgy negotiates these dimensions. The conclusion to the paper will briefly draw out the implications of this patristic heritage for making sense of what liturgy does in a broader sense.

1. Introduction

Several recent and contemporary thinkers argue strongly against a purely mimetic interpretation of liturgy. Alexander Schmemann's entire liturgical project might be summarized as an argument

---

[4]   Although I focus in this paper on Eastern Orthodox liturgy—in keeping with the journal issue's theme of exploring "Orthodox identity"—tracing these sources may also have implications for Western liturgical approaches, especially as at least some contemporary Western liturgical theology is influenced by the work of Schmemann and relies to some extent on historical research on patristic liturgical forms. For a critique of this tendency in liturgical theology, see (Hughes 2003). Hughes is sympathetic to the broader concerns of liturgical theologians such as Schmemann, Kavanagh, and Fagerberg, but judges their approach as too romantic for honestly confronting the contemporary situation. Hughes and others are certainly right to raise these questions, but at the very least a rethinking of the functioning of liturgy today must include as full an understanding as possible of how it was originally meant to function, especially when considering its *meaning*.

for the transformative effect of liturgy on the world, which he interprets in eschatological fashion (as opposed to a merely anamnetic/commemorative interpretation of liturgy) (Schmemann 1987). He does not necessarily argue that liturgy has no anamnetic or mimetic dimensions, but he seriously downplays them in favor of the more transformative and eschatological emphasis he considers to have been lost over the centuries. Liturgy is "for the life of the world"; within liturgy the assembled church enters into the kingdom, celebrates the heavenly mysteries with the larger cosmic reality, and is then sent out to transform all of life into that liturgical vision.[5] His student Aidan Kavanagh carries this further by arguing that liturgy is "doing the world as it is supposed to be done," that liturgy is the "stunningly normal" practice of "world" in the insanity and abnormality of our contemporary culture (Kavanagh 1984).[6] Both proposals, however, are rather short on working out exactly what this means or how it is supposed to be accomplished.[7] David Fagerberg, who strongly shares their overall vision, suggests that ascetic practice must supplement liturgical practice in order to allow liturgy to accomplish what it is supposed to do.[8] These liturgical scholars all move away from a purely mimetic understanding of liturgy to a much more substantively transformative one, although the question of how exactly liturgy *accomplishes* such transformation is often left unanswered.

Andrew White argues heavily against *any* notion of mimesis in Byzantine liturgy. He contends that the Byzantines explicitly and deliberately separated liturgy from theatrical performance (which was concerned with mimesis/representation) and thought of liturgy in purely rhetorical terms (White 2015). Liturgy is not an "enactment" or a "sacred representation"; the Eucharist is completely "non-mimetic" but instead purely symbolic (White 2015, pp. 27, 45, 65, respectively). Indeed, the rejection of mimesis seems to mean for him that liturgy is entirely "spiritual" (White 2015, p. 52).[9] The celebrants "did not do or enact anything" because any such agency in liturgy would have "distracted the congregation from spiritual matters." Liturgy, then, "served to activate a mystical, spiritual presence in the minds of the congregation" (White 2015, pp. 84, 85, 104, respectively). Here liturgy becomes a purely internal, spiritual affair with little connection to its outward, physical performance or material elements. In contrast to White, Terence Cuneo does think that there is a kind of liturgical enactment occurring in Orthodox liturgy, namely one that serves to immerse the listener and participant in liturgy in such a way as to take on certain roles that allows the enactors to appropriate the message and "revise their narrative identities" or shape moral selves (Cuneo 2016).[10] While he does not necessarily claim

---

5   Yet, like Rentel, he also laments the disconnect between liturgy and life: "But the individual believer, entering the church, does not feel he is a participant and celebrant of worship, does not know that in this act of worship he, along with the others who together with him are constituting the Church, is called to express the Church as new life and to be transformed again into a member of the Church." (Schmemann 1986, p. 30). The phase "for the life of the world" refers to his popular lectures *For the Life of the World* (Schmemann 1973).

6   The way in which liturgy is "supreme normality" is explored in the final chapter.

7   For example, Kavanagh claims that liturgy detects shifts in theology: "To detect that change in the subsequent liturgical act will be to discover where theology has passed, rather as physics detects atomic particles in tracks of their passage through a liquid medium" (Kavanagh 1984, p. 74), yet at the same time seems extremely critical of most changes and liturgical development as a kind of degeneration or corruption of some original "purer" form. Similarly, Schmemann can be extremely critical of "corrupt" liturgical forms and mysticizing interpretations, which seem to include almost anything from the fifth century onward. Much of his work seeks to restore the church to an earlier (and presumably better) liturgical interpretation and practice. See W. Jardine Grisbrooke's criticism (Grisbrooke 1990).

8   See (Fagerberg 2004). He works this out more fully in (Fagerberg 2013).

9   He reiterates several times that it is "purely spiritual."

10   This is worked out most fully in chapters four and five. While Cuneo's philosophical interpretations of liturgy are provocative, it is strange that especially in his account of narrative identity he does not at all engage Paul Ricoeur, the philosopher who has developed this topic by far the most fully. Cuneo also repeatedly claims that philosophy has never thought of religion in terms of practice, but treats it entirely as an abstract system of beliefs that does not provide a good account of how believers actually experience their faith. While this may be true of *analytical* philosophy of religion, it is patently untrue of phenomenology, which has engaged in a substantive analysis of experiences and practices for decades. French phenomenologists, especially, have analyzed ritual and liturgy, including Eucharistic practice, for years. This tradition is entirely ignored by Cuneo's account. (E.g., he claims that Christianity "is dedicated to engaging God in various ways by doing such things as blessing, petitioning, and thanking God—activities about which, I should add, philosophers have said virtually nothing" (Cuneo 2016, p. 148). Yet, philosophers like Jean-Luc Marion, Jean-Louis Chrétien, Michel Henry, Jean-Yves Lacoste, Emmanuel Falque, even Emmanuel Lévinas and in a quite different way Martin Heidegger, have said lots about precisely these issues. Similar claims about philosophy's supposed silence on these issues are made throughout the book.)

that liturgy "merely" represents certain aspects of Christ's life, he does attribute mimetic function to our appropriation of the liturgical message, as we strive to imitate the characters who are presented to us as models within the liturgical world. He argues that this is not "to enter into a liturgical time machine in which the past mystically becomes present" but instead a call "to order one's life around the founding events of the church" and "to view one's life as a part of a larger narrative, which includes the founding events of the church," hence effecting a "living relationship with these events" (Cuneo 2016, pp. 122–23). Thus, for Cuneo, any transformation that might occur in our lives on the basis of liturgy does so because of our imitation of the acts and persons represented in the liturgy.

A similar claim is worked out in much more detail and in a close reading of patristic liturgical sources by Derek Krueger, who argues that Byzantine ritual—whether in Romanos' kontakia, in various aspects of the church year, in the praying of the Great Canon of St. Andrew of Crete, or in other penitential hymns—sought to shape a particular liturgical self within liturgy (Krueger 2014). The liturgical texts provide us with models of "salvageable sinners" as "icons of moral development," which serve as "norms for self-understanding and self-presentation" (Krueger 2014, p. 3). In contrast to White, he thinks of this as explicitly mimetic: "In a manner analogous to theater, ritual activities involve playing and ultimately inhabiting the mythic roles of sacred narrative" (Krueger 2014, p. 7). Identifying with the biblical characters enables congregants to "call a sinful identity into being through accusation" and to participate "in their own redemption" (Krueger 2014, pp. 24, 218, respectively). He concludes: "Thus Christians gained access to themselves through penitential rhetoric. Repentant speech provided a mechanism through which to understand themselves. Confidence in the ability of the speaker to inhabit the role lay at the heart of Byzantine ritual theory and undergirded Byzantine ritual practice. Anguished first-person performances of compunction effected the formation of the self. In a moment before their amnesty, the liturgy called selves into being with interpellative force. It produced a communion of liturgical subjects poised between self-recognition and salvation" (Krueger 2014, p. 221). As in Cuneo, liturgy here is taken to have transformative power precisely through its imitative function: the models we encounter in liturgy enable us to understand ourselves and give us access to ourselves; by imitating them, we form a particular version of the self that ultimately functions redemptively.

Krueger seeks to give us a greater understanding of how certain penitential hymns might have served to shape penitential practices leading to particular kinds of self-understanding in historical Byzantium. He leaves open the question of whether these practices and the hymns that remain in contemporary liturgical celebrations can have a similar transformative effect today. Rentel acknowledges that our sensibilities and presuppositions have changed over time and that these changes "push Christian faithful ever so subtly away from the cultural sensibilities that were in place when the liturgical rites were formed," causing "a disconnection from the liturgy of the Church" (Rentel 2015, p. 231).[11] What were these sensibilities and how might they have informed what liturgy was taken to "do"?

This question might be addressed more successfully if we understand more about the larger worldview of late antiquity. Byzantine sensibilities and presuppositions about the world and the human person were significantly shaped by this larger worldview, a worldview that is articulated most fully in what we now identify as "philosophical" texts, such as those of Plato and Aristotle and the commentary tradition that built on them, but also by the contributions of thinkers like Ptolemy and Galen. This is obviously not to claim that patristic "theology" is merely a vulgarization of Greek philosophy or that it appropriated ideas in an unquestioned fashion. Rather, it is to acknowledge that both are worked out against a backdrop of shared assumptions about reality that are not always fully articulated (and which, at least in some cases, we can maybe see more clearly precisely because we no

---

[11]   I am not convinced that the shift is anywhere near as "subtle" as Rentel suggests, even in an Orthodox context. Western liturgical scholars often make much stronger claims, accusing Eastern theologians of deliberately ignoring the ecclesial reality of the twenty-first century, in which very few confessional Christians still experience the kind of liturgical life presupposed by Orthodox liturgical theology. See, for example, the texts by Grisbrooke and Hughes mentioned above.

longer share them and they appear strange to us). It also does not mean that the patristic worldview accords in all points with the ancient philosophical one or that philosophical texts were used explicitly to formulate what might occur in liturgy. Yet, mystagogical texts like that of Maximus the Confessor do draw on broader ancient presuppositions and terminology about the cosmos and the human person within it that are most fully explicated by Plato and Aristotle and taken up explicitly in various ways by the Cappadocians, Nemesius of Emesa, Maximus himself, John of Damascus, and others, which seems to suggest that these shared presuppositions about the world were also operative in what liturgy was taken to do or to accomplish.

A fuller understanding of the philosophical background of this terminology will help us see not only how these assertions might make sense, but could also bring together the often dichotomous or even contradictory claims about what liturgy does, the tension between its mimetic and its transformative functions. *By taking account of the philosophical background to the terminology employed by the patristic thinkers, liturgy can be understood as a metamorphosis into a certain kind of mimesis; that is to say, liturgy tries to effect a "mimetic match" between soul and body, heaven and earth, the invisible and visible realms.*[12] This enables us to hold together mimesis and metamorphosis as connected elements of what occurs in liturgy, but is also a stronger claim than that advanced by Krueger or Cuneo. Liturgy is not only in some general sense about the formation of the self; it is about a unification of soul and body, heaven and earth, invisible and visible in such a way that they begin to match and reflect each other. And it is not just about imitating certain models in order to be personally transformed, but actually calls for the sort of transformation that makes possible a more effective mimesis—one that operates on both anthropological and cosmological planes in such a way as to connect them to each other.

2. Invisible and Visible Realms

Let us return briefly to Maximus' *Mystagogy* to sharpen the question about philosophical presuppositions at work in liturgy. Maximus begins by contending that the "holy Church bears the imprint and image of God since it has the same activity as he does by imitation and in figure" (Maximus the Confessor 1985, p. 186). This means that it brings together various aspects of reality and connects them to each other, yet without abolishing their natures. Such unification of dispersed aspects of reality occurs on several levels: a combination of invisible and visible realms, intelligible and sensory aspects, heaven and earth (identified as the two aspects of the sensory world), human soul and body, and the intellectual or rational and vital or non-rational parts of the soul. Although these are various levels of reality that appear distinct to us, they are also intimately connected, i.e., the two aspects of the soul parallel the two aspects of the human person, which reflect the two aspects of our earthly reality. These in turn parallel the two aspects of the larger cosmic reality, and ultimately the largest distinction between visible and invisible. Bringing together the various levels of reality becomes possible if the soul itself becomes unified through the pursuit of wisdom (*phronesis*), the development of virtues, and the contemplation (*theoria*) of divine reality. Maximus concludes this part of the analysis by saying: "Whoever has been fortunate enough to have been spiritually and wisely initiated into what is accomplished in church has rendered his soul divine and a veritable church of God" (Maximus the Confessor 1985, p. 195). What does he mean by these levels of reality and by their unification? On what conception of the soul does this interpretation of liturgy rely and how is liturgy taken to effect such divinization of the soul? Maximus is using terminology and conceptions of reality that have a long history not only in patristic literature but also in the ancient world more broadly. They are worked

---

[12] This is not to argue that this is the *only* way to understand liturgy or even necessarily the best one. This is merely a first exploration into how taking account of the broader worldview in which liturgy develops might help us understand more fully what it is meant to do, something I hope to work out much more fully in the future.

out most fully in the philosophies of Plato and Aristotle, on whom the fathers draw extensively in their use of these terms.[13]

One of the most fundamental shared presuppositions in the Hellenistic ancient and late antique world concerns the very nature of reality as both visible and invisible. Visible reality is associated with the body and the material world; it undergoes change or motion, comes into being and goes out of being (via *genesis* and *phthora*), and it is physical, i.e., constituted by the four elements (earth, water, air, fire). Invisible reality does not undergo change, is characterized by cyclical motion (which is not really motion in the proper sense but in some form immutable because it has no beginning or end[14]), does not undergo generation or disintegration, and is associated with the soul or the mind. It is often called "intelligible" reality (rather than the "sensory" reality associated with the material world). The fact that it has no beginning or end means that it is eternal; the fact that it is purely intelligible and incorporeal means it is not found in any physical location or place. This invisible reality is often associated with the divine, but also with "spiritual" or intelligible beings (angels, demons, heavenly bodies, and the human soul).[15] These claims about the two-fold nature of reality are already made in Plato's *Timaeus* (28a–37a), where the visible world order is fashioned by its divine maker based on an invisible and beautiful heavenly model, hence imaging its divine inspiration and principles (a possible precedent for Maximus' *logoi* of creation). Already in the *Timaeus* anthropological and cosmological levels are taken to image each other: the cosmos is a living creature and the human is a small cosmos (30c–d, 34b, 44c–46a). Plato also already speaks of the four elements, linear and cyclical motion, and the beginning of time as "a moving image of eternity" (*Timaeus* 37c–39e). This is worked out more fully and with much more concrete detail by Aristotle in the *Physics*, *Metaphysics*, and *On the Heavens*, where he outlines the ways in which the four elements are arranged in a spherical universe, why heavier, denser, colder elements (like earth) are at the center moving in linear fashion, while lighter, thinner, and warmer elements (air and especially fire) are further "up" (i.e., further away from the center and closer to the "heavens," which move in a cyclical fashion around the earth). These assumptions about the basic building blocks of the universe (the four elements) and their respective weight, temperature, and density are universally shared by the ancients.[16]

Various patristic thinkers draw extensively from these treatises for their practically identical divisions of reality. Basil of Caesarea uses the *Timaeus* extensively in his *Hexaemeron*, a series of homilies on the creation accounts in Genesis, including employing the Platonic terms "maker" (*demiourgos*) and "making" (*poēsis*) rather than creation (*ktisis*).[17] Maximus and John of Damascus rely more heavily on

---

13 They do not always do so directly, but often through the commentary tradition or various "digests" of philosophical texts. Philosophical texts continued to be copied and preserved throughout Byzantine history and they were taught as introductions to rigorous thinking and for the formation of rhetorical ability, an immensely important skill for civil servants in the Byzantine politeia. Over a thousand manuscripts of Aristotelian texts alone survive from the hands of Byzantine scribes. The history and legacy of Byzantine philosophy is explored in a number of recent sources (Ierodiakonou and Zografidis 2010; Bydén and Ierodiakonou 2012; Knezević 2015; Ierodiakonou 2002).

14 Aristotle argues this explicitly. Basil challenges the notion that circular motion has no beginning in order to contend that the universe as a whole has a beginning, including the invisible realm, although he does not challenge the broader assumption that visible reality moves in straight and invisible reality in circular ways.

15 There is frequently a problematic slippage between invisible, spiritual, incorruptible, etc. and the divine. While Plato and Aristotle often identify the divine with the invisible and immaterial, which moves in circles and is beyond the lunar sphere, the patristic thinkers increasingly move to speaking of God as beyond even the visible/invisible, sensory/intelligible, corruptible/incorruptible distinction. John of Damascus does this most consistently and most deliberately. Liturgy, however, continually engages in this slippage: sometimes the heavens are merely the invisible realm of the angelic beings, who praise with us (and hence clearly and unambiguously *created*); sometimes it is more closely associated with God. I will have to leave this aside for now, though it is obviously something that would have to be addressed eventually.

16 This includes even such thinkers as the anonymous author of the *Christian Topography* (now called Cosmas Indicopleustes) who argues most strenuously against the spherical nature of the universe and instead favors an image of the cosmos patterned on a tabernacle. He never questions the reality of the four elements, their respective weight and density, or the superiority of cyclical over linear motion, but actually draws on these notions in order to argue for a flat earth.

17 To give just one example: "There are inquirers into nature who with a great display of words give reasons for the immobility of the earth. Placed, they say, in the middle of the universe and not being able to incline more to one side than the other because its centre is everywhere the same distance from the surface, it necessarily rests upon itself; since a weight which is everywhere equal cannot lean to either side. It is not, they go on, without reason or by chance that the earth occupies the

Aristotle's fuller version. To give one concrete example, John of Damascus summarizes the patristic consensus when he says: "The heavens are the outer shell which contains both visible and invisible created things. For, enclosed and contained within them are the spiritual powers, which are the angels, and all sensible things... Furthermore, some have surmised that the heavens surround the universe and have the form of a sphere which is everywhere the highest point; and that the airier and lighter bodies have been assigned by the Creator to the higher positions, while the heavy and unbuoyant have been consigned to the lower, which is the center. Now, the lightest and the most buoyant of the elements is fire, so they say that it comes directly below the heavens. They call it aether. Just below the aether comes the air. Earth and water, since they are heavier and less buoyant, are said to be hung in the midmost position, so that by contrast they are below. The water, however, is lighter than the earth—whence its greater mobility. Everywhere above this, like a blanket, lies the encircling air; everywhere around the air is the ether; and on the outside encircling them all are the heavens. Furthermore, they say that the heavens revolve and that they so bind together the things contained within that they stay firmly together and do not fall apart" (*On the Orthodox Faith* II.6; John of Damascus 1958, pp. 210–11).[18] The patristic vision is insistent that God is the creator and hence the universe (both earth and heaven) must have a beginning (a conviction shared by Plato, though not by Aristotle or later Platonic thinking), is often ambivalent about the existence of aether (as are the ancients), and moves increasingly to "locating" God beyond the division of visible and invisible altogether, but otherwise adopts the ancient worldview.[19] We seriously underestimate today how "real" the "other" (invisible) realm was for the ancients, because the physical and material seems so infinitely more real to us today. For them the intelligible, invisible, incorporeal realm was not only far more real, but also more "extensive" (bigger, albeit it not in spatial terms) and, of course, far more important. And these are precisely the distinctions Maximus refers to when he identifies the nave with the visible, earthly realm and the sanctuary with the invisible, heavenly one. As we will see shortly, these presuppositions about ancient cosmology are operative throughout the Byzantine liturgical texts.

3. Human Soul and Body

The human brings together and participates in both of these two realms: the human is soul and body, "spiritual" and physical, intelligible and material. But the discussion of soul and body has multiple layers. On the most basic level the soul is "most like the divine, immortal, intelligible, uniform, indissoluble, always in the same state as itself," while the body is "most like that which is human, mortal, multiform, unintelligible, soluble, and never consistently the same" (Plato, *Phaedo* 80b). Thus, the soul belongs to the incorporeal, immaterial, invisible, incorruptible, intelligible realm, while

---

centre of the universe. It is its natural and necessary position. As the celestial body occupies the higher extremity of space all heavy bodies, they argue, that we may suppose to have fallen from these high regions, will be carried from all directions to the centre, and the point towards which the parts are tending will evidently be the one to which the whole mass will be thrust together. If stones, wood, all terrestrial bodies, fall from above downwards, this must be the proper and natural place of the whole earth. If, on the contrary, a light body is separated from the centre, it is evident that it will ascend towards the higher regions. Thus heavy bodies move from the top to the bottom, and following this reasoning, the bottom is none other than the centre of the world. Do not then be surprised that the world never falls: it occupies the centre of the universe, its natural place." *Hexaemeron* I.10 (Basil the Great 1995, p. 57). This is a fairly straightforward explication of Aristotle's theory of motion and the arrangement of bodies and elements. Basil does not take over the philosophical tradition uncritically. He (together with pretty much all other Christian thinkers, including the late Platonic philosopher John Philoponus of Alexandria) insists most strongly that the universe has a beginning (and that matter is not eternal, as Aristotle (not, however, Plato) seems to contend (and as the Stoics did, against whom the fathers argue not only in regard to the creation of the world, but also in regard to fate/providence/free will).

18 He goes on to summarize the scientific consensus of his time about the arrangement of the planets and later discusses the four elements in detail, including an outline of ancient meteorology, geography, astronomy, and aspects of the seasons (including exact dates when each season begins). Most of it is a succinct summary of Aristotle, Galen, and Ptolemy, albeit presumably taken from compendia or commentaries and not directly from the primary texts.

19 John of Damascus does this most strongly, often speaking of God as beyond the distinctions between visible/invisible, corporeal/incorporeal, etc. For example, he affirms that "God, then, is substance, and so is every created thing," but immediately qualifies: "God, however, even though He is substance, is super-substantial" (*Fount of Knowledge* I.4; John of Damascus 1958, p. 14). He also makes similar qualifications frequently in *On the Orthodox Faith*.

the body participates in the corporeal, material, visible, corruptible, sensory realm and is made up of the four elements and the four humors.[20] The human is always both, hence already in Plato described as a microcosm, a world in miniature. This is taken up by many of the fathers, such as Maximus: "Hence the Artisan Word, wishing to display this mixture in a single living creature formed from both—I mean from both invisible and visible nature—created man. Fashioning a body from already existing matter and placing within it his own breath, that is, a soul endowed with intellect—the image of God, according to Scripture—he made it a kind of second cosmos, a great creature in a small frame."[21] Or John of Damascus: "Now, a soul is a living substance, simple and incorporeal, of its own nature invisible to bodily eyes, activating an organic body in which it is able to cause life, growth, sensation, and reproduction. It does not have the mind as something distinct from itself, but as its purest part, for, as the eye is to the body, so is the mind to the soul. It is free, endowed with will and the power to act, and subject to change, that is, subject to change of will, because it is also created ... A body is three-dimensional, that is, having height, breadth, and depth or thickness. Every body is composed of the four elements, but the bodies of living things are composed of the four humors."[22] This description of the human soul and body and their interaction is basically indistinguishable from that of Aristotle, especially as appropriated by the late Platonic schools contemporary with early Christian thinkers such as Origen and the Cappadocians. At the same time, it is clear that soul means far more for all of them than it often does today. It is not just some amorphous "spiritual" essence, some possibly dispensable appendix of what we "really" are (bodily); soul is the very identity of the person, the principle of life within the "matter" of the body, moving it and making it into a human being. A soul is what distinguishes a living being from an inanimate corpse, from mere "stuff." Soul for the ancients meant everything irreducible to the purely material (flesh and bones), including emotion, desire, consciousness, rationality, even the capacity to breathe, eat, digest, grow, reproduce, feel, hear, see, taste, and so forth. While we might think of the senses or emotions as primarily associated with the body today, all these were considered functions of "soul."[23]

Already Plato depicts a tripartite version of the soul: mind/reason, spirit/emotion, and appetite/desire. A soul is healthy if it is well ordered and harmonious with all three parts in the right balance (just as a polis is healthy when its guardians, warriors, and laborers are in the right, harmonious balance). In a just soul, a wise reason rules over passions refined by courage and desires tempered by self-control in an overall harmony (*Republic* IV, 433b, 443d–e).[24] Aristotle develops this picture considerably and it is the post-Aristotelian version that is most consistently taken up by the fathers. In Aristotle, the soul is conceived as the "form" or "actuality" of the body (*De Anima* II.1, 412a). It has a rational part (containing both calculative and deliberate functions, i.e., theoretical and practical elements of reason), an appetitive part (containing both spirited/passionate and desirous functions,

---

[20] This final aspect is worked out most fully by the medical thinker Galen. More of his treatises survive than of any other ancient thinker and they were clearly copied extensively. Many patristic thinkers draw on them.

[21] Ambiguum 7 (Ambiguum 7, Maximus the Confessor 2014, vol. I, pp. 125–27). This is precisely the terminology operative also in his *Mystagogy*: "And again using a well-known image he submitted that the whole world, made up of visible and invisible things, is man and conversely that man made up of body and soul is a world. He asserted, indeed, that intelligible things display the meaning of soul as the soul does that of intelligible things, and that sensible things display the place of the body as the body does that of sensible things. And, he continued, intelligible things are the soul of sensible things, and sensible things are the body of intelligible things; that as the soul is in the body so is the intelligible in the world of sense, that the sensible is sustained by the intelligible as the body is sustained by the soul; that both make up one world as body and soul make up one man, neither of these elements joined to the other in unity denies or displaces the other according to the law of the one who has bound them together." (Maximus the Confessor 1985, ch. 7, p. 196)

[22] John of Damascus, *On the Orthodox Faith* II.12 (John of Damascus 1958, p. 236).

[23] This is obviously worked out in the most detail by Aristotle's famous treatise on the soul (*De Anima*), which has detailed discussion on sense perception, emotion, imagination, and so forth.

[24] These four later become the four "cardinal virtues": prudence/practical wisdom, fortitude/courage, temperance/self-control, and justice.

i.e., emotions and desires[25]), and a nutritive part (containing both pulsative and vital functions, i.e., respiratory, reproductive, and nutritive capacities), the rational part distinguishing the human from other living beings (*De Anima* II.2, 413a–b). Nemesius, a late fourth-century bishop of Emesa, summarizes the Platonic and Aristotelian notions of the soul and uses them against various Stoic and other later interpretations to present a refined Christian interpretation of the soul that accords to a large degree with Aristotle's explication, albeit worked out with the use of the commentary tradition that had grown up around Aristotle's texts (Nemesius of Emesa 2008).[26] Nemesius' treatise on human nature was immensely influential for the later patristic tradition and both Maximus the Confessor and John of Damascus draw on it extensively for their own explications, sometimes lifting whole passages literally from Nemesius. For example, the citation from John of Damascus above continues in a straightforward summary of Aristotle on the soul, appropriated from Nemesius: "One should note that man has something in common with inanimate things, that he shares life with the rational living beings, and that he shares understanding with the rational. In common with inanimate things, he has his body and its composition from the four elements. In common with the plants, he has the same things plus the power of assimilating nourishment, of growing and semination of generation. In common with the brute beasts, he has all these plus appetite—that is to say, anger and desire—sensation, and spontaneous movement. Now, the senses are five; namely, sight, hearing, smell, taste, and touch. Belonging to spontaneous movement are the power of moving from place to place, that of moving the entire body, and that of speech and breathing—for in us we have the power either to do these things or not to do them. Through the power of reason man is akin to the incorporeal and intellectual natures, reasoning, thinking, judging each thing, and pursuing the virtues, particularly the acme of the virtues which is piety. For this reason, man is also a microcosm."[27] Here the subsequent patristic literature is completely in accord with Nemesius' summary of Plato and Aristotle on human nature.

Both Plato and Aristotle (and of course the later Platonic tradition in such thinkers as Plotinus, Iamblichus, and Proclus[28]) claim that it is possible for humans to participate in the divine. In Plato this is the very presupposition of the entire theory of forms: the one who loves wisdom is able to ascend from purely corporeal, material, visible, changeable reality to seeing incorporeal, immaterial, invisible, immutable reality, i.e., ultimately joining with the eternal divine: "Therefore we ought to try to escape from earth to the dwelling of the gods as quickly as we can; and to escape is to become like God, so far as this is possible; and to become like God is to become righteous and holy and wise ... God is in no wise and in no manner unrighteous, but utterly and perfectly righteous, and there is nothing so like him as that one of us who in turn becomes most nearly perfect in righteousness" (*Theatetus* 176b). In Aristotle, the activity of *theoria* is the highest kind of activity, the one that provides the best shot at *eudaimonia* (happiness in the sense of a full and flourishing life), and the one that brings us closest to the gods, rendering us divine: "we should try to become immortal as far as that is possible and do our utmost to live in accordance with what is highest in us," namely "the divine element within" us (*Nicomachean Ethics* X.7, 1177b). For Aristotle this is achieved through the intensive practice of habits of excellence (*arete*), i.e., the virtues. For Plato, as we have seen, it is developing a rightly ordered or supremely healthy (hence virtuous) soul achieved through rigorous discipline over passions and desires. The patristic thinkers not only make heavy use of the notion of *theoria* (usually translated as

---

[25] In the Western tradition, relying on the Latin translations, these are often referred to as "concupiscible" and "irascible" elements. These do not, however, seem like optimal translations for the Greek patristic appropriation of the terms, although the "Fathers of the Church" (somewhat problematic) translation of John's *Fount of Knowledge* employs them.
[26] Nemesius' use of various texts is traced carefully by the extensive footnotes of the editors.
[27] John of Damascus, *On the Orthodox Faith* II.12 (John of Damascus 1958, p. 237).
[28] For the sake of brevity, I have focused here on Plato and Aristotle—and even that summary is far too sweeping and superficial—but many middle and late Platonists work aspects of this worldview out more fully or bring Plato and Aristotle together more explicitly. Often the fathers draw on them rather than directly on Plato. The parallel between Christian and late Platonic interpretations and practices is explored far more fully in (Digeser 2012) and specifically for Iamblichus (Shaw 1995).

"contemplation" and seen as one of the major stages of the spiritual life), but often appeal explicitly to Plato's claim from the *Theatetus* that humans can participate in the divine and become like God.[29]

4. Connecting the Dimensions

The crucial question for the ancients (both philosophical and patristic) is this question of participation, not only of the human in the divine, but more broadly of the relationship between the two realms (invisible and visible, heavenly and earthly) and correspondingly the two parts of the human (soul and body). Although contemporary commentary often dismisses this worldview as simplistically dualistic, things are much more complicated.[30] Philosophical and patristic thinkers alike are confident that the two realms relate to each other, participate in each other, and depend on each other. Plato continually tries to work this out in his texts in various forms. Although there are certainly instances when he seems to speak of the two realms (and of soul and body) as utterly separate and even antithetical to each other, at the same time he always affirms that one images and possibly even participates in the other.[31] The famous "allegory of the cave" and its corresponding "divided line" assume that there is a connection between inside and outside the cave and the lower and higher parts of the line (*Republic* VI, 509e–11e; *Republic* VII, 514a–518d). The images in the cave are shadows of the external realities (one cannot have shadows without the realities that cause them); the lesser lights of the cave participate in some way in the abundant and stronger light of the outside world. The visible realities below the line image or represent the ontologically superior invisible realities above the line. The knowledge needed to investigate them is a weaker and less stable form of the knowledge and wisdom needed to apprehend the fuller realities they image.

Indeed, imaging or mimesis itself has an ambivalent status in Plato: it can function both as a positive, good, and beautiful reflection of the divine realities (as in the *Timaeus*) or as an inferior, weak, pale imitation of the real that may distract us away from it (as in *Republic* X, 595b–607c, where poets are banned from the ideal polis precisely for trafficking in such pale imitations and arousing our bad desires and emotions to focus on them).[32] The universe is "a piece of work that would be as excellent and supreme as its nature would allow" (*Timaeus* 30b), imaging the divine as much as possible, because its creator "believed that likeness is incalculable more excellent than unlikeness" (*Timaeus* 33b). There has to be a bond enabling such relationship, "making it a symphony of proportion"

---

[29] Obviously, they also appeal to biblical texts, often far more explicitly than to philosophical ones. To highlight the continuity in worldview is not to imply that this somehow constitutes a denial or betrayal of the biblical heritage. The two are often read in harmony with each other or biblical passages are interpreted through a philosophical lens, i.e. with these presuppositions about cosmology and anthropology. (This latter tendency is particularly strong in Origen, the Cappadocians, and Maximus.)

[30] Often the accusation of dualism itself seems sufficient to reject a particular view. But not all dualisms are of necessity pernicious. Far more nuance is required in this discussion; one must examine how the two spheres interact with or relate to each other, how the supposed dualism functions and what effects it has, etc.

[31] Gregory Nazianzen often expresses a similar ambivalence: "How I am connected to this body, I do not know, nor do I understand how I can be an image of God, and still be mingled with this filthy clay; when it is in good condition, it wars against me, and when it is itself under attack, it causes me grief! I love it as my fellow servant, but struggle against it as an enemy; I flee it as something enslaved, just as I am, but I show it reverence as called, with me, to the same inheritance. I long that it be dissolved, and yet I have no other helper to use in striving for what is best, since I know what I was made for, and know that I must ascend towards God through my actions...So I treat it gently, as my fellow worker; and then I have no way of escaping its rebellion, no way to avoid falling, weighed down by those fetters that drag me or keep me held down to the earth. It is a cordial enemy, and a treacherous friend. What an alliance and what an alienation! What I fear, I treat with honor; what I love, I fear. Before we come to war, I am reconciled to it, and before we have made peace, I am at odds with it again. What wisdom lies behind my constitution? What is this great mystery?" Gregory Nazianzen, Oration 14.6–7 (Daley 2006, p. 79).

[32] Plato uses strong language: "So, imitation [*mimesis*] is an inferior thing that consorts with another inferior thing to produce inferior offspring" (603b); "But we haven't yet brought our chief charge against imitation. For its power to corrupt all but a very few *good* people is surely an altogether terrible one" (605c). The language in the *Timaeus* is equally strong in the other direction. The "maker and father of this universe" is described as "most excellent," making our universe "most beautiful" by using an "image" or "eternal model" for its construction (29a–b). As reason for the likeness of the universe to the divine, Timaeus says: "Now why did he who framed this whole universe of becoming frame it? Let us state the reason why: he was good, and one who is good can never become jealous of anything. And so, being free of jealousy, he wanted everything to become as much like himself as was possible" (30a). Therefore, "divine providence brought our world into being as a truly living thing, endowed with soul and intelligence" (30c).

(*Timaeus* 32c).[33] Well satisfied with the beauty of creation, its "Father" "in his delight thought of making it more like its model still" and created time as "a moving image of eternity," "an eternal image, moving according to number, of eternity remaining in unity" (*Timaeus* 37d). To fall away from this unity and likeness or to imitate it in deceptive and ignorant fashion, as the artist is taken to do, is the most horrible kind of evil and misfortune.[34] There are hence two forms of mimesis: "bad" imitation that distracts from the reality by focusing attention on mere appearance and "good" imitation, which represents the eternal model well and participates in it in some form. Aristotle will wed these two possibilities of mimesis to some extent by arguing that appropriate presentation of emotion on stage can lead to cathartic release of difficult or even destructive emotions (such as fear and pity) in such a way as to lead to moral formation through imitation of the heroic actions of superior ethical characters (*Poetics* 6, 1449b, 13–15, 1452b–54b).[35]

The same ambivalence characterizes the relation of soul and body. While the *Phaedo* (maybe the most "Platonic" of all the dialogues) presents philosophy as a "practice of dying," namely the effort to free "the soul from association with the body as much as possible" to the point where "it takes leave of the body and as far as possible has no contact or association with it in its search for reality" (64a, 65a, 65c), other dialogues instead advocate a rule of the soul over the body and the soul's rational element over its spirited and desirous parts, rather than a total separation. Such rule can be depicted quite violently: in the *Phaedrus* the mind is pictured as a charioteer who guides two horses and has to assert control over them by pulling back on the reins so sharply that the horses are covered with foam and the unruly horse of desire finally gives up in exhaustion (245c–256d).[36] Only such a well-ordered soul has access to the intelligible realm. This pursuit and self-discipline is not only beneficial inasmuch as it gains true wisdom through access to eternal realities, but it is also supremely valuable in itself, as Plato argues through Socrates in several crucial texts. This claim is worked out the most fully in the *Republic* (e.g., 433a–445e), but also returns in several other dialogues. For example, in the *Gorgias* Socrates seeks to convince his interlocutor of the value of philosophy over rhetoric or sophistry by showing that Gorgias' version of rhetoric would ultimately endorse an unjust life and is useful only for escaping punishment, while Socratic questioning helps us realize that such an unjust soul would be supremely unhappy, because it is an eminently unhealthy soul, a "soul that is rotten with injustice and impiety," which is a "most serious kind of badness" surpassing "others by some monstrously great harm and astounding badness" (479c, 478d, 477e). It is much better to undergo punishment for injustices than to get away with them, because at least these measures will begin

---

[33] Plato stresses that "the best bond is one that really and truly makes a unity of itself together with the things bonded by it" (31c). He describes the right proportion as a kind of permanent friendship: "They bestowed friendship upon it, so that, having come together into a unity with itself, it could not be undone by anyone but the one who had bound it together" (32c). The immediate context here is the connection between the four elements, but also the larger bonding of the entire cosmos.

[34] It is fairly clear in the argument about banning the poets from the ideal republic that they are condemned not for imitation *as such*, but for lacking knowledge about the reality they are trying to imitate and therefore creating a false beauty that is deceptive and leads people *away* from the true reality they ought to know (e.g., *Republic* X, 599b).

[35] Indeed, Aristotle argues explicitly that imitation is natural to human beings and that it is conducive to learning (*Poetics* 4, 1448b). He also stresses that tragedy is not about imitation of persons, but a representation of "actions and life" (*Poetics* 6, 1450a16, 1450b3–5). Ricoeur has worked this into a far fuller analysis of narrative identity and plot, including the ways in which texts open a world for us in which we are challenged to envision ourselves differently. I have tried to show the relevance of this for analyzing liturgy in my "Toward a Ricoeurian Hermeneutics of Liturgy" (Gschwandtner 2012).

[36] This is also taken up by some of the fathers. Basil argues, for example, that "the body in every part should be despised by everyone who does not care to be buried in its pleasures, as it were in slime; or we ought to cleave to it only in so far as we obtain from it service for the pursuit of wisdom, as Plato advises, speaking in a manner somewhat similar to Paul's when he admonishes us to make no provision for the body unto the arousing of concupiscences. Or in what way do those differ, who are solicitous how the body may be as well off as possible, but overlook the soul, which is to make use of it, as utterly worthless, from those who are much concerned about their implements but neglect the art which uses them for its work? Hence we must do quite the opposite—chastise the body and hold it in check, as we do the violent chargings of a wild beast, and by smiting with reason, as with a whip, the disturbances engendered by it in the soul, calm them to sleep; instead of relaxing every curb upon pleasure and suffering the mind to be swept headlong, like a charioteer by unmanageable horses riotously running at large." Basil of Caesarea, "On Greek Literature" IX (Basil of Caesarea 1934, pp. 420–23).

to work a cure in the soul. Thus, such a person should be courageous, "grit his teeth and present himself with grace and courage as to a doctor for cauterization and surgery, pursuing what is good and admirable without taking any account of the pain," even if this involves flogging, imprisonment, fines, exile, or even execution (*Gorgias* 480d). While Socrates' audience reacts with revulsion at this counsel to voluntary punishment, this is precisely the pedagogical and therapeutic language much of the patristic literature will use to speak of the battle against sin and injustice in both soul and body.[37]

What is evident here is that soul and body cannot be separated in the simplistic fashion we often read Plato. Clearly punishment of the body results in improvement of the soul. Disciplining one's body enables disciplining one's soul. And there are also less violent measures in Plato's dialogues. The attraction of beauty, for example, is consistently taken to help us remember the realm from which we came and to draw us back toward it. In the *Symposium*, the lover with the help of beauty's attraction learns to move from a love of concrete, particular, physical, and transitory beautiful things to a love of the universal, immaterial, incorporeal, immortal reality of beauty as such (206c–208b).[38] The true lover generates such beauty in another (*Symposium* 209b–c). In the *Republic*'s allegory of the cave and divided line, knowing the "reality" helps in negotiating the appearances. A process of education leads us from darkness to light, from the shadows of the cave to the brilliant reality of the good (*Republic* VII, 518a–d). Plato consistently assumes that what we do in this corporeal, transitory life matters to what happens to our soul after death. The *Republic* culminates in the powerful "Myth of Er" in which souls pick their next life based on how they have behaved in the previous one (Book X, 614b–621c). Indeed, "it was a sight worth seeing how the various souls chose their lives" because "their choice reflected the character of their former life" (620a). Although they must drink from the river of forgetting before being reborn, their new bodies match their souls better and this ought to be

---

[37] For example, Basil says: "As, therefore, the physician is a benefactor even if he produces distress or pain in the body (for he fights the illness, not the sick person), so also God is good, who provides salvation to all, through particular punishments. And you do not accuse the physicians of any wrong in his cuttings and burnings and complete mutilations of the body; but rather you probably pay him money and you call him a savior, since he has produced illness in a small part of the body to prevent the suffering from spreading throughout the whole of it." "Homily Explaining that God is Not the Cause of Evil" 3 (Basil the Great 2005, p. 68). Or John Chrysostom: "In the case of diseases and injuries we do not grieve for those who are being cured, but for those who have incurable diseases. Sin is the same as disease or injury; retribution is the same as surgery or medicine. Do you understand what I am saying? Pay attention: I want to teach you a word of wisdom. Why do we grieve for those who are being punished, but not for those who are sinning? Punishment is not as grievous as sin, for sin is the reason for the punishment. If you see someone with a putrifying sore, and worms and discharges coming from his body, and you see him neglecting his infection, but you see another person with the same affliction benefiting from the hands of physicians, from cautery and surgery and bitter-tasting medicines, for whom will you grieve? Tell me, for the one who is ill and is not being treated, or for the one who is ill and is being treated? In the same way imagine two sinners, one being punished, the other not being punished. Do not say, this one is lucky because he is rich, he strips orphans of their property, and he oppresses widows. Apparently he is not ill, he has a good reputation in spite of his thefts, he enjoys honor and authority, he does not endure any of the troubles which afflict mankind—no fever, no paralysis, nor any other disease—a chorus of children surrounds him, his old age is comfortable; but you should grieve most for him, because he is indeed ill and receives no treatment. I shall tell you how. If you see someone afflicted with dropsy, his body swollen with a painful spleen, and not hurrying to the doctor, but drinking cold water, keeping a Sybaritic table, getting drunk every day, surrounded with body-guards, and aggravating his disease, tell me, do you call him lucky or unlucky? If you see another person afflicted with dropsy, benefiting from the care of doctors, purging himself with hunger, with great difficulty braving his bitter medicines which are painful but bring forth health through pain, do you not call this person more fortunate than the other? It is agreed: for one is ill and is not treated, but the other is ill and benefits from treatment. But, you may say, the treatment is painful. But its purpose is beneficial. Our present life is like this also, but you must change the words from bodies to souls, from diseases to sins, from the bitter taste of medicines to the retribution and judgment from God. What the medicines, surgery, and cautery are for the physician, chastisement is from God. Just as fire is often used to cauterize, to prevent the spread of infection, and as the steel removes decayed flesh, bringing pain but providing benefit, so hunger and disease, and other apparent evils, are used on the soul instead of steel and fire to prevent the spread of disease, by analogy with the body, and to make it better...When you see a bad person faring well, then weep: for there are two evils, the disease and its incurability." "Sixth Sermon on the Rich Man and Lazarus" (John Chrysostom 1984, pp.101–3).

[38] At the same time, there is a similar ambivalence as that noted above in regard to imitation: beautiful bodies can lead us to beautiful souls, but they can also distract and deceive. And not all beautiful souls necessarily inhabit beautiful bodies: Socrates is consistently pictured as snub-nosed and generally ugly despite his eminently beautiful soul. The tradition of "match" between soul and body, including the conviction that moral and immoral behaviors are somehow visibly expressed in one's countenance, has a long and rich tradition. One particularly striking more recent example is Oscar Wilde's novel *The Picture of Dorian Gray*.

borne out by the subsequent life lived, which can work at better match and thus be reborn at a higher level in the next life. At other points, too, Plato suggests that present behavior is both an indicator of the state of one's soul and a predictor of one's future body (*Phaedrus* 248d, *Laws* 944e, *Timaeus* 42b–c). This implies that somehow soul and body must match each other, that there must be a "fit" between the two.[39] And the goal obviously is not just any kind of "fit": a "bad" soul also suits a "bad" body. But such a bad soul is supremely unhealthy and disordered, at variance with itself and the universe. A healthy soul, in contrast, "becomes entirely one, temperate and harmonious," acting externally in order to "preserve this inner harmony" (*Republic* IV, 443e).[40] Hence, soul and body only truly match each other if their harmonious and well-ordered unity also matches the larger cosmic order. For Plato, such fit is assured through the practice of philosophy and the succession of reincarnations, where each life provides the chance to achieve a better match between soul and body and to exercise the soul to greater purity and justice.[41]

This notion of the transmigration of souls was obviously rejected by the patristic tradition. While some of the earlier fathers still allow that the soul might in some form preexist its body (dwelling in some heavenly realm before it is sent into the one body in which it lives out its one mortal life), most insist that soul and body are created together.[42] Just as the cosmos has a beginning and is created by God together with space and time, so souls have a beginning created by God together with their material bodies. And they certainly do assume that soul and body are closely connected. Nemesius consistently argues that various aspects of the soul are concretely expressed in parts of the body and visible in their functioning.[43] Maximus is quite emphatic that soul and body always go together: "Moreover, if the body is the instrument of a soul endowed with intellect (since it is the soul of a human being), and if the whole soul permeates the whole body, giving it life and motion (since the soul by nature is simple and incorporeal), without however being divided or enclosed by the body, then the soul is present to the whole body and to each of its members (for each member by nature is able to receive it, consistent with its innate potential to receive the soul's energy). Being present to the body in this way, the soul binds together the members that variously receive it, in proportion to each member's way of maintaining the unity of the body" (Ambiguum 7, Maximus the Confessor 2014, vol. I, p. 135).

---

[39] Plato's assumptions about the need for a "fit" between soul and body or even a possible "mismatch" between the two is particularly evident in his comments about gender: although women can be trained and even govern in the ideal republic, Plato is fairly clear that they have "male souls" in "female bodies" and that somehow the two do not match. Cowardly men really have female souls in their male bodies and will be reborn in female bodies. Comments of this sort are quite frequent throughout the dialogues.

[40] In Aristotle also, an excellent person is one whose soul is supremely in harmony with itself, all its parts well-ordered and honed to greatest excellence of character. In both Plato and Aristotle, the same applies to the larger *polis* or *koinonia*. For Plato, a disordered and unjust state is one in which someone self-indulgent or "puffed up by wealth" governs. Such bad ruling and disorder among classes will "destroy the city" and "is the greatest harm that can happen to the city and would rightly be called the worst evil one could do to it" (*Republic* IV, 434b). For Aristotle, excellent friendship creates the same kind of harmony and balance as rules in an excellent individual soul and the relation evil people have with each other similarly reflects the disordered soul of the unjust person who is at variance with himself (*Nicomachean Ethics* IX.4, 1166a–1166b).

[41] In the interest of space, I'm leaving Aristotle aside here, who obviously holds soul and body far more closely together than Plato in the first place. The patristic thinkers consistently treat the Platonic–Aristotelian heritage as a whole and read them as corroborating each other. Aristotle is interpreted as the logical and introductory basis for Plato's more elevated and more difficult theories. In either case, the Aristotelian pursuit of excellence supports a similar philosophical "program" for improvement of the soul within its body (and larger social and political context) and its "imaging" of the divine as much as humanly possible.

[42] "And as for anyone who idly asserts this nonexisting 'preexistence' of souls, let him confine himself to rational arguments. For if the body and soul are parts of man, as has already been explained, then as parts they necessarily admit of reciprocal relation…Therefore, insofar as soul and body are parts of man, it is not possible for either the soul or the body to exist before the other, or indeed to exist after the other in time, otherwise what is known as the principal of reciprocal relation would be destroyed." Ambiguum 7 (Ambiguum 7, Maximus the Confessor 2014, vol. I, p. 137). John of Damascus asserts the same: "The body and the soul were formed at the same time—not one before and the other afterwards" *On the Orthodox Faith* II.12 (John of Damascus 1958, p. 235).

[43] He is extremely detailed in his account of how various powers of the soul are located in and expressed in concrete parts of the body, even adducing particular illnesses or malfunction of the body that have an impact on emotional and intellectual functioning (presumably relying on Galen for much of this information). See especially *On the Nature of Man*, sct. 6–15 (Nemesius of Emesa 2008, pp. 100–27).

John of Damascus also insists: "The soul is united with the body, the entire soul with the entire body and not part for part. And it is not contained by the body, but rather contains it, just as heat does iron, and, although it is in the body, carries on its own proper activities."[44] The soul moves and permeates the body, is present to all of it, and the body is nothing without this animating principle within it. Yet, the two are not just naturally united, but we must work at bonding them together in order for a good and healthy soul to dwell in a well-functioning body. Health of soul and proper functioning of soul and body together are efforts to pursue and result in a larger harmony, not only between these two parts, but also with the order of all things.[45]

Even in the ascetic tradition, where the Platonic injunction to focus on the soul and separate it as far as possible from the passions and the body is maybe taken up most fully, a fit between soul and body is often implied. In Athanasius' famous depiction of Saint Antony's emergence from the cave, the holiness of his "soul" is visible in the vigor and youthfulness of his body (Athanasius of Alexandria 2003). And ascetic practice itself assumes that a rigorous disciplining of our body and the soul's corporeal desires (e.g., for food and sleep) are conducive toward the more difficult task of disciplining the higher elements of the soul (ruling over anger, pride, sloth, etc.).[46] In Evagrius and Maximus, various vices can be attributed to various elements of the soul and they are correspondingly healed by virtues corresponding to similar parts of the soul.

This desire for a "match" between the mortal and the immortal or corporeal and incorporeal reality is perhaps adopted most expressly in the distinction between image and likeness. While the human is created in the image of God, likeness to the divine has to be achieved through virtuous and holy living.[47] While not all the fathers make the distinction between image and likeness, the ones who do consistently speak of achieving likeness through the transformative effort of combatting vices and cultivating virtues. At the same time, as in Aristotle, cultivation of virtues and especially the practice of *theoria*, bring us closest to the divine and allows us to imitate the divine, to become like God as closely as possible. This may be precisely what the idea of the microcosm exemplifies: the two realms come together in the human in some way; they begin to match and achieve a "fit," a fit not only between an individual soul and its body, but also between the human (on personal and communal levels) and the larger cosmos.[48]

5. "Fit" in Liturgy

This finally gets us back to our original question of how these presuppositions operate within liturgy. The "fit" between body and soul, that is to say, the unification of the realms and their full participation in each other, is achieved most fully within and through liturgy. What Plato works out with a theory of the transmigration of souls, the patristic tradition tries to work out in liturgy: liturgy is the space where we strive for a greater "match" or "fit" between body and soul, between heavenly and earthly, between visible and invisible—and of all of them together via a match between anthropological and cosmological dimensions. In liturgy bodies come to match their "souls," "spirits," or "minds" and to cultivate the health of both through their harmony with the cosmos. The beauty of invisible

---

44 *On the Orthodox Faith* I.13 (John of Damascus 1958, p. 198).

45 As has often been pointed out, the Byzantines were obsessed with order, proper position, and harmony. Maybe this was not just a peculiar obsession, but a reflection of a deeper belief in the harmony of the universe that was part of a larger worldview.

46 This is constantly assumed and even explicitly argued in the ascetic literature. To give just one example from Evagrius' *Eulogios*: "Do not delay in paying the debt of prayer when you hear a thought by reason of the approach of work and do not make loud noises, troubling your body, during manual labour, lest you trouble as well the eye of the soul... When you do not give your heart to considerations of material things, at that moment you may drive away captive the crowd of thoughts." (Evagrius of Pontus 2003, pp. 36, 38).

47 "Since this was the case with his own hands he created man after his own image and likeness from the visible and invisible natures. From the earth he created his body and by his own inbreathing gave him a rational and understanding soul, which last we say is the divine image—for the 'according to his image' means the intellect and free will, while the 'according to his likeness' means such likeness in virtue as is possible." *On the Orthodox Faith*, II.12 (John of Damascus 1958, pp. 234–35).

48 The fullest and most explicit expression of this is probably found in Maximus' Ambiguum 41, where he outlines Christ's and the human unification of all levels of reality (Ambiguum 7, Maximus the Confessor 2014, vol. II, pp. 102–21).

reality becomes continually expressed in the visible, but the visible cannot "replace" it, just as liturgy constantly exhorts us to "see" the invisible in the visible, but we can only see it there if they truly match and are not in discordance or disharmony. Real transformation would mean total mimesis—every moment of time would be imbued with the eternal, every physical reality would bear at the same time the invisible, each body would perfectly match its soul, everything human would become suffused with the divine, everything earthly would somehow bear the heavenly. This cannot be fully achieved in personal ascetic labor, because it is not merely about the match between one individual soul and its particular body. Only in liturgy can the larger "fit" between heaven and earth, invisible and visible realms be accomplished. Yet, what exactly does that mean? How do invisible and visible, incorporeal and corporeal, heavenly and earthly realms come together in liturgical practice?

First of all, patristic and contemporary Orthodox liturgy is suffused with language referring to both realms, including the frequent claims that heaven and earth celebrate together. Some feasts accomplish the fit particularly well. The liturgical texts for the feast of the Annunciation announce such unification on several levels: "Lo, our restoration is now made manifest to us: God is ineffably united to men. At the words of the Archangel error is laid low; for the Virgin receives joy, and the things of the earth have become heaven. The world is loosened from the ancient curse. Let the creation rejoice exceedingly."[49] The divine is united to the human, the heavenly to the earthly, the invisible to the visible. These are "glad tidings of joy" because "things below are joined to things above" (Mother Mary and Ware 1998, *Festal Menaion*: 445). Christ is taken to gather "together all the creation" (Mother Mary and Ware 1998, *Festal Menaion*: 455). Similarly, Christ's birth by the virgin is (in every liturgy) affirmed to be without "corruption" or "defilement," i.e., literally without disintegration, decay, or perishing (*phthora*). Unifying the invisible, imperishable, incorruptible with the visible and mortal, as occurs in the nativity, renders such birth incorruptible and without decay.[50] The feast of Christ's Nativity creates harmony, both in the larger creation and, more narrowly, in human social and political arrangements.[51] "Heaven and earth are united today," a unification that concerns both heaven and earth and divine with human; it also always goes in both directions: descending (of Christ into the virgin, "bowing down" the heavens) and ascending (of the human via Christ into heaven, taking up the earth into it).[52] The constant affirmation that heaven and earth celebrate together (reiterated in all of the feasts) is surely also significant. The texts for Ascension speak repeatedly of Christ's body ascending from "earth" to "heaven" and therefore bringing together earthly and heavenly, corporeal and incorporeal realms, simultaneously "renewing" the world. Therefore, "the earth celebrates and dances for joy, and heaven rejoices today on the Ascension of the Maker of creation, who by his volition clearly united that which was separated."[53] The kontakion also explicitly affirms that Christ's ascension "unites things on earth with the heavens."[54] Hence the transformation worked by the feasts is that of the kind of unification in which earth images the heavens, where they come together and penetrate each other, yet without confusion or total assimilation.

---

[49] Lity at Compline, Feast of the Annunciation of the Most Holy Theotokos (Mother Mary and Ware 1998, *Festal Menaion*: 445).

[50] This affirmation ("without corruption you gave birth to God the Word") hence does not mean—as it is often interpreted—that sexual activity involves some sort of sinful defilement or is morally objectionable. *Phthora* is a basic characteristic of the material as undergoing change and decay, coming into being and going out of being; it is not a moral judgment and has nothing to do with sexual activity (or its lack) in the divine conception.

[51] Vespers for the Nativity According to the Flesh of our Lord and God and Savior Jesus Christ (Mother Mary and Ware 1998, *Festal Menaion*: 254). It is maybe also not coincidental that Christ is called the "sun" (and not just the "son") throughout many liturgies, festal and otherwise.

[52] Lity for Nativity (Mother Mary and Ware 1998, *Festal Menaion*: 263).

[53] Ode 3 at Matins for the feast of the Ascension.

[54] Proclus of Constantinople also claims this in a homily on Ascension: "The nature of creation is distributed in heaven and on earth,/but the grace of today, having bridged the division of these things,/does not permit me to see the division./For who would in future say that heaven is separated from things on earth..." Homily 21.1 (Proclus of Constantinople 2001, p. 193).

Similar assertions are made about the dormition of the theotokos. Her entry into paradise is not just on her own behalf, but in some way reunifies earth and heaven.[55] Indeed, "by thy deathless Dormition thou hast sanctified the whole world."[56] In some patristic homilies, she is explicitly said to bless all of the four elements as she is borne to paradise: "The air was blessed by your passing through it, the aether of the upper regions was sanctified"; "I imagine that the elements of nature were stirred up and altered... the air, the fiery aether, the sky would have been made holy by the ascent of her spirit, as earth was sanctified by the deposition of her body. Even water had its share in the blessing; for she was washed in pure water, which did not so much cleanse her as it was itself consecrated."[57] Mary's body perfectly matches her spirit or soul and hence enables a transformation of the elements in a manner that achieves a better mimetic fit with their heavenly reality.[58] Mary "blesses" the elements, transforms them mimetically so they are imbued with the holiness of the divine. (Maybe that is precisely what blessing ceremonies do: they try to effect the "match" of earthly and heavenly.) And the bodily matters here. John of Damascus assures his audience of this in vivid imagery: "And this holy temple—truly holy, truly worthy of God—I seemed for a moment to embrace with my own arms! I pressed my eyes, my lips, my forehead, my neck, my cheeks to her limbs, rejoicing in these sensations as if her body were present and I could touch it."[59] Such vivid attention to the physical and corporeal reality maybe finds its apex in the cult of relics, where the bodily and material is taken to be a bearer of the divine, but precisely in and through its very physicality.[60]

The continual insistence—especially in the festal services but also more broadly—that all this takes place "today" similarly assumes that the eternal "reality" of the feast becomes present in the particular moment of the celebration. The events of annunciation, nativity, theophany, and so forth, really occur "today" because in them the eternal is manifested in time. The liturgical "today" is always simultaneously the concrete "today" of physical reality and the eternal "today" without temporality. They meet and come to merge in the celebration of the feast. At the same time it is continually recognized that the "fit" is not perfect, that the match is not yet achieved. We have to work at "fit," it does not happen magically by itself. As we have seen, in Plato the path to it is dual: via beauty and via gnosis or ascesis—one is intrinsically attractive, the other more difficult, but there is always the danger that we will stop too early, remaining only with beautiful bodies and not going on to the contemplation of immortal, immaterial beauty (or that we might be distracted by mere appearances rather than proceeding to the reality). Similarly, liturgy is constantly torn between the attempt to match (in the feasts) and the recognition that the "fit" isn't quite there (or maybe far from there), resulting in an attempt to work at better fit via repentance. Maybe we need to repeat all this continually precisely in order to achieve a better match; we try again at each liturgy, each Eucharist, during each Lent, at each Pascha.

Constant exhortations to repentance and especially the penitential time of Great Lent—and to a lesser degree the other fasting periods, including the kneeling prayers at the end of the Pentecost season—are hence also characterized by such a desire to achieve a match, but here the disconnect

55 Paradise itself is often portrayed as a more beautiful version of the *oikoumene*. This can take quaintly amusing forms as when heaven is pictured by various medieval Byzantine sources as an enlarged, more beautiful and more harmonious Constantinople (e.g., Baun 2007).
56 Sticheron at Vespers for the Dormition of Our Most-Holy Lady the Theotokos and Ever-Virgin Mary (Mother Mary and Ware 1998, *Festal Menaion*: 504).
57 See especially John of Damascus' cycle of three homilies on the feast of the Dormition (Daley 1998, *Dormition of Mary*: 183–239). The quotes above are from Homily I.11: 196 and Homily II.11: 214–15. Germanos speaks of her as a "bridge" that will enable others to "bear the weight of all of humanity" (Daley 1998, *Dormition of Mary*: 171). This is a common theme; John also mentions it several times (Daley 1998, *Dormition of Mary*: 193). It is surely also significant that Christ's and Mary's *bodies* are said to ascend or be carried up into the heavens, in the feasts of Ascension and Dormition, respectively. It is the touch of Mary's body (obviously united with its soul) that effects the sanctification of the elements.
58 John affirms this also about her preparation for the conception: "she preserved the virginity of her soul no less than that of her body, and thus her bodily virginity was also preserved." Homily I.7: 190. (Daley 1998)
59 Homily II.5: 209. (Daley 1998)
60 This is at least what Patricia Cox Miller argues (Miller 2009), especially ch. 1.

and lack are stressed rather than the accomplishment (maybe paralleling the tension in Plato's dual proposal of attraction through beauty and stern pedagogy). The liturgical texts for the Lenten periods consistently counsel a greater match to the divine through a unification of soul and body. This is particularly obvious in the Great Canon of St. Andrew of Crete: "I have defiled my body, I have stained my spirit, and I am all covered with wounds: but as physician, O Christ, heal both body and spirit for me through repentance."[61] Many liturgical prayers (whether in preparation for communion or in various litanies and not just during Lent) pray for the sanctification of *both* soul and body. This is evident not only in texts, but maybe even more strikingly in actions: fasting, abstaining from various activities and foods, and the bodily exercises of bowing and prostrations are all training the body to greater concordance with the soul as it should become.[62] Our bodily postures should reflect and match the dispositions of our minds and hearts. Repentance is always an effort of both body and soul, together. Many homilists upbraid their listeners precisely for lack of "match": Chrysostom chides his congregation for running to the games and races: "On a Friday, when your Master was being crucified on behalf of the world and such a sacrifice was being offered, and paradise was being opened, and the robber was being led back to his old native land, the curse was being undone, and sin was disappearing, and temporal war was being destroyed, and God was being reconciled to human beings, and everything was being changed—on that day, you should have been fasting and giving praise and sending up prayers of thanksgiving for all the blessings in the world to the one who made them. Then why did you leave the church and the spiritual sacrifice, and the gathering of brothers and sisters and the sobriety of fasting? Were you carried off to that spectacle as the devil's captive?"[63] Clearly Chrysostom thinks something is actually presently occurring within the liturgy and participating in it requires one's behavior to match the content of the celebration and the events that are taking place within it.

In a different vein, John of Damascus argues that celebrating Mary's dormition should result in concrete acts of mercy: "Let us delight in her holiness of soul and body; after all, she is truly, after God, the holiest of all beings, for like always delights in like! Let us do her homage by our mercy and our compassion for the poor. For if God is honored by nothing so much as by mercy, who can deny that his mother is glorified, too, by the same thing?"[64] Near the end of the homily he asks how we can celebrate a proper remembrance of her and suggests that this should involve avoiding impurity, "frivolous talk," self-indulgence, "seductive perfumes," "puffed-up arrogance," "an unforgiving mind," and "all vice," instead pursuing their opposites "in fasting, in self-control, in singing of psalms...the peaceful and gentle heart," "love and mercy and humility."[65] Here, celebrating the feast requires a lifestyle that matches its content. Basil similarly exhorts his congregation to put what they are doing within liturgy into practice (Basil the Great 2009). He also bemoans the lack of match in their actions: "I

---

[61] *The Lenten Triodion*: 392 (Mother Mary and Ware 2002). Such examples could be endlessly multiplied, not only from the canon but from the Lenten liturgical texts more generally.

[62] Indeed, many homilies stress this need for repentance to be the united effort of body and soul. E.g., John Chrysostom: "Do you see, dearly beloved, what true fasting really is? Let us perform this kind, and not entertain the facile notion held by many that the essence of fasting lies in going without food till evening. This is not the end in view, but that we should demonstrate, along with abstinence from food, abstinence also from whatever is harmful, and should give close attention to spiritual duties. The person fasting ought to be reserved, peaceful, meek, humble, indifferent to the esteem of this world." Homily on Genesis 8.15 (John Chrysostom 1986, vol. 82, p. 114). In a later homily he says: "I am not making this point [that fasting is not worthwhile if one skips church] to undermine the importance of fasting—God forbid: on the contrary, I'm all in favor of it. Instead, my intention is to teach you to take an active part in spiritual matters with an alert mind, not just follow along out of habit. The shameful thing, you see, is not attendance at this spiritual teaching after partaking of food, but attendance with an attitude of sloth, addiction to passion, and failure to control the movements of the flesh. There is nothing wrong with eating—God forbid; the harmful thing is gluttony, stuffing yourself with food in excess of need, and ruining your stomach—something, after all, that destroys even the pleasure that comes from food. So, too, in like manner, there is nothing wrong with drinking in moderation, but rather surrendering to drunkenness and losing control of your reasoning through excess." Homily 10.2 (John Chrysostom 1986, p. 128).

[63] "Against the Games" 164; in (Mayer and Pauline 1999, pp. 119–120).

[64] John of Damascus, Homily II.16 (Daley 1998, *Dormition of Mary*: 220).

[65] Homily II.19 (Daley 1998, *Dormition of Mary*: 223).

know many who fast, pray, sigh, and demonstrate every manner of piety, so long as it costs them nothing, yet would not part with a penny to help those in distress."[66] After describing all sorts of vain luxuries in detail, he exclaims: "when I go into the house of one of these tasteless newly rich individuals, and see it bedecked with every imaginable hue, I know that this person possesses nothing more valuable than what is on display; such people decorate inanimate objects, but fail to beautify the soul."[67] He upbraids them for their lies, which do not match their actions: "you profess this to be true with your tongue, but your hand gives you the lie" (namely by flashing with expensive rings when claiming to have no money to help the poor).[68] Liturgical practice and Christian living requires one's deeds to match one's words, requires bodily actions to fit the "spiritual" content of the message.

While the focus in these homilies is on the human, the "fit" of body and soul parallels and participates in the match of earth and heaven, visible and invisible realms. This helps us understand the many references to visibility and invisibility in liturgical texts: we "mystically represent the cherubim," so that we may "receive the king of all" who comes to us "invisibly." The powers of heaven "invisibly" serve with us, as we visibly serve the liturgy of the presanctified gifts. We "taste and see" that the Lord is good, we see and taste the "pure, immortal, heavenly, and life-creating, and awesome mysteries" and pray that therefore our "whole evening may be perfect, holy, peaceful, and sinless."[69] It may well be (although this cannot be worked out in detail here) that the circular movements around the sanctuary in which the celebrants engage evokes and in some way instantiates the invisible, eternal reality (which the ancients thought to move in a circular fashion). Similarly, the cyclical nature of time in the liturgical calendar is significant.[70]

This makes much better sense of Maximus' vision and of many liturgical texts. Maximus' vision is not purely eschatological, as it is often interpreted, but it is depicting what ought to occur in every liturgy: here the invisible and immaterial realm enters into and becomes one with the visible and material celebration. Maximus actually maintains this in the *Mystagogy*: "For the whole spiritual [intelligible] world seems mystically imprinted on the whole sensible world in symbolic forms, for those who are capable of seeing this, and conversely the whole sensible world is spiritually explained in the mind in the principles which it contains."[71] It is not that we long for the day when we will finally leave our bodies behind and float as immaterial souls into some eternal, heavenly realm. Nor is liturgy best understood as departing the earth for heaven. Rather, liturgy seeks to bring together earth and heaven, tries to achieve a match between physical and spiritual realities, a fit between soul and body,

66 "To the Rich" 3 (Basil the Great 2009, p. 46). Basil uses very strong language. After describing in detail the suffering of parents who are selling their own children in order to have something to eat, he tells the rich that they are utterly deluded and have a completely false conception of reality: "In everything you see gold, you imagine everything as gold; it is your dream when you sleep and your first thought when you awaken. Just as those who are out of their mind do not see reality, but rather imagine things out of their malady, thus also your soul, being seized with avarice, sees everything as gold or silver. You would rather see gold than the sun itself. You wish that everything could be transformed by nature and become gold, and for your part you intend to turn as many things into gold as you can." "I Will Tear Down My Barns" 4 (Basil the Great 2009, p. 65). Indeed, in a later homily Basil suggests that heaven may begin to match our unjust behavior by withholding rain and causing famine.
67 "To the Rich" 4 (Basil the Great 2009, pp. 48–49).
68 "To the Rich" 4 (Basil the Great 2009, p. 49). Throughout these homilies Basil constantly accuses his listeners of deception and exhorts them to care for their souls precisely by divesting themselves of their superfluous and even damaging wealth. He chides them for the lack of consistency between their beliefs and their actions: "But you are not such a person. How do I know this? You begrudge your fellow human beings what you yourself enjoy; taking wicked counsel in your soul, you consider not how you might distribute to others according to their needs, but rather how, after having received so many good things, you might rob others of their benefit" "I Will Tear Down My Barns" 2 (Basil the Great 2009, p. 62).
69 "Hymn of the Entrance," "Communion Hymn," and Litany after Communion from the Liturgy of the Presanctified Gifts.
70 Andrew Louth points to this and explicitly connects it to the notion of time as a moving image of eternity in Plato's *Timaeus* (Louth 2009; Louth 2013).
71 *Mystagogy* 2 (Maximus the Confessor 1985, p. 189). Also: "Then the body will become like the soul and sensible things like intelligible things in dignity and glory, for the unique divine power will manifest itself in all things in a vivid and active presence proportioned to each one, and will by itself preserve unbroken for endless ages the bond of unity." *Mystagogy* 7 (Maximus the Confessor 1985, p. 197).

precisely so the earthly and corporeal, including human body and soul, can fully image and therefore represent the heavenly and incorporeal while wholly remaining itself.[72]

For Maximus, Christ is the supreme microcosm who most excellently combines soul and body. In Christ, there is a perfect match between soul and body, invisible and visible, incorporeal and corporeal. In him, they are no longer two divergent natures, but they are perfectly integrated, albeit without confusion.[73] As we have seen, the liturgies, especially those for the major feasts, also stress this. Similarly, John of Damascus affirms about Christ in a homily on Dormition: "You are not simply God or merely human, but one who is both Son of God and God enfleshed, God and human at the same time; you have not undergone confusion or endured division, but you bar in yourself the natural qualities of two natures essentially distinct, yet united without confusion and without division in your concrete existence: the created and the uncreated, the mortal and the immortal, the visible and the invisible, the circumscribed and the uncircumscribed, divine will and human will, divine activity no less than human activity; two self-determining realities, divine and human at the same time; divine miracles and human passions."[74] Or, to use different patristic imagery: in Christ image and likeness of the divine match perfectly—he is the very icon of God—while we still have to work on the fit between the two through pursuit of the virtues and by battling what keeps us from such fit between image and likeness. Christ is affirmed to be both fully human and fully divine; they come together perfectly in his person, without schizophrenia, but also without confusion and without suppression of one nature by the other. Similarly, the Eucharistic "transformation" means that mimesis between the two is achieved: the physical bread and wine in some way "match" the body and blood of Christ, the earthly and heavenly come together. In physically consuming the gifts, the participants assimilate this reality to their own bodies: the "match" between earthly and heavenly, physical and "spiritual" becomes in some way performed in them.

6. Conclusions

What are we to make of these claims today? Can they still describe what liturgy does for us? Can we recover this sensibility for the meaning of invisible and visible reality, heavenly and earthly realm, human soul and body? Maybe because these terms (body/soul, physical/spiritual) are so loaded, bear so much baggage, are understood so differently today, we need new language.[75] While a full retrieval, re-appropriation, or rephrasing into new language (or even a full argument about whether this would be necessary today) is beyond the bounds of this paper, maybe we can draw at least some preliminary conclusions about implications for liturgy today.

Unlike what we often assume (both Christians themselves and their critics), the match between the two cosmological realms and the two aspects of the human is not and cannot be a flight from this earthly reality into some otherworldly, heavenly one. This is so because the incorporeal can only be "seen" in the corporeal—it is otherwise "invisible"—, can only be touched and tasted in the

---

[72] And Maximus puts this in terms of the formation of habits: "When the soul is moved by them to make progress it becomes united to the God of all in imitating what is immutable and beneficent in his essence and activity by means of its steadfastness in the good and its unalterable habit of choice." *Mystagogy* 5 (Maximus the Confessor 1985, p. 191).
[73] This might actually also make sense of the many liturgical statements that affirm Christ to be simultaneously in heaven and on earth (lying in a manger, riding on a donkey, hanging on the cross, while still reigning in heaven). Rather than positing a schizophrenic split in Christ, where one nature dwells in some realm far away, while the other one walks around physically on earth at a particular point in historical time, the two "natures" combine the two realms fully within the liturgical celebration so as to make them inseparable. It is not that Christ is in two places at once, but that the two have become one in him.
[74] John of Damascus, Homily I on Dormition (Daley 1998, *Dormition of Mary*: 186). This is interpreted to remove *phthora*: "you transformed what was corruptible into incorruption" (Daley 1998, *Dormition of Mary*: 186).
[75] It is possible that contemporary phenomenology can help us with this, partly because it tries to overcome divisions between "objective" and "subjective" as they have become cemented in the (Western) tradition and partly because it is far more attentive to experience and hence an especially appropriate methodology for investigating liturgical praxis. Maybe it can provide resources also for articulating more fully and more authentically how liturgy functions (helping us hear again what the ancients heard at least some of the time and in some places). This is not something that can be worked out here, but I hope to explore it more fully in the future.

material—it is otherwise immaterial—, can only be encountered in the spatial and temporal—it has no other "place" or "time" because on its own it is without either.[76] And yet we frequently use spatial, temporal and physical language for the invisible, intelligible, heavenly, maybe because it is almost impossible to do otherwise in human language that reflects our human experience in space and time. The visual and physical metaphor of "entry" in Schmemann, for example, certainly makes it seem like heaven is a place (located in the sanctuary?) to which we (magically?) ascend.[77] Yet, liturgy is not a "weekly trip" from earth to heaven. Khaled Anatolios describes such a view as a "temporary excursion to an otherworldly reality" or even a "magical replacement of earth by heaven," judging such an interpretation a "misconstrual" that "can be disastrous for a proper appreciation of Byzantine liturgy and spirituality" (Anatolios 2000, pp. 1–2). If the invisible realm truly is incorporeal and immaterial, if it is truly eternal (i.e., atemporal and non-spatial), then the only way in which it can become visible, the only way in which it can be "entered," the only way in which we can "live" in it, is *if it becomes instantiated in space and time, in bodies and in materiality*. Just as the soul always has to be expressed in, with, and through a body, so the invisible and immaterial reality has to be expressed in the visible and material realm. The only "place" the invisible (or the "soul") can "be," if they are to be united, is "here," in the visible; the only time is "now." The only "place" for a soul is in a body, the only place for heavenly liturgy is on earth; it must be "here" because it cannot be "there" (and has no spatial "there"). Earth does not just mirror heaven in the false sense of mimesis as mere shadow or deceptive imitation, but it becomes imbued with it as the two are transformed in a union without confusion where they match up, where the "feasting above" is entirely comingled with and occurs in the "feasting below."[78]

Liturgy, then, enacts not just any kind of transformation, but a very specific one in which heaven and earth come together, where earth opens onto heaven—not in some magical other "place" but here and now. Liturgy is not a merely "spiritual" endeavor, but is profoundly and deeply physical and material, precisely because it brings the two together and seeks to establish harmony between them. Liturgy does not shape just a penitential self, but forms a self whose "body" perfectly comes to express a healthy "soul" in harmony with other human beings, and with the visible and invisible cosmos. And this cannot occur solely in private spirituality or personal ascetic pursuit, because it is never just about individual souls and their particular bodies, but also always about the unification of heaven and earth, intelligible and sensory, invisible and visible realms. The visible, physical, material is not merely a negligible conduit for accessing the invisible, incorporeal, intelligible realms, to be dismissed and abandoned as soon as one has tapped into the more "spiritual" reality. There is no access to the spiritual but through, via, and *within* the physical. This also means that liturgy is not primarily about some far-away eschatological reality, a mere preparation for the afterlife in "heaven." Rather, liturgy does the important work of unification here and now. Liturgy is the deliberate practice of *together* shaping our bodies and identities to be in harmony with each other and in harmony with all of reality. Liturgy continually aims at such health and harmony and engages in the difficult labor that

---

[76] This may also be at least one way of understanding more fully in what way the Eucharistic elements are "truly" the body and blood of Christ: they match perfectly, in them the visible and invisible accord, the incorporeal is entirely "present" within the corporeal, the "heavenly" bread is "there" in the earthly loaves (it could not be elsewhere). "Make this bread the precious body of your Christ" and "that which is in this cup the precious blood of your Christ" is maybe less a purely ontological claim than a claim about fit, where the two realities come together and truly "are" one.

[77] Aristotle has the same issue: he clearly argues that spherical motion is purely intelligible and yet it is somehow "located" beyond the moon. It is not physical in the sense in which earth, water, air and fire are physical (they can change into each other), yet he introduces "aether" as a subtle fifth element of "aetherial" reality.

[78] Again, there really is no "above," technically speaking, because the heavenly/intelligible/invisible is not spatial; in all these cases, we are using spatial and temporal language for something that is not corporeal, material, or physical and hence not subject to space and time. Even the question of whether the two realms or parts are "even" is in some way a red herring, because such a comparison assumes proportion and measurement and those are "physical" terms. Only the spatial can have volume and extension.

makes it possible. It is in this sense that liturgy renders us fully alive, most truly ourselves, and at the same time most authentically open to each other and to all of creation.

The questions raised by Rentel still stand, however: "Do we need liturgy? Why do we Orthodox Christians do this? Celebrate our services like this? Do they have to be this way? What do they mean? Do we even have to do liturgy as Christians?" (Rentel 2015, p. 213). If we no longer share this worldview, if we no longer conceive of the cosmos as the conjunction of visible and invisible realities, if we no longer think of the human as ensouled body, if we no longer experience liturgy as cosmic in scope but as a purely personal matter, can any of this still work? Is it still possible to subscribe fully to this ancient worldview today? And even if this can be done, would it be desirable or would it simply constitute an unsustainable denial of the contemporary world in which we actually live? Yet, can Orthodox believers continue the same liturgical practices while simultaneously subscribing to a different cosmological worldview and an individualist conception of the self? Will liturgy still function in the same way if that is the case? And these questions must also be confronted, albeit in a different way, by Western liturgical theology: Can Western liturgies retrieve aspects of this liturgical worldview if their practices are now fundamentally different? What do those practices mean and what worldview do they communicate? What does post-Vatican II Roman Catholic liturgy do and how does it function? How do the great varieties of Protestant liturgies function and what do their practices mean? How do those practices shape personal selves and communal identities? These are absolutely crucial questions for liturgical theology and practice—East and West—today. They must be pursued vigorously and honestly. Yet, such questioning or even possible retrievals cannot happen without exploring the original presuppositions of liturgy in depth and understanding as fully as possible how liturgy—in a place and time crucial for the formation of Christianity—was meant to function.

Conflicts of Interest: The author declares no conflict of interest.

References

Anatolios, Khal. 2000. Heaven and Earth in Byzantine Liturgy. *Antiphon* 5: 1–10.

Athanasius of Alexandria. 2003. *The Life of Antony*. Translated by Tim Vivian and Apostolos N. Athanassakis. Kalamazoo: Cistercian Publications.

Basil of Caesarea. 1934. Address to Young Men on Reading of Greek Literature (Loeb Classical Library No. 270). In *Basil: The Letters, Vol. 4 (Letters 249–386)*. Translated by Roy J. Defferari. Cambridge: Harvard University Press.

Basil the Great. 1995. Nine Homilies of the Hexaemeron. In *Basil: Letters and Select Works*. Edited by Philip Schaff and Henry Wace. Peabody: Hendrickson Publishers.

Basil the Great. 2005. *On the Human Condition*. Translated by Nonna Verna Harrison. Crestwood: St. Vladimir's Seminary Press.

Basil the Great. 2009. *On Social Justice*. Translated by C. Paul Schroeder. Crestwood: St. Vladimir's Seminary Press.

Baun, Jane Ralls. 2007. *Tales from Another Byzantium: Celestial Journey and Local Community in Medieval Greek Apocrypha*. Cambridge: Cambridge University Press.

Bydén, Börje, and Katerina Ierodiakonou. 2012. *The Many Faces of Byzantine Philosophy*. Athens: The Norwegian Institute at Athens.

Cabasilas, Nicholas. 1960. *A Commentary on the Divine Liturgy*. Translated by J. M. Hussey and P. A. McNulty. London: SPCK Press.

Cuneo, Terence. 2016. *Ritualized Faith: Essays on the Philosophy of Liturgy*. Oxford: Oxford University Press.

Daley, Brian E. 1998. *On the Dormition of Mary: Early Patristic Homilies*. Translated by Brian E. Daley. Crestwood: St. Vladimir's Seminary Press.

Daley, Brian E. 2006. *Gregory of Nazianzus*. London: Routledge.

Digeser, Elizabeth DePalma. 2012. *A Threat to Public Piety: Christians, Platonists, and the Great Persecution*. Ithaca: Cornell University Press.

Evagrius of Pontus. 2003. *The Greek Ascetic Corpus*. Translated by Robert E. Sinkewicz. Oxford: Oxford University Press.

Fagerberg, David. 2004. *Theologia Prima: What is Liturgical Theology? A Study in Methodology*. Mundelein: Hillenbrand Books.

Fagerberg, David. 2013. *On Liturgical Asceticism*. Washington: University of America Press.

Germanos of Constantinople. 1984. *On the Divine Liturgy*. Translated by Paul Meyendorff. Crestwood: St. Vladimir's Seminary Press.

Grisbrooke, W. Jardine. 1990. Liturgical Theology and Liturgical Reform: Some Questions. In *Liturgy and Tradition: Theological Reflections of Alexander Schmemann*. Edited by Thomas Fisch. Crestwood: St. Vladimir's Seminary Press, pp. 31–37.

Gschwandtner, Crina. 2012. Toward a Ricoeurian Hermeneutic of Liturgy. *Worship* 86: 482–505.

Hughes, Graham. 2003. *Worship as Meaning: A Liturgical Theology for Late Modernity*. Cambridge: Cambridge University Press.

Ierodiakonou, Katerina. 2010. *Byzantine Philosophy and Its Ancient Sources*. Oxford: Clarendon Press.

Ierodiakonou, Katerina, and George Zografidis. 2010. Early Byzantine Philosophy. In *The Cambridge History of Philosophy in Late Antiquity*. Edited by Lloyd P. Gerson. Cambridge: Cambridge University Press, vol. II, pp. 843–68.

John Chrysostom. 1984. *On Wealth and Poverty*. Translated by Catharine P. Roth. Crestwood: St. Vladimir's Seminary Press.

John Chrysostom. 1986. Homilies on Genesis 1–17. In *Fathers of the Church*. Translated by R. C. Hill. Washington: The Catholic University of America Press.

John of Damascus. 1958. Writings. In *The Fathers of the Church*. Translated by Frederic H. Chase. Washington: The Catholic University of America Press.

Kavanagh, Aidan. 1984. *On Liturgical Theology*. New York: Pueblo Publishing.

Knezĕvić, Mikonja. 2015. *The Ways of Byzantine Philosophy*. Alhambra: Sebastian Press.

Krueger, Derek. 2014. *Liturgical Subjects: Christian Ritual, Biblical Narrative, and the Formation of the Self in Byzantium*. Philadelphia: University of Pennsylvania Press.

Louth, Andrew. 2009. Space, Time and the Liturgy. In *Encounter between Eastern Orthodoxy and Radical Orthodoxy: Transfiguring the World through the Word*. Edited by A. Pabst and C. Schneider. Farnham: Ashgate, pp. 215–31.

Louth, Andrew. 2013. Experiencing the Liturgy in Byzantium. In *Experiencing Byzantium. Papers from the 44th Spring Symposium of Byzantine Studies, Newcastle and Durham, April 2011*. Edited by Claire Nesbitt and Mark Jackson. Farnham: Ashgate, pp. 79–88.

Maximus the Confessor. 1985. The Church's Mystagogy. In *Selected Writings. The Classics of Western Spirituality*. Translated by George C. Berhold. Mahwah: Paulist Press.

Maximus the Confessor. 2014. *On Difficulties in the Church Fathers: The Ambigua*. 2 vols. Translated by Nicholas Constas. Cambridge: Harvard University Press.

Mayer, Wendy, and Pauline Allen. 1999. *John Chrysostom*. New York: Routledge.

Miller, Patricia Cox. 2009. *The Corporeal Imagination: Signifying the Holy in Late Ancient Christianity*. Philadelphia: University of Pennsylvania Press.

Mother Mary, and Kallistos Ware. 1998. *The Festal Menaion*. Translated by Mother Mary and Kallistos Ware. South Canaan: St. Tikhon's Seminary Press.

Mother Mary, and Kallistos Ware. 2002. *The Lenten Triodion*. Edited by Mother Mary and Kallistos Ware. South Canaan: St. Tikhon's Seminary Press.

Nemesius of Emesa. 2008. *On the Nature of Man*. Translated by R. W. Sharples and P. J. van der Eijk. Liverpool: Liverpool University Press.

Proclus of Constantinople. 2001. *Homilies on the Life of Christ*. Translated by Jan Harm Barkhuizen. Brisbane: Centre for Early Christian Studies.

Rentel, Alexander. 2015. Where is God in the Liturgy? *St. Vladimir's Theological Quarterly* 59: 213–33.

Schmemann, Alexander. 1973. *For the Life of the World: Sacraments and Orthodoxy*. Crestwood: St. Vladimir's Seminary Press.

Schmemann, Alexander. 1986. *Introduction to Liturgical Theology*. Translated by Asheleigh E. Moorhouse. Crestwood: St. Vladimir's Seminary Press.

Schmemann, Alexander. 1987. *The Eucharist: Sacrament of the Kingdom*. Crestwood: St. Vladimir's Seminary Press.

Shaw, Gregory. 1995. *Theurgy and the Soul: The Neoplatonism of Iamblichus*. University Park: Pennsylvania University Press.

Taft, Robert. 1992. What Does Liturgy Do? Toward a Soteriology of Liturgical Celebration: Some Theses. *Worship* 66: 194–211.

Taft, Robert. 2006. *Through Their Own Eyes: Liturgy as the Byzantines Saw It*. Berkeley: InterOrthodox Press.

White, Andrew Walker. 2015. *Performing Orthodox Ritual in Byzantium*. Cambridge: Cambridge University Press.

religions

MDPI

Article

Service and Pro-Existence in the Thought of the Romanian Theologian Dumitru Staniloae: A Path for the Orthodox Church Facing the Challenges of Globalization

Ionut Untea

School of Humanities, Department of Philosophy and Science, Wenke Building A, Jiulonghu Campus, Southeast University, Nanjing 211189, China; untea_ionut@126.com or 108109055@seu.edu.cn

Academic Editor: John A. Jillions
Received: 3 April 2017; Accepted: 9 May 2017; Published: 16 May 2017

Abstract: "Pro-existence" is a concept developed by 20th century western Christian theologians to describe the service of the Church facing contemporary challenges. The leading Romanian theologian Dumitru Staniloae (1903–1993) took this further by expressing his Orthodox understanding of the relationship between service and pro-existence. The article explores Staniloae's call for Orthodox Christians to serve not only people from other denominations, but those from other religions, as well as atheists. He depicted human pro-existence as an "existential impetus" towards serving the one in need, an impetus that the Orthodox Church should more visibly exercise. In a gentle, non-critical approach, Staniloae argues that the Orthodox Churches concentrated on liturgical service to God, while leaving service to people underdeveloped. The path ahead for the Orthodox Church will be the development of a harmonious multi-level understanding of pro-existence to hear and respond, as a "Serving" Church, to the needs of any human being.

Keywords: pro-existence; co-existence; Christian service; Orthodox Church; Christology; ecclesiology

---

1. Introduction

The term "pro-existence" appeared in various theological sources at the beginning of the second half of the twentieth century. In the late twentieth century, the term was already being used in Catholic and Protestant Christologies and Ecclesiologies. The Romanian theologian Dumitru Staniloae took the term from the Christian Peace Conference, founded in 1958, and in 1963 he dedicated an article to the relationship between service and pro-existence; an article which is practically unknown in international scholarship. Dumitru Staniloae's development of the relationship between service and pro-existence in the life of the Church shares many of the insights proposed by western Christian theologians, to which Staniloae adds a number of genuine views, which can be considered the fruit of his Orthodox understanding of the Church's mission to put into practice the relationship between service and pro-existence. Nonetheless, Staniloae's aim is not so much to enter into a debate with western theologians as to reinvigorate the Orthodox Church's understanding and practice of the pro-existential "impetus" of human nature into concrete acts of service between the members of a local Church and between local Churches themselves. In the first section of the article, I propose a brief analysis of the Catholic and Protestant understandings of service and pro-existence in the thought of a number of renowned theologians such as Dietrich Bonhoeffer, Josef Hromádka, Elisabeth Adler, Jon Sobrino, Aidan Nichols, Michel Deneken, Edward Schillebeeckx, François Xavier Durrwell, Walter Kasper, Heinz Schürmann, and Walter Klaiber, while in the second section, I will emphasize first the Romanian theologian's specific Orthodox contribution, and subsequently show the implications of Staniloae's ideas for the reception of a renewed sense of service within the Orthodox Church.

2. Two Approaches in Catholic and Protestant Theologies of Service and Pro-Existence in the Twentieth-Century and Beyond

Early twentieth-century developments of the pro-existential aspect of the Church can be traced back to the Reformed theologian Karl Barth's Christology and especially to the Christological developments of his student, Dietrich Bonhoeffer, a theologian engaged in the ecumenical dialogue who was also a vocal preacher against the Nazi persecution of Jews and a concentration camp victim (Deneken 1988, pp. 286–87). In his letters from captivity (1943–1945), Bonhoeffer writes about the life of the Church (by which he understands the concrete manifestation of the Church's mission regarding the concrete needs of each parish, preaching, and the life of a Christian in a "religionless world"), and the necessity to take Christ as a model in "turbulent times" as the only hope for remembering "what it is that makes life really worth while "by virtue of Christ's example" as one whose only concern is for others" (Bonhoeffer 1959, pp. 123, 179, 184). This perspective of Jesus "being for" each individual has mainly generated two approaches in twentieth-century western theological thinking.

2.1. The First Approach: Experiencing Pro-Existence as a Christian Immersed in Concrete Socio-Political Problems

Without downgrading the theological implications of the attitude of "being for", and actually using theological arguments as a point of departure, the first approach consisted in emphasizing the essential vocation of each Christian to follow Christ's example in serving their neighbor, identifying the "neighbor" beyond confessional and religious boundaries. As in Bonhoeffer's case, this approach emerged more in contexts where political settings or social and economic infrastructures would be unfavorable for members of Christian Churches. The Christian Peace Conference founded in 1958 in Prague by the Czech Protestant theologian Josef Hromádka used the term *pro-existence* in its gatherings dedicated to promoting peace among countries of the Eastern bloc and in the world at large (Staniloae 1963, p. 1019). Hromádka's hopes, sometimes judged as naive by western interlocutors, were that the Soviet system would rather change over time, renouncing its oppressive character and making way for eastern European Christian heritage into the social application of Marxism (Bock 1992, p. 82). In a similar fashion, in the late 1950s and early 1960s, Christians of the German Democratic Republic (GDR) were using the term *pro-existence* to promote reciprocal relations of tolerance and mutual aid between Marxists and Christians, as part of their effort to show Marxist fellow citizens that Christians should not be viewed as enemies. In the preface of an 1964 English-language translation of several sermons of anonymous pastors of the GDR, Elisabeth Adler aims to counter two preconceived western attitudes towards Christians in Eastern Europe: the first, that they were "heroes of the faith", since they had chosen to be witnesses of faith and even martyrs in the social and political contexts prevailing under atheistic regimes; the second, that they were "traitors to the faith", having chosen certain degrees of compromise with those regimes. Neither of the two, Adler contends, can fully account for the realities encountered by Christians in such contexts in everyday life (Adler 1964, p. 7). That is why the term *pro-existence* was meant to invite a reconsideration of the relationships with the neighbor. She quotes a 1959 report of Protestant Student Congregations in the GDR that aimed at going "beyond the controversial thesis of co-existence to a practical 'pro-existence'", and adds: "The word 'pro-existence' does of course run the risk of being little more than an attractive slogan. But it does seem to sum up in some measure what for Christians in the DDR [GDR] is the order of the day. [...] We have learnt that in our country there is no case to be made out for Christians simply going into hibernation, or just trying to save the Church alive during a period of atheistic attacks. [...] We have learnt, too, that we have no business breaking off relations with Communists and fellow-travelers, or with anxious and even apathetic souls outside the Church; instead, it is our business to create such relationships. [...] So it is not the Church we try to preserve now, but the Gospel. Preserving the Gospel means living the Gospel, and living the Gospel means pro-existence—being there for the world, just as Christ was there for the world" (Adler 1964, p. 13).

As Elisabeth Adler has put it, the pro-existential vocation does not inspect the religious, intellectual, or social profile of the person in need, whether this person is an atheist, a non-Christian believer, or simply a fellow-traveler, but calls every Christian to service simply by virtue of the neighbors' sharing of human nature, since Christ came for all humankind. Viewing the atheists and non-Christians as fellow travelers in this world, side by side with Christians, would at the same time promote more peaceful relations between members and non-members of the Church and would encourage every Christian to live a more concrete life in the Gospel.

This focus on the specific need rather than on the specific profile of the neighbor and the image of a pro-existent Christ as a model for the Christian engaged in dealing with specific circumstances of life, be it political, economic, or religious, also attracted the theoretical attention of Jon Sobrino, a Catholic theologian known for his contributions to liberation theology. Sobrino understands that Jesus has come for all human beings, including the "oppressors" (Sobrino [1987] 2004, p. 34). Echoing the term "preferential option for the poor" established in Catholic theology by the Latin American Episcopal Council (CELAM) (Allen 2007), Sobrino's Christology sees Christ's person as transmitting to the world an example of "partisan pro-existence", by which he understands Christ's "existence in favor of certain other", the poor: "Stated systematically, Jesus's pro-existence consists, in a first moment, in a proclamation and toil calculated to further the passage of the poor from infra-existence to the existence of daughters and sons of God." (Sobrino [1987] 2004, p. 34). Given the official endorsement of the phrase "preferential option for the poor" by Pope John Paul II, by Cardinal Joseph Ratzinger, and by Pope Francis (Allen 2007; Gibson 2015), Sobrino's version of Jesus's "partisanship" of the poor shows how concrete social needs, in this case those of the Church in Latin America, can generate theological renewal in the Church.

Later developments of the term *pro-existence* as part of an approach dedicated to the concrete circumstances of life can also be identified in the ecclesiology of the Catholic theologian Aidan Nichols, in his reflection on the Anglican theologian John Milbank, founder of the Radical Orthodoxy movement, which attracted theologians from different confessions and aimed at a deeper engagement of the Church within the social and political sphere. Nichols believes that Millbank's ecclesiological attitude is to radically assert a pro-existence of the Church in the sense of Richard Hooker's *respublica Christiana*, which would confound Church and civil society in an indistinguishable mass, marginalizing the "story of grace and sin" in which not everything can be solved by the application of charity: "The Church 'pro-exists' for all humanity; but in the meanwhile, before her mission is divinely completed, she must 'co-exist' with other aggregates of the human members of the creation" (Nichols [2014] 1992, pp. 331–32). Nichols thus emphasizes the key issues of the second approach regarding the term *pro-existence*: a search not only for the cultivation of respectful and fraternal relations towards the neighbor, but also for the manifestation of the living body of Christ as a means of nourishment of Christians from the reality of Christ's presence, which would give them the capacity to recognize organizations that do not perceive, or are themselves the product of, the manifestation of sin in the world. With such "aggregates" (organizations, governments) being incompatible with the Church's mission, the Church should simply learn how to coexist.

If in the first approach, there is a tendency towards radical affirmation of Christ's life as a gift "for" every human being, sometimes giving the impression of a relativization of the distinction inside-outside Church, the second approach depicts pro-existence as a vocation inside the Church, cultivated and nourished by the Church's sacramental life. With minor variations, Catholic, as well as Protestant theologians producing views that can be integrated into a second approach see pro-existence in a close relationship with *diakonia*, a call to service emanating from the centrality of the Eucharistic sacrament of the Church.

2.2. The Second Approach: Christian Service and Pro-Existence Immersed in the Institutional and Sacramental Life of the Church

The Catholic theologian Michel Deneken identifies in the theology of Edward Schillebeeckx, one of the most active theologians during the Second Vatican Council, an intimate relationship between Christ's ministry, the Christian vocation towards service to the neighbor, and the partaking by Church members of the sacrament of Eucharist (Deneken 1988, p. 268). Indeed, Schillebeeckx calls to meditation on Christ's words during the Last Supper, depicting the phrase "for you", together with the submission to the Father's will and with Christ's own human will to serve the whole of humanity as the founding moment of human pro-existential life (Matthew 26:28,39): "The 'for you' (*hyper* formula), in the sense of Jesus's entire pro-existence, was the historical intention of his whole ministry and was substantiated by his very death" (Schillebeeckx [1987] 2004, p. 311). In this light, pro-existence is something to be achieved by somebody by simply taking Jesus's humanity as a model and orienting one's personal life towards the service of people, but always with the goal of honoring God, as Jesus did, in his founding pro-existential attitude of honoring the Father by serving humanity. Commenting on the same passages of the Scripture, Walter Kasper defines pro-existence as shared humanity, after the model of Jesus: "Human pro-existence (or shared humanity), but proceeding from God and to the honor of God: to that end Jesus was filled with God's Spirit and his very existence as a man was the work of God's Spirit" (Kasper [2007] 1976, p. 558).

Michel Deneken also sees in the Eucharistic theology of Karl Rahner and that of François Xavier Durrwell elements of Christological pro-existence. In Deneken's reading, Rahner's "anthropo-theology" of Christ's death as service to humanity represents a "key-moment" in "the understanding of Jesus" (*un moment-clé de la compréhension de Jésus*), since the moment of sacrifice is transformed in a moment of love for humanity (Deneken 1988, p. 274). In this point, Deneken shows the important place of theological reasoning on pro-existence in the framework of Christology, as it allows a renewal of theological reflection, a departure from old theological interpretations on Christ's service as sacrifice. Deneken acknowledges the twentieth-century Catholic departure from a sacrificial or legalistic interpretation of the phrase *hyper*, interpretations that had occurred due to a misleading exegetical reading of *hyper* as "in lieu of" (*à la place de*) instead of "for" (Deneken 1988, p. 270). In Deneken's view, the theology of the Eucharist facilitates "the shift from sacrificial to pro-existential" (*le passage du sacrificiel au pro-existentiel*) (Deneken 1988, p. 268).

According to Deneken, in the Eucharistic "gesture" (Deneken 1988, p. 267) during the Last Supper, Walter Kasper sees, as does Rahner, the moment of Christ's revealing as "the-man-for-the others" (*l'homme-pour-les autres*) (Deneken 1988, p. 271). When discussing the words "for us", "for the multitude", Kasper appreciates that the dimension of Jesus's service for the whole of humanity received a central place in the post-Paschal preaching of the Apostles (Deneken 1988, p. 271; Kasper 1980, p. 325), which explains their centrality in the sacrament of the Eucharist. In this spirit, Deneken concludes that the Last Supper of Jesus with the Apostles represents the essential place of pro-existence (*la topique de la pro-existence*) (Deneken 1988, p. 271). Arguing that, in his service, Jesus showed himself as "the brother" of all humans (Deneken 1988, p. 271; Kasper 1980, p. 325), Walter Kasper also argues for integrating the service for non-Christians and even the oppressors, the aspect so much emphasized by the first approach to pro-existence, into a Christian attitude of following the man Jesus's example: "Following Jesus meant following him in this service: If anyone would be first, he must be last of all and servant of all (Mark 9:35). Service, love which includes one's enemies, in short living for others, is the new way of living which Jesus inaugurated and made possible. A life like this involves being prepared for anything, leaving everything (Mark 10:28), even risking your life (Mark 8:34)" (Kasper [2007] 1976, p. 377). This is similar to Schillebeeckx's approach to Jesus's examples in his humanity. The interpretations of both Kasper and Schillebeeckx leave the door open to interfaith dialogue, since the accent placed on following Jesus in his submission to God and service to people as a human does not necessarily imply faith in his divinity.

If Kasper and Schillebeeckx widen the perspective of Jesus's example for each Christian, but also to all humans by virtue of their quality of "brothers" of Jesus in his humanity, Heinz Schürmann bases his reflection on Jesus's pro-existential service on the relationship of Jesus's submission to the Father's will, leading to a new anthropological dimension of pro-existence that follows the model of Christ's *kenosis*. First of all, Schürmann emphasizes that, when taking Jesus as an example, one should not forget that his attitude of service is an attitude of "submission" and "total self offering" to God, before being a gesture of accepting the sacrifice for all human beings (Deneken 1988, p. 272; Schürmann 1977, p. 166). The importance of Jesus's example lies in the fact of his human kenosis: if the kenosis in the incarnation of the Son is a widely discussed aspect in Christology, Schürmann initiated the reflection on a new type of kenosis, a "contemplative kenosis" (Deneken 1988, p. 277; Schürmann 1977, p. 181): in his pro-existential submission to Father's will and acceptance of the sacrifice for the whole of humanity, Jesus becomes "the man truly free, freed of his self", freed of the fears of his human self (*Jésus est donc l'homme vraiment 'libre', libéré de lui-même*) (Deneken 1988, p. 273; Schürmann 1977, p. 167). Following Jesus in this "contemplative kenosis", every Christian has to embrace the same pro-existential attitude of becoming free of his human self, free of everything that makes him fearful for his life, safety, or wellbeing.

This is indeed a bold understanding of Jesus's prayer to the Father (Matthew 26:39; Luke 22: 43–44; John 17:4), aligning the reflection with other theologians' embracing of the second approach to pro-existence, by reasserting Jesus's gift to God and humanity, during the founding moments of the sacrament of the Eucharist, at the center of every human search for service. Nonetheless, Schürmann's reflection also remains inclusive regarding the first approach to pro-existence, by the exhortation towards Christians to accept the "contemplative kenosis", which, during service to the non-Christian "brother", may sometimes require a self-inflicted deprivation of everything that makes a Christian life: a voluntary renouncement to the safe zone of one's own community while searching for the brother in need in the territories of different faiths, social systems, or political regimes. Furthermore, Schürmann talks about a process of "inculturation" of Christology according to different historical periods, as new ways of understanding Christ according to the ways in which the Scripture's message is understood in the midst of concrete historical situations (Deneken 1988, p. 276). Schürmann dedicates an entire article to this reflection on Jesus's pro-existence, an article published in the 1970s, but suggestively entitled as a question addressed to Christians everywhere: "Will the "pro-existent" Christ remain at the heart of tomorrow's faith?" (Schürmann 1977, pp. 145–87). By his call to total renouncement to our human fears, by which he may also understand giving up the fears of being deprived of the sacramental life of the Church, Schürmann's theology of pro-existence combines the two approaches of the reflection on pro-existence, making the first seem less radical, and the second become more dynamic.

Another perspective that seems to reconcile the two approaches comes from the Evangelistic theologian Walter Klaiber, who expands the Christological reflection of the words "for us" to Ecclesiological dimensions. Klaiber already sees, in the fact that the New Testament is composed of different writings addressed to specific needs of local communities, a post-Paschal application of Christ's Eucharistic words: "The New Testament is not a missionary writing [...]. It is a collection of writings for certain churches which cite this basic missional gospel in very different situations and utilize it for theological or teaching purposes. [...] Nonetheless a unity is recognizable. [...] The basis and power of this message lies in the certainty that 'God is for us', which is guaranteed by Jesus's message and his offering of life for us. The reality of God's pro-existence reaches human need in its entire complexity and breaks through the power of sin which draws its power from the isolation and the ego-centricity of humankind. The mission of the Church of Jesus Christ, whose witness, communion, and ministry is filled and formed by God's existence *for us*, is grounded in this" (Klaiber [2003] 1997, pp. 75–77). Klaiber's insistence on the application of Jesus Christ's attitude of "being for" God and people to the concrete situations of each community, brings his thought closer to the first approach in the theological reflection on pro-existence. The novelty of Klaiber's perspective lies in the fact that it alludes to the importance of recreating the unity of the Church from the bottom up, from the way diverse communities respond in the application of Jesus Christ's service to concrete local needs regarding the help due to the neighbor. Since the New Testament itself has emerged as a unified missionary and educational message in spite of its writings being dedicated to specific applications of Christ's message, there is no reason to suppose that a firmer institutional grounding in God's pro-existence at different levels like the ministry of the clergy, communion of the members, and the mission of being Christ's witnesses in a world ravaged by deep social unrest would not recreate the unity of the Church of Jesus Christ.

The continuity of the reflection on pro-existence in the twenty-first century can be seen in Pope Benedict XVI's use of the term "pro-existence" in his *Jesus of Nazareth* (Pope Benedict XVI 2011, pp. 134, 174); the ecological dimensions of pro-existence raised by the publication of the Evangelical theologian Udo Middleman in 1974 and the republication of the book in 2012 (Middelmann [1974] 2012); or the use of the term in feminist theology (Rösener 2002, p. 3). However, as my short presentation of the two approaches suggests, further work on pro-existence is needed in order to give more detailed answers to the challenge of integrating the service to "brothers" in concrete needs within the unity of Christ's body, the Church. The next section, dedicated to Dumitru Staniloae's Orthodox perspective on service and pro-existence, shows a series of aspects that resonate well with many elements of either of the two approaches emphasized in this section, and his further theological reflection on integrating the need for concrete service into the environment of a pro-existence sustained by the sacramental life of the Church.

3. Dumitru Staniloae's Distinctive Orthodox Contribution to the Theological Reflection on Service and Pro-Existence

"So it is not the Church we try to preserve now, but the Gospel" asserted Elisabeth Adler (Adler 1964, p. 13). Likewise, Sobrino's understanding of "partisan pro-existence" (Sobrino [1987] 2004, p. 34) suggested that the Church should more radically cultivate love to the one in special need than simply talking about God's love for all Christians or all humankind. The first approach can thus be interpreted as an attempt to apply to the concrete circumstances of life Christ's pro-existence as expressed in the parable of the Lost Sheep, where the good shepherd is ready to leave the ninety-nine sheep in order to rescue the one in danger (Matthew 18:12–14; Luke 15:3–7). The second approach in Catholic and Protestant theology, which faces the relativizing danger of a call to service aiming at transgressing religious boundaries, has generally maintained that fullness of service can only be experienced if Christians are nourished by Church's sacraments, especially by the founding words of the Eucharist as the full expression of Christ's self giving to God and absolute service to humans, and guided by the ministry of the clergy. At the same time, Heinz Schürmann's and Walter Klaiber's perspectives can be read as contributions in which elements of the first approach are considered essential to the life of Jesus Christ's Church, without necessarily having to assert a radical attitude of service. For instance, both theologians assert the need of the Church to regard the specific problems of a certain community or space in which a community lives as opportunities to inform and renew the Christian understanding of pro-existence, just as different historical periods have shaped new understandings of Christology, as part of a larger process of "inculturation".

In the manner of the second approach to pro-existence, the Romanian Orthodox theologian Dumitru Staniloae reflects on the possibilities of living service to the human brother as fully as possible, in relation to the beating heart that sets into motion the life of the Church: the Eucharist. Nevertheless, a closer look at both Staniloae's experience as a member of the Romanian Orthodox clergy under Communist persecution, and his theological understanding of service and pro-existence will show that, for him too, the concrete circumstances of life should play an essential role in situating oneself as a Christian within the Church, and situating the local Orthodox Church itself, led by a bishop, and all the Orthodox Churches, within the larger body of Christ.

3.1. Pro-Existing in Humbleness: The Oppressed, Their Need for Christ's Presence and the Response of the Incarcerated Orthodox Priests

Fr. Dumitru Staniloae personally experienced the horrors of an oppressive system, his marginalization from the center of Romanian intellectual life having reached its peak in September 1958, when he was incarcerated due to his membership of *Rugul Aprins* (*The Unburnt Bush*). This cultural organization had organized small meetings in members' houses, and public conferences at the Antim monastery in Bucharest, having thus contributed to Romanian cultural life and to keeping alive the spirit of intellectual resistance to Soviet ideology (Botez 1992, p. 212). In an article published in 1990, Father Staniloae describes with modesty, in just a few words, some of the physical torments that he and his fellows endured during imprisonment, and gives the names of his cellmates who died in prison or shortly after being released. He also adds: "In prison, the Orthodox priests and monks did not just dwell, but taught people Akathist hymns and other prayers, written on pieces of soap with broken bars taken from cell doors; they gave lessons in the Christian catechism. In spite of all persecution and surveillance, the priests and monks continued practising their service, celebrating the Divine Liturgy, as well as baptisms, marriages and funerals. They continued preaching the word of God, and nobody ever heard any priest mentioning the tyrant in their sermon" [Author's transl.] (Staniloae 2003b, p. 284). Father Dumitru Staniloae shows the two attitudes shared by the incarcerated: first of all, the rituals of the Church helped them gain a sense of normalcy of life, a degree of inner freedom that no persecution could have taken away from them; secondly, while coming together in prayer, they never uttered words of contempt regarding their persecutors, suggested by the symbolic name "the tyrant". They simply followed Christ's example (Isaiah 53:7) that was included by the Christian Orthodox Tradition in the prayers of the Proskomedia, the ritual of the preparation of bread and wine for the Sacrament of the Eucharist. It is also striking that Orthodox priests and monks could have celebrated the Divine Liturgy and other Church sacraments and hierurgies without that which makes a Church visible in the eyes of a common Christian: without the building itself, without liturgical garments, without the bride and the groom being physically present in the same room, and even without bread or wine for the Eucharist. Fr. Staniloae does not give details on how all of this had been materially possible, since, according to his testimony, many of his fellow inmates died of starvation, a fact which would have practically made procuring bread very difficult, and practically impossible when it came to procuring wine for the Eucharist. He simply states that all these sacraments and hierurgies did actually take place, as a facet of the Church's service to the special need of Christ's brothers. Nonetheless, this did not weaken the Church in her visible presence, but rather intensified it, as the Church took the concrete situation in the prison as the starting point of her service, and continued her mission of bringing Christ at the table of the ones who needed his presence.

3.2. Service as the "True" Dimension of the Church in the "New Social Era"

In 1965, two years after his release, Father Staniloae was reinstated as a professor of theology in Bucharest, following a response by the regime who wished to generate a more positive impression among western intellectuals who were themselves demanding information on Staniloae's fate (Botez 1992, pp. 212–13). Already in 1963, the year of his release from prison, Dumitru Staniloae published in the Romanian Orthodox theological journal *Glasul Bisericii* (The Call of the Church) an article simply entitled "Servire şi proexistenţă" (*Service and Pro-existence*), mentioning that he took the term *pro-existence* from the proceedings of the Christian Peace Conference (Staniloae 1963, p. 1019). Staniloae's contribution to the reflection on pro-existence that generated the two approaches mentioned in the first section of this article places in balance both the need for Christians to take as a point of departure the concrete situations of certain persons or communities in order to find the best answer to their needs, and the Church's vocation of offering the plenitude of her gifts to those animated by faith in Christ's pro-existence.

Given the fact that the concrete circumstances may inform the pro-existential attitude of Christians towards concrete service to people in need for specific solutions, in his 1963 article Staniloae chooses to talk first about service, by pointing to the fact that Catholic and Protestant Churches have a long and uncontested experience in serving, not only individuals, but especially communities. In the opening of his 1963 article, Staniloae quotes from the Japanese Protestant theologian Masao Takenaka's intervention during the World Council of Churches's third General Assembly of New Delhi (1961), emphasizing that, although the "dimension of service" remains the essential feature of Christ's Church, it is the concrete "new", "communitarian structure" of the international context that has "helped" the Church "rediscover" new ways of accomplishing her call (Staniloae 1963, p. 1019). Staniloae goes as far as asserting that this "new" dimension emphasized by Takenaka actually represents the Church's "true" dimension (Staniloae 1963, p. 1020), an attitude that might seem compatible with the aspect of "inculturation" in Christology discussed in Schürmann's case, this time also extended to Ecclesiology.

Staniloae advances further towards a peculiar argument of "inculturation" regarding Ecclesiological renewal given the opportunity of the reevaluation, within each local Church, of the role of service that is becoming more and more necessary under the pressure of international instability. The growing necessity of serving not only individuals, but also entire communities, has led to the emergence of international organizations dedicated to service. According to Staniloae, right from the first meeting of the Second Vatican Council, the Catholic Church has reacted to this situation by the official "renouncement" of any "tendency of domination" in the Church, a measure accompanied by the more practical rule for the clergy to divest themselves of the "royal garment" and instead to don the "coat of humility". Moreover, "a special merit for the emphasis placed nowadays on Christian 'service' within the Ecumenical Movement belongs to Protestant theology". Staniloae believes that the "salutary rediscovery" of service in the Protestant theology has come as a "special joy" for the Church, since this rediscovery "represented a return from the individualism of the original protestant doctrine, which had dissolved the community" [Author's transl.] (Staniloae 1963, p. 1021).

3.3. The Necessity of a Renewed Sense of Service in the Orthodox Church: From Humbleness in the Face of Oppressive Political Authority, to Humbleness Regarding the Authority of the Clergy

By contrast, service in the Orthodox Church "has always been practised as something self-evident". However, this also explains the insufficiency of the Orthodox theological reflection on the dimensions of service in "the new social era": "What is needed today from the Orthodox Church as well is both the necessary theological clarification of the notion of service, and its increased application in an Orthodox spirit" [Author's transl.] (Staniloae 1963, p. 1021). In other words, given the new special circumstances of the "new social era", both Catholic and Protestant Churches have come closer to the Orthodox understanding of service, although paradoxically, the Orthodox Church does not respond adequately to this phenomenon, but rather follows the old trends of those western Churches. An "inculturation" process in Ecclesiology as a new understanding of Church unity based on Christ's "act of boundless service" is not only desirable, but necessary, not only because the Orthodox Church is not sensitive enough, or does not organize herself well enough to respond more urgently to situations requiring concrete help, but also because, throughout her history, the Orthodox Church has not been able to fully observe the complexity of Christ's example, in spite of her openness to doing so: "The Orthodox Church preserved, as much as circumstances allowed, a part of the spirit of community of early Christianity" [Author's transl.] (Staniloae 1963, p. 1021).

The striking assertion that the Orthodox Church has only preserved a "part" of Christ's example of service should not be understood as a radical call, similar to the first approach to service and pro-existence emphasized above, but rather as a call to humbleness: the Orthodox Church has always been under the negative pressure of the "structure and mentality of an individualistic society", which she always chose to counter by humbleness. "Humbleness, united with the feeling of fraternity and equality, preached and applied throughout her area of jurisdiction, had bridled the tendency towards arrogance" [Author's transl.] (Staniloae 1963, p. 1021). This a humble way of suggesting that, at the time of the article, the Orthodox Church was, as in the past, under the pressure of a certain "structure and mentality" that was promising "equality" and "fraternity" without liberty. Thus, the

Church's mission had always consisted in the work of proposing humbleness as a substitute for liberty, humbleness as internal liberty paired with Christ's attitude of readiness to suffer without retaliation, as prophesied: "He was oppressed, and he was afflicted, yet he opened not his mouth" (Isaiah 53:7). At the same time, this carries the risk of an incorrect understanding of humbleness by the clergy themselves, who, in their great eagerness to escape being supervised by a superimposed earthly authority and their great confidence that some truths are "self-evident" in the teaching of the Church, would rather renounce any further enquiry and try to look for discourses complacent with the ideological trends of the time. The humbleness of the Orthodox way is thus not the one that transforms the clergy into a quiet instrument of a political regime that, in spite of its official endorsing of equality and fraternity, leads in practice to a more acute individualism. Admitting that the hierarchy of the Orthodox Church made mistakes every time the clergy tried to borrow attitudes preached by the political power in the name of equality and fraternity, would be an important step towards embracing a kind of humbleness that would reorient the Orthodox Church towards the true meaning of Christ's teaching and example.

There are three challenges ahead for the Orthodox clergy, Staniloae believes. The first is the harmonious joining of both service to God, which he renders by the Greek term *leitourgia*, which in Romanian has been translated by the term "slujire", and service to people, represented by the term *diakonia*, in Romanian being called "servire", although in practice the first term, "slujire" is wide enough to express both meanings in Romanian, service to God (worship) by service to people: "It is fair to admit that the Church has been preoccupied in the past rather with the service to God in the strict sense of the word, that is with the "divine service" (*sfintele slujbe*). Still, the refreshing of the Christian life from the spring of the New Testament should help us avoid dissociating "service-worship" (*slujirea*) to God from "service" (*servirea*) to people. Only in the "service" (*servirea*) to people is the "service-worship" (*slujirea*) to God fully accomplished" [Author's transl.] (Staniloae 1963, p. 1025).

The second challenge, even for the common priest, will be to find adequate ways of serving "beyond the divine service and the preaching of the word", especially because even small communities may be affected by problems which the priest "will not define himself" to his community, but will be "imposed to him by the specific needs of the people among whom he lives, believers or non-believers" [Author's transl.] (Staniloae 1963, pp. 1025–26). This is a special reminder for the Church hierarchy not to fall into ideological rigidity, or mislead the members of the Church by defining in an erroneous way the specific need for service of a certain person or number of persons as a potential threat for the integrity of faith of the community as a whole, even when the persons in need are not believers.

3.4. The Necessity of a Unified and Coherent Effort of the Orthodox Churches in the Context of Global Challenges

The third challenge for the Orthodox Church hierarchy is to find ways to allow local Churches to come together and produce a coherent message that would be translated into a visible unified effort comparable to the effort of other Churches and non-Christian institutions dedicated to the service of specific human problems: "When emphasizing the requirement of service that is to be expected from the Church as a whole, as distinguished from the personal service of each Christian, we need to take into consideration the fact of the existence of iniquities or threats of a more general order, which cannot be overcome simply by individual actions, but which require the common action of all peoples and institutions. It is the case with the contemporary world's threat of an atomic war. Tackling this threat requires the firm action of the humanity as a whole and necessitates at the same time the service of the Church, or to put it more clearly, the service of the Churches as integers (*întreguri*) in each part. There are also other problems, which inflict suffering to peoples and large numbers of human beings, and preclude the development of humanity: racial persecutions, cultural backwardness, extreme poverty and sickness of a large segment of population from different parts of our planet" [Author's transl.] (Staniloae 1963, p. 1026). Catholic and Protestant Churches have proven their ability to respond to the new problems of the humanity as a whole by coming closer to the spirit of the Orthodox understanding of service, whereas the Orthodox Churches have major difficulties in finding ways to organize themselves around the principle according to which each local Church is the whole Church manifested according to the particular political, social, or cultural settings. The solution envisaged by Staniloae is only suggested in the article dedicated to service and pro-existence, and is developed subsequently.

In the 1963 article, Staniloae believes that one reason for this insufficiency in bringing about a unified decision and action comes from the import of the distinction between Militant and Triumphant Church in the Orthodox ecclesiology, a separation abandoned by the Catholic Church at the Second Vatican Council. This distinction is damaging for the Orthodox Church in the sense that her clergy embrace either a political messianic mission, against the existing structures, or simply slip into collaboration with the political power, since at first sight, the ideology of equality and fraternity seems compatible with the mission of the Church, praising both social stability and the establishment of a social order capable of offering a certain degree of safety from the external potential threats. The second attitude, nourished by concrete social and political situations, leads local Churches to reach an "individualistic" mentality, with the consequence of arrogating for themselves in practice, although not theologically, the authority of the whole Church: "It is not for nothing that Dionysius the Areopagite assimilates the role of the three hierarchical ranks of the Church (deacons, priests, bishops) with that of the angels, something that the Book of Revelation had done with the rank of bishop (in Chapters 2 and 3), because angels themselves are servants. The 'fight' of the Christian or the Church can only be understood as service" [Author's transl.] (Staniloae 1963, p. 1026).

In another article, published in 1977, Staniloae went on to propose a theological term intended to clarify the ways in which each local Church may present herself as a representative of the Church as a whole. This term is "sinodicity" (*sinodicitate*), which he first describes as similar to the term "sobornicity" (*sobornicitate*) (Staniloae 1977, p. 611). In the field of Ecumenical studies, Dumitru Staniloae is known for having proposed the term "Open Sobornicity" to express the inclusive attitude of the Orthodox Church towards the doctrinal and spiritual advancement of the Catholic and Protestant Churches towards an Orthodox perspective (Turcescu 2002). This time, he intends the term "sinodicity" to mean not interconfessional dialogue, but the dialogue between the Orthodox Churches in their goal of regenerating the understanding of sobornicity and coming together in one coherent body. Describing the function of the bishop leading the local Church, Staniloae asserts that the bishop helps manifest the whole presence of the Church in the local part led by him, in a similar way to Christ's presence in the Eucharist: "The transformation of the gifts into the Lord's body and blood is accomplished by the priest with the invocation of the Holy Spirit, although not in isolation from the atmosphere of prayer of the community; similarly, the ordination of the bishop is accomplished by the invocation of the Holy Spirit by the ordaining hierarchs, although within the atmosphere of a liturgical community [...]. That is why, right from the initial moment of his quality and service, the bishop is 'pars in toto', not 'pars pro toto'"[Author's transl.] (Staniloae 1977, p. 613).

Thus, the bishop cannot simply substitute, in an individualistic way, the wholeness of the Church for the wholeness or the "integer" of his community. Moreover, Staniloae argues that, by virtue of this ordination accomplished by several bishops as a visible sign of the "liturgical community" across the Orthodox Churches, the bishop has the prerogative of participating in a general council "without having to receive a special empowerment from the members of the Church, although he represents the pleroma of his Church during the council and at all times." Staniloae is aware that the preparation for a "synod" of the Churches requires a considerable amount of time and work spent in creating an agreement and unity of perspective not only between the participating groups of clergy, but also an internal coherence of each local Church before the departure of the clergy to take part in the synod: "In other words, the Church prepares the statements, and is preparing herself for the resolutions to be taken by the synod, and within this framework the bishops are preparing themselves as well; and it is still up to the Church to establish later if the formula agreed upon [during the Council] corresponds to the essence of the preliminary conclusion that had emerged from her experience and reflection as it was reasoned prior to the Council" [Author's transl.] (Staniloae 1977, pp. 613–14).

This extended argument shows Dumitru Staniloae's view that a more decisive response of the Orthodox Church as a whole regarding global challenges is possible, provided that the local Churches renounce their individualistic inclinations that have affected the functioning of sobornicity, and embrace the humility of acknowledging that the ambition of a local Church to talk "pro toto", for the entire body of the Church, should be countered with the attitude of following the example of Christ who "washed the feet of his disciples and gave the parable of the Samaritan who washed the wounds of the one who fell among robbers" [Author's transl.] (Staniloae 1963, p. 1026). In the framework of Staniloae's argument, the figure of the Samaritan may account for the Catholic and Protestant Churches, since he chose to open the article dedicated to service and pro-existence with examples of their advancements in following the biblical service. The actions of the Catholic and Protestant Churches should not be overlooked by the Orthodox Church, and neither should the Orthodox Church overlook the actions of other international organizations. Given the situation created by the new international context—a situation dominated by urgent problems like nuclear threats, racial discrimination, cultural backwardness, extreme poverty, sickness, and the like—service becomes not only a desideratum, but a necessary activity of the secular international world, so that "no human being and no human organization can elude this general trend, far less the Church, as she has at her very foundation an act of boundless service" [Author's transl.] (Staniloae 1963, p. 1020). This perspective places Staniloae in a position which is incompatible to that of Aidan Nichols, who had disapproved of the idea of compatibility between the Church and other human "aggregates", with which, in Nichols's view, the Church can only have a relation of "co-existence", in spite of their philanthropic activities. As we will see further, the reason for the peculiar position of Fr. Dumitru Staniloae comes from his theological understanding of the attitude of pro-existence.

3.5. Staniloae's Specific Understanding of "Pro-Existence" and Its Implications for the Orthodox Church's Attitude to Service

If the Catholic and Protestant theologians emphasize Christ's self-sacrifice as the initiator of human pro-existence, in Staniloae's thought, the perspective is much wider: pro-existence is seen as an "ontological fact" (Staniloae 1963, p. 1027), being given by God to Adam and Eve from their creation, and it is not lost with the fall, because it has always been, in human history, closely connected to co-existence: "The term 'pro-existence' means the existence for the other. It emphasizes a certain aspect of the term 'co-existence'. 'Co-existence' means the together existence of many. But it does not express only an appended existence, but rather a certain community of existence [...]. In a way, the ones that co-exist reciprocally help each-other to exist. This community of existence is stated more clearly from a certain perspective by the term 'pro-existence'. For each of those that co-exist, to exist together with the other means also, among other meanings, to exist for the other. It is obvious that, in this way, pro-existence expresses a deeper, more fundamental engagement of each human being towards others than service, but also the want that each one has for the existence of the other. [...] 'It is not good for the man to be alone' says already the first page of the Holy Book of the Christian Revelation. 'I will make a helper suitable for him'; this is the role of a human being side by side with another human being: to be 'a helper suitable for him' (Genesis 2:18)" [Author's transl.] (Staniloae 1963, p. 1027). First of all, pro-existence is identified by Staniloae even in the attitude of co-existence, since existence for each other is unavoidable, as this is a condition of society. The dimension of pro-existence thus only serves to emphasize the existing aspect of reciprocal existence implied in co-existence. However, this doesn't mean that the minimal pro-existence included in the reciprocal help manifested with co-existence fully accounts for all the generous acts manifested in the world since the beginning of human existence. The minimal level of pro-existence included in co-existence would not explain the philanthropic acts that are carried out in the complete absence of any self-interest. Staniloae's argument for this second, autonomous level of natural pro-existence is "the want that each one has for the existence of the other".

In other words, one can feel the need to be in the presence of the others in a more practical way, the division of labor being among the aspects that would correspond to a level of "being for" included in co-existence, but it would be hard to explain by this aspect of co-existence the need to love and be loved, or the need to help and be helped in a non-selfish way, as these needs are given by God to Adam and Eve, and manifested by all human beings before Christianity. Pro-existence is an "ontological fact", asserts Dumitru Staniloae. Indeed, Staniloae admits, the ontological restoration accomplished by Christ in his pro-existent attitude enlarges the horizons of pro-existence: "The ultimate cause and finality for Christians is God" (Staniloae 1963, p. 1027).

This perspective explains Staniloae's claim that Christians should serve not only believers, but unbelievers as well, and that the service to God or worship (*leitourgia*) should not exclude service to people (*diakonia*). In another article focusing on the topic of service and published in the "Pastoral Guidance" section of the journal "Romanian Orthodox Church", being thus intended as a theological resource for priests, Fr. Staniloae argues: "By Serving people we do not give the tithe of our service to God, we do not steal from the time and full attention owed to the service of God, but actually we serve God by accomplishing His commandment" [Author's transl.] (Staniloae 1970, pp. 409–10). If the project of the Catholic theologians was to go beyond a sacrificial and legalistic understanding of Christ's pro-existential gesture of suffering death for all humankind (Deneken 1988, p. 270), Dumitru Staniloae's project was to go beyond a ritualistic understanding of worship in the Orthodox Church, which was, in his view, linked to a kind of sacrificial understanding of the service to people. If co-existence means occasionally existing for others, with the feeling of sacrificing one's own time and energy, this might appear acceptable for an Orthodox Christian, since this would involve giving the tithe of our own profit for the glory of God, but having to give the tithe of our own worship, this would seem unacceptable, first, because even if Christians prayed day and night, they would still not bring enough service to God by worship, and second, because this may engender a bad habit of choosing to sacrifice time for prayer when trying to help the other, rather than sacrificing from our private time and, thus ultimately endangering our own hope for salvation. As we have seen, Staniloae does not agree with this kind of attitude, first of all because a natural pro-existence inclines even non-Christians to carry out unselfish acts, even if they do sacrifice a large part of their own time and profit, and also because if the Christian embraces a renewed pro-existence in Christ, s/he will choose in a non-selfish way to serve God by serving the neighbor.

Furthermore, it can be argued that there is an undeniable degree of compatibility between the natural pro-existence and the Christian pro-existence, by taking into account Fr. Dumitru Staniloae's view on the place of the world as a space of communion between people and of people with God. Fr. Marc-Antoine Costa de Beauregard, who spent the summer of 1981 at the Monastery Cernica interviewing the Romanian theologian, writes that, in Staniloae's thought, the world itself becomes "a space of communion and a space of liberty", and that it is in this space that God showed that his creation is for the human being, as all the animals are brought to him as God's gift, "revealing thus the trinitarian, that is, relational form of the created space" [Author's transl.] (De Beauregard 2002, p. 149; De Beauregard 1983, pp. 169–79). Indeed, Staniloae's vision on the vocation of Christian pro-existence to embrace all natural pro-existence and co-existence with human beings, animals, and the entire material universe as a space of love can be observed from an article published in 1972: "When we share in the material goods of the universe we must be conscious that we are moving in the sphere of Christ, and that it is by making use of these material things as gifts for the benefit of one another that we progress in our union with Christ and with our neighbor. [...] Thus the universe is called to become the eschatological paradise through the agency of fraternal love. It is our duty to free the universe from the vanity of the blind and selfish use we make of it as sinners, and to see that it shares in the glory of the sons of God (Rom. 8:21), the glory which is an inseparable part of our union as brothers" (Staniloae 1980, p. 212).

It remains to be clarified why Fr. Dumitru Staniloae sees pro-existence as a deeper engagement than service. Staniloae's explanation resides in the way he defines pro-existence as compared to service:

"The term 'service' expresses a voluntary engagement. It expresses the idea that, once I exist, I can and I am obliged to work towards others. Service is added to my existence; and through service I add something to others' existence. The term 'pro-existence' expresses the fact that in my very existence is imprinted the dynamic reference towards the other, as a primary finality in this world, and that [this imprinted reference] is given and is being fulfilled through the reference of other existences towards myself. Service is nothing but the moral consequence of the ontological fact of pro-existence. If serving means working for the other, pro-existing means more: to exist for others. Pro-existence ontologically excludes egoism. Egoism is a perversion, an 'alienation' of human nature" [Author's transl.] (Staniloae 1963, p. 1027). If human beings can be forced to serve, they cannot be forced to pro-exist, since pro-existence is an ontological feature of humanity given from Creation. Moreover, we can learn how to serve, but pro-existence is fundamental to human nature. By their egoism, human beings merely deter pro-existence from manifesting itself in their hearts: "When we impeach the pro-existential impetus coming from our inner selves, we impeach the manifestation of other people's pro-existence towards us" [Author's transl.] (Staniloae 1963, p. 1029).

This assertion is essential in the context of Staniloae's advice to priests not to define the concrete problems themselves, but to wait for the persons affected by those particular problems to define them. The danger that the priest may generate is to spread fear or "individualistic" mentality among the members of the community, which would effectively deter the "pro-existential impetus" to be manifested towards those that the members of the community perceive as potential enemies. Staniloae is thus aware that an ideological reading of the neighbors' problems may reorient towards a more limited or safer manifestation of love, limited only to those we completely know and trust. However, this means advancing towards a biased understanding of the Christian imperative of love for the enemy.

There is, indeed, an important risk associated with pro-existing towards, or communing with, the enemy. Staniloae gives a series of Scriptural arguments to show that Christians should embrace this calling and face the danger, even when this means being sacrificed (John 5; 7:19; 10:10; I John 3: 14–16) (Staniloae 1963, p. 1029). Nonetheless, Christians should not be afraid of this extreme situation, because the extreme cases can be avoided by using the most characteristic medium of communication of human beings, the word: "The pro-existential character of the human person is probably nowhere manifested to such a high extent than in the word which constitutes the person's most defining and comprehensive spiritual attribute, according to the Holy Fathers' definition: the human being is an animal endowed with speech. [...] Through the word, human beings become attached to each other, they support each other, they weave connections and make communal advancements. Within the word, human beings themselves join each other, ceasing to be distant from each other. [...] This is adequately suggested by the Romanian term 'cuvânt', which comes from the Latin 'conventus', encounter, fusion, coming to the same place. [...] The word-command, when it is not covered by the authority of the whole community [...], represents an 'alienation' of the role of the word, an 'alienation' of nature from its thirst for communion and a deprivation of the chance to advancement in communion and meaning. [...] The human being has the power of refusing to serve and the capacity to use the word towards discord and disunion, and this tends to the weakening of the humanity" [Author's transl.] (Staniloae 1963, pp. 1027–28). The individualistic word does not reflect the communal liturgical experience and reasoning of the ways in which the pro-existential impetus should be expressed in actual service. Even if endowed with a special status and ministry, the members of the hierarchy cannot use the word towards strengthening their authority, and should not use their influence to predefine the problems to be tackled by the community. The concrete problems will be acknowledged directly from those who suffer and, according to the principle of sinodicity, the whole Church will become active in each particular local community thanks to an active consultation and reasoning among her members and a fraternal debate between the clerics of different localities, thus opening up the possibility of reaching a decision that would reflect the service involving all the love the community can give.

Serving Christ's brothers in need, not necessarily through a preferential treatment of some of them, but rather by using the exchanged word in order to reach to the understanding of the concrete

Churches will also discover new capabilities in bringing back the lost sheep, and make way for God's work of faith in the hearts of all humanity.

Conflicts of Interest: The author declares no conflict of interest.

References and Notes

Adler, Elisabeth, ed. 1964. *Pro-existence: Christian Voices in East Germany*. London: SCM Press LTD.

Allen, John L., Jr. 2007. CELAM update: The Lasting Legacy of Liberation Theology. *National Catholic Reporter*, May 24. Available online: https://www.ncronline.org/news/celam-update-lasting-legacy-liberation-theology (accessed on 14 March 2017).

Pope Benedict XVI (Joseph Ratzinger). 2011. *Jesus of Nazareth. Part Two: Holy Week, From the Entrance into Jerusalem to the Resurrection*. San Francisco: Ignatius Press.

Bock, Paul. 1992. Protestantism in Czehoslovakia and Poland. In *Protestantism and Politics in Eastern Europe and Russia: The Communist and Post-Communist Eras*. Edited by Sabrina Petra Ramet. Durham and London: Duke University Press, pp. 73–106.

Bonhoeffer, Dietrich. 1959. *Prisoner for God; Letters and Papers from Prison*. Edited by Eberhard Bethge. Translated by Reginald H. Fuller. New York: The Macmillan Company.

Botez, Victor. 1992. Missionaire du sacré: Une interview du Père Dumitru Staniloae. In *Philosophes Roumains; Repères Universels*. Edited by Victor Botez, Valentin F. Mihaescu and Nicolae Sarambei. Bucharest: Rédaction des Publications Pour L'étranger, pp. 200–19.

De Beauregard, Marc Antoine Costa. 1983. *Dumitru Staniloae: Ose Comprendre Que je T'aime*. Paris: Cerf.

De Beauregard, Marc-Antoine Costa. 2002. Le cosmos et la croix. In *Dumitru Staniloae: Tradition and Modernity in Theology*. Edited by Lucian Turcescu. Iasi and Oxford: The Center for Romanian Studies, pp. 147–65.

Deneken, Michel. 1988. Pour une christologie de la proexistence. *Revue des Sciences Religieuses* 62: 265–90. [CrossRef]

Gibson, David. 2015. Liberation Theology's Founder Basks in a Belated Rehabilitation under Pope Francis. *National Catholic Reporter*, May 7. Available online: https://www.ncronline.org/news/people/liberation-theologys-founder-basks-belated-rehabilitation-under-pope-francis (accessed on 14 March 2017).

Klaiber, Walter. 1997. *Call and Response: Biblical Foundations of a Theology of Evangelism*. Nashville: Abingdon, pp. 75–77. Quoted in Scott J. Jones. 2003. *The Evangelistic Love of God and Neighbor: A Theology of Witness and Discipleship*. Nashville: Abingdon Press.

Kasper, Walter. 1976. *Jesus the Christ*. Wellwood: Burns and Oates, p. 120. Quoted in Eamonn Mulcahy. *The Cause of Our Salvation: Soteriological Causality according to Some Modern British Theologians 1988–1998*. Rome: Editrice Pontificia Univesità Gregoriana, 2007.

Kasper, Walter. 1980. *Jésus, le Christ*. Paris: Cerf.

Middelmann, Udo. [1974] 2012. *Pro Existence: The Place of Man in the Circle of Reality*. Eugene: Wipf & Stock.

Nichols, Aidan. 1992. 'Non tali auxilio': John Milbank's Suation to Orthodoxy. *New Blackfriars* 73: 326–32. Quoted in Alan Thomson. 2014. *Culture in a Post-Secular Context: Theological Possibilities in Milbank, Barth and Bediako*. Cambridge: James Clarke & Co., p. 138.

Rösener, Christiane. 2002. 'Your People Shall Be My People, and Your God My God.' The Shared Life of Ruth and Naomi as a Model for Women Transgressing Intercultural Boundaries. In *Transgressors: Toward a Feminist Biblical Theology*. Edited by Claudia Janssen, Ute Ochtendung and Beate Wehn. Collegeville: The Liturgical Press, pp. 1–8.

Schillebeeckx, Edward. 2014. *Collected Works, Vol. VI: Jesus: An Experiment in Christology*. London and New York: Bloomsbury T & T Clark.

Schürmann, Heinz. 1977. *Comment Jésus A-T-Il Vécu sa Mort*. Paris: Cerf.

Sobrino, Jon. [1987] 2004. *Jesus in Latin America*. Eugene: Wipf & Stock, 2004.

Staniloae, Dumitru. 1963. Servire si Proexistenta (Service and Pro-existence). *Glasul Bisericii (The Voice of the Church)* 11–12: 1019–30.

Staniloae, Dumitru. 1970. Slujitori ai lui Dumnezeu, slujitori ai oamenilor (Servants of God, Servants of People). *Biserica Ortodoxa Romana* 3–4: 408–16.

Staniloae, Dumitru. 1977. Natura Sinodicitatii (The Nature of Sinodicity). *Studii Teologice* 9–10: 605–14.

Staniloae, Dumitru. 1980. The Orthodox Doctrine of Salvation and Its Implications for Christian Diakonia in the World. In *Theology and the Church*. Written by Dumitru Staniloae. Translated by Robert Barringer. Foreword by John Meyendorff. Crestwood: St. Vladimir's Seminary Press, pp. 181–12. Originally published in Romanian, in *Ortodoxia* 24 (1972): 195–212.

Staniloae, Dumitru. 2003a. Crestinism si traditie in viata nationala (Christianity and Tradition in the Life of the Nation). In *Dumitru Staniloae: Natiune si Crestinism*. Edited by Constantin Schifirnet. Bucharest: Clion, pp. 123–33. Originally published in *Luceafărul*, I, nr. 2,1941: 42–48.

Staniloae, Dumitru. 2003b. Prigonirea Bisericii Ortodoxe stramosesti sub comunism (The Persecution of the Orthodox Church of Our Ancestors). In *Dumitru Staniloae: Natiune si Crestinism*. Edited by Constantin Schifirnet. Bucharest: Clion, pp. 283–85. Originally published in *Ortodoxia XLII* 1 (1990): 197–200.

Turcescu, Lucian. 2002. Eucharistic Ecclesiology or Open Sobornicity? In *Dumitru Staniloae: Tradition and Modernity in Theology*. Edited by Lucian Turcescu. Iasi and Oxford: The Center for Romanian Studies, pp. 83–103.

Article

Green Patriarch, Green Patristics: Reclaiming the Deep Ecology of Christian Tradition

Elizabeth Theokritoff

Institute for Orthodox Christian Studies, Cambridge CB4 1ND, UK; e.theokritoff@some.oxon.org

Received: 23 May 2017; Accepted: 16 June 2017; Published: 30 June 2017

Abstract: In environmental circles, there is an increasing awareness of the Orthodox tradition, largely thanks to the speeches and initiatives of Patriarch Bartholomew of Constantinople. Less widely known is the considerable body of other Orthodox writing, which is less concerned with specific ecological problems, but addresses in greater depth the theological themes found in his pronouncements. This paper looks at the continuing development of Orthodox thinking in this area, and the increasing tendency to go deep into the sources of Orthodox tradition—theological, ascetic, liturgical, and hagiographic—to address underlying questions of the spiritual significance of the material world and the rôle of man within God's purposes for it. It takes as examples four themes: the unity of creation and divine presence; cosmic liturgy/eucharist and 'priest of creation'; 'ecological sin'; and asceticism. It concludes that the Orthodox tradition goes beyond the dichotomy of man and nature to offer a 'deeper ecology' in which the physical interrelations between creatures are set within the divine economy for all creation.

Keywords: Orthodox; unity of creation; cosmic liturgy; eucharistic; ecological sin; asceticism; patriarch bartholomew; deep ecology; greening of religion

---

1. Introduction

The past sixty years or so, which have seen the rise of the modern environmental movement, have simultaneously been a time of philosophical and religious soul-searching: what was it about modern Western civilisation that had triggered such environmental destruction here and now? Starting from the 1960s (though with earlier antecedents), some writers began to point the finger at monotheism and in particular Christianity. The time-line of environmental destruction, even apart from other considerations, should have raised serious questions about this diagnosis, and indeed its simplistic historical claims have been widely and repeatedly contested (Heckscher 2013, p. 138; e.g., (Khalil 1978)). Yet, 'sweeping generalisations based on unexamined assumptions' (Khalil 1978, p. 195) notwithstanding, the idea of Christianity as anti-ecological has lodged itself in the popular mind and created among environmentalists a widespread 'group think' which dismissed the Christian tradition out of hand as a possible source for solutions to the environmental crisis. On the positive side, this critique at least agrees that beliefs make a difference to the way we treat the earth. It has often been pointed out since that correlations between belief and behaviour are not straightforward (e.g., (Taylor et al. 2016; Taylor 2001, p. 279)), yet Christians have been spurred to think seriously about their faith and its implications. What is perhaps surprising is the degree to which environmentally-aware Protestants and Roman Catholics, especially the former, have accepted the negative assessment of Christian tradition, so that the widespread 'greening' of denominations and congregations often presents itself as a radical revision of traditional church practice and even doctrine (Heckscher 2013, pp. 147–49).

A striking feature of this whole story is that Orthodox Christianity is edited out of the picture almost completely. Some of the early critics of the historical rôle of Christianity did mention in passing that environmentally catastrophic practices and technologies failed to develop in the Christian East (see (Khalil 1978, pp. 193–98; Heckscher 2013, pp. 136–37)). But they then hurried on to make their case against 'Christianity' as if the Christian East did not exist; and for those who followed in their footsteps, it did not, or at best it disappeared from view after about the fourth century (Heckscher 2013). As Jurretta Heckscher has shown in a brilliant and devastating critique of this 'failure of environmental history' (Heckscher 2013), the silence surrounding Orthodox Christianity is vital to the case against 'Christianity': not just its historical record, but much more importantly the alleged 'ecological bankruptcy' of its tradition. Once Eastern Christianity is taken seriously as a continuing and vital part of the Christian tradition, the case unravels completely.

One consequence of all of this is that the rise of an ecological consciousness among the Orthodox follows a rather different path from that of Western Christianity. Orthodox would typically see the ideological roots of a damaging domination of nature as being both Western and secular, so that in our efforts to correct ecologically harmful attitudes and behaviours—and no Orthodox theologian is denying that as members of modern society, we need to do this—we are not trying to reform or reinterpret the traditional Christian understanding of man's place in the world, but to reclaim it. As the Oriental Orthodox Metropolitan Paulos mar Gregorios remarked trenchantly almost 40 years ago, the very concept of 'nature' as something over against 'man' 'became prominent in the Western tradition only in its post-Renaissance, secularist phase, when the centrality of God began to give place to anthropocentrism'. For the church Fathers, the crucial distinction lies between all that is created and God (Gregorios 1978, pp. 19, 23).

Another consequence of the above narrative is that discovering from the literature the part played by Orthodoxy can resemble the search for sub-atomic particles: the presence of Orthodoxy has to be inferred from its effects. Thus Bron Taylor, purporting to cover a broad sweep of 'religions', describes how a prominent American environmentalist repented of his 'simplistic view' that Christianity was inherently anti-nature, with no more than a bibliographic reference to the Orthodox environmental symposium that had caused the scales to fall from his eyes (Taylor 2016, p. 277, n. 11). He later discusses Pope Francis's encyclical '*Laudato Si*'' without reference to its prominent acknowledgement of the Pope's especial debt to Ecumenical Patriarch Bartholomew (§7–9), as did much of the media when the encyclical was launched with significant Orthodox participation.

In more cosmopolitan environmental circles, however, there is an increasing awareness of the Orthodox tradition largely because of the speeches and initiatives of Patriarch Bartholomew (Chryssavgis 2016, pp. 175–208), dubbed the 'Green Patriarch'. Indeed, the many symposia, seminars, and conferences that he has initiated in various parts of the world feature a remarkable roll-call of people of all faiths and none who are deeply committed to practical environmental action, but also often agree with him that the external environmental crisis is rooted in the human heart.

Some commentators would see Bartholomew's concern with the environment as an engagement with contemporary issues, and 'part of his agenda to modernise a deeply conservative church that can seem distant and insular, with its focus on long Byzantine rituals and mysticism' (Simons 2012). But the reality of Orthodox environmental thinking is a much more complex one, in which 'rituals' and 'mysticism', not to mention Byzantine theological treatises and Saints' Lives, are vital resources for reclaiming the Christian vision of creation.

It may seem curious that the Patriarch so often begins his addresses by explaining why a spiritual leader should be talking about environmental issues (e.g., (Bartholomew 2015)). His belief that environmental problems have spiritual roots and hence spiritual solutions is shared with a high proportion of grass-roots environmentalists, at least (cf. (Taylor 2001)). But Bartholomew stands out in two ways. Firstly, he is exceptionally effective in bringing that spiritual dimension to high-level secular audiences—political and economic leaders, civic and academic institutions—who are indeed accustomed to talking about the environment in terms of technology, economics, and policies. Secondly, he shows publicly and cogently that 'spiritual solutions' do not have to be sought in Eastern religions or neo-paganism, but can be deeply rooted in the Christian tradition. This is where the work of the many other Orthodox theologians to whom we shall refer below is of importance in filling in the background and showing how the ideas fit together. In the words of environmentalist Bill McKibben's jaunty Foreword to an important recent collection of Orthodox ecological writings (which I will cite repeatedly below), their work shows how the Patriarch's 'forthright activism' is not 'some personal tic' but 'an expression of an underlying spiritual tradition with deep connections to the natural world and remarkable gifts to offer' (Chryssavgis and Foltz 2013, p. xiii). Insofar as the Patriarch is 'out on a limb', in the words of his environmental advisor John Chryssavgis (in (Chryssavgis 2012, p. 20)), the 'limb' is shared by a number of Orthodox hierarchs, clergy, and lay people: pastors, theologians, and practical environmentalists, not to mention hugely influential self-effacing visionaries such as Costa Carras and the late Maria Becket.

It must also be said that there are also plenty of other Orthodox at all levels (especially, it seems, the most official) for whom 'the environment' occupies quite a separate compartment from liturgy or theology. In a 2004 encyclical addressed to his own flock, Patriarch Bartholomew states with evident frustration that Orthodox reveal their greatest vulnerability in putting theory into practice, often finding it easier to blame 'Western' development and technology (Chryssavgis 2012, p. 54). But there is a widespread if usually tacit recognition that even before practising what we preach, we need to preach what we practise: to raise awareness among Orthodox themselves of how their rich tradition of worship and theology, sacramental life and ascetic discipline, and even traditional customs encapsulates an entire view of creation as a whole and its relation to God.

A key advocate of this approach has been Metropolitan John (Zizioulas) of Pergamon, who is definitely the most systematic Orthodox thinker in ecological theology; contemporary Orthodox writers owe a considerable debt to him, whether or not they agree with him on all details. Metropolitan John has insisted from the beginning, in language often echoed by the Patriarch, that confronting the ecological problem has to be a matter of ethos rather than moral rules (Metropolitan John (Zizioulas) of Pergamon 1992, p. 28). The choices that people make must be grounded in an attitude to matter as part of our relationship with God, and this attitude is shaped above all in worship. Zizioulas' comments on the actual state of Orthodox worship (primarily addressing his own Greek tradition) are frequently scathing, which helps explain why learning from worship in turn requires a process of educating clergy and theologians.

2. Themes and Terms

Since environmental issues first emerged as a challenge to theology, there has been a subtle yet discernible shift in emphasis in the Orthodox response. The themes have changed little since the still-impressive booklet put out by Constantinople in 1990 under Patriarch Demetrios (Ecumenical Patriarchate 1990): the paradigm of the Eucharist and man's priestly role; 'God meets us in the very substance of His creation'; 'creation, ourselves included, is of God'; the whole universe offers worship; the call for repentance and asceticism; and man's responsibility under God to care for creation. Indeed, many enduring themes are already assembled in the writings of Olivier Clément in the 1950s and 1960s (Clément 1958; Clément 1967). But in statements and writings from the 1980s and 1990s, (e.g., (Limouris 1990; Ecumenical Patriarchate 1990; Belopopsky and Oikonomou 1996)) the theological themes may seem in some degree props for a call to environmental action. Since then, there has been an increasing inclination among Orthodox theologians to take a step back and explore these themes in greater theological depth, so that whatever we 'do about' environmental threats flows out of what God has done and is doing in all His creation. One might speak loosely of a growing cosmological emphasis, but it is really not a matter of focussing on the cosmos rather than man. Rather, we are talking about a vision of creation—material created being—*as a whole* in its relationship to its Creator: what the late Philip Sherrard called a 'theanthropocosmic vision' of the sacredness of ourselves and the world (Sherrard 2013, p. 218).[1]

In the language of environmental philosophy, this could be seen as a progression from a 'shallow' to a 'deep' ecological approach. This might seem a startling choice of terminology given that writers representing the Deep Ecology movement are 'typically strongly anti-Christian' (Taylor 2001, p. 294, n. 45), and promote a rigorous 'ecological egalitarianism' (Sessions 1987, p. 112) sharply at odds with the Orthodox understanding of the rôle of the human. Yet if one considers what some call the 'intuition of deep ecology' (Devall 2001, pp. 22–24)—the experience of ecological interrelatedness, of human ignorance before the complexity of nature, and an awareness of the *telos* of all beings which is to be respected (Sessions 1987, pp. 108, 112, 115)—this looks remarkably like a secularised version of the vision of all things as the creation of the infinite God before whom we stand in awe. Such a vision is the matrix within which human 'dominion' has to be understood: a fact self-evident to pre-modern Christians, but fatefully easy to overlook today. The Anglican theologian Willis Jenkins captures well the similarity, as well as the difference, between ecocentric and theocentric 'deep ecologies' when he characterises the theology of Sergei Bulgakov (with a nod to Aldo Leopold) as 'thinking like a transfigured mountain' (Jenkins 2008, pp. 207–25).

This is just one of the more unexpected ways in which Orthodox theologians, in their quest to rediscover the fullness of their own tradition, are not working in isolation from Western thought. The theological 'cosmology' of the church Fathers is a resource of great importance; but patristic texts often need to be creatively interpreted and indeed re-envisioned, not least because today's understanding of the physical world and its relationships differs so dramatically from that of the church Fathers. In the process of interpretation, contemporary Orthodox often draw wittingly (and perhaps more often unwittingly) from a wide range of Western philosophical, theological, and literary sources as well as current ecological thought; and the process of fashioning all this into a coherent whole is far from complete.

While some 'borrowings' are very felicitous, as we shall see, in seeking to apply the Church's tradition to new problems Orthodox writers also find themselves adopting expressions that do not serve well to convey Orthodox theology. A prime example would be the use of 'creation' as a pious synonym for 'the environment': originally intended, no doubt, to underline the relationship between the non-human world and God, this terminology ends up undermining the very basis of unity between man and all other creatures. It is hard to reclaim an integrated vision of creation if the available vocabulary constantly undermines it.

Another example is the continued use of 'stewardship' language, alongside statements of why it is unsatisfactory. The term seems to have become conventional shorthand for environmentally responsible behaviour, but it carries considerable theological baggage (see e.g., (Jenkins 2008, pp. 77–92, 153–87)) jarringly at odds with the bigger picture of creation and humans' place in it. The 1990 Constantinople statement (Ecumenical Patriarchate 1990) tries to introduce the very rich scriptural imagery of 'shepherd' for man's relationship to the earth, but unfortunately this failed to catch on. So what does it mean if we are forced to admit, apparently, that our day-to-day interactions with the world are just property management after all? Terminology can involve difficult choices, because ostentatious idiosyncrasies of language are best avoided; but these examples illustrate the work still to be done if we are to express the Orthodox vision in a coherent way.

Another through subtler, linguistic hurdle confronting those writing in English today is the difficulty of conveying the sense of *anthropos*, the human being/race considered as one. Metropolitan Kallistos (Ware) of Diokleia emphasises that the 'corporate character of our humanness' is today

---

[1] Zizioulas has suggested that Orthodox theological writing (in Greek) should replace the term 'cosmology' with 'ktisiology' (*ktisis* = creation) (Zizioulas 2006, p. 35). This would be rather an unmanageable neologism in English, but he is right about the need for a term that embraces all things including humans, and expresses the ontological dependence of the whole on God.

more important than ever (Metropolitan Kallistos (Ware) of Diokleia 2013, p. 100); this is a theme prominent also in Metropolitan John (Zizioulas) of Pergamon (e.g., (Metropolitan John (Zizioulas) of Pergamon 1992, pp. 22–23)). But the increasing taboo in theological publishing against the term 'man' in its generic and comprehensive sense results in subtle shifts in meaning, as authors substitute 'humans' in the plural (suggesting an aggregate of individuals), or 'the human person', or the more abstract 'humanity'.

To illustrate some of the resources in the Orthodox tradition and the way they are brought to bear on environmental problems, we will turn now to four themes prominent in Orthodox writers: the unity of all creation, humanity included, and the divine presence within it; the imagery of cosmic liturgy/eucharist and 'priest of creation'; human responsibility and Bartholomew's language of 'ecological sin', which has attracted considerable attention in recent years; and finally the key rôle of *asceticism* as the practical path to perceiving and treating all creation rightly.

3. Unity of Creation and Divine Presence

'Human beings and the environment compose a seamless garment of existence, a multi-coloured cloth which we believe to be woven in its entirety by God,' declares Patriarch Bartholomew (Chryssavgis 2003, p. 289); and again, 'the Lord suffuses all creation with His divine presence in one continuous legato from the substance of atoms to the mind of God' (Chryssavgis 2003, p. 222). Modern Orthodox thinking on the unity of creation and the relationship of all things to God can be traced back to the quest for 'pan-unity' in the 'sophiological' thought of nineteenth-century Russian religious philosophy, associated especially with the names of Vladimir Soloviev (1853–1900), Pavel Florensky (1882–1937) and Sergei Bulgakov (1871–1944) (see further (Smith and Theokritoff 2012, pp. 11–29)). Their thought can be seen as a reaction against the sort of post-Enlightenment rationalism and dualism that is often now seen as the root of the ecological crisis, and they drew their initial inspiration from Western reactions to those tendencies, adopting ideas such as 'panentheism'. The figure of 'Sophia', the divine wisdom, is invoked to account for the possibility of communion between God and His creation (see (Papanikolaou 2013a)).

It has become fashionable in theological discussions to draw a sharp distinction between this 'Russian school', and the 'neo-patristic school' in twentieth-century Orthodox theology (Papanikolaou 2013b), which is represented by Georges Florovsky and Vladimir Lossky. This schematic portrayal can be useful in elucidating the presuppositions of different writers; but it also risks misrepresenting the degree to which Orthodox today, particularly if they are not academically trained theologians, may draw on both 'sides' in their understanding of creation (sometimes with unresolved inconsistencies as a result). Certainly, the figure of 'Sophia' is viewed with suspicion by most contemporary Orthodox, finding more resonance in non-Orthodox 'eco-theology' (e.g., (Deane-Drummond 2004)), although it is less likely now to be dismissed out of hand.[2] But the underlying desire to reclaim a unified vision of creation and affirm God's presence in the material world has defined the agenda for much modern Orthodox thinking, just as the desire to re-appropriate patristic thought has largely defined the way it is pursued.

We do however find distinct differences, sometimes more in tone than in substance, which correspond to the different theological tendencies. There is the spirit we see in Olivier Clément (who draws quite extensively on the sophiological thinkers, as well as many other sources), Paul Evdokimov, or Philip Sherrard: more affective, 'mystical', and sensitive to divine presence in non-human nature. Then there is the more intellectual and philosophical approach, which is more jealous of human privilege and alive to any threat of romanticism or paganism. This is exemplified in Zizioulas and to a great extent Staniloae, and is typical of Greek academic theology and official church pronouncements. But it is noteworthy that many important writers on ecology, such as Metropolitan Kallistos (Ware)

---

[2] See for instance the discussions in Chryssavgis (1999, pp. 139–164) and Papanikolaou (2013a).

of Diokleia and John Chryssavgis, are impossible to pigeon-hole according to these categories, and Patriarch Bartholomew's work presents a veritable mosaic of the two tendencies.

Returning to the idea of the unity of creation, this understanding is no nineteenth-century invention. It is underlined, as we saw above, by Paulos mar Gregorios, drawing on Gregory of Nyssa (331–395) (Gregorios 1978, pp. 64–66). In a key passage, Gregory of Nyssa emphasises that in comparison with the exalted nature of God, all created things are inferior to the same degree (*Great Catechism* 27). Createdness is thus a bond uniting all things that exist, from molecules to man. Man, a creature who blends spiritual and material, is in a unique position, but by virtue of the unity of creaturehood it is also a *mediating* position: when man receives the divine inbreathing it is *for the sake of the whole creation*, so that nothing in creation should be deprived of a share in communion with God (*Great Catechism* 6).

This brings us to the firm conviction, no less axiomatic, that God is not only absolutely other than creation: He also pervades it. In seeking to explain how this works, the theologian that Orthodox keep coming back to is St Maximus the Confessor. It is encouraging to see that as a result, his importance is increasingly being recognised by Western eco-theologians as well (e.g., (Jenkins 2008; Southgate 2008)).

Central to Maximus' understanding of creation is the concept of the *logoi*: the 'words', rationales or essential principles of everything that exists. The *logos* of a creature expresses the creative will of God, but equally, as Bishop Kallistos Ware sums it up,

> the divine presence in that thing, God's intention for it, the inner essence of that thing, which makes it to be distinctly itself and at the same time draws it towards God. By virtue of these indwelling *logoi*, each created thing is not just an object but a personal word addressed to us by our Creator. The divine Logos, the Second Person of the Trinity, the Wisdom and the Providence of God, constitutes at once the source and the end of the particular *logoi* and in this fashion acts as an all-embracing and unifying cosmic presence (Metropolitan Kallistos (Ware) of Diokleia 2013, p. 91).

While 'existing in Himself without confusion' (*Ambiguum* 7, PG91: 1077C), the Word of God is yet wholly present in the infinite variety of creatures, and inscribed upon them as if by letters: rather as a work of art embodies the *logos* of the artist, as Patriarch Bartholomew says. This is one of three ways in which the Word of God is 'embodied', the second being in the words of Scripture. So when the Word of God in person enters into his creation by becoming incarnate, he is fulfilling a pattern laid down at the moment of creation. This is why the incarnation can be seen as a 'normative spiritual movement', as John Chryssavgis says (Chryssavgis 1999, p. 54).

The 'inscription' of the Word on all things is also what enables us to 'read' something of the Creator in his creation. This is the prime way in which all things serve to bring humans to God, the purpose being that humans will return the favour. Man was intended to be 'a natural bond' and 'a workshop of unity', bringing into harmony in his own person the divisions within creation, and ultimately uniting all creation with the Uncreated (*Ambiguum* 41, PG 91:1304D-1312B). In order to be this focus of unity, man has to be himself focused on God; when he 'inclined towards his senses from the moment of his creation' (*To Thalassius* 61, PG 90:628A), he became a force for division instead. This failure is redeemed by Christ when he comes in the flesh in order to 'fulfil the great purpose of the God the Father' and recapitulate all things in himself (Eph. 1:10).

Maximus' schema makes it abundantly clear that the human is functionally 'central' to God's purposes for creation, and equally how little this has to do with 'anthropocentrism' as 'a power-term ... imply[ing] that humanity is in the centre *without* God' (Bordeianu 2009, p. 111). As in Gregory of Nyssa, man can play this key role precisely because he shares the nature of all creation; he is *microcosm* and the world is man writ large, so that there is a correlation between their destinies (cf. (Bordeianu 2009)). It is in this spirit that Metropolitan John Zizioulas states unequivocally that 'the fact that man is also an animal is a *sine qua non* for his glorious mission in creation' (Metropolitan John (Zizioulas) of Pergamon 1990). Furthermore, the recognition of *logoi* in all creation illumines how our particular human form of 'rationality' (*logos*), far from separating us from other creatures, connects us in a unique way to the logos-filled totality. To quote Andrew Louth, '[b]ecause humans participate in the divine Logos, they are *logikoi* and therefore capable of discerning meaning, that is, logos; they are capable of discerning the logoi of creation...' (Louth 2004, p. 189). This also entails that there is no rivalry between the complexity, wisdom, and depth manifest in the human person, and those same qualities manifest 'proportionately', as Maximus would say, in the rest of creation. This license to look seriously at the workings of God in the physical universe is starting to be reflected in Orthodox writing (cf. (Knight 2007, pp. 111–123; Woloschak 2011; Theokritoff 2013)).

Many recent scholars have commented on the 'strong motivation for an ecological consciousness' provided by Maximus' vision of creation (Tollefsen 2008, p. 1), and recognised its enormous importance for those who see environmental problems as rooted in alienation from the world, and are looking for answers often anywhere but in the Christian tradition (cf. (Bordeianu 2009; Louth 2004, p. 195)). Indeed, it is striking how a 'logos cosmology' finds echoes in beliefs of indigenous religions that are sometimes seen as 'greener' *alternatives* to Christianity. Thus Fr Michael Oleksa described how the nineteenth-century Russian missionaries in Alaska 'could affirm that the spiritual realities those societies worshipped were indeed *logoi*, related to the divine *Logos*, whose personal existence these societies had simply never imagined' (Fr Michael Oleksa 1992, p. 61). Patriarch Bartholomew will sometimes talk in the same vein: speaking at his Symposium on the Amazon, he commends the belief of the indigenous people of the Amazon that all life is connected and that every living thing has what might be called its own 'logos' (Chryssavgis 2012, pp. 192, 283–84; cf. (Chryssavgis 2003, pp. 130, 243–244)). Both of them acknowledge here a process of learning from others how to re-discover our own tradition: as Oleksa writes, 'there are some insights which pre-modern societies that have become Orthodox automatically understand better than we do', in relation to 'the cosmos as ... God's icon, God's self-portrait, God's revelation to us' (Fr Michael Oleksa 1983, p. 21).

A 'logos cosmology' may offer an answer to what many people are looking for in nature-worship, but it does so without in any way compromising the absolute distinction between Creator and creation. It affirms the *paradoxical* presence of the Word who 'is not participated in in any way' (*Ambiguum 7*, PG 91: 1081B). Some writers also invoke the terminology of Gregory Palamas to affirm that 'the whole God is radically transcendent in His essence, and the whole God is radically immanent in His energies' (Bishop Metropolitan Kallistos Ware, p. 166). On the other hand, 'reading' God in creation, and thus seeing visible things as revelatory and symbolic of the divine, in no way conflicts with valuing them for themselves, since one and the same *logos* makes a thing itself, orientates it towards its Creator, and enables us to perceive Him in it. As Evdokimov says of the scriptural understanding, 'the more nature is firm, living, and full of sap in its own right, the greater is its symbolic meaning' (Evdokimov 1965, p. 7).

This vision is also clearly distinct from 'ecological egalitarianism' in its insistence that the unity of creation does not negate a special position for man; indeed, the unity of all creation with God requires it. This points to an order that is *hierarchical* in the sense used by Dionysius the Areopagite (who after all coined the term); and Eric Perl has suggested persuasively that this unfashionable concept may actually be the key to understanding the value of all creatures, the continuity between them, and the divine presence in all, without claiming that all are on the same level. In this understanding of the world, it is not that 'nature is ordered to man and man is ordered to God..., rather, all things are ordered to God, each in its own proper way' (Perl 2013, p. 29). This is an important correction, because many Orthodox would indeed subscribe to what Fr John Meyendorff (more than thirty years ago, admittedly) called 'an anthropocentric cosmology' and 'a theocentric anthropology' (Meyendorff 1983). In an 'articulated continuum', by contrast, 'the higher any being is, the more—not the less! it is in the service of ... all that is below it'. Perl suggests that this might be a 'metaphysical commentary' on Mt 20:25–27; a text that the Athonite Archimandrite Vasileios, too, has applied to human lordship of 'nature' (Archimandrite Vasileios of Iviron 2013). Perl acknowledges that it is a modern extrapolation to explore how the Areopagite's hierarchical ontology might apply to non-human material creation, but it is certainly an intriguing one.

What does it mean to live in a world thus defined by connection, among created things, and with God? Relationship is a central theme for Metropolitan John Zizioulas, and he has given more attention in recent years to the idea of relationship between *all* created things, not just humans. Drawing extensively on Maximus, he posits a 'relational ontology' that 'consists in conceiving of all that is said to exist as a constant movement of change and modification that preserves (or rather brings about?) unity and otherness at the same time' (Zizioulas 2010, p. 151). 'If we live in a relational universe', he concludes, 'not as external visitors to it but as parts of it, any individualistic approach to existence is bound to contradict not only the will of God but also the truth of our own being' (156). Although his context here is physics rather than ecology, I think the relevance is obvious. The interdependence of creatures, humans included, charted by ecological science is not only something we have to recognise to avoid disastrous physical consequences: it is something we must embrace and learn from in order to be fully human. What Zizioulas is saying here, I think, is essentially the same as Fr Lev Gillet's exhortation to 'integrate our spiritual lives with the life of the universe' (Gillet 1976, p. 19), but in a different key, and in a way less likely to be dismissed as romantic cosmicism.

4. Cosmic Liturgy: Eucharist and Priesthood

Maximus' thought is valued in modern Orthodox theology not only for its holistic character, but also for its evocation of a 'cosmic liturgy'. This term strikes such a chord with Orthodox writers that it is not infrequently attributed to Maximus himself; but like some other supposedly patristic phrases, it has a more complex history. The phrase was coined by the distinguished Roman Catholic scholar H. U. von Balthasar to describe Maximus' vision both of the Divine Liturgy and of the universe (Von Balthasar 2003), but Michael Donley has pointed out that it carries distinct echoes of the poet Paul Claudel, who was also a significant influence on Clément and on Fr Alexander Schmemann (Donley 2016, pp. 5–8).

Various strands came together to form the liturgical cosmology which is so important for much Orthodox ecological thinking. One is the ecclesial approach to cosmology, and indeed to life as a whole, which blossomed first in the Russian emigration (but can also be traced back to St Maximus) (e.g., (Lossky 1957, pp. 174–95; Evdokimov 1965)). The entire universe is called to enter into the Church, says Vladimir Lossky; it was created in order to participate in the fullness of divine life (Lossky 1957, pp. 111–13; cf. (Chryssavgis 1999, pp. 16–21)). Another strand is the liturgical renewal that began in the Russian emigration of the twentieth century, in dialogue with the liturgical movement in Roman Catholicism. The renewed liturgical consciousness was given eloquent expression in the work of Fr Alexander Schmemann, for whom sacraments reveal matter in its true reality, the world is the matter of a cosmic eucharist, and man is first and foremost *homo adorans*, a priestly figure who 'becomes himself' in offering the world back to God in thankfulness, in 'eucharist' (Schmemann 1973, p. 60). The ecological significance of the liturgical renewal begins with the rediscovery of sacramental life not as 'more or less isolated acts of the Church', but as expressions of 'the world as sacrament', 'holy materialism', and 'some healing of man's estrangement from the good creation' (Schmemann 1979, p. 221, cf. (Evdokimov 1965)). Not that Schmemann himself was thinking in terms of ecological implications, but he was trying to counter the 'progressive ... alienation of our culture ... from the Christian experience and "world view" which initially shaped that culture' (Schmemann 1973, p. 7); an 'alienation' that most Orthodox today would see as a key factor in human abuse of the world. The cosmological—and cosmic—implications of 'a universe created to become eucharist' are explored much more fully by Clément, writing at much the same time (Clément 1958; Clément 1967, p. 253; cf. (Clément 2000)); the reader should not be misled by the anthropological emphasis of his titles. The ecological relevance of such a sacramental vision, and indeed of the Incarnation in which sacraments are grounded, does come across a few years later when Archimandrite Kallistos Ware (1971) takes up themes from Schmemann and liturgical texts, including the rite perhaps most obviously emblematic of cosmic sanctification—the Great Blessing of Waters, performed in celebration of the baptism of Christ at which 'the nature of water is sanctified'. The fact that this rite is traditionally performed out-of-doors makes clearer the connection between sacrament and matter as a whole. The Blessing of Waters is not confined to the feast day, and indeed is often celebrated as part of ecological events, such as Patriarch Bartholomew's ship-board environmental symposia.

Orthodox writers have developed the liturgical approach to creation in two rather different ways. One focuses more on the Eucharist, the *offering* of *thanks,* as the paradigm for human action and attitudes, and, increasingly in recent years, on the idea of man as 'priest of creation'. The other explores the idea of praise and worship as the characteristic activity of all things, which is actually the most ancient strand in the 'liturgical' understanding of creation. Underlying these different developments we may discern different understandings of the communion between creation and God, and the degree to which it is necessarily channelled through the human being (cf. (Papanikolaou 2013a)).

The image of eucharistic offering: '[o]ffering Thee Thine own of Thine own, in all things and for all things we praise Thee, we bless Thee...', is ubiquitous in Orthodox writings on creation. 'Human beings are eucharistic animals, capable of gratitude and endowed with the power to bless God for the gift of creation', as Patriarch Bartholomew says (Chryssavgis 2012, p. 125). This is the essence of the 'eucharistic ethos' in using the world, which Bartholomew and others so often call for. The language of creation as a gift to man, worked out in some detail by Fr Dumitru Staniloae (e.g., (Staniloae 2000, pp. 21–63)) and taken up by Patriarch Bartholomew, must always be heard in the context of the *eucharistic* gifts; it never means that the world is simply handed over to humans! Everything remains 'God's own'; it is 'given' in order that we have something to give back, in order that all our use of creation should be a way of relating to a Giver. And by the same token, since it is a gift to all, the world is 'a sacrament of communion with God and neighbour' (Patriarch Bartholomew, in Chryssavgis 2003, p. 315).

In this connection, the language of man as 'priest' has been used for many years; initially, alongside that of 'king' (the primary image), prophet, mediator, and other images (e.g., (Archimandrite Kallistos Ware 1971; Lossky 1957, p. 111)). But it is a step further to couple the idea of priest/offerer with Maximus' language of the human as *bond* or *link*, to produce the image of man as 'priest of creation'. Like 'cosmic liturgy', this terminology is often attributed to the church Fathers (and increasingly, glibly cited as the traditional Orthodox view); its origins are obscure, but it probably owes more to Claudel and other modern thinkers than to any patristic writing.

It is John Zizioulas, once again, who has set out systematically the case for the language of 'priest of creation': for seeing man as a creature who, as an integral part of creation, takes creation into his hands and refers it to God, through which action creation is brought into communion with God. He argues that 'priest' should be at the very least complementary to the managerial image of 'steward': it is preferable both because it relates man to nature not by what he *does* but by what he *is,* and because it leaves room for creativity and development (Metropolitan John (Zizioulas) of Pergamon 2013; cf. (Metropolitan John (Zizioulas) of Pergamon 1996; Gregorios 1978, pp. 84–85)). There might seem to be a tension between these two justifications, and it is not obvious that 'priesthood' is the most appropriate image for the latter (see further (Theokritoff 2005)). But even if we take the metaphor on its own terms, it could be argued that Zizioulas, let alone other writers who use 'priest of creation' language much less reflectively, does not properly take account of the fact that a priest celebrates only as the representative of a congregation.

This brings us to the idea that we live in a worshipping cosmos. The modern interest in the human activity of worship brings us back to the vision of early liturgical texts (prominently including, of course, the Psalms), according to which human worship takes its place within the worship offered by all things in heaven and earth (cf. (Clément 1967, p. 290; Clément 1993, p. 193; Patriarch Bartholomew, in Chryssavgis 2012, p. 129)). Among the texts in current use, the prayers for the Great Blessing of Waters are often quoted: '[t]he sun sings Your praises; the moon glorifies You; the stars supplicate before You; the light obeys You; the deeps are afraid at Your presence, the fountains are Your servants.' It has long been recognised that such texts emphasise the cosmic dimension of worship and the sacramental quality of the world, or at the very least the potential for the material world to be 'rendered articulate in praise of God' (Bishop Kallistos Ware, p. 54); here many writers like to quote the words of Leontius of Cyprus, saying that 'creation does not venerate the Maker directly and by itself, but it is through me that the heavens declare the glory of God...'.[3] But there is some interest now in rejecting a purely anthropocentric interpretation of texts describing cosmic worship, and exploring what it means to take them more at face value (Theokritoff 2013). This includes exploring liturgical texts, some less well known, that describe the response of all created things to the incarnation of their Creator (Gschwandtner 2013; Theokritoff 2001).

Far more significant than academic studies, however, is the testimony of contemporary monasticism. The monastic tradition provides a spectacular exception to the rule-of-thumb articulated above, namely that the Greek tradition shows less 'cosmic' sensibility. When St Nectarios of Aegina (1846–1920), for instance, enables his nuns to hear the grasses praising the Lord (Clément 1967, p. 261), or the highly-respected contemporary Elder Porphyrios describes the nightingale singing in praise of God (Porphyrios 2005, p. 32), they are heirs to an extremely ancient tradition of the direct experience of that cosmic worship which human worship both emulates and affirms. In more recent centuries, this experience is often associated with the Jesus Prayer, as in the nineteenth-century Russian classic *The Way of a Pilgrim* (cited for instance in Archimandrite Bishop Kallistos Ware, p. 15). If we think of the praise from all creatures as yet another aspect of the *logos* or 'word' of each creature—'ontological praise' as Clément calls it (Clément 1967, p. 261)—then it makes perfect sense that invoking the Name of the incarnate Word of God should allow us to tune in to it. A remarkable contemporary instance is the life-changing experience of Elder Aemilianos of Simonopetra, one of the pioneers of the twentieth-century Athonite revival, and a major international influence on Orthodox spiritual life today: his night-time vision in which the stars unite themselves with the earth and everything is praying the Jesus Prayer, which leads into the celebration of the Divine Liturgy. One of his monks comments on the 'deeply ecclesial character' of this experience: the worship of all creation is 'a kind of matins service, in which creation literally responds to the call of the Psalmist' in the Lauds psalms (Fr Maximos [Constas] 2007, pp. 24–5). This has profoundly influenced the way the Elder has organised his monasteries, with daily celebrations of the Divine Liturgy, and a strong sense of the entire life of the community as a liturgy in which the whole environment joins (Aemilianos 1996).

This profound sense of all creation as *participants*, as the 'congregation' of a cosmic liturgy, is, I would suggest, the context in which the language of human 'priesthood' could be most usefully be applied. Unfortunately, however, the two approaches more often come across as *alternatives*. An exception is provided by another Athonite, Hieromonk Gregorios, who begins an essay on '[t]he cosmos as a realm of liturgy' (Gregorios 2006) with the declaration that '[m]an is the priest of God's world. When man offers the eucharistic sacrifice, the entire creation stands at his side and joins him in glorifying the Creator'. Even here, one of the recurrent difficulties with 'priest of creation' language (e.g., (Bauckham 2002)) comes up: why should man need to 'transform creation in such a way that it too sings a hymn of praise', given that it 'utters a trinitarian hymn to the Creator simply by existing'? But it later becomes apparent that Hieromonk Grgeorios is talking about the same trajectory as Elder Aemilianos: the cosmos inspires man to join it in offering praise, and man takes it forward with him so that both 'become eucharist', and thereby 'attain their appointed goal and prepare for the ultimate End'.

This eschatological framework should make it clear that the crucial rôle of man in taking all creation to its appointed end need not diminish the praise offered by all creatures, either before or since man's appearance on earth. A more cogent reservation about 'priest of creation' language concerns the idea that man has to turn the world into something of his own in order to perform his eucharistic or 'priestly' task of offering it up to God. This was emphasised in a different era by Dumitru Stanilaoe, for whom the world as gift *and task* is a central theme; and it is strongly emphasised today by Zizioulas,

---

[3]   *Fifth Homily of Christian Apologetic against the Jews, and on the Icons*, PG 93: 1604B.

who in his argument for speaking of man as 'priest of creation' talks about a development of nature not to satisfy human needs, but *for* [nature's] *own sake, in order to fulfil its own being* (Metropolitan John (Zizioulas) of Pergamon 2013, p. 170). This emphasis is one of the features that disturbs critics of 'priest of creation' language, some Orthodox among them (e.g., (Gschwandtner 2015; Theokritoff 2016)). It is of course perfectly true, as we are so often reminded, that the eucharistic elements are the fruits of the earth *shaped by man*. But they are 'shaped' and brought in by the congregation, not the priest. This just highlights the difference between saying that our attitude to the world should be eucharistic, even 'priestly', and elevating priesthood-as-creativity so that it is identified with man's function as the link between creation and God. There is an unresolved question of what it implies to take the Eucharist as our paradigm. Does it mean that everything must be transformed and 'humanised' (Staniloae 1969) before it can be offered to God? Or does it mean something that is, I would argue, more realistic and helpful: that our creative impulse, being integral to *our* nature, is not essentially in tension with the integrity of 'nature' as a whole? In practical terms, it can at least be agreed that our 'shaping' must be such that we can offer the human 'product' back to God, acknowledging it as totally His own gift. The icon, in which humans shape the matter of this world into a literal image of Christ, is the most compelling illustration of this (cf. (Aidan Hart [Monk Aidan] 1998)). But culture and daily living can equally transform matter 'into an instrument of communion with man and with God' (Metropolitan John (Zizioulas) of Pergamon 1992, p. 27), as Clément (Clément 2000) and Zizioulas both affirm. This is surely central to the environmental ethos arising out of Orthodoxy: we are not faced with the grim choice that nature will be 'either virgin or violated'; there are cultural monuments that testify to 'a mastery [that] does not obliterate, but releases prayer from things' (Clément 2000, pp. 120, 35).

5. Human Responsibility and 'Ecological Sin'

What has been said so far makes it clear that Orthodox have no compunction about affirming the importance of the human being for all creation; and that this must be sharply distinguished from an idea that *only* humans count, which Zizioulas and others describe as *anthropomonism*. Rather, it has to do with the connectedness and reciprocity built into the structure of creation.

In the big picture, 'nature needs man' for its eternal survival no less than 'man needs nature' for his physical survival (Metropolitan John (Zizioulas) of Pergamon 1997a). In explaining why, Metropolitan John Zizioulas starts from St Athanasius' account of why creation requires salvation: mortality, flux, and decay are *natural* to the created order precisely because it is created out of nothing. There should be no reason to see in this any contempt for the material world: it is a purely realistic description of the state in which all material creatures find themselves, humans no less than others. But it does mean that creation has to *transcend itself* in order to survive. And this movement, Zizioulas continues, is possible only through man, the animal in the divine image, who as *person* can realise his true self only by going beyond himself. The human is created to relate to God and to refer back to God everything he touches (Metropolitan John (Zizioulas) of Pergamon 1990).

But what happens if man fails to relate to God? The key position of man means that he also has a destructive potential exceeding the nightmares of the most misanthropic deep ecologist. Typically in Orthodox thinking, contemporary anthropogenic environmental destruction simply re-runs an ancient story: disorder, conflict, and suffering in creation have their root in human apostasy from a proper relationship to God. 'Sin has cosmic consequences ... I myself ceaselessly perpetuate the transgression of Adam and destroy the harmony of creation, by abandoning the Creator ... and in return nature turns itself against me' (Fr Makarios 1992, p. 43).

As Schmemann already reminds us, the Fall story is all about how humans use the world: whether that use is within or outside a relationship with its Creator. Adam 'chose not to be a priest but to approach the world as consumer' (Schmemann 1976, p. 96). Orthodox are generally happy using the traditional language of Genesis, whether or not they believe in a historical Fall which objectively changed the conditions of life for all earth's creatures. Others may find this unhelpful, especially as there is rarely any attempt to explore how such language may be interpreted in a world where mortality and predation evidently antedate *Homo sapiens* by millions of years. Not that such attempts are wholly absent (see e.g., (Knight 2007, pp. 86–91; Theokritoff 2009, pp. 79–88; Yannaras 2012)); and we may also note that in adopting the language of St Athanasius, Zizioulas gives us a scheme in which the Fall is a failure to transcend an *existing* state of mortality. It would be a grave mistake to see the Orthodox view as wedded to a literal interpretation of Genesis. The core intuition here is that even the condition of 'nature' is in a sense anomalous, or at least does not represent God's ultimate intention for it; and that humans hold the key to its transformation, not by their skills and technologies but through setting right their relationship with God. This would seem to be supported by the many well-attested stories of holy people, some of them our contemporaries, whose relationships with animals and their natural surroundings image in some degree a paradisal state (see e.g., (Stefanatos 1992; Ioannikios 1997; Sheehan 2013)).

The same connections underlie the services for 1 September commissioned by the former Patriarch Demetrios when he established this first day of the church year as a day of prayer for the protection of the natural environment. The Old Testament readings in the original text of the service (Belopopsky and Oikonomou 1996, Appendix) clearly link environmental calamity with human unfaithfulness to God: '[i]f you will not listen to Me... your land will be desert and your farms will be desert...' (Lev 26: 14, 33). But when, in his annual encyclical for this day, Bartholomew calls us to 'repent for our actions against God's gift to us' (Chryssavgis 2003, p. 46), this seems to be going a step further: the devastation of the land is not the *consequence* of sin but its *content*.

The Patriarch received considerable publicity (Chryssavgis 2016, pp. 176–178) by declaring in Santa Barbara in 1997 that 'committing a crime against the natural world is a sin' and enumerating examples such as climate change, pollution, and deforestation (Chryssavgis 2003, p. 221). 'Sin against nature' is avowedly a new concept, and it is not apparent that it has been fully thought through. Some of the attempts to define what it consists in, apart from wanton damage to another creature, seem on close inspection to be either circular or less than coherent. Thus it is not obvious what it means to apply the language of 'sin' to *outcomes* such as climate change, especially when they result from the *aggregate* of actions that are often individually blameless, or the least of evils, or even intended to avoid some other form of environmental damage (e.g., 'clean diesel' cars). Granted, Bartholomew does refer to voluntary *and involuntary* sins in this context (Chryssavgis 2003, p. 221). And it is both spiritually and practically important to recognise that we are implicated willy-nilly in systems and chains of events that damage the environment; we cannot pride ourselves on our green virtues and look for someone else to demonise. But it is equally important to recognise that the causes of environmental destruction are far more complex than 'corrupt, egoistic, insatiable, irresponsible, and deeply sinful conduct' stretching the earth's resources to breaking point (Chryssavgis 2003, p. 335), plus acts of deliberate disrespect to nature, all of which the Patriarch rightly decries.

This does not mean that theology has nothing useful to say about the practical causes of environmental damage. Rather, the fateful environmental consequences of even our 'best' desires and decisions can be connected with the limitations—the mortality—of the world, which Orthodox theology connects with its 'fallen' state. Helpful here is the very nuanced doctrine worked out by the Greek theologian Panayiotis Nellas based on Gregory of Nyssa, according to which all aspects of human physical and social life—marriage, work, science, politics, art etc.—are aspects of the 'garments of skin' which become man's 'second nature' after the Fall. These things are blessings that, used rightly and with restraint, enable us to regain our 'original' (intended) state; but if we 'make them autonomous' and place all our hope in them, those hopes will be dashed (Nellas 1987, pp. 46, 61, 95–96).

There is a risk that the language of 'environmental sin' wins approval from secular environmentalists for the wrong reason: because of an idea that the Church's job is to lay down moral rules (see for example the praise for the Patriarch's 'new environmental dogma' (*sic*) (Tal 2006, p. 203), with the implicit threat that they will be divinely policed. This feeds the sort of guilt-driven environmentalism that is increasingly seen as counter-productive and, more to the point, sets up a false opposition between 'human sinfulness' and 'human dignity' (cf. (Prins 2010, p. 5)).

But none of this is what Zizioulas or Bartholomew want to convey. There are two core points, which are not at all new in Orthodox theology. One is that the world serves humans as a means of their relationship with God. Inasmuch as the exploitation or destruction of nature is a refusal of this relationship (e.g., (Chryssavgis 2003, pp. 148–49)), that is by definition sin. Zizioulas actually says that 'any harm inflicted upon nature would render it incapable of performing its function as a vehicle of communion between us and with God' (Metropolitan John (Zizioulas) of Pergamon 1997b); cf. Patriarch Bartholomew, in (Chryssavgis 2003, p. 221)), which may be clarified when he goes on to say that harming nature prevents *us* fulfilling *our* relational nature. The other core point is quite simply the compassion for all creatures that flows from love of God and neighbour: Orthodox repeatedly invoke Isaac the Syrian's image of the 'merciful heart', which grieves over the slightest harm done to any creature (cf. Patriarch Bartholomew, in (Chryssavgis 2012, p. 230)). Traditionally, this would not have been seen as a moral imperative (cf. (Sophrony 1999, pp. 94–96)). Talking about 'sin' in this context is a paedagogical tool, educating the conscience by establishing as normative something that saints down the ages have discovered through a holy life: that what we self-centredly call 'our environment' is also our 'silent neighbour' (Patriarch Bartholomew, in (Chryssavgis 2012, p. 234)).

6. Asceticism

Asceticism is the third leg of the ethos that Patriarch Bartholomew so often calls for. As with the *eucharistic* and *liturgical* ethos of thankfulness and sharing, this approach takes an attitude to material things already deeply enshrined in the Christian spiritual tradition and connects it with the demands of the present environmental crisis. The ascetic way has been refined in the monastic tradition into a highly sophisticated science of the soul, and is most tangibly experienced by Christians 'in the world' in the form of fasting discipline. According to the Church's fasting rules, Orthodox abstain from meat and animal products for about half the year. Eating, that most basic interaction with the world, ceases to be a matter of individual fancy and becomes a communal event.

It was recognised some years ago that there is a remarkable coincidence between the ascetic practices of fasting and self-restraint in the use of material things, and the way of living habitually advocated by ecologists (Gschwandtner 2010): '[a]sceticism offers practical examples of conservation. By reducing our consumption—what in Orthodox theology we call *enkrateia* or self-control—we seek to ensure that resources are left to others in the world ... [a]sceticism provides an example whereby we may live simply' (Patriarch Bartholomew, in (Chryssavgis 2003, p. 219)). Asceticism teaches us to 'walk lightly on the earth' and distinguish wants from needs, providing an antidote to a 'consumerist' approach to the world (e.g., (Bishop Kallistos (Ware) of Diokleia 1996)). The direct practical effects of an ascetic 'life-style' are often emphasised; thus clergy have been known to parry questions about the environmental impact of human population by pointing out that fasting rules preclude conjugal relations on fast days.

It is important to be clear, however, that such practical bonuses resulting simply from the application of a set of rules are *not* the point of ascetic discipline. Asceticism is a process of purification; but paradoxically, as Andrew Louth points out, '[t]he personal life of struggle against temptation and growing in virtue is not simply a personal matter ... ; it is a matter of cosmic significance, for such ascetic struggle restores the human capacity of being priest of nature, interpreter of the cosmos' (Louth 2004, p. 190). We began this article with the *logoi* of all things wherein all creation, including human affairs and relationships, coheres and *makes sense*. Now we come to the practical side of this doctrine: until we purify ourselves from *passions*, our disordered appetites and desires, we are not actually able to apprehend these *logoi*. 'We tend not to see God's meaning in the world and all its parts, rather we tend to see the world in relation to ourselves and read into it *our* meaning. As a result the world becomes an arena for human conflict...' (Louth 1996, p. 37). This is what lies behind Bartholomew's words (Chryssavgis 2003, p. 214) that 'to fast is to love, to see more clearly, to restore the primal vision of creation, the original beauty of the world...'. The 'wondering and respectful distance' between us and the world, as Clément calls it (Clément 1993, p. 141), opens up to us another, very profound sense in which we receive all creation as a 'gift': it is the means whereby God speaks to us and educates us (Patriarch Bartholomew, in Chryssavgis 2012, pp. 128–42).

I believe that the 'ascetic ethos' is of enormous practical importance for dealing with the environmental crisis, but not for the more obvious, superficial reasons. First, it casts in quite a different light the 'sacrifices' that are inevitably demanded of the better-off especially in order to address large-scale environmental problems. It is not merely that a simpler life is more fulfilling, as many environmentalists have already remarked; the demands of our times cease to be an imposition and become a path of spiritual growth. The crisis itself affords us an opportunity to change the mentality that helped to cause it. Hence the Patriarch's emphasis on what he calls the 'missing dimension' of sacrifice, which he characterises as 'primarily a spiritual issue and less an economic one' (Chryssavgis 2003, pp. 304–8). The ascetic tradition turns on its head the identification of 'freedom' with 'consumer choice', which is often a barrier to environmental measures: as Metropolitan Kallistos says of fasting, 'Lent is a time when we learn to be free' and 'the process presupposes obedience, discipline and self denial' (Bishop Kallistos (Ware) of Diokleia 1996, p. 66).

The second reason why asceticism is so significant has to do with the paradox of the world. John Chryssavgis points out that the Christian vision of creation consists of three fundamental intuitions: the world is created *good*; the world is *evil*, fallen; and the world is *redeemed*. He points out that 'when one of these is either isolated or violated, the result is an unbalanced and destructive vision of the world' (Chryssavgis 1999, p. 38). The physicist and theologian Christopher Knight observes that 'on the one hand, by its stress on the effects of the Fall, the Eastern Christian tradition has tended in many respects to be more pessimistic about the empirical world than has the Western tradition. Paradoxically, however, it has in other respects been more optimistic' (Knight 2007, p. 80). The important environmental consequence of this 'pessimism' is that we are more likely to accept the limitations of the world and make fewer demands on it. This is an important antidote to the 'emphasis on human progress and achievement, together with the optimistic development of civilisation', which, as John Chryssavgis writes, will otherwise 'lead us to the post-Christian determinism that has influenced much of Western technology and culture during the last centuries' (Chryssavgis 1999, p. 41). Yet the pessimism is often overlooked because the Fall is treated quite matter-of-factly, as we saw with Nellas' 'garments of skin': it is *in the world of the Fall* that we are given the conditions that allow us to survive and attain our original goal in Christ (Nellas 1987, p. 61). And the key to using the 'fallen' world to positive effect is that characteristic ascetic virtue of *moderation* (Nellas 1987, p. 100). The paradox of creation finds its practical counterpart in the paradox of asceticism. Our fallen, dysfunctional relationship with the material world, beginning with our own bodies, has to be rejected before a proper relationship can be restored (cf. (Fr Makarios 1992)): we have to 'kill the flesh to acquire a body', in the oft-quoted words of Fr Sergei Bulgakov (cf. (Metropolitan Anthony of Sourozh 1987, p. 45)). The affirmations of harmony, order, and cosmic celebration in the natural world are not a willfully blinkered or scientifically naïve gloss on the fallen world accessible to our senses: they are statements—for most of us, taken on trust—of the world as perceived by purified senses, as received back after ascetic renunciation: the world perceived according to its *logoi*. It seems that Orthodox theologians do not always do a good job of conveying the balance between the three aspects of creation, however, since the lack of zeal among Orthodox for transforming the world by human efforts is sometimes taken to have quite the opposite meaning, and associated rather with the sunny optimism of 'creation spirituality' (e.g., (Southgate 2008, p. 112–13)).

Without denying that 'spiritualising' tendencies have sometimes found their way into the Christian ascetic tradition, Orthodox theologians have contributed significantly to an understanding of the essentially positive character of Christian asceticism: Florensky was already extolling it as being 'in love with creation' (Florensky 1997, p. 212), recalling his spiritual father whose loving care extended to uprooted weeds and broken branches (Florensky 1987, p. 71). The greatest witness to this re-discovery of the beauty of creation lies in the stories of the ascetics themselves, from the earliest anchorites of the Egyptian desert up to a present-day figure such as Amphilochios of Patmos (1889–1970), who talked of an additional commandment to 'love the trees' and was largely responsible for the dramatic re-forestation of the island (Metropolitan Kallistos (Ware) of Diokleia 2013, pp. 86–87), or the renowned Athonite Elder Paisios who could see a blade of grass as an icon, full of the energies of God. John Chryssavgis has written eloquently about the Desert Fathers who attained 'equilibrium with the whole of (their) environment' (Chryssavgis 1999, p. 95). His studies present these severe ascetics in their harsh landscape in an unexpected light: as witnesses to the sacredness of creation, characterised by a love for the land, a harmonious relationship of mutual care with the animals and even the elements, and joy, humility, and veneration of the neighbour. (Chryssavgis 1993; Chryssavgis 1999, pp. 90–118). And it is hardly a coincidence that in the Orthodox Church, monasteries have been at the forefront of implementing organic farming and conservation measures, seeing this as the most natural contemporary manifestation of the traditional relationship between monastics and their environment.

It could be objected that it is unrealistic as a 'programme' to declare, in effect, that environmental problems will be solved only if humans all become saints. Orthodox might respond that that is precisely the point: on the level of 'programmes', we are talking about palliative measures which may solve one problem, but are more than likely to create new ones. Environmental problems, like social problems, are but symptoms of a deeper imbalance in our relationship with God, and therefore with all His creation.

7. Conclusion: A Deeper Ecology?

So we see once again the Orthodox instinct to go beyond questions of 'what should we do?' to explore root causes at the deepest level. Few Orthodox would welcome the suggestion that they share this quest with 'deep ecologists': compare Patriarch Bartholomew's vehement objection that deep ecology 'classifies humanity within the natural ecosystem' and considers the human 'of equal significance with every other living being' (Chryssavgis 2003, p. 301; cf. (Bordeianu 2009, p. 107)). Yet even Bartholomew can talk elsewhere about the unique place of *all* creatures and objects, and of 'begin[ning] to see our own place within nature' as we recognise nature as a work of God (Chryssavgis 2003, p. 46). Defensive (over-)reactions to the 'ecological egalitarianism' of the Deep Ecology movement obscure the fact that 'deep questioning, right down to fundamental root causes' rather than 'technological fixes ... based on the same consumption-oriented values and methods of the industrial economy' (Drengson) is precisely the approach that typically comes out of the Orthodox tradition. Compare Bartholomew's frequent insistence that no real protection of the environment can be based on the same utilitarian logic that has led to its destruction (e.g., (Chryssavgis 2003, p. 144)). And these congruences matter, because we are talking about intuitions that resonate with millions of environmentally concerned people who would never call themselves deep ecologists, and, equally, sometimes for the reasons sketched out at the start of this paper, would never identify themselves with Christianity either.

If Orthodox have a criticism of the ecocentric emphasis of the Deep Ecology movement, it is that this is still too shallow, and too narrow; one must also take account of the divine economy, which as Bartholomew says, 'is always the solid support of ecology as a whole' (Chryssavgis 2012, p. 141). This is what gives the natural world its 'deep significance' (Chryssavgis 2003, p. 267). The notion of natural systems being embedded in the divine economy, inasmuch as the process of salvation is 'systemic and ecological in the broadest sense' (Chryssavgis and Foltz 2013, p. 4), allows man to fit into the 'system' as the sort of creature he actually is: at once physical and spiritual, able to shape and transform his surroundings far beyond what is 'natural' to other creatures, yet called to 'wonder humbly and obediently at the sacred laws *which govern the function of the microcosm* (i.e., man) *and the macrocosm*' (Chryssavgis 2003, p. 335) (my italics). This very ancient and very important principle does not refer only to physical laws (which is obvious): the point is that physical, spiritual, and moral laws mirror each other because they come from the same source.

This theological insight should, and increasingly does, allow Orthodox to draw on the wisdom of the natural world (i.e., ecology) for guidance in how to live our lives, and not only on the level of 'sustainability'. It allows us to see the natural world and its systems not just as something we take care of but as something we listen to, because it speaks to us of God who cares for all His creatures. To give the last word to another 'green hierarch' of the Orthodox Church, we can affirm that there *is* a path 'through the creation to the Creator' (Metropolitan Kallistos (Ware) of Diokleia 2013).

Conflicts of Interest: The authors declare no conflict of interest.

References

Aemilianos, Archim. 1996. The Experience of the Transfiguration in the Life of the Athonite Monk. In *Alexander Golitzin, The Living Witness of the Holy Mountain*. South Canaan: St. Tikhon's Press, pp. 194–215.

Aidan Hart [Monk Aidan]. 1998. Transfiguring Matter. The Icon as Paradigm of Christian Ecology. Available online: www.aidanharticons.com/category/articles/ (accessed on 20 May 2017).

Archimandrite Kallistos Ware. 1971. The Value of the Material Creation. *Sobornost* 6: 154–65.

Archimandrite Bishop Kallistos (Ware) of Diokleia. 1974. *The Power of the Name*. Oxford: SLG Press.

Archimandrite Vasileios of Iviron. 2013. Ecology and Monasticism. In *Towards an Ecology of Transfiguration: Orthodox Christian Perspectives on Environment, Nature and Creation*. Edited by John Chryssavgis and Bruce V. Foltz. New York: Fordham University Press, pp. 348–55.

Bartholomew. 2015. Creation Care and Ecological Justice, Address to the Oxford Union. November 4. Available online: http://www.orth-transfiguration.org/wp-content/uploads/2016/09/HAH-Creation-Care-and-Ecological-Justice.pdf (accessed on 23 March 2017).

Bauckham, Richard. 2002. Joining Creation's Praise of God. *Ecotheology* 7: 45–59. [CrossRef]

Belopopsky, Alexander, and Dimitri Oikonomou. 1996. *Orthodoxy and Ecology Resource Book*. Bialystok: Syndesmos.

Bordeianu, Radu. 2009. Maximus and ecology: The relevance of Maximus the Confessor's theology of creation for the present ecological crisis'. *Downside Review* 127: 103–26.

Bishop Kallistos (Ware) of Diokleia. 1996. Lent and the Consumer Society. In *Living Orthodoxy in the Modern World*. Edited by Andrew Walker and Costa Carras. London: SPCK, pp. 64–84.

Bishop Kallistos (Ware) of Diokleia. 1999. *The Orthodox Way*. Crestwood: St. Vladimir's Press.

Bishop Metropolitan Kallistos (Ware) of Diokleia. 2004. God immanent yet transcendent: The Divine Energies according to Saint Gregory Palamas. In *Whom We Live and Move and Have Our Being: Panentheistic Reflections on God's Presence in a Scientific World*. Edited by Philip Clayton and Arthur Peacocke. Grand Rapids and Cambridge: Eerdmans, pp. 157–68.

Chryssavgis, John. 1993. *The Sacredness of Creation'. Studia Patristica XXV*. Leuven: Peeters Press, pp. 346–51.

Chryssavgis, John. 1999. *Beyond the Shattered Image*. Minneapolis: Light and Life Publishing.

Chryssavgis, John. 2003. *Cosmic Grace, Humble Prayer: The Ecological Vision of the Green Patriarch Bartholomew I*. Grand Rapids, Michigan and Cambridge: Eerdmans.

Chryssavgis, John. 2012. *On Earth as in Heaven: Ecological Vision and Initiatives of Ecumenical Patriarch Bartholomew*. New York: Fordham University Press.

Chryssavgis, John, ed. 2016. *Bartholomew, Apostle and Visionary: Twenty-Five Years of Guiding the Christian East*. Nashville: W [Thomas Nelson].

Chryssavgis, John, and Bruce V. Foltz, eds. 2013. *Towards an Ecology of Transfiguration: Orthodox Christian Perspectives on Environment, Nature and Creation*. New York: Fordham University Press.

Clément, Olivier. 1958. L'homme dans le monde. *Verbum Caro XII* 45: 4–22.

Clément, Olivier. 1967. Le sens de la terre (Notes de cosmologie orthodoxe). *Contacts* 59–60: 252–323.

Clément, Olivier. 1993. *The Roots of Christian Mysticism*. London: New City.

Clément, Olivier. 2000. *On Human Being: A Spiritual Anthropology*. London: New City.

Deane-Drummond, Celia E. 2004. The Logos as Wisdom: A Starting Point for a Sophianic Theology of Creation. In *Whom We Live and Move and Have Our Being: Panentheistic Reflections on God's Presence in a Scientific World*. Edited by Philip Clayton and Arthur Peacocke. Grand Rapids and Cambridge: Eerdmans, pp. 233–45.

Devall, Bill. 2001. The Deep, Long-Range Ecology Movement: 1960–2000—A Review. *Ethics & the Environment* 6: 18–41.

Donley, Michael. 2016. *Claudel: Poet of the Sacred Cosmos and Prophet of a Christian Ecology*. Leominster: Gracewing.

Drengson, Alan.   n.d.   Some Thought [sic] on the Deep Ecology Movement.   Available online: http://www.deepecology.org/deepecology.htm (accessed on 28 May 2017).

Ecumenical Patriarchate. 1990. *Orthodoxy and the Ecological Crisis*. Constantinople: Ecumenical Patriarchate/WWF.

Evdokimov, Paul E. 1965. Nature. *Scottish Journal of Theology* 18: 1–22. [CrossRef]

Florensky, Pavel. 1987. *Salt of the Earth*. Platina: St Herman of Alaska Brotherhood.

Florensky, Pavel. 1997. *The Pillar and Ground of the Truth. Translated by Boris Jakim*. Princeton: Princeton University Press.

Fr Makarios. 1992. The Monk and Nature in Orthodox Tradition. In *So that God's Creation might Live*. Constantinople: Ecumenical Patriarchate, pp. 41–48.

Fr Maximos [Constas]. 2007. Charisma and Institution at an Athonite Cloister. Friends of Mount Athos Annual Report. pp. 17–34. Available online: http://www.johnsanidopoulos.com/2011/09/charisma-and-institution-at-athonite.html (accessed on 27 June 2017).

Fr Michael Oleksa. 1983. The Confluence of Church and Culture. In *Perspectives on Religious Education*. Edited by Constance Tarasar. Syosset: Syndesmos/OCA Department of Religious Education, pp. 5–26.

Fr Michael Oleksa. 1992. *Orthodox Alaska: A Theology of Mission*. Crestwood: SVS Press.

Gillet, Lev. 1976. *The Burning Bush*. Springfield: Templegate.

Gregorios, Metropolitan Paulos mar. 1978. *The Human Presence*. Geneva: WCC.

Gregorios, Hieromonk. 2006. The cosmos as a realm of liturgy. In *Synaxis: An Anthology Volume I: Environment-Anthropology-Creation*. Edited by John Hadjinicolaou. Montreal: Alexander Press, pp. 245–49.

Gschwandtner, Christina M. 2010. Orthodox ecological theology: Bartholomew I and Orthodox contributions to the ecological debate. *International Journal for the Study of the Christian Church* 10: 1–15. [CrossRef]

Gschwandtner, Christina M. 2013. "All Creation Rejoices in You": Creation in the Liturgies for the Feasts of the Theotokos. In *Towards an Ecology of Transfiguration: Orthodox Christian Perspectives on Environment, Nature and Creation*. Edited by John Chryssavgis and Bruce V. Foltz. New York: Fordham University Press, pp. 307–23.

Gschwandtner, Christina M. 2015. Creativity as Call to Care for Creation? John Zizioulas and Jean-Louis Chretien. In *Being-in-Creation: Human Responsibility in an Endangered World*. Edited by Brian Treanor, Bruce Ellis Benson and Norman Wirzba. New York: Fordham University Press, pp. 100–12.

Heckscher, Jurretta Jordan. 2013. A "tradition" that never existed: Orthodox Christianity and the Failure of Environmental History. In *Towards an Ecology of Transfiguration: Orthodox Christian Perspectives on Environment, Nature and Creation*. Edited by John Chryssavgis and Bruce V. Foltz. New York: Fordham University Press, pp. 136–51.

Ioannikios, Archimandrite. 1997. *An Athonite Gerontikon: Sayings of the Holy Fathers of Mount Athos. Translated by Maria Derpapa Mayson and Sister Theodora (Zion)*. Thessaloniki: Kouphalia.

Jenkins, Willis.   2008.   *Ecologies of Grace: Environmental Ethics and Christian Theology*.   Oxford: Oxford University Press.

Khalil, Issa J. 1978. The Ecological Crisis: An Eastern Christian Perspective. *St Vladimir's Theological Quarterly* 22: 193–211.

Knight, Christopher C. 2007. *The God of Nature*. Minneapolis: Fortress Press.

Limouris, Gennadios. 1990. *Justice, Peace and the Integrity of Creation: Insights from Orthodoxy*. Geneva: WCC.

Lossky, Vladimir. 1957. *The Mystical Theology of the Eastern Church*. London: James Clarke and Co.

Louth, Andrew. 1996. *Maximus the Confessor*. London: Routledge.

Louth, Andrew. 2004. The Cosmic Vision of Saint Maximus the Confessor. In *Whom We Live and Move and Have Our Being: Panentheistic Reflections on God's Presence in a Scientific World*. Edited by Philip Clayton and Arthur Peacocke. Grand Rapids and Cambridge: Eerdmans, pp. 184–96.

Meyendorff, John. 1983. Creation in the History of Orthodox Theology. *St Vladimir's Theological Quarterly* 27: 27–37.

Metropolitan Anthony of Sourozh. 1987. Body and Matter in Spiritual Life. In *Sacrament and Image, 3rd*. Edited by A. M. Allchin. London: Fellowship of St Alban and St Sergius.

Metropolitan Kallistos (Ware) of Diokleia. 2013. Through the Creation to the Creator. In *Towards an Ecology of Transfiguration: Orthodox Christian Perspectives on Environment, Nature and Creation*. Edited by John Chryssavgis and Bruce V. Foltz. New York: Fordham University Press, pp. 86–105.

Metropolitan John (Zizioulas) of Pergamon. 1990. Preserving God's creation (Part 3). *King's Theological Review* 13: 1–5. Available online: https://www.resourcesforchristiantheology.org/preserving-gods-creation-1/#more-130 (accessed on 25 May 2017).

Metropolitan John (Zizioulas) of Pergamon. 1992. Orthodoxy and the Problem of the Protection of the Natural Environment. In *So That God's Creation might Live, Ecumenical Patriarchate of Constantinople*. Istanbul: Ecumenical Patriarchate of Constantinople, pp. 19–28.

Metropolitan John (Zizioulas) of Pergamon. 1996. Man the Priest of Creation. In *Living Orthodoxy in the Modern World*. Edited by Andrew Walker and Costa Carras. London: SPCK, pp. 178–88.

Metropolitan John (Zizioulas) of Pergamon. 1997a. The Book of Revelation and the Natural Environment. In *Revelation and the Environment: AD 95- 1995*. Edited by Sarah Hobson and Jane Lubchenco. Singapore: World Scientific.

Metropolitan John (Zizioulas) of Pergamon. 1997b. Ecological Asceticism: A Cultural Revolution. *Sourozh* 67: 22–25.

Metropolitan John (Zizioulas) of Pergamon. 2013. Proprietors or Priests of Creation? In *Towards an Ecology of Transfiguration: Orthodox Christian Perspectives on Environment, Nature and Creation*. Edited by John Chryssavgis and Bruce V. Foltz. New York: Fordham University Press, pp. 163–71.

Nellas, Panayiotis. 1987. *Deification in Christ: Orthodox Perspectives on the Nature of the Human Person*. Crestwood: SVS Press.

Papanikolaou, Aristotle. 2013a. Creation as Communion in Contemporary Orthodox Theology. In *Towards an Ecology of Transfiguration: Orthodox Christian Perspectives on Environment, Nature and Creation*. Edited by John Chryssavgis and Bruce V. Foltz. New York: Fordham University Press, pp. 106–20.

Papanikolaou, Aristotle. 2013b. Orthodox Theology in the Twentieth Century. In *Key Theological Thinkers: From Modern to Post-Modern*. Edited by Staale Johannes Kristiansen and Svein Rise. Farnham and Burlington: Ashgate Publishing Ltd., pp. 53–64.

Perl, Eric. 2013. Hierarchy and Love in St. Dionysius the Areopagite. In *Towards an Ecology of Transfiguration: Orthodox Christian Perspectives on Environment, Nature and Creation*. Edited by John Chryssavgis and Bruce V. Foltz. New York: Fordham University Press, pp. 23–33.

Porphyrios, Elder. 2005. *Wounded by Love: The Life and Wisdom of Elder Porphyrios*. Limni: Denise Harvey.

Prins, Gwyn. 2010. The Hartwell Paper: A New Direction for Climate Policy after the Crash of 2009. Available online: http://www.lse.ac.uk/researchAndExpertise/units/mackinder/theHartwellPaper/Home.aspx (accessed on 20 May 2017).

Schmemann, Alexander. 1979. The World as Sacrament. In *Church, World, Mission*. Crestwood: SVS Press, pp. 217–27. First published in 1965.

Schmemann, Alexander. 1973. *For the Life of the World*. Crestwood: SVS Press. (American edition of The World as Sacrament. London, 1965).

Schmemann, Alexander. 1976. *Water and the Spirit*. London: SPCK.

Sessions, George. 1987. The deep ecology movement: A review. *Environmental Review* 11: 105–25. [CrossRef]

Sheehan, Donald. 2013. The Spirit of God moved upon the Face of the Waters: Orthodox Holiness and the Natural World. In *Towards an Ecology of Transfiguration: Orthodox Christian Perspectives on Environment, Nature and Creation*. Edited by John Chryssavgis and Bruce V. Foltz. New York: Fordham University Press, pp. 365–76.

Sherrard, Philip. 2013. Human Image, World Image: The Renewal of Sacred Cosmology. In *Towards an Ecology of Transfiguration: Orthodox Christian Perspectives on Environment, Nature and Creation*. Edited by John Chryssavgis and Bruce V. Foltz. New York: Fordham University Press, pp. 210–25.

Simons, Marlise. 2012. Orthodox Leader Deepens Progressive Stance on Environment. *New York Times*, December 3.

Smith, Oliver, and Elizabeth Theokritoff. 2012. Eastern Christian Thought. Introduction. In *Creation and Salvation Volume 2: A Companion on Recent Theological Movements*. Edited by Ernst M. Conradie. Zurich and Berlin: Lit Verlag.

Sophrony, Archimandrite. 1999. *Saint Silouan the Athonite*. Crestwood: SVS Press.

Southgate, Christopher. 2008. *The Groaning of Creation. God, Evolution and the Problem of Evil*. Louisville and London: Westminster John Knox Press.

Staniloae, Dumitru. 1969. The world as gift and sacrament of God's love. *Sobornost* 5: 662–73.

Staniloae, Dumitru. 2000. *The Experience of God: Orthodox Dogmatic Theology, The World: Creation and Deification*. Brookline: Holy Cross Orthodox Press, vol. 2.

Stefanatos, Joanne. 1992. *Animals and Man: A State of Blessedness*. Minneapolis: Light and Life.

Tal, Alon. 2006. *Speaking of Earth: Environmental Speeches that Moved the World*. New Brunswick: Rutgers University Press.

Taylor, Bron. 2001. Earth and Nature-based Spirituality (Part I): From Deep Ecology to Radical Environmentalism. *Religion* 31: 175–93. [CrossRef]

Taylor, Bron. 2016. The Greening of Religion Hypothesis (Part One). *Journal for the Study of Religion, Nature and Culture* 10: 268–305. [CrossRef]

Taylor, Bron, Greta van Wieren, and Bernard Zaleha. 2016. The Greening of Religion Hypothesis (Part Two): Assessing the Data from Lynn White, Jr, to Pope Francis. *Journal for the Study of Religion, Nature and Culture* 10: 306–78. [CrossRef]

Theokritoff, Elizabeth. 2001. Creation and Salvation in Orthodox Worship. *Ecotheology* 10: 97–108.

Theokritoff, Elizabeth. 2005. Creation and Priesthood in Modern Orthodox Thinking. *Ecotheology* 10: 344–63. [CrossRef]

Theokritoff, Elizabeth. 2009. *Living in God's Creation: Orthodox Perspectives on Ecology*. Crestwood: St. Vladimir's Seminary Press.

Theokritoff, Elizabeth. 2013. Liturgy, cosmic worship and Christian cosmology. In *Towards an Ecology of Transfiguration: Orthodox Christian Perspectives on Environment, Nature and Creation*. Edited by John Chryssavgis and Bruce V. Foltz. New York: Fordham University Press, pp. 295–306.

Theokritoff, Elizabeth. 2016. Priest of creation or cosmic liturgy? In *Rightly Dividing the Word of Truth: Studies in Honour of Metropolitan Kallistos of Diokleia*. Edited by Andreas Andreopoulos and Graham Speake. Oxford: Peter Lang, pp. 189–211.

Theokritoff, George. 2013. The Cosmology of the Eucharist. In *Towards an Ecology of Transfiguration: Orthodox Christian Perspectives on Environment, Nature and Creation*. Edited by John Chryssavgis and Bruce V. Foltz. New York: Fordham University Press, pp. 131–35.

Tollefsen, Torstein Theodor. 2008. *The Christocentric Cosmology of St Maximus the Confessor*. Oxford: Oxford University Press.

Von Balthasar, Hans Urs. 2003. *Cosmic Liturgy: The Universe According to Maximus the Confessor*. San Francisco: Ignatius Press.

Woloschak, Gayle. 2011. The Broad Science-Religion Dialogue: Maximus, Augustine and Others. In *Science and the Eastern Orthodox Church*. Edited by Daniel Buxhoeveden and Gayle Woloschak. Farnham and Burlington: Ashgate Publishing Ltd., pp. 133–40.

Yannaras, Christos. 2012. *The Enigma of Evil*. Brookline: Holy Cross Orthodox Press.

Zizioulas, John. 2006. Christology and Existence. The Dialectic of Created and Uncreated and the Dogma of Chalcedon. In *Synaxis: An Anthology Volume I: Environment-Anthropology-Creation*. Edited by John Hadjinicolaou. Montreal: Alexander Press, pp. 23–35.

Zizioulas, John. 2010. Relational Ontology: Insights from Patristic Thought. In *The Trinity and an Entangled World: Relationality in Physics and Theology*. Edited by John Polkinghorne. Grand Rapids and Cambridge: Eerdmans, pp. 146–56.

religions

MDPI

Article

Sex, Abortion, Domestic Violence and Other Unmentionables: Orthodox Christian Youth in Kenya and Windows into Their Attitudes about Sex

Joseph William Black [1,2]

[1] Faculty of Theology, St. Paul's University, PO Private Bag, Limuru 00217, Kenya; wblack@spu.ac.ke
[2] Makarios III Patriarchal Orthodox Seminary, Po Box 46119, Nairobi 00100, Kenya

Academic Editor: John A. Jillions
Received: 28 February 2017; Accepted: 2 April 2017; Published: 27 April 2017

Abstract: This article is based on the results of a survey of Orthodox Youth in Kenya and their attitudes about sex, abortion and domestic violence. This survey was taken of the participants of an all-Kenya Orthodox youth conference held in western Kenya in August of 2016. The results give insight into the participants' sources for first learning about sexual matters, as well as the sources that are preferred today. The youths' perception of the Orthodox Church's handling of sexual matters and sexual education is also revealed. Difficult moral issues facing Orthodox Kenyan youth are raised, such as premarital sex, domestic violence, the impact of HIV-AIDS on behavior, and responses to unintended pregnancy, with results providing insight as to how Orthodox youth are navigating the challenges facing them as they grow up into modern life both as Kenyans and as Orthodox Christians. After relating the story told by each set of survey results, conclusions are drawn from each of the issues addressed, with suggestions made as to a way forward, or further questions to pursue.

Keywords: Orthodox Church of Kenya; youth; sex; sources of information about sex; internet; pre-marital sex; domestic violence; HIV-AIDS; unintended pregnancy; abortion

---

1. Introduction

While the Orthodox Church in Kenya has existed since the 1930s, its real expansion began after the British colonial authorities ended the 10-year-long Emergency in 1962, during which the Orthodox Church had been banned and shuttered by the authorities [1]. With Kenyan independence in 1963, the Orthodox were finally able to reopen Churches, ordain clergy, buy property and build new buildings and schools. In the more than 50 years since this new start for Orthodoxy in Kenya, the Church has expanded across the country and includes more than 300 parishes, with a trained and educated clergy, along with numerous schools, clinics and development projects [2]. With such a growing number of parishes, it should not be surprising that there is a thriving youth movement throughout the Church. These young people meet on a regular basis at the parish level and also hold regional and national meetings on an annual basis. It should be noted that the word 'youth' is used in Kenya (and in many parts of sub-Saharan Africa) differently than the way it is often used in many Western countries. In the United States, for example, 'youth' is most often used to refer to those in high school or perhaps even middle school. In Kenya, 'youth' is an inclusive term that encompasses young people from puberty until even 30 years of age. One is no longer considered a 'youth' when one gets married. One of the unexpected reasons behind this extension in the age of Kenyan youth are the challenges that arise for many young men in raising sufficient funds to cover the required amount for the bride price or dowry. This is one of the major reasons why Kenyan men may wait until their late twenties or early thirties before getting married.

Delayed marriage means that youth groups in Kenya, Orthodox and otherwise, may be made up of both young teenagers and young unmarried adults. This age range presents a particular challenge to youth leaders, both in the community and in churches, who are attempting to address issues that concern all of their members. However, because this way of viewing 'youth' is a cultural given, the young people themselves do not feel out of place when participating in such groups, even though they themselves may be much older or much younger than many of the other members.

Over the period 17–21 August, 2016, a conference was held for Orthodox Youth in Serem, Nandi County, in the Diocese of Kisumu and Western Kenya. More than 500 youth attended, representing Orthodox Churches from across Kenya. The author participated in this conference as a speaker. Such a large number of Orthodox Kenyan youth gathered together presented the author with a further opportunity, to gather information on a subject that is not much discussed in Kenyan Orthodox circles, much less explored. The author decided to devise a survey that would access the attitudes of these young people with respect to a number of different issues having to do with sex and related controversial issues such as abortion and domestic violence. The survey was distributed, explained, completed, and collected during the Conference's morning session on Thursday, 18 August 2016 [3,4][1].

It must be stated at the outset that the group of youth taking this survey was not a scientifically controlled set in the traditional mold of social science research. Survey takers were self-selected participants in a Kenyan Orthodox-sponsored conference. As such, the participants were all Orthodox Christians and were all participants in local Orthodox youth groups. They were active enough in their youth ministries and motivated enough to travel to a remote spot in western Kenya for four days of meetings, speakers and fellowship. Some were leaders, others local members. Most had grown up in Orthodox Christian homes. A very few were from other Christian backgrounds.[2] The conference, which occurs annually, is considered important enough to the Orthodox Church that both the Archbishop of Nairobi, His Eminence Makarios, and the Bishop of Kisumu and Western Kenya, His Grace Athanasios, were both in attendance (His Grace Bishop Neophytos of Nyeri and Central Kenya was unable to attend at the last minute).

The wide range of ages presented a particular challenge when tabulating the results of the survey. The decision was made to tabulate the results not just according to the total responses to all of the questions, but also to separate the responses both by gender and by age range, to see if the responses were the similar across the board or if there might be any interesting differences in response, either according to age or gender. The full survey completed by the Kenyan Orthodox youth is found in Supplementary Materials.

The results of the survey were tabulated according to the following scheme:

- All respondents of both genders and all ages.
- Males of all ages
- Males 14 years old and younger
- Males 15–17 years old
- Males 18–22 years old
- Males 23–30 years old
- Males 31 and older

---

[1] This survey was opportunistic in nature and did not involve the controlled sort of sampling seen in many other social science research surveys. As a result, this survey and article are not seeking to uncover information about Kenyan youth in general, or to make scientifically verifiable statements about the attitudes of Kenyan youth on matters of sex or domestic violence. Rather this survey provides insight into what the participants in a national Orthodox youth conference in Kenya believe about these issues. Even within the limits of what a survey like this can accomplish, it will be undoubtedly useful in the hands of Kenyan Orthodox Church leaders and will be of interest to those in the wider Christian mission community and others interested in the impact of Christian values in African faith communities. For a more accurate reflection of what Kenyan youth in general believe on these issues, a more controlled study will need to be undertaken.

[2] The information contained in this paragraph was obtained informally through conversations with the conference leaders.

- Females of all ages
- Females 11–14 years old
- Females 15–17 years old
- Females 18–22 years old
- Females 23–30 years old
- Females 31 and older

There were also a number of surveys that were handed in which indicated gender but failed to indicate age. These surveys have been included under the category of Male—no age indicated; and Female—no age indicated. Their responses were included in the 'All respondents of both genders and all ages' category and in the 'Males of all ages' and 'Females of all ages' categories.

A word should be said about my choice of age range for tabulating the results of the survey. For both males and females, the age ranges follow the usual ages for the different levels of school, i.e., middle school, high school and college or university. However, this is not as straightforward as it seems, as the Kenyan government has restructured the education system recently, and plans are circulating to do so again. Moreover, age at the time of matriculation into university studies can vary wildly, with some beginning their studies immediately after their high school exams, and others delaying studies until their twenties or even thirties [5].

There are inherent challenges with any survey seeking to understand sexual behavior [6]. This is even more so in the Kenyan context, where there is an even more profound cultural reticence to discuss such matters. Turner et al. state that "We know that adults typically underreport many sexual activities and that important gender-related differences are present in the error structure of the data [7]." These researchers are commenting on studies done primarily in the United States in the context of American cultural norms and issues. Similar studies in the African context are rare, and even if there are methodological studies undertaken in South Africa, for example, the cultural contexts in Kenya or Nigeria or Senegal are so different as to make it unwise to assume that the results from a study of one or even ten African cultures can be applied to the other several thousand without significant revision [8,9].[3]

This study has a different purpose than just a contribution to the general understanding of attitudes towards sexual behavior of young people in Kenya. The context of this study is within the Orthodox Church of Kenya, and the participants are religiously active Orthodox Church members. The social science community will, of course, have an interest in the results. In addition, the leaders of the Orthodox community in Kenya (as well as other religious groups) for reasons of its own catechesis, will be keenly concerned with what this survey reveals about its youth.

2. Goals of the Survey

The survey consists of ten questions (including an initial question concerning the gender of the respondent), with both males and females answering eight questions, and then males only answering a gender-specific ninth question and females alone answering a similar but gender-specific tenth question (the survey itself may be found in Supplementary Materials below). Questions 2 and 3 are concerned with determining where the respondent gets his or her information about sex, both initially and currently. Question 4 asks when it is alright for a man and a woman to initiate sexual relations, i.e., "is premarital sex ok or not?" Questions 5 and 6 asks respondents to choose the source that is most influential in their current attitudes towards sex, be it media, culture or Church. Question 7 raises

---

[3] Researchers of sexual behavior in other non-African cultures have met with similar issues. The research team of a study among Thai students observe that "An enduring problem of research on sexual behavior and other sensitive topics is that the validity and reliability of the data collected depend on the accuracy of the answers provided by respondents who, for a variety of reasons, may not wish to disclose personal information. Indeed, there exists well-documented literature on the problems of reliability and validity of data on sexual behavior collected through standard surveys."[8]

the issue of domestic violence between a man and a woman and asks if this is always, sometimes or never acceptable. Question 8 asks if the presence of HIV-AIDS has altered the respondent's attitude and behavior with respect to sex. Finally, question 9 asks men about what their response would be if they got a woman pregnant, with choices ranging from marrying the girl to encouraging her to get an abortion. Question 10 asks a similar question of girls/women, concerning their response if a boy got them pregnant, with answers again ranging from marrying the boy to seeking an abortion.

The matter of abortion is actually what drove me to better understand the motives driving Kenyan youth and their choices concerning their own sexual behavior. I had been asked to give a talk at a local high school in a Nairobi slum. As part of my presentation I presented a kind of case study of a high school boy who got his girlfriend pregnant. I asked the students what this boy and this girl should do, and almost in unison they replied, 'Get an abortion.' I had heard anecdotally that this was becoming the preferred solution to teenage pregnancy, but I was still shocked that when given the opportunity to suggest options for this couple, the student body chose abortion. I began looking for an opportunity to explore these issues more fully, mainly as a way to help myself and others engaged in working with Kenyan youth in general and Kenyan Orthodox young people in particular better understand the moral context in which youth find themselves and to come up with more effective ways to help them cope with the increasingly terrible choices that confront them.

My observation has been that sex and related topics such as abortion and domestic violence are almost never discussed within families (an observation confirmed by the responses to this survey, as we shall see). Nor is information about sex handled effectively by schools or churches. Instead, it seems there is a vast cone of silence over this issue between the generations which is buttressed and further enabled by local societal institutions. Because of this, I wanted to find out what was actually happening in the lives of Orthodox young people, how they were getting their information, and how their sources influenced their own moral choices. Again, a survey like this does not enable one to say conclusively that Kenyan youth, or even Orthodox youth believe this and do that. However, it does provide a fascinating window into a significant sample of Orthodox young people and how they chose to answer these particular questions. It provides grounds on which to make a few tentative suggestions as to how Orthodox parishes and Orthodox leaders may respond so as to help their young people navigate increasingly stormy moral waters.[4]

3. Results

After the surveys were printed but before they were distributed, the author determined that it would also be useful to know how old the respondents were. When the surveys were distributed, I requested that everybody stop what they were doing, listen and write the number of their age at the top of the page. While some surveys were turned in without an age written on it, the vast majority did include the age of the respondent, enough to enable me to make tabulations by age as well as by gender.

The first question asks one simply to identify oneself as male or female. At least 457 Orthodox young people took part in the survey, of whom 271 or 59.3% were females and 186 or 40.7% were male.

4. Sources for Information about Sex

I was concerned to find out where the Orthodox youth attending this conference would say that they first learned about sex. I was also interested in where they currently went for information about sexual matters. To this outsider from a different culture, their responses were unexpected.

---

4   This article is not interested in arguing the morality of the various issues raised in the survey, but rather accepts as the starting point the traditional teachings on sexual and relational morality of the Orthodox Churches, not just of Kenya but globally.

Allowing that the survey's first question asked the gender of the person completing it, the survey's second question asks—"You first learned about sex from: my mother; my father; my brother; my sister; another relative; my friends; movies or TV; the internet; other (school, books, etc.)?"(Tables 1 and 2) The respondent was to choose one from that list of possible sources. What follows immediately below are the responses by the male respondents of question 2. The first column records the responses for all the males who answered. The following six columns breaks down the male responses by age.

Table 1. First Learned About Sex—All Males.

1. First learned about sex from:	All Males: all ages (186 resp)	Males 14 and younger (10 resp)	Males 15–17 (55 resp)	Males 18–22 (61 resp)	Males 23–30 (33 resp)	Males 31+ (5 resp)	Males: no Age (21 resp)
Mother	3% (6 resp)	0% (0)	0% (0)	4.9% (3)	3% (1)	20% (1)	0% (0)
Father	1.2% (2)	0% (0)	3.6% (2)	0% (0)	0% (0)	0% (0)	0% (0)
Brother	0.0% (0)	0% (0)	0% (0)	0% (0)	0% (0)	0% (0)	0% (0)
Sister	0.0% (0)	0% (0)	0% (0)	0% (0)	0% (0)	0% (0)	0% (0)
Another relative	8.6% (16)	10% (1)	1.8% (2)	3.3% (2)	9.1% (4)	0% (0)	4.8% (1)
Total for family members	12.9% (24)	10% (1)	5.5% (3)	8.2% (5)	15.2% (5)	20% (1)	4.8% (1)
My friends	44% (82)	10% (1)	47.3% (26)	47.5% (29)	33.3% (11)	60% (3)	57.1% (12)
Movies or TV	23% (42)	60% (6)	21.8% (12)	21.3% (13)	24.2% (8)	20% (1)	9.5% (2)
Internet	17% (32)	10% (1)	12.7% (7)	21.3% (13)	18.2% (6)	0% (0)	23.8% (5)
Other (school, books, etc)	7% (13)	10% (1)	12.7% (7)	1.6% (1)	9.1% (3)	0% (0)	4.8% (1)

Table 2. First Learned About Sex—All Females.

1. First Learned about sex from:	All females: all ages (271 resp)	Females 11–14 and (49 resp)	Females 15–17 (104 resp)	Females 18–22 (55 resp)	Females 23–30 (32 resp)	Females 31+ (3 resp)	Females no age (28 resp)
Mother	9.2% (25 resp)	18.4% (9)	4.8% (5)	5.5% (3)	9.4% (3)	0% (0)	17.8% (5)
Father	0.7% (2)	0% (0)	0% (0)	1.8% (1)	0% (0)	0% (0)	3.6% (1)
Brother	0.4% (1)	0% (0)	0% (0)	1.8% (1)	0% (0)	0% (0)	0% (0)
Sister	1.8% (5)	0% (0)	1.9% (2)	1.8% (1)	3.1% (1)	0% (0)	0% (0)
Another relative	2.6% (7)	6.1% (3)	1.9% (2)	1.8% (1)	0% (0)	0% (0)	0% (0)
Total for family members	14.8% (40)	26.5% (13)	8.7% (9)	12.7% (7)	12.5% (4)	0% (0)	21.4% (6)
My friends	33.9% (92)	22.4% (11)	29.8% (31)	34.5% (19)	56.3% (18)	33.3% (1)	42.9% (12)
Movies or TV	33.9% (92)	34.7% (17)	40.2% (43)	30.9% (17)	21.9% (7)	33.3% (1)	25.0% (7)
Internet	11.4% (31)	12.2% (6)	11.5% (12)	18.2% (10)	6.3% (2)	33.3% (0)	3.6% (1)
Other (school, books, etc.)	5.9% (16)	4.1% (2)	8.7% (9)	3.6% (2)	3.1% (1)	0% (0)	7.1% (2)

The striking thing emerging from the responses to this question, seen across both genders and all ages, is how few of these young people got their initial information about sex from either their mother or their father or another family member. The women had slightly elevated percentages of those who first learned about sex from their mother. Even allowing for that, more than 85% of the female respondents got their initial information about sex from outside the home or extended family. The percentage was even higher for males, with more than 87% learning about sex from sources outside the home or extended family. For both males and females, the most cited source for their initial information about sex was from friends, with media sources such as movies and TV and the internet coming in second and third, respectively, as information sources. In fact, for young women, TV, movies and the internet, taken together, were the most cited initial source of information about sex, accounting for 45.3% of the responses, whereas friends accounted for 33.9% of responses. In contrast, 44% of young men indicated that their friends were the source of their initial information about sex, while 40% got their information from media sources (movies, TV and internet). This corresponds with other studies of young people in other sub-Saharan African contexts that show friends and mass media to be the major sources of information about sex, as opposed to learning about sexual matters from parents or other relatives [10,11].

At the very least, one can say that sex is simply not discussed in the homes of the Orthodox youth represented in this survey. There are undoubtedly cultural reasons informing this silence. However, the effect is driving Orthodox youth outside the home to find other sources for their information about sex.

In a recent conversation with the principle of a local Orthodox primary school, I was told that just last week, a group of six or seven 8 year olds (both boys and girls) were discovered 'pretending to have sex' in their class room. When asked where they learned about this behavior, they said they were trying to do what dad and mom did. Many of these children live in what could be termed a slum, in houses that have one or two rooms for both parents and multiple children. Privacy in such conditions is a luxury at best, and most usually non-existent. So these children, at least, are taking what they have seen and heard at home and then trying it out with their playmates. Notice that none of the parents of these children offered to have a conversation with their children about what their son or daughter had been hearing or seeing, or offered a more age-appropriate way to understand what sex is all about. That lack of parental engagement would be consistent with the responses to question 2.

The third question of the survey asks: "Where do you go for information about sex today?" Respondents were given a list of possible answers identical to the second question. The difference was respondents were allowed to tick more than one response to allow for multiple sources of information. The responses (Tables 3 and 4) are as follows:

Given the lack of consultation with family members, particularly parents, about sex that we saw in the first question concerning one's initial information about sex, it should surprise no one that the trend continues when it comes to current sources of information about sex. With respect to this lack of parental engagement with their children with respect to sexual issues, it is worth noting that fathers in particular all but disappear from the conversation, with marginally more than 2% of males citing their fathers as sources of information about sex. Slightly more than 5% of females said their mothers were their main informants. For reasons that this survey does not reveal, mothers play a marginal role and fathers almost no role at all in their children's sex education.

Table 3. Sources of Information about Sex—All Males.

2. Sources of Information about sex today?	All males: all ages (216 resp)	Males 14 and younger (11 resp)	Males 15–17 (69 resp)	Males 18–22 (61 resp)	Males 23–30 (77 resp)	Males 31+ (5 resp)	Males: no age (20 resp)
Mother	0.9% (2 resp)	0% (0)	0% (0)	4.9% (3)	1.3% (1)	0% (0)	0% (0)
Father	2.3% (5)	0% (0)	3.6% (2)	1.4% (1)	2.6% (2)	0% (0)	0% (0)
Brother	0.5% (1)	0% (0)	0% (0)	4.3% (3)	0% (0)	0% (0)	0% (0)
Sister	0.5% (1)	0% (0)	0% (0)	1.4% (1)	1.3% (1)	0% (0)	0% (0)
Another relative	2.5% (13)	0% (0)	1.8% (2)	4.3% (3)	3.9% (3)	0% (0)	0% (0)
Total for family members	10.2% (22)	0% (0)	5.5% (3)	11.6% (8)	9.1% (7)	0% (0)	0% (0)
My friends	15.3% (33)	0% (0)	47.3% (26)	15.9% (11)	20.8% (16)	20% (1)	15% (3)
Movies or TV	23.6% (51)	27.3% (3)	21.8% (12)	21.7% (15)	26.0% (20)	40% (2)	20% (4)
Internet	45.4% (98)	63.3% (7)	12.7% (7)	42.0% (29)	39.0% (30)	40% (2)	55% (11)
Other (school, books, etc)	7.9% (17)	9.1% (1)	12.7% (7)	8.7% (6)	5.2% (4)	0% (0)	10% (2)

Table 4. Sources of Information about Sex—All Females.

3. Sources of Information about sex today?	All females: all ages (311 resp)	Females 14 and younger (56 resp)	Females 15–17 (122 resp)	Females 18–22 (60 resp)	Females 23–30 (35 resp)	Females 31+ (3 resp)	Females: no age (20 resp)
Mother	5.1% (16 resp)	16.1% (9)	1.6% (2)	3.3% (2)	0% (0)	0% (0)	0% (0)
Father	0.9% (3)	3.6% (2)	0% (0)	1.7% (1)	0% (0)	0% (0)	0% (0)
Brother	0.9% (3)	0% (0)	1.6% (2)	1.7% (1)	0% (0)	0% (0)	0% (0)
Sister	0.9% (3)	0% (0)	0.8% (1)	1.7% (1)	0% (0)	0% (0)	0% (0)
Another relative	1.9% (6)	1.8% (1)	1.6% (2)	1.7% (1)	0% (0)	0% (0)	0% (0)
Total for family members	10.0% (31)	21.4% (12)	5.7% (7)	10.0% (6)	0% (0)	0% (0)	0% (0)
My friends	18% (56)	10.7% (6)	18.9% (23)	16.7% (10)	25.7% (9)	20% (1)	0% (0)
Movies or TV	33.1% (103)	37.5% (21)	40.2% (49)	21.7% (13)	28.6% (10)	40% (2)	66.7% (2)
Internet	34.7% (108)	26.8% (15)	29.5% (36)	48.3% (29)	45.7% (16)	40% (2)	33.3% (1)
Other (school, books, etc)	4.2% (13)	3.6% (2)	5.7% (7)	3.3% (2)	0% (0)	0% (0)	0% (0)

The biggest surprise from this question is how the human factor in terms of learning about sex has been almost entirely replaced by media. When it comes to current sources of information about sex, 69% of males and 68% of females find their information from either the internet or movies and TV. With females, the divide between internet and movies/TV is about half and half. With males, the internet is almost twice as popular as TV and movies as their go-to source for information about sex (45.4% vs. 23.6%). This is actually astonishing, to me at least. Kenya is a developing country not known for its robust infrastructure. The Orthodox youth represented in this survey come from major Kenyan metropolitan areas such as Nairobi, Kisumu, Nakuru and Eldoret, but they also come from smaller towns and villages in the rural areas. Understand that these young people most likely do not have access to desktop computers or laptops; rather, they are, for the most part, using smartphones (with a few tablets thrown into the mix). Relatively inexpensive smartphones have made the internet accessible to millions of young people across Kenya, including the young people filling out this survey. It is almost a cliché now to say that this new technology is revolutionizing communications across Africa in general and Kenya in particular. That being the case, it should give one pause when almost a majority of young men are citing their smartphone-accessed internet as their current source for information about sex. Given that online information sites to answer one's questions about sex are rare, and given that internet filter usage in Kenya is even rarer, it would not be leaping to unfounded conclusions to suggest that for most of these young men, using the internet as their current source for 'information about sex' is a safe way to say that the internet is their current source for access to pornography. It would take a more specific set of questions and a more controlled set to survey to say more conclusively just what their online sources are for information about sex. While my speculation in this instance about pornography use cannot be proven on the basis of the current evidence, it is also not entirely unwarranted.

For purposes of organizing the data, it is appropriate to include question 5 in this section: "Your attitudes towards sex are influenced most by (one of the following)—what I hear on the radio or watch on TV; what I see or read on the internet; what I read in books; what my friends say; what the Church teaches; what my parents say". The results are as follows (Tables 5 and 6):

Table 5. Attitudes about Sex Most Influenced by? All Males.

5. My attitudes about sex most influenced by:	All males: all ages (179 resp)	Males 14 and younger (9 resp)	Males 15–17 (52 resp)	Males 18–22 (61 resp)	Males 23–30 (32 resp)	Males 31+ (4 resp)	Males: no age (21 resp)
Radio/TV	22.3% (40 resp)	55.6% (5)	25.0% (13)	19.7% (12)	21.9% (7)	25% (1)	9.5% (2)
Internet	43.0% (77)	33.3% (3)	36.5% (19)	36.1% (22)	53.1% (17)	25% (1)	71,4% (15)
Books	2.2% (4)	0% (0)	3.8% (2)	3.3% (2)	0% (0)	0% (0)	0% (0)
Friends	20.7% (37)	0% (0)	19.2% (10)	29.5% (18)	15.6% (5)	50% (2)	9.5% (2)
Church teaching	8.9% (16)	11.1% (1)	11.5% (6)	9.8% (6)	6.3% (2)	0% (0)	4,8% (1)
Parents	2.8% (5)	0% (0)	3.8% (2)	1.6% (1)	3.1% (1)	0% (0)	4.8% (0)

Table 6. Attitudes about Sex Most Influenced by? All Females.

5. My attitudes about sex most influenced by:	All females: All Ages (261 resp)	Females 14 and younger (50 resp)	Females 15–17 (104 resp)	Females 18–22 (54 resp)	Females 23–30 (31 resp)	Females 31+ (3 resp)	Females: no age (25 resp)
Radio/TV	28.3% (74 resp)	30% (15)	28.9.0% (30)	22.2% (12)	38.7% (12)	100% (3)	28% (7)
Internet	34.5% (90)	18% (9)	33.7% (35)	44.4% (24)	41.9% (13)	0% (0)	36% (9)
Books	5% (13)	8% (4)	6.7% (7)	0% (0)	3.2% (1)	0% (0)	4% (1)
Friends	20.3% (53)	20% (10)	21.2% (22)	22.2% (12)	9.7% (3)	0% (0)	24% (6)
Church teaching	6.5% (17)	10% (5)	5.8% (6)	7.4% (4)	6.5% (2)	0% (0)	0% (0)
Parents	5.3% (14)	14% (7)	2.9% (3)	3.7% (2)	0% (0)	0% (0)	8% (2)

The answers to this question continue to show that a majority of both males and females of all ages are looking to media, not only for answers to their questions about sex, but also for how they should think about sex. Nearly 63% of young women and 65% of young men indicated that the internet and then TV and radio carried the most influence when it came to their thinking about sex and sexual matters. Given that we have already seen that parents are rarely consulted by their children about sex, it is not surprising that only 5% of women and 3% of men considered their parents influential in shaping their perspectives on sex. What is most surprising to this observer, given that this is a survey of Orthodox youth gathered for a spiritual conference, is that 93.5% of the young women and 91.1% of the men indicated that their attitudes about sex were shaped by other factors than by Church teaching or input. Possible reasons for this include that the Churches are doing an excellent job in teaching young people about sexuality and Christian sexual behavior, but that young people are ignoring the Church's teachers and being influenced by other sources. It may be a combination of neglect on the part of Church leaders and choices to behave otherwise on the part of Orthodox youth. It could be that the Churches, like most parents, are saying nothing and doing nothing with regards to their young people and matters of sexual morality. Regardless of the reasons, even this small statistical sampling raises challenging questions for Orthodox priests and hierarchs in Kenya (and beyond) to consider, not least of which is, what are we actually teaching our young people and is it making any difference and if not, why not?

The participants in this survey had an opportunity to address their own attitudes towards the Orthodox Church and how Church leaders were handling the various issues relating to sexuality. The statement posed to them was: "When it comes to Christianity and the Church and their message about sex and relationships"—with four options from which to choose: "(1) My local Church is very clear in its teaching on sex and very supportive to me as a young person and the issues I have; (2) My local Church is very clear in its teaching about sex and relationships but is not very supportive and helpful to me as a young person and the issues I have; (3) My local Church is not very clear in its teaching about sex and relationships and is not very supportive and helpful to me as a young person and the questions that I have; (4) My local Church pretends that sex doesn't exist". In hindsight, I regret the wording of the fourth option, as sometimes sarcasm does not translate into Kenyan cultures, and sarcasm is never the best option when trying to conduct research. Also, the question itself is a difficult one, being posed to a group of people who are guests of the Church who may feel that it is to their advantage to give the 'right' answer to the question. Certainly the moral ambiguity reflected in subsequent answers raises the question of how far the responses to this question can be taken. In any case, problem or no, their answers reflect their opinion when they were given the opportunity to grade the performance of their local parishes when it comes to Christian teaching and guidance about sex (Tables 7 and 8).

Table 7. Church's Teaching about Sex—All Males.

6. My Church's teaching about sex	All males: all ages (179 resp)	Males 14 and younger (9 resp)	Males 15–17 (52 resp)	Males 18–22 (60 resp)	Males 23–30 (33 resp)	Males 31+ (5 resp)	Males: no age (20 resp)
Clear, supportive and helpful	59.8% (107 resp)	66.7% (6)	57.7% (30)	68.3% (41)	48.5% (16)	80% (4)	50% (10)
Clear but not supportive and helpful	18.4% (33)	33.3% (3)	17.3% (9)	16.7% (10)	12.1% (4)	0% (0)	35% (7)
Not clear, not supportive, not helpful	13.4% (24)	0% (0)	15.4% (8)	11.7% (7)	21.2% (7)	0% (0)	10% (2)
Sex might as well not exist as far as my parish is concerned	8.4% (15)	0% (0)	9.6% (5)	3.3% (2)	18.2% (6)	20% (1)	5% (1)
Percentage less than satisfied with the Church's input on sex	40.2%	33.3%	42.3%	31.7%	51.5%	20%	50%

Table 8. Church's Teaching about Sex—All Females.

6. My Church's teaching about sex	All females: all ages (265 resp)	Females 14 and younger (47 resp)	Females 15–17 (101 resp)	Females 18–22 (54 resp)	Females 23–30 (32 resp)	Females 31+ (3 resp)	Females: no age (28 resp)
Clear, supportive and helpful	67.5% (179 resp)	78.7% (37)	71.3% (72)	61.1% (33)	59.4% (19)	33.3% (1)	57.1% (16)
Clear but not supportive and helpful	15.4% (42)	12.8% (6)	13.9% (14)	14.8% (8)	15.6% (5)	66.7% (2)	25% (7)
Not clear, not supportive, not helpful	11.3% (30)	8.5% (4)	7.9% (8)	18.5% (10)	18.7% (6)	0% (0)	7.1% (2)
Sex might as well not exist as far as my parish is concerned	5.3% (14)	0% (0)	5.9% (6)	5.6% (3)	6.3% (2)	0% (0)	10.7% (3)
Percentage less than satisfied with the Church's input on sex	32.5%	21.3%	28.7%	38.9%	40.6%	66.7%	42.9%

Even with the prospect of some respondents feeling obligated to support their parish and not speak ill of their leaders, 40% of young men and nearly one-third of young women felt their parish was lacking when it came to providing meaningful help for youth navigating the issues of sexuality as Orthodox Christians. Given that the actual percentages of the dissatisfied may be significantly higher, and that the ones responding to this survey are the Orthodox Church of Kenya's youth leaders and most active members, these responses should at the least alert Orthodox Church leaders that all is not well with the new generation of Orthodox Christians in our parishes, and motivate these leaders to find new more effective ways to raise the children of their parishes as responsible Orthodox Christians. Young people who are dissatisfied with their Church have a tendency simply to disappear [12].[5]

5. Orthodox Youth in Kenya and Challenging Moral Issues—Premarital Sex

The remainder of the survey addresses several of the difficult moral issues facing Orthodox Christian young people. These are not issues particular to the Orthodox Churches, but they affect young people across the ethnic, economic and societal divides of Kenya. The first of these issue-oriented questions deals with premarital sex. Respondents were asked to check the statement with which they agreed. The first statement for consideration is: "A man and a woman should wait until they are married before they begin a sexual relationship." The second statement reads: "It is OK if a man and a woman want to have a sexual relationship before they are married." The results are as follows (Tables 9 and 10):

Table 9. Attitudes about Premarital Sex—All Males.

4. With respect to premarital sex	All males: all ages (181 resp)	Males 14 and younger (10 resp)	Males 15–17 (54 resp)	Males 18–22 (60 resp)	Males 23–30 (31 resp)	Males 31+ (5 resp)	Males: no age (21 resp)
Couple should wait until married before having sex.	76.2% (138 resp)	90% (9)	79.6% (43)	78.3% (47)	64.5% (20)	60% (3)	76.2% (16)
Sex before marriage is OK	23.8% (43)	10% (1)	20.4% (11)	21.7% (13)	35.5% (11)	40% (2)	23.8% (5)

Table 10. Attitudes about Premarital Sex—All Females.

4. With respect to premarital sex	All females: all ages (264 resp)	Females 14 and younger (47 resp)	Females 15–17 (102 resp)	Females 18–22 (54 resp)	Females 23–30 (32 resp)	Females 31+ (3 resp)	Females: no age (26 resp)
Couple should wait until married before having sex.	83.3% (220 resp)	87.2% (41)	86.3% (88)	83.3% (45)	81.3% (26)	100% (3)	65.4% (17)
Sex before marriage is OK	16.7% (44)	12.8% (6)	13.7% (14)	16.7% (9)	18.7% (6)	0% (0)	34.6% (9)

Given then conservative nature of Kenyan society, and the morally conservative culture that characterizes Orthodox parishes, any deviation from the bedrock moral teaching of the Church should be cause for concern. In this case, nearly a quarter of young Orthodox men have no problem with premarital sex, and almost 17% of young Orthodox women concur. Of course there are many factors at play in an issue such as premarital sex, such as the very long delays in Kenya before marriage, the sexualization of popular culture through both music, internet, film and TV, the lack of supervision for teenagers and the seeming disengagement of parents from positive roles in their children's character and moral development—all of these play a role in creating a context in which is seems impossible to make positive, intentionally Christian choices when it comes to moral issues pertaining to sexual behavior. There is also a concern as to whether the terms used in the question are fully comprehended by the respondents. An earlier survey of Kenyan youth found that less than half understood what terms such as 'abstinence' actually mean [13]. In an atmosphere of heightened religious expectations,

---

5   Other studies across other Kenyan denominations reveal a similar level of discomfort among young people concerning their church's engagement with sexual issues.

there may be a need to give the right answer to questions such as this may be perceived as more important than giving an accurate answer.

6. Orthodox Youth in Kenya and Challenging Moral Issues—Domestic Violence

Domestic violence is simply not discussed in Kenyan society. This silence is reflected in Orthodox Churches in Kenya. But as we will see, people 'keep quiet' not because domestic violence is not happening, but for reasons that are beyond what one question in a survey can unravel. The question was phrased in this manner: "Physical violence between a man and a woman is (choose one): (1) Ok. No problem; (2) Sometimes it's alright, sometimes it's wrong, depending on the situation; Or (3) Never right, always wrong." Here is how these Orthodox youth responded (Tables 11 and 12).

Table 11. Attitudes towards Domestic Violence—All Males.

7. With respect to domestic violence	All males: all ages (184 resp)	Males 14 and younger (10 resp)	Males 15–17 (53 resp)	Males 18–22 (61 resp)	Males 23–30 (33 resp)	Males 31+ (5 resp)	Males: no age (22 resp)
Physical Violence between a man and woman is OK	4.9% (9 resp)	30% (3)	3.8% (2)	3.3% (2)	3% (1)	0% (0)	4.5% (1)
Physical violence between a man and woman is sometimes all right, sometimes wrong	57.6% (106)	50% (5)	71.7% (38)	54.1% (33)	48.5% (16)	60% (3)	50% (11)
Physical violence between a man and woman is never right, always wrong	37.5% (69)	20% (2)	24.5% (13)	42.6% (26)	48.5% (16)	40% (2)	45.5% (10)

Table 12. Attitudes towards Domestic Violence—All Females

7. With respect to domestic violence	All females: all ages (267 resp)	Females 14 and younger (48 resp)	Females 15–17 (102 resp)	Females 18–22 (55 resp)	Females: 23–30 (32 resp)	Females: 31+ (3 resp)	Females: no age (27 resp)
Physical violence between a man and woman is OK	4.5% (12 resp)	12.5% (6)	2.9% (3)	5.5% (3)	0% (0)	0% (0)	0% (0)
Physical violence between a man and woman is sometimes all right, sometimes wrong	61.4% (165)	60.4% (29)	59.8% (61)	58.2% (32)	75% (24)	100% (3)	55.6% (15)
Physical violence between a man and woman is never right, always wrong	34.1% (91)	27.1% (13)	37.3% (38)	36.3% (20)	25% (8)	0% (0)	44.4% (12)

Clear majorities (more than 62%) of young men of all ages responded that physical violence between men and women was all right, given the circumstance (with a small percentage—4.9%—indicating that such violence was ok at any time). An even greater percentage of women (nearly 66%) answered that physical violence between men and women was acceptable depending on the circumstances (again with a small percentage of that number—4.5%—seeing no problem with violence between men and women at any time) [14,15]. These results were unexpected and startling, and I endeavored to find out if my question had been misunderstood or if I had misunderstood the responses or if the results were somehow simply wrong. Numerous conversations with sources within and without the Orthodox Church reassured me that the question was clear and that the results, to them, reflected reality on the ground.[6] The most-repeated explanation for the apparent prevalence of domestic violence in Orthodox marriages and families was that 'this is our culture. Indeed, the fact that young women who are presently or who stand to become the objects of physical violence at the hands of their partners think that such violence is allowable under certain circumstances indicates the likelihood of powerful cultural factors overriding fears of personal safety or personal shame in the experience of these women. If this is the case (and a better analysis of the issue may be found or forth-coming), then it means that physical violence between a man and a woman is not being addressed from the standpoint of New Testament morality or Church Tradition and teaching on the matter. It could mean that such perspectives and teachings are being ignored by the majority of Orthodox married couples. It may mean that culture rather than Orthodoxy is informing behavior in marriages, or it may be a combination of all three. The fact that a significant minority (37.5% of men and 34.1% of women) understand physical violence between men and women to be never right and always wrong may show that some Kenyan Orthodox leaders have attempted to address domestic violence and have met with some success in changing hearts and minds on the issue. However, the fact that these Kenyan Orthodox youths are so accepting of domestic violence as simply what men do to women demonstrates that there is still a considerable gap among Orthodox Christians in Kenya between Christian profession and Christian behavior, at least on this issue.

7. Orthodox Youth in Kenya and Challenging Moral Issues—The Impact of HIV-AIDs on Attitudes and Behavior

HIV-AIDS has left the headlines of western news outlets, but it is still silently spreading across Africa, infecting men who engage in risky sexual behavior (with sex workers, for example), who then unknowingly come home and infect their wife (or wives) and any children who may be born to an infected mother. Massive efforts to educate sexually active men and women concerning HIV-AIDS and how it is spread has had some success. The work of activists to push western governments into providing the latest anti-retroviral medication for those infected has meant that HIV-AIDS is not the death sentence that it once was. However, the availability of education, testing, and medication will not stop anyone who chooses to live a sexually reckless life or who lives in denial that they could become ill or even are ill. As a result, the newspapers are still full of funeral notices for young, professional-aged men and women, whose cause of death is never mentioned, but for that reason alone it is safe to suspect they died of complications to HIV-AIDS. The upshot of this is simply that HIV-AIDS is still a massive problem in Kenya and across the continent, and while great strides have been made to manage the spread of the disease and to help those who have been infected, the disease is still touching, changing and destroying lives [16].[7]

For this reason, I wanted to find out if, among a group of Orthodox Kenyan youth, there was awareness of HIV-AIDS, and whether or not the push to educate people in Africa over the past 20 years had trickled down to affect the lives of these young people. With that in mind, the eighth question is simply: "HIV-AIDS: (1) has influenced my attitude and behavior when it comes to sex; (2) is something that I think about from time to time; (3) is something I never think about". There have been many similar and more in-depth surveys covering the issue of HIV-AIDS and sexual behavior across many cultures and populations. Similar challenges are faced by almost everyone who makes use of surveys to better understand the issues [17]. The topic is considered by most to be private and by many to be even threatening. Therefore responses can be evasive, causing the conclusions to be misleading.

---

[6] Compare these attitudes with this study of actual abuse which indicates that fully 40% of married women in Kenya have experienced physical and or sexual abuse at the hands of their partner [14]. Another study indicates that more than half of the married women in rural Kenya experience domestic violence at the hands of their spouse during their lifetime [15].

[7] The circumstances that prompted widespread "Western" Christian concern for and engagement with the HIV-AIDS pandemic, especially in sub-Saharan Africa, are still very much present in Kenya and for the participants of this survey, even if certain medical advances have meant that the virus is no longer the almost certain death sentence that it was.

There are methods of interviewing that can be adopted that mitigate such responses, but the challenges are never entirely done away with. In this case, the question about HIV-AIDS and sexual behavior is one among a number of other questions, and the issue being addressed is not one of behavior but of attitude. Nevertheless, it is useful to keep in mind the wealth of experience others have when attempting to understand the very complicated situation that has arisen, especially in a Sub-Saharan country like Kenya, with respect to the ongoing impact of HIV-AIDS on the lives of young people, and even the young people of the Orthodox Church in Kenya. Here are the results for the young men (Tables 13 and 14):

Table 13. Influence of HIV-AIDS on Attitudes and Behavior About Sex—All Males.

8. HIV-AIDS ...	All males: all ages (183 resp)	Males 14 and younger (10 resp)	Males 15–17 (53 resp)	Males 18–22 (61 resp)	Males 23–30 (33 resp)	Males 31+ (5 resp)	Males: no age (21 resp)
Influences my attitude and behavior when it comes to sex	76.0% (139 resp)	70% (7)	83.0% (44)	73.8% (45)	84.8% (28)	80% (4)	52.4% (11)
Is something I think about from time to time	16.9% (31)	10% (1)	7.6% (4)	21.3% (13)	12.2% (4)	20% (1)	38.1% (8)
Is something I never think about	7.1% (13)	20% (2)	9.4% (5)	4.9% (3)	3% (1)	0% (0)	9.5% (2)

Table 14. Influence of HIV-AIDS on Attitudes and Behavior about Sex—All Females.

8. HIV-AIDS ...	All females: all ages (261 resp)	Females 14 and younger (49 resp)	Females 15–17 (98 resp)	Females 18–22 (55 resp)	Females 23–30 (29 resp)	Females 31+ (3 resp)	Females: no age (27 resp)
Influences my attitude and behavior when it comes to sex	75.9% (198 resp)	77.6% (38)	75.5% (74)	76.4% (42)	79.3% (23)	66.7% (2)	70.4% (19)
Is something I think about from time to time	13.8% (36)	18.4% (9)	11.2% (11)	10.9% (6)	17.2% (5)	33.3% (1)	14.8% (4)
Is something I never think about	10.3% (27)	4% (2)	13.3% (13)	12.7% (7)	3.4% (1)	0% (0)	14.8% (4)

8. Orthodox Youth in Kenya and Challenging Moral Issues—Youth Pregnancy and Abortion

Anecdotal evidence indicated to me that teen pregnancy was an issue, at least in the expansive Nairobi slum of Kawangware where I live. Informal discussion with local high school students and several youth pastors suggested that abortion was a more common solution to the 'problem' of teenage pregnancy than is being reported. I included the last two questions of my survey in an effort to find out if any of this was true among Orthodox youth. Because of the great stigma involved in admitting sexual behavior (even anonymously) and owning attitudes about abortion, it is difficult to know for certain how accurately the responses below reflect actual behavior, or if it merely reflects what these young people think the right response should be. Charles Nzioka, who surveyed the responses of young men in a particular district in Kenya with respect to their attitudes towards unwanted pregnancy and abortion, found that:

"In Kenya, where abortion is permitted only to save a woman's life, unsafe abortion accounts for over one-third of maternal deaths and hospital emergency rooms are overcrowded with women suffering complications of induced and spontaneous abortions. Adolescents constitute the majority of those who die or present with pregnancy-related complications due to unsafe abortion in most medical facilities in Kenya" [18].

Given the limits of this instrument, it must be left to others to devise a more precise way to resolve some of these issues. Even so, as Nzioka observes, the few studies that exist on this issue have focused mainly on the perspective of young women with regards to on pregnancy and abortion [18]. With this present study we now also have a record of how both Orthodox male and female young people from across Kenya answered questions about roles and responsibilities in pregnancy and abortion. Even so, given the cultural factors involved, it is impossible to give any assurance that the responses reflect the actual perspectives of the respondents. In the case of his own survey, Nzioka summarizes some of the challenges:

"Some young men are responsible for a proportion of unwanted pregnancies, but accurate data on the level of their involvement in causing these pregnancies is lacking and difficult to capture owing to the unwillingness on the part of young men to own up to causing these unwanted pregnancies. Relatively few young men are willing to admit to playing any role in the abortion procurement decision-making process. Young men appear to admit to fatherhood but few are ready to accept parenthood due to the heavy responsibility associated with parenting" [18].

While Nzioka's study relates to actual behavior, my questions do not require admitting responsibility but create a hypothetical situation and invite a response. In this case, the responses reflected in this survey are aspirational, carrying a sense of how one might want to respond if faced with this situation. As such, these questions are asking different things than Nzioka's. But even though 'how I might want to respond' may be different from 'how I actually responded', the way these Orthodox youth answered still gives valuable insight concerning the moral context these young people are assuming.

I posed this question to the young men completing their survey:

"If I got a girl pregnant, I would:

(1) Encourage her to carry our baby to term and take steps to marry her.
(2) Encourage her to carry our baby to term by not marry her but rather take steps to support her and the child.
(3) Break off my relationship with her.
(4) Encourage her to get an abortion and continue to have relationships with girls."

Here is how these young men answered (Table 15):

Table 15. Pregnancy Options—All Males.

9. If I got a girl pregnant:	All males: all ages (185 resp)	Males 14 and younger (10 resp)	Males 15–17 (52 resp)	Males 18–22 (63 resp)	Males 23–30 (32 resp)	Males 31+ (5 resp)	Males: no age (21 resp)
Encourage her to carry baby to term and marry her	48.6% (90 resp)	20% (2)	36.5% (19)	54% (34)	71.9% (23)	60% (3)	42.9% (9)
Encourage her to carry baby to term but not marry, support instead	42.7% (79)	30% (3)	61.5% (32)	38.1% (24)	21.9% (7)	40% (2)	52.4% (11)
Break off my relationship with her	3.8% (7)	20% (2)	3.8% (2)	1.6% (1)	3.1% (1)	0% (0)	4.7% (1)
Encourage her to get an abortion	4.8% (9)	30% (3)	1.9% (1)	6.3% (4)	3.1% (1)	0% (0)	0% (0)

Here is how these young women answered a similar set of questions (Table 16):

Table 16. Pregnancy Options—All Females.

10. If a boy got me pregnant:	All females: all ages (269 resp)	Females 14 and younger (48 resp)	Females 15–17 (103 resp)	Females 18–22 (56 resp)	Females 23–30 (32 resp)	Females 31+ (3 resp)	Females: no age (27 resp)
Want to have my baby and marry the boy	59.9% (161 resp)	47.9% (23)	58.3% (60)	60.7% (34)	62.5% (20)	66.7% (2)	63% (17)
Want to have my baby but not marry the boy	33.8% (91)	39.6% (19)	37.9% (39)	28.6% (16)	37.5% (12)	33.3% (1)	14.8% (4)
Get an abortion and continue to have relationships	6.3% (17)	12.5% (6)	3.9% (4)	1.8% (1)	0% (0)	0% (0)	22.2% (6)

The way these questions are phrased for both the young men and the young women mean the answers are aspirational—how I would want to respond, as opposed to how I have responded. One obviously would need to have a control set of respondents who were not necessarily so obviously Christian in their morality, but I suspect that if we had access to a wider sampling of young people that included those outside the circle of Christian faith, we might see the above responses as reflective of Christian self-identity—in other words, this is what one as a Christian *should* believe and do. Even so, the fact that abortion is considered an option by 4.8% of the young men and 6.3% of the young women at a gathering that is so self-consciously Christian is another way of indicating that many of these young people are getting their information about sex and morality from sources other than the Church. One wonders, if presented with the same questions in a different context, such as their local school, if the percentages would remain the same or if the numbers of those opting for abortion would be much higher [19–21]. I suspect the latter, but given the limitations of this survey, my suspicions remain just that.

9. Summary Discussion

Christian morality has always mixed with local culture in unexpected ways in places where there are churches. In the case of Kenya, Christianity was introduced from the outside by Western missionaries, for the most part. Christianity became one of the colonial-era tools for maintaining social control, both through the teaching of what was understood by the missionaries as 'Christian morality' but which was perceived by many local people as 'western morality'. Enforced by both missionary church rules and by the law of the land, Christian morality quickly began legalistic religion in the hands of many mission churches and their subsequent denominations. Morality in general, and sexual morality in particular, became a list of dos and do nots, imposed from up high, demanding conformity as opposed to culturally-sensitive application. The results have been predictable across the board in countries like Kenya, with the widespread pretense of keeping the law and widespread disregard when it comes to one's actual personal behavior. Morality as legalism has created a nation where the vast majority claim to be 'Christian' (84% according to recent surveys), but whose legalistic understanding of Christian morality has created a nation of hypocrites as well. The fear of being found out, of being hauled before a church board and sanctioned means that many people opt to keep their private, relational, sexual, and business lives separate from their religious lives. As such, Christianity never effectively touches who many of these people actually are or what they actually do.

This survey is an effort to get behind the assumptions and the religious postures and to raise questions about sexual and relational morality that are rarely if ever discussed in Orthodox Church contexts at least. The sampling is of Orthodox young people from parishes all across Kenya participating in an annual spiritual life conference. Though such a sampling is limited, it does give insight into how many Orthodox youth are thinking and behaving when it comes to matters of sexuality and relationships.

Several results (those with respect to domestic violence and unintended pregnancy, for example) call for further corroboration and a deeper study of the implications for both the individuals and the life of the Churches. Other results shed unexpected light on family dynamics, for example. It will surprise many Western readers that both parents and the Church disappear when it comes to sources from which young people learn about sex. This puts young people effectively at the mercy of the culture and of cultural morals when it comes to sex. My sources in Kenya acknowledge that this is the case and assume that this is normal. Obviously there are cultural issues at play here. However, is this a case of culture being used as an excuse for parents and local parishes not taking responsibility for teaching their own children about sex and relationships? This is not a question that I can answer for my friends who are doing the hard work of raising children in this place. But it is a question surely worth asking.

A second result concerns the immense power technology and social media are exercising over the youth of Kenya. Solid majorities of young men and young women indicate the internet (first) and movies and TV (second) are their primary sources for information about sex today. I think it is a safe assumption that using the internet for information about sex is another way of saying using the internet to gain access to pornography. The amazing and growing spread of smartphone use means that young people now have unfettered and unmonitored access to the internet. I believe it is safe to say they are not using it just to look up football scores. This should be deeply troubling to parents and to Churches. As far as I know, no Christian organizations, certainly no Orthodox ones, are providing parents and young people with help and guidance as to how to use responsibility the powerful technologies available to youth, far more powerful than anything they or any previous generation ever had. More study needs to be done to determine if access to pornography means actual use of pornography and what impact that may actually have on morality and relationships. If the results of this survey come close to measuring reality, the Orthodox youth in Kenya are in serious trouble.

A third result to highlight concerns youth satisfaction with the input on sex and relationships they have received/are receiving from their Orthodox priests and parishes. The fact that 40% of young men and 32% of young women had problems with the Church's input on these issues should be a flashing red light for Church leaders that all is not well in their parishes. Given the denial that exists on the part of priests, parents, young people and parishes on matters of sex and relationships, the fact that a random sampling of youth would put up these numbers of unhappiness means that the Church is not helping to solve the problem but is rather part of the problem. It is not the role of this paper to suggest yet more culturally-inappropriate ways of responding to this need, but rather to challenge those in positions of responsibility to help the youth under their care as Christian leaders.

A fourth result concerns the prevalence of domestic violence, even in Orthodox homes, and the assumption of the majority of young people that violence between a man and a woman, under certain circumstances, is normative. This is a classic example of the clash between Christian values and cultural values, with Christian values simply routed from the field. There is a significant minority who understand that this behavior is never right and always wrong, which is encouraging. Clearly the Church has been delinquent when it comes to explaining what love is, what marriage is, what self-sacrifice means, what loving your wife as Christ loves the Church means, etc. Even though parents are refusing to teach their children when it comes to sex, we can see that a majority of fathers (and mothers) are teaching their children all the wrong lessons about love, relationships and marriage through the ongoing battering of their spouses. Their children are learning that it is acceptable, in fact desirable to treat women badly. The Orthodox Church should be at the forefront in leading the charge against this travesty of marriage and family life. As far as I can tell, nothing is being done, nothing is being said. Once again, if we Orthodox are not part of the solution, we are a significant part of the problem.

Such a survey can, at best, provide a window into what a certain set of young people believe about the questions with which they were presented. It is hoped that this effort will provoke even better studies, which will not only provide more clarity with regards to the attitudes and behavior of

Orthodox Christians on these matters, but also even more helpful suggestions for youth, parents and Church leaders as to a way forward. The moral landscape of Kenya is changing, and the youth are the ones driving that change across the country. The fact that Orthodox youth in Kenya turn out not to be that much different from their non-Orthodox neighbors in this regard should be, for Orthodox leaders, a call to action.

Supplementary Materials: The following are available online at http://www.mdpi.com/2077-1444/8/4/73/s1.

Conflicts of Interest: The author declares no conflict of interest.

References

1. Black, Joseph William. "Offended Christians, Anti-Mission Churches and Colonial Politics: One Man's Story of the Messy Birth of the African Orthodox Church in Kenya." *Journal of Religion in Africa* 43 (2013): 261–96. [CrossRef]
2. Tillyrides, Archbishop Makarios. "Continued Growth of the Orthodox Church in Kenya for the Last 50 Years." In *Yearbook and Review 2012*. Nairobi: Greek Orthodox Archbishopric of Kenya, 2012, pp. 197–98.
3. Buga, Geoffrey A., Donald H. Amoko, and Daniel J. Ncayiyana. "Adolescent sexual behaviour, knowledge and attitudes to sexuality among school girls in Transkei, South Africa." *East African Medical Journal* 73 (1996): 95–100. [PubMed]
4. Uthman, Olalekan A., Stephen Lawoko, and Tahereh Moradi. "Sex disparities in attitudes towards intimate partner violence against women in sub-Saharan Africa: A socio-ecological analysis." *BMC Public Health* 10 (2010): 223–31. [CrossRef] [PubMed]
5. Embassy of the Republic of Kenya. "Education in Kenya." Available online: https://www.kenyaembassy.com/aboutkenyaeducation.html (accessed on 2 February 2017).
6. Parker, Richard. "International Perspectives on Sexuality Research." In *Researching Sexual Behavior: Methodological Issues*. Edited by John Bancroft. Bloomington: Indiana University Press, 1997, pp. 9–20.
7. Turner, Charles, Heather G. Miller, and Susan M. Rogers. "Survey Measurement of Sexual Behavior: Problems and Progress." In *Researching Sexual Behavior: Methodological Issues*. Edited by John Bancroft. Bloomington: Indiana University Press, 1997, pp. 37–60.
8. Rumakom, Patchara, Philip Guest, Waranuch Chinvarasopak, Watit Utarmat, and Jiraporn Sontanakanit. "Obtaining Accurate Responses to Sensitive Questions among Thai Students: A Comparison of Two Data Collecting Techniques." In *Sex without Consent: Young People in Developing Countries*. Edited by Shireen J. Jejeebhoy, Iqbal Shah and Shyam Thapa. London: Zed Books, 2005, pp. 318–32.
9. Dare, O. O., and J. G. Cleland. "Reliability and Validity of Survey Data on Sexual Behavior." *Health Transition Review* 4 (1994): 93–110. [PubMed]
10. Bankole, Akrinrinola, Ann Biddlecom, Georges Guiella, Susheela Singh, and Eliya Zulu. "Sexual Behavior, Knowledge and Information Sources of Very Young Adolescnts in Four Sub-Saharan African Countries." *African Journal of Reproductive Health* 11 (2007): 28–43. Available online: https://www.ncbi.nlm.nih.gov/pmc/articles/PMC2367131/ (accessed on 28 February 2017). [CrossRef] [PubMed]
11. Crichton, Joanna, Latifat Ibisomi, and Stephen Obeng Gyimah. "Mother-daughter Communication about Sexual Maturation, Abstinence and Unintended Pregnancy: Experiences from an Informal Settlement in Nairobi, Kenya." *Journal of Adolescence* 35 (2012): 21–30. [CrossRef] [PubMed]
12. Kangara, Lucy. "Youth, Church, and Sexuality in Kenya." *Post-Sexuality Leadership Development Fellowship Report Series* 7 (2004): 1–33. Available online: http://www.arsrc.org/downloads/sldf/FinalReportLucyKangara2004.pdf (accessed on 3 February 2017).
13. Pulerwitz, Julie, and Barbara Curbow. "Kenyan In-School Youths' Level of Understanding of Abstinence, Being Faithful, and Consistent Condom Use Terms: Implications for HIV-Prevention Programs." *Journal of Health Communication—International Perspectives* 14 (2009): 276–92.
14. Kimuna, Sitawa R., and Yanyi K. Djamba. "Gender-based Violence: Correlates of Physical and Sexual Wife Abuse in Kenya." *Journal of Family Violence* 23 (2008): 333–42. [CrossRef]
15. Hatcher, Abigail M., Patrizia Romito, Merab Odero, Elizabeth A. Bukusi, Maricianah Onono, and Janet M. Turan. "Social Context and Drivers of Intimate Partner Violence in Rural Kenya: Implications for the Health of Pregnant Women." *Culture, Health and Sexuality* 15 (2013): 404–19. [CrossRef] [PubMed]

16. World Council of Churches Study Document. *Facing AIDS: The Challenge, the Churches' Response.* Geneva: WCC Publications, 1997.

17. Giami, Alain, Helene Olomucki, and Janine de Poplavsky. "Surveying Sexuality and AIDS: Interviewer Attitudes and Representations." In *Researching Sexual Behavior: Methodological Issues.* Edited by John Bancroft. Bloomington: Indiana University Press, 1997, pp. 61–83.

18. Nzioka, Charles. *Willing Fathers, Reluctant Parents: Young Men's Perspectives on Unwanted Pregnancies and Abortion in Kenya.* Addis Ababa: Organization for Social Science Research in Eastern and Southern Africa, 2009.

19. Izugbara, Chimaraoke O., Kennedy J. Otsola, and Alex Chika Ezeh. "Men, Women, and Abortion in Central Kenya: A Study of Lay Narratives." *Medical Anthropology* 28 (2009): 397–425. [CrossRef] [PubMed]

20. Adaji, Sunday E., Linnea U. Warenius, Antony A. Ong'any, and Elisabeth A. Faxelid. "The Attitudes of Kenyan In-School Adolescents toward Sexual Autonomy." *African Journal of Reproductive Health* 14 (2010): 33–41. [PubMed]

21. Ikamari, Lawrence, Chimaraoke Izugbara, and Rhoune Ochako. "Prevalence and Determinants of Unintended Pregnancy among Women in Nairobi, Kenya." *BMC Pregnancy and Childbirth* 13 (2013): 69. [CrossRef] [PubMed]

religions

MDPI

Essay

Reflections on Reading the Scriptures as an Orthodox Christian

Mary Ford

St. Tikhon's Orthodox Theological Seminary in South Canaan, PA 18459, USA; mary.ford@stots.edu

Received: 13 April 2017; Accepted: 15 June 2017; Published: 5 July 2017

Abstract: The heart of the differences between an Orthodox understanding and use of Scripture, and what has prevailed in most non-Orthodox scholarly circles since the time of Spinoza, is not primarily anything to do with methodologies, or techniques as such, but fundamentally it is about the theological context within which the methods are used. Hence this paper begins by outlining the fundamentals of theology that undergird all traditional Orthodox exegesis. These fundamentals of Orthodox theology and life provide a radically different interpretive context for the use of any methods or tools of interpretation from that of the essentially agnostic approach promoted by Spinoza and those following him, who have exclusively used the historical critical method, whose foundational principle was to "interpret as if there is no God." Hence, from an Orthodox perspective, all the basic technical aspects of historical criticism—linguistic studies, looking at the historical context, etc.—when used within a traditional Christian interpretive context can be valuable tools leading to a deeper understanding. However, the ultimate purpose of properly interpreting Scripture–salvation, becoming holy—is achieved primarily through living the gospel.

Keywords: Orthodox Christian Tradition; Biblical interpretation; Fathers; historical criticism; the historical-critical method; salvation; gospel

---

"The Church does not give us Holy Scripture as a book to study and interpret on our own. Rather, it opens to us the door of that beauty to which we are called by the Bridegroom Himself."(Vasileios 2012, p. 105)

All understandings of, uses of, and methodologies for interpreting Scripture ultimately arise from the theology and world-view of those who develop and embrace them—and these include *why* interpreting Scripture is considered a valuable undertaking in the first place. Thus, for a proper understanding of the interpretation of Scripture in the Orthodox Church and her Tradition, it is important to give a little of the theological foundation. Of course, in a short article only a brief overview can be given.

In this article I will focus on eight foundational beliefs and a few additional key elements necessary for understanding how Scripture is used and interpreted within the Orthodox Church.

I. First, and most foundational, is the fact that *God is real and has revealed Himself most fully in Jesus Christ as the good God Who loves mankind (a phrase repeated frequently in Orthodox worship services). Thus, because He is this good God, He does everything for our benefit* in the sense of our ultimate benefit, our salvation—even to the point of the extreme humility of a voluntary death on the cross for our sakes. Therefore, Holy Scripture is considered to be a great gift of this good God, inspired by His Holy Spirit, in order primarily to help people in all times and places in their life's journey to come to know this good God through communion with Him, and to come to know various spiritual realities.

Thus, Scripture is seen as a kind of guide book on how to benefit spiritually from reality as it truly is (in contrast to how it is often perceived by the fallen mind), and on how to live in such a way as to be healed and transformed—to be able to purify one's heart so that one can acquire grace and live eternally in loving communion with God in Christ through the Holy Spirit. In other words, to fulfill the purpose for which we were created, to be saved. This is the approach we find in the New Testament itself—as for example, when St. Paul says about people and events recorded in the Old Testament, "Now all these things happened to them for examples, and they were written for our admonition..." (1 Cor. 10:11).

To use a different analogy, we could say that Scripture's intended role is understood to be not primarily to provide us with interesting historical information (though it can do that), but ultimately to provide us with "glasses" permitting us to see more and more clearly the way things truly are—so that we can move forward on the spiritual journey that is our life, so that we can move forward and eventually "take off."

As Archimandrite Vasileios, a highly respected Athonite spiritual father and theologian, says:

> I listen to some theories or "theologies" which are like airports with no runway for takeoff. These are the things which restrict man and abuse the aeroplane. The aeroplane has to take off—it is not a push-cart you can use to sell tomatoes from in the market. It has a different destiny. And man too has a different destiny (Vasileios 1997, pp. 49–50).

> Before the runway ends, it [the airplane] has found a different means of support, and so it doesn't have a crash. Before this life ends, man has to find a different means of support. And by the time death comes, he no longer treads this earth (Vasileios 1997, pp. 49–50).

Scripture, properly interpreted, helps people to find that "different means of support." We can see that for the Church Fathers and Saints, this personal transformation through grace is the primary purpose of reading/interpreting Scripture. We see this not only from their explicit statements, but also from the analogies they have frequently made through the ages about Scripture. In Scripture itself, we find it being compared to a light—"Thy word/law is a lamp unto my feet" (Ps. 119:105)—which illumines a way of life which, when we follow it, enables us to see Jesus Christ, the God-Man, Who most perfectly reveals the One True God—and to know that this God is the good God Who loves mankind.

The Scriptures are described by the Fathers as being like wells (holding the water of the Holy Spirit, Who transforms our lives); water; living water; succulent food; medicines; healing plaster for wounds; tree leaves that heal; yeast (that transforms the whole lump of dough); a weapon; armor; leaves that protect and shield; a beacon light, guiding us safely; and a counselor, keeping us on the right path, protecting us from error, so we can grow in the new life. Scripture is understood, then, to support and encourage movement and positive change: nourishment for growth (and growth is change), movement from sickness to health, while also providing safety and protection for both growth and good health.

These images also strongly imply that part of what it means to say we live in a fallen world is that people are in a weakened state, in poor spiritual health, likely to stray from the good path, likely to be tempted to leave the path that leads to fullness of health; and that therefore we all *need* the healing, nourishing, guiding, and protecting which the Scriptures are intended to provide as one important part of a whole treasury of healing in the Church. These various images also imply that entering into the new life in Christ isn't just a matter of mentally accepting some ideas as being true. If we need protection, then it isn't an easy process; it involves struggle, *deep* change, a cross.

II. Of course, if we are weak and sick with sin, we need healing and help—we need corrective lenses, a light to illumine the darkness we find ourselves in. And if we need to be changed, or transformed or purified, that also means that *fallen humanity unaided and untransformed cannot properly see or perceive, hear or understand, true reality* (see Mark 4:12)—especially spiritual realities, as one can notice many times in the gospel accounts.

The gospel accounts—and the New Testament as a whole—are full of exhortations about the need for positive change, the need to "bear fruit," to *keep* Jesus' words/commands—to "do the truth" (John 3:21), to live the gospel life. And we are called to do this, not because these are arbitrary rules like the speed limit, but because this is the only way to achieve the most profound personal transformation—a transformation which will be life-giving for ourselves and others, leading to true health, to "life in abundance," to eternal life in Christ. That's why this level of interpretation has been called "transformative (Fr. Theodore Stylianopoulos 1997). And because this personal transformation is understood to be the primary purpose of interpreting Scripture (and of life as a whole), it is the primary focus of the exegesis of those following the Orthodox Tradition—which is continuous with that of the early Church Fathers and the Apostles before them. This transformation always begins with a specific kind of change, often misunderstood today, called *repentance*.

Jesus often called for repentance. His first word in Matthew's gospel account is "Repent," and His first words in Mark's account concern the same theme (Matt. 4:17; Mark 1:15). In the Greek of the Fathers, repentance (*metanoia*) "signifies primarily a 'change of mind' or a 'change of the intellect' (*nous*): not only sorrow, contrition or regret, but more positively and fundamentally the conversion or turning of our whole life towards God (Palmer 1979, vol. 1, pp. 363–64)." According to St. John of Damascus, "Repentance is the returning from the unnatural into the natural state, from the devil to God, through discipline and effort." (St. John of Damascus 1979, vol. IX, p. 43)

So, secondly, all this means that there is real knowledge which is, as St. Paul says, "spiritually discerned"; and therefore, the "natural man," the unrepentant, uninspired, worldly person *cannot* perceive or have access to this knowledge as long as he or she is in that state (see I Cor. 2:14; see also Matt. 12:33–35). In other words, *one's spiritual state determines whether one can perceive/know the most fundamental truths of Scripture*, such as who Jesus Christ is and why this matters.

There is no sense here, or elsewhere in the gospel accounts, that one can acquire the kind of knowledge which Scripture is most concerned to impart by merely finding information about certain topics, or trying to be an "objective" observer, trying to interpret Jesus' actions and words accurately from a detached position. Again, *how* one interprets, one's very ability to interpret, or "see," depends directly upon one's spiritual state.

That's why St. Athanasius says, in concluding his classic work *On the Incarnation*[1],

> For the searching of the Scriptures and *true* knowledge of them, *an honorable life is needed*, and a pure soul, and that virtue which is according to Christ. So that the intellect, guiding its path by it, may be able to attain what it desires, and to comprehend it, in so far as it is accessible to human nature to learn concerning the Word of God. For without a pure mind and a modeling of one's life after the saints, a man could not possibly comprehend the words of the saints. For just as, if a man wished to see the light of the sun, he would wipe and brighten his eyes, purifying himself in some way like what he desires, and then he may see the light of the sun...thus he who would comprehend the mind of those who speak of God must begin by washing and cleansing his soul, by his manner of living, and approach the saints themselves by imitating their works. So that, associated with them in the conduct of a similar way of life, he may understand also what has been revealed to them by God. (St. Athanasius the Great 1979, vol. IV, p. 67)

III. So what does Scripture, and the Orthodox Church's Tradition as a whole, tell us about acquiring this kind of knowledge? What kind of training do we need to live an "honorable life" like the Saints? In a nutshell, we need to "put on Christ," to acquire the virtues, and free ourselves from the control of the negative passions (like anger towards others), and demonic deception, so that these passions like anger are only used as intended—as weapons against sin, especially our own sin, in order to build up the Body of Christ, and not to hurt others.

There is unanimity in the Tradition that *the best way to acquire the Holy Spirit, the virtues, the good spiritual state necessary for fully understanding Scripture, is to live the gospel, which includes keeping ascetic*

---

[1] See also, e.g., (St. Ignatius Brianchaninov 1983), the chapter on carnal zeal; and St. Symeon the New Theologian, *The Discourses*, Chapter XXIV.

practices, especially prayer, fasting, almsgiving. These disciplines help us overcome the negative passions, the lusts of the flesh that enslave us, our egotism, self-centeredness—the things that make it hard for us to be truly loving and for our hearts to be open to receive the Holy Spirit, to be illumined by Christ with "divine knowledge." We have to live the gospel in order to properly understand it.

And again, the fact that we need such illumination for a proper understanding of Scripture is also clear from the gospel accounts. Perhaps the most famous example is Christ walking with Luke and Cleopas on the road to Emmaus; but also in Luke 24:45, when the risen Jesus opened the eyes of all the apostles so that they could understand the Scriptures—especially, of course, those pertaining to Him. One could also include St. Paul's Damascus Road experience. This opening of their eyes involves much more than simple information about correct interpretations. "Did not our hearts burn within us...while he opened to us the scriptures?" the disciples say.

We can see this also, for example, in the prayer before the gospel in the Orthodox Liturgy of St. John Chrysostom, which begins,

> Illumine our hearts, O Master, Who loves mankind, with the pure light of Thy divine knowledge, and open the eyes of our mind to the understanding of Thy gospel teachings; implant in us also the fear of Thy blessed commandments, that trampling down all lusts of the flesh, we may enter upon a spiritual way of life... (St. John Chrysostom)

There is a great emphasis on knowing and obeying the gospel commandments in virtually all writings of spiritual direction in our Tradition: that *only if we obey the commandments, living the gospel way of life, can Scripture be life-giving to us.* Christ Himself says in John 14:15, "If you love Me, you will keep My commandments. And I will pray the Father, and He will give you another counselor, to be with you for ever, even the Spirit of truth..." Living the gospel leads to communion with God, which means communion with the Spirit of truth, and such communion is necessary for properly understanding that truth.

St. Silouan of Mt. Athos, from the 20th century, repeats from his own experience the Church's same understanding from a different angle: "We may study as much as we will, but we shall still not come to know the Lord unless we live according to His commandments; for the Lord is not made known through learning, but by the Holy Spirit...To believe in God is one thing, to know God is another. Both in heaven and on earth the Lord is made known only by the Holy Spirit, and not through ordinary learning." (quoted by (Fr. Theodore Stylianopoulos 1980))

This also means, as indicated above, that many of the key aspects which Scripture is primarily concerned with (including, as in Matthew 12, who Jesus truly is) can only be fully, properly understood by being in a good spiritual state—by having a pure heart, or at least being repentant and striving for a pure heart, striving to live the gospel, and thus having one's heart illumined by the light of Christ. This reality—that one must live the gospel to fully/properly understand it, that one must be like the Saints in order to fully understand their words—has even been called by others "the fundamental rule" of traditional patristic exegesis[2]. This principle has also been called "the desert hermeneutic (Burton-Christie 1988; quoted by Paul Blowers (Blowers 1991))," though actually it is emphasized in all times and places by those following the apostolic and patristic Tradition.

Since this key principle has been entirely overlooked, or considered to be irrelevant, for several centuries in most non-Orthodox biblical studies, it is worth repeating: *how you live your life is inseparable from being able to receive the illumination necessary to properly understand Scripture in its most important dimensions.*

---

[2]   St. Justin Popovich, a contemporary Serbian Orthodox saint and scholar, says "the fundamental rule of Orthodox exegesis" is that you have to live the gospel in order to fully, properly understand it (see, e.g., (Popovich n.d.)). And that is why, for those in the patristic Tradition, and for those who follow them, Jesus Christ is the only true 'exegete of God.' Because He is God, He alone fully lives that reality (see John 1:18).

IV. The fact that this spiritual knowledge is real and essential, and that you have to live the gospel to acquire this kind of knowledge that comes along with acquiring God's grace, is also why we in the Orthodox Church depend upon the Church Fathers and Saints for discerning the fundamentals of the Faith, and for providing the best interpretive context for our exegesis—why we base our interpretations of Scripture on their works, which are such a crucial part of our entire written Church Tradition. These are all people who are knowledgeable about God and the things of God from their own experience, whose interpretations/teachings as a whole have been confirmed by the Church as a whole, especially in the Ecumenical Councils (which in our Church have to be accepted by the people as a whole). That is why the Fathers are trustworthy guides for our reading of Holy Scripture, though we do not consider that anyone, other than Jesus Christ Himself, is somehow "infallible." The whole must be considered—or as St. Photius the Great (9th century) said, "The safe criterion of Orthodoxy is the majority [of Church Fathers]."[3]

St. John Chrysostom (4th century) explains this further with a helpful analogy:

> It behooves us therefore to explore everything carefully. For the words of the Scripture are our spiritual weapons; but if we do not know how to fit those weapons and to arm our scholars rightly, they keep indeed their proper power, but they cannot help those who receive them. For let us suppose there to be a strong corselet [a piece of armor that covers the trunk of the body], and helm(et), and shield, and spear; and let one take this armor and put the corselet upon his feet, the helmet over his eyes instead of on his head, and let him not put the shield before him..., but perversely tie it to his legs: will he be able to gain any advantage from the armor? Will he not rather be harmed? It is plain to anyone that he will. Yet this is not on account of the weakness of the weapons, but on account of the unskillfulness of the man who knows not how to use them well. So with the Scriptures—if we confound their order, they will even so retain their proper force, yet will do us no good. (St. John Chrysostom 1979, vol. XIV, p. 105)

We depend on the Fathers and the interpretive context of Tradition in order to best learn how to use the "spiritual weapons" which Scripture provides us with, so that we too can have spiritual victory in our lives. At this point in time, we have many hundreds of years and many thousands of people (including living saints) to verify the effectiveness of the Fathers' and Saints' understanding in helping us to become holy, so we very reasonably accept it to be true. Additionally, in the Orthodox Church, although the early Fathers have a special pre-eminence for a variety of reasons, the period of the Fathers never ends; there are a number of holy, learned theologians even in our own time who are widely recognized in the Church as ranking among the Fathers of the Church—though more time must pass before we see how influential their writings and lives have been and how lasting their influence will be.

V. The idea of depending on the Fathers for our basic interpretive context for Scripture, and even for their wisdom about specific passages, never has meant that people were not encouraged to read Scripture themselves. From the beginning of Church history, except when in a situation of oppression and general lack of education (or habits derived from those times!), those in the mainstream Tradition have emphasized the importance of reading and studying Scripture for all who are able to.

To give a quick cross-section through time—in the 4th century, St. John Chrysostom, who urged all his parishioners to read Scripture at home and discuss the sermon as a family, says, "for this is the cause of all evils—not knowing the Scriptures."[4] St. John of Damascus in the 8th century wrote:

---

[3] (Ford 2015, p. 315). Some of the material in this paper appears in this book.
[4] (St. John Chrysostom 1979, vol. XIII, p. 301). By Chrysostom's time, he can assume that in large cities almost every parishioner will have at least a copy of the four gospels that they can read at home. There were *scriptoria* where up to 100 scribes would make copies of Scripture as it was being dictated—producing up to 1000 copies a month.

> To search the Scriptures is a work most fair and most profitable for souls. For just as the
> tree planted by the channels of waters, so also the soul watered by the divine Scripture is
> enriched and gives fruit in its season... Wherefore let us knock at that very fair garden of
> the Scriptures.... let us not knock carelessly but rather zealously and constantly. For thus it
> will be opened to us. If we read once or twice and do not understand what we read, let us
> not grow weary, but let us persist, let us talk much, let us inquire... let us luxuriate, let us
> revel insatiate." (St. John of Damascus 1979, vol. IX, p. 89)

And from the 19th century, St. Ignatius Branchianinov says (of a monk, but, as Metr.
Kallistos [21st century] has explained, it applies to lay people as well): he/she "should devote
all possible care and attention to the reading of the Holy Gospel. He should study the Gospel so closely
that it is always present in his memory...Keep on studying the gospel until the end of your life. Never
stop. Do not think that you know it enough, even if you know it all by heart." (Ware 1987, p.147)

VI. A sixth fundamental is that because God is the good God Who loves mankind, He has arranged
for the fallen world a salvation economy (the Incarnation, etc.) that includes *an ascetic economy*, to help
us in our healing, our transformation, our repentance. This means in part that difficulties and trials
are a crucial aspect of the "spiritual pedagogy" that the Lord has arranged in this world ultimately
for the salvation of humankind. You have to properly enter into that asceticism, you have to use the
tools reality gives you, so to speak, in order to make spiritual progress and to properly understand
both Scripture and life. You have to undergo ascetic efforts in the proper spirit to purify your heart
in order to become holy, to acquire the Holy Spirit—or however you may wish to talk about this
spiritual reality.

In other words, the spiritual struggle, or any difficulties in life, are not punishments,
or "imperfections" that should not be there—something that is wrong. Rather, they are an important
and valuable aspect of reality that we should not only expect to be there, but if approached in the
proper way, we should expect them to benefit us, and thus we can actually also be grateful for them.
As St. Gregory the Theologian (4th century) says even about the expulsion of Adam and Eve from
Paradise, and everything that came with their Fall, "the penalty becomes an act of compassion.[5]" And
as St. John Chrysostom says of death, the greatest "difficulty" in the fallen world, "even though death
entered as a result of sin, nevertheless such is the superiority of God, His lovingkindness, and the
excess of His care that He employs even this to the advantage of our race." (St. John Chrysostom 1999,
vol. 2, p. 37, on Psalm 111)

Indeed, Archimandrite Vasileios can even say,

> In the end, the faithful will thank God only for great sufferings, for complete "perplexities."
> In other words, everything will be swept away by the fire of praise. And the cooling flame
> of unbearable fire will leap up from the painful occurrences, the temptations and the thorns
> that we did not wish to undergo, considering them to be obstacles, a curse making our
> lives miserable. For we had not realized that for the man who is placed rightly... obstacles
> blocking the road are nothing other than steps which take him upwards and opportunities
> to give praise. For it is the Lord who is at work in everything (Vasileios 1984).

This understanding is simply the direct continuation of what is very evident in many places in
the New Testament. For example, St. James says, "Consider it *pure joy*, my brethren, whenever you
face trials of many kinds, because you know that the testing of your faith develops perseverance"
(James 1:2–3; my emphasis). And as Christ Himself says in St. John's gospel, "In the world you have
tribulation; but be of good cheer, I have overcome the world" (John 16:33).

---

[5]   Quoting from St. Gregory the Theologian's Oration 45, on Easter, part 8, excerpt given in Panayiotis Nellas (Nellas 1987), *Deification in Christ: The Nature of the Human Person.*

VII. Another fundamental presupposition to be discussed here is related to that just above. Reality is set up with many analogous aspects; in this case, difficulties in everyday life are analogous to difficulties in interpreting Scripture, and thus should be approached in the same spirit. More will be said about this shortly.

VIII. The last foundational principle is that a critical part of the interpretive context for Orthodox Christians is *the liturgical use of Scripture*. In a real way, this is first—it's the context in which Scripture was primarily intended to be encountered. Every service in our Church is filled with references to Scripture, quotations from Scripture, as well as the reading of entire passages. During the services of the Church, the faithful are "bathed" in Scripture, its phrases and images, and reflections on it.

A very clear example of how important and valuable this is can be seen in the services celebrating the Transfiguration of Our Lord on August 5th and 6th. In these services, in the context of many beautiful hymns explaining the proper understanding of this event described in the gospel accounts, one finds not only the gospel accounts of Matthew and Luke read, but also 2 Peter 1:10–19, where Peter speaks of the Apostles being "eyewitnesses of His majesty." During Vespers, several key Old Testament theophanies are read which illuminate how this event should be understood: Exodus 24:12–18—the children of Israel seeing the glory of the Lord on Mt. Sinai; Exodus 33:11–23 and 34:4–6, 8—Moses seeing the "back parts" of God; and 1 Kings 19:3–9, 11–13, 15–16—the theophany in the still small voice given to Elijah.

Below are a few of the hymns from the Vespers service, in which we notice how key foundational principles of the interpretive context mentioned above are reinforced in a way very characteristic of Orthodox services:

> Before Thy Crucifixion, O Lord, taking the disciples up into a high mountain, Thou wast transfigured before them, shining upon them with the bright beams of Thy power. From the love of mankind and in Thy sovereign might, Thy desire it was to show them the splendour of the Resurrection. Grant that we too in peace may be counted worthy of this splendour, O God, for Thou are merciful and lovest mankind (Mother 1969, p. 470).

> When Thou wast transfigured, O Saviour, upon a high mountain, having with Thee the chief disciples, Thou wast shone forth in glorious majesty, proving thereby that those who surpass in the height of their virtues shall be counted worthy of the divine glory. Talking with Christ, Moses, and Elijah showed that He is Lord of both the living and the dead [Romans 14:9], the God Who spoke of old through the Law and the Prophets. And the voice of the Father testified to Him from the cloud of light, saying, "Hear ye Him, Who through His cross harrows hell and gives the dead eternal life (Mother 1969).

> O Christ our God, Who wast transfigured in glory on Mount Tabor, showing to Thy disciples the splendour of Thy Godhead, do Thou enlighten us also with the light of Thy knowledge, and guide us in the path of Thy commandments, for Thou alone are good and lovest man (Mother 1969, p. 474).

> He Who once spoke through symbols to Moses on Mount Sinai, saying, "I am He Who is" [Ex. 3:14], was transfigured today upon Mount Tabor before the disciples; and in His own person He showed them the nature of man, arrayed in the original beauty of the Image. Calling Moses and Elijah to be witnesses of this exceeding grace, He made them sharers in His joy, foretelling His decease through the Cross and His saving Resurrection (Mother 1969, p. 476).

Another important element of the patristic analogies for Scripture which many emphasize is the enjoyment of beauty in reading/hearing Scripture. Scripture is compared to a fragrant garden; a garden with many beautiful flowers; a beauty of treasures leading to delight, wonder, and praise. Orthodox liturgical services, in which hymns such as those above are sung, very much emphasize this "atmosphere" of beauty as well. All the senses are involved through the sung services, the beautiful icons, the fragrant incense, various movements—indeed, the whole body is being "soaked" in beauty as an essential part of worship wherever possible. This is a way to physically experience that the God we worship is the good God Who loves us, Who does everything for our benefit, Who is worthy of our worship.

The beautiful services intend in part to inspire "good eros"—the desire for union with this good God in Christ through the Holy Spirit. St. Basil the Great said after his dramatic experience of God's uncreated light (or glory), "What is more marvelous, more worthy of love, than the beauty of God." Our services intend to evoke a similar feeling and awareness in worshipers, giving a foretaste of the paradise that is the heavenly kingdom, and increasing our desire for that inexpressibly beautiful life in union with the One most worthy of love.

Even from these brief examples and description, hopefully the non-Orthodox reader can get a glimpse of what Archimandrite Vasileios describes when he says, "The Church does not give us Holy Scripture as a book to study and interpret on our own. Rather, it opens to us the door of that beauty to which we are called by the Bridegroom Himself." This beauty is meant to inspire us to undertake with love and joy the ascetic labors necessary for real spiritual transformation.

St. Macarios the Great (4th century) gives a helpful analogy when he says that a Christian

> should every day have the hope and the joy and the expectation of the coming kingdom and deliverance, and to say, "If today I have not been delivered, I shall tomorrow." As the man who plants a vine has the joy and the hope in himself, before he ever embarks upon the toil, and sketches out vineyards in his mind, and reckons up the income, when there has been no wine yet, and so enters upon the toil—for the hope and expectation make him labour cheerfully...and in like manner the man who builds a house and the man who tills a field, are at much expense to themselves first, in hope of the advantage to come; so it is here. If a man does not keep before his eyes the joy and the hope, "I shall find deliverance and life," he cannot endure the afflictions, or the burden, and adopt the narrow way. It is the presence of hope and joy that make him labour and endure afflictions (St. Macarius the Great 1974, p. 190).

It is also the ascetic dimension that helps prevent all the beauty from being merely aesthetic, superficial appreciation or pleasure.

These fundamentals of Orthodox theology and life—the truth of which has been experienced by myriads of Christians through the centuries, and have been confirmed by the Church as a whole—provide a radically different interpretive context for the use of any methods or tools of interpretation from the essentially agnostic approach promoted by Spinoza and those who have followed in his footsteps who have exclusively used the historical critical method, whose foundation was to "interpret as if there is no God." Indeed, the whole "Enlightenment" project, which began to dominate biblical studies after the intense and sometimes violent conflicts following the Reformation, with its impossible attempt to have "Scripture alone," rejects all of the Orthodox fundamentals mentioned above.

The "Enlightenment" world-view does not believe in a "good God Who loves mankind, Who does everything for our benefit"; so it cannot understand the ascetic dimension of reality in a positive way, but regards difficulties in biblical interpretation (as in life) as imperfections, things that shouldn't be there (especially if God were good, or if this were a divinely inspired text). Difficulties are then usually regarded as indications that the biblical author/redactor failed in some way (clumsy editing, etc.). The assumption often seems to be that such difficulties surely would not be there if the biblical authors were as intelligent and well-informed as their later interpreters! Of course, this secular view does not see the world as a revelation of God, or His careful organizing of reality for our salvation. Rather, things are as they are, it is claimed, as a result of impersonal, purposeless natural forces with no meaning beyond their own existence.

This seems to me to be the heart of the difference between a truly Orthodox understanding and use of Scripture and what has prevailed in most non-Orthodox scholarly circles.[6] This means that the differences are not primarily anything to do with methodologies, or techniques as such—though these do differ in various ways—but fundamentally they are about theology.

From an Orthodox perspective, all the basic technical aspects of historical criticism—linguistic studies, looking at the historical context, etc.—when removed from the agnostic interpretive context of historical criticism can be valuable tools leading to a deeper understanding. That is why I believe it is helpful to distinguish these techniques used apart from that Spinozan interpretive context by calling them "the techniques of biblical criticism" as distinct from "historical criticism." Nevertheless, regardless of how helpful these techniques may be in understanding certain passages, they cannot be considered essential for the primary purpose of Scripture to be fulfilled: for people to become holy, to know God through their purified hearts—to be in loving communion with Him and one another. For that goal/*telos*, living the gospel is the essential "method."

Of course, the need to find a way to determine authoritative interpretations of Scripture in the aftermath of the Reformation and the so-called "Wars of Religion" led many to look for a "scientific" approach that all reasonable people would have to accept—an approach which could safely ignore or bypass not just the Church and her Tradition, but also any sense of the need for purifying the heart, of a gospel way of life necessary before proper interpretation could take place.

Gradually in many circles, the focus shifted from things which cannot be determined by any scientific method, which are not even appropriate subjects for scientific study alone—such as what is true? what leads to holiness, communion with God, fulness of life, salvation?—to aspects that *could* be studied by the new scientific methods, such as attempts to determine the "original" text, historical circumstances, etc. Certainly, technical information has been valued by the highly educated Church Fathers and used when available; but because it was not germane to the primary purpose of Scripture, these aspects were never primary, and certainly could not properly be the exclusive focus.

Hence, while taking advantage of any information or insights gained through biblical critical techniques, archaeology, etc., the Orthodox exegete today who wishes to follow our Tradition will always start with the principles given above, along with the entire interpretive context provided by the Tradition; and they will consult the patristic witness where possible on specific passages.

The following analogy of Macarios the Great about spiritual life is equally true for the work of interpreting Scripture. As he says,

> In the outer world, the husbandman tills the ground; but in spite of his tilling, he needs rain and showers from above. If no moisture comes from above, the husbandman has no profit from his tilling of the ground. So it is with the spiritual world... The man must cultivate with a will the ground of his heart, and labour upon it.... But unless clouds of heaven make their appearance from above, and showers of grace, the husbandman does not profit by his toil (St. Macarius the Great 1974).

Partly because this is the case, it does not follow that exegetes who follow the Orthodox tradition believe the Fathers have exhaustively interpreted Scripture, and all that's left to do is to restate what they've said. The Holy Spirit can inspire exegetes in all eras. This is clear from the analogies for Scripture of the early Fathers themselves stressing its endless depths and riches—that there is no end to what one can see and learn. There is no trace of the idea that exegetes must find the one original historical meaning in order to really understand Scripture. Rather, it is compared to a vine with endless fruit; endless wealth, a never-failing spring; a meadow with diverse flowers, copious fruit,

---

6   Protestant Fundamentalists also share the attitude that difficulties in the interpretation of Scripture are imperfections which shouldn't be there, since every verse must have a clear interpretation. And there can be no small, incidental factual errors of any kind, even if they were believed by everyone at the time the passage was written. Of course, this is all also a legacy of the untenable "Scripture alone" approach.

and abundant fragrance—a paradise of flowers and fruit; a fair garden with varied sounds; a treasure chest with inestimable riches and precious stones; and the rock which Moses struck with oceans of water springing from it. It is said to possess inexhaustible grace.

So, while basing our interpretations on those of the exegetes who have gone before us whose wisdom is confirmed by the Church, and its "rule of Faith"—those truths of the Faith which will never change—we realize that there is always more to say. And we can pray for wisdom and guidance to say what those who are hearing or reading what we say need to hear for their spiritual benefit.

Finally, in evaluating certain exegetes and the worth of their exegesis, it is not enough only to discern if they have given readers correct information. I would suggest that readers would do well to ask about some things that are just as important: are these exegetes being "nourished and renewed by their own theology"? Are they "a support and joy for the Church" (Ford 2015, p. 282)? Are they "passing on the joy" of life in Christ in a life-giving way as the Fathers always have (Vasileios 1984, p. 35)? This is certainly a vital part of what traditional Orthodox Christian exegetes of all times and places hope to do!

Conflicts of Interest: The author declares no conflict of interest.

References

Blowers, Paul. 1991. *Exegesis and Spiritual Pedagogy in Maximus the Confessor: An Investigation of the Quaestiones ad Thalassium.* South Bend: University of Notre Dame Press, p. 38.

Burton-Christie, Douglas. 1988. Scripture and the Quest for Holiness in the *Apophthegmata Patrum.* Ph.D. Dissertation, Theological Union, New York, NY, USA.

Ford, Mary. 2015. *The Soul's Longing: An Orthodox Perspective on Biblical Interpretation.* South Canaan: St. Tikhon's Monastery Press.

Fr. Theodore Stylianopoulos. 1980. *Bread for Life: Reading the Bible.* Brookline: Dept. of Religious Education, Greek Orthodox Archdiocese of North and South America, p. 37.

Fr. Theodore Stylianopoulos. 1997. *The New Testament: An Orthodox Perspective.* Brookline: Holy Cross Orthodox Press, chp. 3.

Mother, Mary. 1969. *The Festal Menaion.* London: Faber and Faber.

Nellas, Panayiotis. 1987. *Deification in Christ: The Nature of the Human Person.* Crestwood: St. Vladimir's Seminary Press, p. 204.

Palmer, G.E.H. 1979. *The Philokalia.* London: Faber and Faber, vol. 1, pp. 363–64.

Popovich, Justin. n.d. How to Read the Bible and Why. Available online: http://www.sv-luka.org/library/howtoread_jp.htm (accessed on 16 March 2017).

St. Athanasius the Great. 1979. On the Incarnation. In *Nicene and Post-Nicene Fathers.* Second Series. Grand Rapids: Eerdmans, vol. IV, p. 67.

St. Ignatius Brianchaninov. 1983. *The Arena.* Jordanville: Holy Trinity Monastery, pp. 140–44.

St. John Chrysostom. 1979. Homily IX on Colossians. In *Nicene and Post-Nicene Fathers.* First Series. Grand Rapids: Eerdmans.

St. John Chrysostom. Divine Liturgy of St. John Chrysostom. In *Service Books of the Orthodox Church.* South Canaan: St. Tikhon's Seminary Press, vol. 1.

St. John Chrysostom. 1999. *Commentary on the Psalms.* Translated by Hill Robert Charles. Brookline: Holy Cross Orthodox Press, vol. 2, p. 37.

St. John of Damascus. 1979. Exact Exposition of the Orthodox Faith. In *Nicene and Post-Nicene Fathers.* Second Series. Grand Rapids: Eerdmans.

St. Macarius the Great. 1974. *Fifty Spiritual Homilies.* Willits: Eastern Orthodox Books.

St. Symeon the New Theologian. 1980. *The Discourses.* New York: Paulist Press.

Vasileios, Archimandrite. 1984. *Hymn of Entry.* Crestwood: St. Vladimir's Seminary Press.

Vasileios, Archimandrite. 1997. *The Christian in a Changing World*. Montreal: Alexander Press.
Vasileios, Archimandrite. 2012. *Hymn of Dismissal*. Crestwood: St. Vladimir's Seminary Press.
Ware, Bishop Kallistos. 1987. *The Orthodox Way*. Crestwood: St. Vladimir's Seminary Press.

![religions logo] *religions*

MDPI

Article

The Healing Spirituality of Eastern Orthodoxy: A Personal Journey of Discovery †

Kyriacos C. Markides

Department of Sociology, University of Maine Orono, Maine 04469, USA; Markides@maine.edu;
Tel.: +1-207-581-2390

† I am grateful to my colleague Michael Lewis and my wife Emily Markides for their critical reading of the first draft.

Academic Editor: John A. Jillions
Received: 4 April 2017; Accepted: 2 June 2017; Published: 8 June 2017

Abstract: It is generally assumed by western scholars and spiritual seekers that mystical, experiential religion and spirituality are primarily a hallmark of the far East, as exemplified by Hinduism, Buddhism, Taoism, and tribal religions like native American shamanism. In this overview, based on thirty years of field research as a sociologist, I have tried to show that such mystical practices and spiritual approaches exist in Eastern Christianity among groups of lay people, as well as in ancient monasteries like those found on Mt. Athos in northern Greece. It is argued that these thousand-year-old practices in the Christian East may contribute to what some thinkers have called the "eye of contemplation", namely the cultivation of the intuitive, spiritual side of human beings that has been repressed over the centuries because of the dominance of rationalism and scientific materialism.

Keywords: Eastern Orthodoxy; mysticism; religion; spirituality; healing

---

It is said that Christianity has two "lungs" one Western and the other Eastern, and that both are needed for proper breathing. It is a metaphor put forward by those who long for the re-establishment of unity that was torn asunder in 1054 when the Pope of Rome and the Patriarch of Constantinople excommunicated each other. As is well known, the trigger for the Great Schism was the notorious—for eastern Christians—Filioque. This was the addition to the Christian creed by the Roman Pope of a word signifying that the Holy Spirit proceeded from the Father "and from the Son", instead of simply "from the Father", as was traditionally stated and continues to be recited to this day during Divine Liturgy by Orthodox Christians.

It is beyond the scope of this paper to explore the theological complexities of that detail in the Christian creed or to elaborate on the historical and geopolitical forces that, over the preceding centuries, had built up the pressures that led to the split. However, what is important to underscore here is the fact that this episode in Christian history had monumental and unintended consequences, not only for Christianity but for the way European Civilization and the world at large have developed. The Western part of Christianity followed a radically different historical experience than its Eastern counterpart. Whereas Roman Catholicism became increasingly more involved in the affairs of this world and more rational in its theological formulations on how to know God, the Eastern part of Christianity became more otherworldly and more focused on the inward and mystical experience of Divinity. The Roman Catholic Church adopted the massive work of Thomas Aquinas, who incorporated into Christian theology the philosophy of Aristotle. This innovation set the foundation for the scientific revolution and the parallel development of capitalism.[1] God was conceived in rational terms, the One who created the universe, governed by rational laws and principles. Therefore, human beings, made in the image of God, are encouraged to apply their God-given reason to understand their world and their Maker. The great monasteries of the West, as leading sociologist of religion Rodney Stark so convincingly demonstrates, became workshops in studying nature.[2] Western monks were given the green light to experiment and study nature, and in doing so they would come to understand how God governs his Creation. This rational approach to God opened the way for the scientific revolution and the eventual and increasing rationalization of the West. In other words, modernity, material prosperity, technological innovation, social progress and secularism have their roots in theology as developed in the Western "lung" of Christianity.

The Eastern part of Christianity, on the other hand, turned inward, emphasizing an approach to God that was more contemplative, meditative and experiential.[3] This difference in the approach to God was sealed when Eastern Christianity was taken over by Islamic warriors, culminating at the Fall of Constantinople in 1453 and, later on, the communist takeover of Russia in 1917. The Eastern part of Christianity remained cut off from Western history, such as the further rationalizing developments ushered in by the Protestant Reformation and the on-going disputes between, on the one hand, a science that disentangled itself from its religious origins and moorings and, on the other hand, with Christian theology. The Eastern part of Christianity, playing hardly any role in the external developments of western history, remained pretty much insular in its outlook and more focused on its contemplative approaches as practiced in monasteries like those of Mt. Athos.

Today's Westerners, spiritually exhausted from the dominance of rationalism and materialism, and disenchanted with western, organized religions, have been seeking an outlet in the religions of the Far East like Zen Buddhism, Taoism and Hinduism. They have been looking for a healing spirituality that somehow they could not find within the secularizing ethos dominant in contemporary western culture, particularly as it prevails in universities, which have been my professional world as a sociologist for over forty years. The Eastern part of Christianity, with its experiential, mystical focus and methodologies related to spiritual healing, remains largely unknown in the West. In the rest of this paper I will share my own personal quest and "discovery" of the richness of Eastern Orthodox spirituality and its potential relevance for the future of Christianity and the world at large. It is my quest for the other "lung" of Christianity that may contribute to the healing of what many feel is our spiritually broken world.

My "discovery" of the healing tradition of Eastern Orthodoxy came by way of a serendipitous encounter with a group of lay healers and mystics in Cyprus during the 1980's. This encounter led to several years of field research exploring the world of these uncommon individuals. During this period I became, among other things, a witness to extraordinary feats of healing that defied, at least for me, a rational explanation. Following my exposure to the Cypriot healers and my sensitization to the possibility of the "miraculous" as part of human experience, the way was opened for me through certain coincidences to take a renewed and closer look at the religion of my upbringing. Consequently, since the mid-90's I have been researching and studying the mystical and miracle-filled culture of Eastern Orthodoxy as it is preserved to this day in ancient monasteries like those of Mount Athos, the isolated peninsula in northern Greece. Otherwise known as the Holy Mountain, it has served since the tenth century as a refuge for monks and hermits.

---

[1] See the work of leading sociologist of religion Rodney Stark in several of his pioneering works such as his seminal opus (Stark 2006), and his more recently published (Stark 2014).
[2] Ibid.
[3] The four-year theological debate in the 14th Century between Orthodox theologian St. Gregory Palamas (monk from Mt. Athos and later Archbishop of Thessaloniki) and the Calabrian Monk Barlaam set the seal of the different approaches in Christian theology between East and West. (See (Meyendorff 1974; Lossky 1997; Ware 1995)). It should be noted, however, that some recent scholarship has focused on areas of convergence between Gregory Palamas and Thomas Aquinas. See for example, (Plested 2012).

I should point out from the outset that these two pivotal experiences—my work with the lay healers and mystics of Cyprus, followed by my explorations of the spiritual healing tradition of Eastern Orthodoxy—had a profound effect on my worldview and outlook on life. Not surprisingly, the experiences had a radical impact on my academic career as well. Originally trained as a political sociologist studying problems related to nationalist movements and international terrorism, I shifted my focus and research towards the study of religion, spirituality and mysticism. In the following pages, I will share some aspects of this thirty-year intellectual and spiritual odyssey, and try to summarize the key features of the healing spirituality of Eastern Orthodoxy as I have experienced and studied it through my interactions with Athonite elders and hermits. I will then venture to suggest its potential relevance and contribution to contemporary western culture and identify possible weaknesses and obstacles that prevent such a development from occurring.

I must confess that, like most academics, I was at first suspicious of any claims related to presumed miracle healings and the "paranormal" phenomena so much in vogue today in popular culture, and so routinely debunked by the established academic community. My training in social science made me wary of any unusual and extravagant-sounding claims about "miracle" healings, clairvoyant visions and the like that could not be supported by "hard" scientific evidence, meaning controlled and replicable experiments. Furthermore, I have accepted as a matter of course, albeit reluctantly, the underlying tacit assumptions within which modern academic discourse operates; assumptions based on positivism, reductionism, relativism and determinism. That is, that the only truth is the truth discovered by our sense observations aided by the scientific method (positivism); that the only reality "out there" is the reality of the observable physical universe (reductionism); that there is no objective basis for values other than what cultures and societies construct (relativism); and that human beings are ultimately and exclusively products of biological and socio-cultural forces (determinism). These taken-for-granted tenets of scientific materialism that allow no room for the workings of spiritual or non-materialistic forces in our lives are driven into our consciousness very early in our academic training.

But what if, as a result of field research in cultures outside the dominant orbit of western, "post-modern" understanding of reality, we become witnesses to phenomena that contradict the assumptions I mentioned above. Then what? How do we negotiate in our minds the severe cognitive dissonance that unavoidably results from the gross disparity between what we were led to believe is the true nature of the world, on one hand, and the way we experience that world on the other? This has been a recurrent dilemma among some anthropologists, who as participant observers studied shamanism in tribal societies (Harner 1982). Being fully aware of the possibility of trickery, they became witnesses to what they considered authentic phenomena that could not be accommodated within the limits and dominant paradigms of contemporary, western science.

This is what happened to me as I first encountered the healers of Cyprus, which led me to reconsider the dominant assumptions of academic, scientific culture about the nature of reality (Markides 1990, 1987, 1990). When we are confronted with such dilemmas, questions are bound to pop up in our minds: perhaps reality is much more than the physical universe; perhaps we are much more than what we permit ourselves to assume we are, namely biological organisms determined by our DNA and the cultural milieu within which we happen to be born; perhaps there is knowledge that goes beyond the rational mind, as many sages have argued from Pythagoras and Plato to the founder of sociology at Harvard Pitirim Sorokin (Sorokin 1947), to contemporary transpersonal theorists like Ken Wilber, to medical researchers like Larry Dossay and experimental psychologists like Dean Radin (Wilber 1998; Dossey 2014; Radin 1997) as well as leading scholars of comparative religions like Huston Smith (Smith 2002). These sages would argue that it is a mistake to assume that knowledge of the world is attained only through our rational faculty (philosophy and mathematics) and our senses (experimental science) but also, and most importantly, through intuition. Before his retirement from Harvard, Pitirim Sorokin argued for the honoring of all three strands of knowledge, for a more "integralist" and holistic understanding of Reality. In his dramatic writing style he claimed that:

> Side by side with the subconscious (or unconscious) and conscious levels in human
> personality, a third stratum—the supraconscious—is gaining increasing recognition. It is
> not the subconscious or unconscious, but the supraconscious energies that are beginning to
> be considered as the real source of all great human creations, discoveries and inventions
> in all fields of culture—science, philosophy, law, ethics, fine arts, technology, politics and
> economics ... .Such phenomena as extrasensory perception and psychokinesis, as the
> supraconscious religious experience of the great mystics; as precognition; as the so-called
> "calculating boys" or "arithmetical prodigies", as the state of samadhi of the yogi, or satori
> of the Zen Buddhists; as cognitive and creative intuition are neither subconscious nor
> unconscious, but supraconscious, and, as such are not reducible to the lower forms of vital
> and mental energy.[4]

To illustrate what I have suggested I will share some of my direct field experiences of healing
phenomena with the Cypriot lay mystics; phenomena that I believe cannot be handled within
the boundaries of established rationalistic and scientific paradigms. It is for this reason that,
recognizing this problem right from the start, I preferred to employ a phenomenological approach
in my field research. That is, I avoided imposing my own sociological categories in explaining the
world of my subjects. Instead I asked them to explain their world from within their own categories
of understanding.

One day, I received a phone call from a man in New York whose wife was suffering from a serious
chronic illness that the doctors could not diagnose or identify. This man, who read my first book on
the healers, asked me whether I could take along a picture of his wife to Daskalos (the leading healer I
was studying) with the hope that he could perhaps identify the source of her problem. I volunteered
to do so during my upcoming trip to Cyprus. When I gave Daskalos the picture he closed his eyes and
with his hands began stroking and "feeling" the "vibrations" of the middle-aged woman in the picture.
Then he opened his eyes and claimed that the problem of that woman was in her teeth. He said that her
gums were all infected and that her teeth should be taken out and replaced with dentures. Because I
thought his diagnosis was too outlandish, I was at first reluctant to write a letter to the person in
New York. But at the insistence of Daskalos I overcame my initial hesitation, wrote the letter with his
prescription and mailed it from Cyprus. Two months after I returned to Maine, I received another
call from the same person (whom I had never met) to inform me that when he received my letter he
threw it away considering Daskalos' radical suggestion sheer nonsense. Soon after, however, two of
the front teeth of his wife fell out and infectious pus was dripping from her gums. She then went to an
oral surgeon who took care of the infection and her physical problems disappeared. What were the
probabilities, I wondered at the time, of someone making such an accurate diagnosis of the illness of a
woman seven thousand miles away by simply touching her picture? In fact, some medical doctors
today, based on their own experience, accept this unusual phenomenon as resting within the realms
of possibility. A board-certified neurologist and psychiatrist like Dr. Mona Lisa Schulz, who calls
herself a "medical intuitive", employs such an unconventional approach in her medical practice when
traditional approaches to diagnosing illnesses do not work (Schulz 2005).

Daskalos, a high school graduate, not only healed an Israeli woman suffering from psychiatric
problems that reputable psychiatrists could not cure, but also healed a local woman from spine
problems after leading doctors in Cyprus and in Israel concluded that there was no cure for her
problem. These experts suggested to her that she should get used to the idea that she would spend
a large part of her life lying in bed. After Daskalos's intervention (a matter of forty-five minutes of
barely touching her back, a procedure that I witnessed with my own eyes) the patient got out of bed
and was able to live a normal life from that very day. After the healing, the X-rays that she took that

---

[4] In Willis Harman and Howard Rheingold, Higher Creativity: Liberating the Unconscious for Breakthrough Insights (Jeremy
P. Tarcher 1984)—quoted in (Markides 1990, pp. 181–82).

same afternoon showed a healthy, normal spine, in contrast to the X-rays she had taken a week earlier. On another occasion, the Cypriot healer accurately alerted a friend of mine, the late Leonard Doob, Yale psychology professor, of a liver infection by simply casually chatting with him. The healer warned him that he should never donate blood to another person since, even though he reassured him that his illness was not life threatening, he would always be a carrier of the virus. My friend dismissed Daskalos' uninvited diagnosis and advice. He had just had a physical examination in New Haven, and had been declared perfectly healthy by his physicians. But three months later, after we returned to the States, he contacted me from Yale. He said the doctors discovered Hepatitis B on his liver, exactly as mentioned by "your healer", as he referred to Daskalos. His doctors claimed that it was impossible for anyone to detect the virus on his liver, as it takes three months to incubate and thus become noticeable through medical instruments. That means that when Daskalos told him that he had a virus infection the virus was already on his liver at the early stages of incubation, but could not have been detected by any traditional physician using state-of-the-art medical technology. Yet the healer in Cyprus "saw" the infection, not with any instrument, but with his consciousness. As Daskalos explained to Leonard the following summer, he used a different faculty of cognition unknown to medical science. In another instance, using such a special faculty, he accurately described in minute detail the inside of our house in Maine when he had never been to the U.S. He even suggested humorously that we needed to install a telephone on the second floor of our house to avoid the risk of falling down the steps every time the telephone would ring in the kitchen! One time, he contacted us to urge Emily to see a doctor about a problem on her knee, when we had told nobody in Cyprus that she had a knee problem.

Of course these are anecdotal experiences and stories that cannot be supported scientifically. Speaking for myself, however, I cannot deny my own experience. Additionally, an increasing number of reputable observers have been reporting similar experiences in other social and cultural settings. Even as long ago as the early sixties Dr. Jerome Frank, hard-nosed scientist and professor of psychiatry at Johns Hopkins University, could state in his classic work Persuasion and Healing:

> Some individuals may have a gift of healing that defies scientific explanation. . . . Nor can one rule out the possibility—indeed the evidence for it is quite persuasive—that some healers serve as a kind of conduit for a healing force in the universe, often called the life force, that, for want of a better term, must be called supernatural (Frank 1974).

Another scientist with impeccable credentials that drew similar conclusions is the neurologist and acclaimed brain researcher Dr. Wilder Penfield, who pointed out in The Mystery of the Mind (Penfield 1975) that for most of his life he had been a total materialist, believing that mind cannot exist independently of the brain. Yet on the basis of his research, he recognized that certain functions of mind could not possibly be explained on the basis of the material brain. That led him to the conclusion that the mind cannot be contained within the brain and that the latter is simply a vehicle for the former. One reviewer stated that:

> "The Mystery of the Mind is Widler Penfield's apology for his belated conversion from monism to dualism. That may not sound like much, but Professor Penfield, now at the end of his career as a pioneering neurosurgeon and explorer of the brain, has come to the conclusion that brain and mind are separate entities and that, while the mind is ordinarily dependent on the brain for its activity, it cannot be explained entirely by brain mechanisms. In a field where many workers will not even admit the existence of nonphysical realities like mind, that is quite a conclusion . . . I once heard a Hindu yogi tell a group of Western scientists that 'all of the brain is contained within the mind, but not all of the mind is in the brain.' To hear a Western neurosurgeon say something similar is most remarkable." (No Author 1976).

Unusual phenomena have also been studied and recorded diligently by parapsychologists, carrying out their work under controlled experimental conditions. A vast body of such studies has been accumulated during the last one hundred years, ever since the establishment of the Society for the Study of Psychical phenomena by British scientists at the close of the 19th Century.[5] Yet, with very few exceptions, mainstream scientists would refuse even to consider the evidence, presuming that such phenomena are not phenomena at all. Reacting to this prejudicial attitude on the part of mainstream scientists, British author and philosopher Colin Wilson wrote:

> Skeptical scientists living in London or New York have already concluded that the paranormal does not exist because it cannot exist. Almost without exception they would not take the trouble to go and see a psychic surgeon even if one lived round the corner: they tell you wearily that they know nothing will happen, or that if it does it will be trickery. All they are prepared to do is to consider the evidence at second hand, preferably in some easily digestible form, for they all lack patience, and then think up objections. And the result of their deliberations is then accepted by the rest of the scientific community as the unbiased conclusions of hard-headed scientists. In fact it is little more than a regurgitation of the opinions they have been expressing for years, opinions which are change-proof because the scientists have no intention whatever of studying the evidence (Wilson 1988).

To consider "paranormal" phenomena (in the Athonite language, "miracles") seriously would imply a willingness to radically revise our materialistic and reductionist assumptions about reality, and seriously entertain the notion that the mind is not confined within the brain; that it may be, in fact, "non-local", and that soul and spirit may be realities that must be factored in for a fuller understanding of self, society and cosmos (Fontana 2003). Furthermore, we must be open to the possibility that a sizable number of people who live ordinary, normal lives also have experiences that can be called "paranormal" or "non-ordinary", or "miraculous", but because of the dismissal of such experiences by mainstream scientists as nothing more than delusions or hallucinations, such individuals prefer to remain silent, lest they be stigmatized as mentally ill. I have been a witness to this problem time and again. When my books came out on the healers and mystics of Cyprus, scores of individuals contacted me to reveal that they themselves live within the realities that I described in my books, but prefer to remain quiet about them lest they be ridiculed, stigmatized and/or fired from their jobs. And these are individuals from all walks of life, including scientists and academics!

As I mentioned earlier, the extraordinary healing phenomena and "paranormal" abilities that I had witnessed in my work with Daskalos and his circle of mystics and healers prepared me for my personal "discovery" of Mount Athos. A friend familiar with my work urged me to join him on a journey to Mount Athos to meet "real saints." (Markides 1995) Their prayers, he claimed, are so powerful that healing miracles and other extraordinary phenomena are routine matters. I took up his invitation and my exploration and life took another turn.

In my years studying Athonite elders, I have heard of similar miraculous recoveries from physical and psychological illnesses after an elder prayed for the healing of the suffering individual. In recent years there emerged a plethora of books (mainly in Greek) on the miraculous lives of contemporary saints like elders Porphyrios and Paisios that, even though not "scientific" in the traditional sense, could dispel doubts related to the authenticity of the extraordinary lives of these elders. Having personally and directly witnessed healing phenomena during my work with the Cypriot lay mystics I was now open to such possibilities in the lives of venerated elders and Athonite monks and hermits.

Here is one of many concerning Elder Paisios, whom I met two years before his death in the early 90's. He was seeing pilgrims all day long in his hermitage on Mount Athos. By four o'clock in the afternoon, he announced that he was tired and could not see any more pilgrims. One of his visitors was very distressed, as he was eager to have a private meeting with the Elder. "Please Father," he implored, "I must see you. It is for my wife." "Sorry my son, but I am very, very tired." "But Father,

---

[5] See for example the extensive survey of such research (Brown 2005).

my wife is dying. I need to talk to you." This pilgrim wanted to ask Elder Paisios to intercede with God and pray for the healing of his wife who was dying from cancer. The Elder tapped his visitor on the back and said, "Go my son, and your wife is okay".

That pilgrim went back to Athens feeling that his journey several hundred miles away had all been in vain. When he entered his house his wife, who had been bedridden, was up and moving about the house. Later the doctors verified that, miraculously, her tumor had disappeared. She explained that as she was lying in bed, she felt heat all over her body, as if her cancer was melting away. It was during the hour when Elder Paisios told her husband "Go my son, and your wife is okay".

The Athonite culture is replete with tales not only of healing phenomena like the one I just described, but also of other types of extraordinary mystical experiences, of stories about the materialization and dematerialization of sacred icons, of teleportation, out-of-body travel, levitation and the bi-location of holy elders. These are stories that one usually reads about in the mystic traditions of Hinduism and Tibetan Buddhism (Yogananda 1987; Sogyal 2012). I was fascinated when I realized that such tales are much alive in the very heart of Christianity. I further noticed that Mount Athos preserved a system of "eldership", of a master/disciple relationship that again I had assumed up to that point was the exclusive hallmark of the religions of the far east. I am saying this because what attracted contemporary westerners, myself included, to the religions of India and Tibet is the emphasis on an experiential, mystical approach to the Divine, something that we felt was lacking in western Christianity. But since my encounters with Daskalos and his group, and my experiences with Athonite elders, I have realized that mystical spirituality is very much alive within the bounds of western civilization, in the cultural remnants of the eastern part of the Roman Empire. We have simply ignored that reality because of the triumph of scientific rationalism and certain other historical and sociological reasons that are beyond the scope of this paper.

The person who served as my key informant and mentor in the healing, mystical culture of Eastern Orthodoxy was Father Maximos, the thirty-three-year-old monk whom I met on my first visit to Mount Athos in 1991. He had already lived more than a decade as an Athonite ascetic intending to spend the rest of his life on the Holy Mountain. But following the requests of his elders he left Mount Athos in 1993 and became the abbot of the Panagia monastery in the Troodos mountains in Cyprus. There, he served as the spiritual guide to about thirty-five monks and forty nuns from a near-by women's monastery. Quickly developing a reputation as a spiritually gifted elder, he was sought by hundreds of lay people for confession and counseling; so much so that he was considered the person mostly responsible for a monastic renaissance on the island. It was in Cyprus that I joined him as a resident scholar studying his life and work, while also serving as his temporary chauffer, a task that allowed me more time to converse with him. During many hours of direct observation on my part, and conversations related to the subject matter of my work, I came to appreciate the spiritual tradition within which I had grown up. I had been alienated from that tradition since my arrival in America, which began the inevitable process of my secularization and absorption into the skeptical culture of academic social science. Father Maximos exposed me in a direct, personal way to the healing culture of Orthodoxy and its "apophatic" theology. It is from him that I first heard the novel idea that the Ecclesia must be seen first and foremost as a spiritual hospital, a healing institution; and that theology as a discipline should be part of medicine and not the humanities, as it has traditionally been considered. Like medicine, the central focus of the Ecclesia must be healing; most importantly the healing of the self, which is alienated from its true divine homeland. This is accomplished, as I will show later, through the application of specific healing methodologies that have practical and observable results (Markides 2001, 2005, 2012).

Perhaps a good way to introduce this Orthodox healing tradition is to briefly narrate two interrelated stories. The first story is that of a death row inmate that I will call David, who several years back wrote to me after reading the books I wrote related to the Cypriot lay healers. He asked for my assistance in connecting him with someone who could offer him spiritual advice. In his letter, he stressed the urgency of his request, as he did not know how much time he had left before his execution. He did not reveal what his offence was, other than that he had been involved with drug trafficking. I assumed he was convicted for murder. He also pointed out that he was a college graduate and in fact held a masters degree in English literature. It was clear from the quality of his letter that he was an educated person.

Without hesitation, I sent him the address of Father Maximos. Several months later David wrote to me again. He thanked me for the contact and claimed that in his entire life he had never experienced so much love coming to him as he felt coming through the letters of Father Maximos. They maintained regular correspondence as Father Maximos offered spiritual advice while providing him with classical texts on Orthodox spirituality (such as The Way of the Pilgrim and The Philokalia). This contact was decisive in David's personal transformation and atonement, as will become clear from the second story, which is, in a most unusual way, linked to David's fate.

About the same time that I received David's letter, a Texan businessman called me to relate an experience he had undergone while a pilgrim on Mount Athos. He introduced himself as a very wealthy man who had made his fortune in real estate. At one point in his life he had had a car accident that had left him mentally incapacitated. He had lost most of his memory and was unable to do simple arithmetic; a man with a masters degree in mathematics, and a second masters in business administration. At the urging of a friend—an Orthodox priest—this Texan (as I will refer to him), who was not Orthodox, decided to join him on a pilgrimage to Mount Athos. While walking from one monastery to another, they spotted a hermit dressed in rags plowing his garden. The Texan felt pity on him and offered him some money. When the hermit refused his generous offer, his friend explained that the reason why he is a hermit is precisely to live beyond worldly temptations. "But if you wish to give him some money to buy candles and light them in church for your healing he will do so", the Orthodox priest suggested. When that was clarified, the hermit accepted a small sum. He then placed his hands on the head of the Texan and began murmuring some Greek prayers that the Texan could not understand. "I thought for a moment", he told me over the phone, "that the old hermit living by himself in the wilderness was half demented." When the Athonite hermit finished his prayer, he turned to the Greek American priest and said "Your friend is whole now." Then they continued their hike. Just as they reached their destination, outside the gate of the next monastery, the Texan's memory was suddenly restored. He was "whole" again. Overwhelmed by his experience, he decided to devote time and money to help set up an Athonite monastery in the United States. And this is what happened. A septuagenarian elder from Mount Athos, reputed for his charismatic and prophetic gifts migrated to the United States and, with the help of the Texan and other patrons, set up a monastery in the middle of a desert in the American South West. The story of how it was located in the desert is a "miracle" in itself. I was told that while they were roaming the desert in a jeep searching for an appropriate location to buy land, they heard bells ringing. For the elder, that was a sign from heaven that they had found the right place, and he asked his companions to buy the land. They pointed out, however, that there was no water anywhere nearby and that the state would not allow the building of anything without a reliable water supply. The elder insisted. Obedient to their spiritual guide and elder, the Texan and the others bought a large portion of desert land knowing that they were "throwing their money away." As they predicted, the state refused a permit without first securing a water source. Then according to the story the elder, like an Old Testament prophet, went into the desert for three days of fasting and ceaseless prayer. On the third day he came out of his fasting and prayer and announced the spot where they should dig to find water. Lo and behold, after drilling deep into the desert floor they discovered a huge underground lake. The monastery was built and in a matter of six years the desolate land was transformed into a veritable oasis with thousands of pilgrims visiting each year hosted by over forty monks. In the meantime, plans were made to create a women's monastery nearby.

Interestingly, the monastery was an hour away from the maximum-security prison where David was being held. Furthermore, the abbot of the monastery (not the spiritual elder who created the monastery) was a friend of Father Maximos from their years together on Mount Athos. Father Maximos requested that his friend take up the case of David, and after nine months of persistent effort, the authorities eventually gave permission to the bearded black-robed monks from the monastery to meet with David. They designed for him a program of spiritual practices and prayer meditations for his spiritual recovery. It was a program based on the ascetical traditions of Orthodox monks and hermits.

In his last letter to me, David said that the best thing that happened to him was to be arrested and sentenced to death. On death row, he said, he had discovered God. Had he remained out in the world, living the kind of life he had lived would have led him to a spiritual death. Now he is spiritually alive. No longer fearing death, his prison cell is his Athonite hermitage that helped him find himself and heal his soul. There is no question, according to Father Maximos and the monks who guided him on his spiritual journey, that David's metanoia (radical change of heart and mind, repentance) is genuine. He may eventually be executed, but he has been healed at the very core of his being. And this is what ultimately matters as far as Orthodoxy is concerned.

I believe these two parallel stories, the radical transformation of David and the mental recovery of the Texan businessman, are archetypal of the salient features of Eastern Orthodoxy: a healing tradition, a miracle tradition and a desert tradition. It is a healing tradition insofar as its ultimate goal is to heal the soul at its very core. David, through deep metanoia, was in the process of being spiritually healed from the vast chasm between him and God that had resulted from the kind of life he had carried on while living in the world. According to Orthodoxy, the ultimate goal of all human beings is in fact to re-establish this unity between us and God that was originally shattered as a result of the mythic Fall of Adam and Eve.

Furthermore, Orthodoxy is a miracle tradition in that the life of those who are reputed for establishing that direct connection with God—that is, the saints and holy elders—become vehicles for the healing energy of the Holy Spirit, which can cause miracles to happen not only on the spiritual and psychological levels, but also on the physical level, as in the case of the Athonite hermit who is credited for healing the Texan pilgrim, and Elder Paisios healing the woman who suffered from cancer. In fact, miracles are the sin qua non of what is, as a rule, required before one can be declared a saint by the Ecclesia. And these miracles must take place while the saint is alive and after he or she departs from this world. Mount Athos and Orthodoxy in general are filled with miracle stories of healing phenomena.

Lastly, in Eastern Orthodox mystical spirituality, the desert plays a prominent role, both literally and figuratively, in the development of its theology and spiritual practices. Once Christianity was established as the official religion of the Roman Empire in the early part of the fourth century, the new "martyrs", as living witnesses to the faith, were hermits, like the Great Anthony, who abandoned the comforts of city life and entered the desert to find God through ceaseless prayer, contemplation and spiritual exercises. This tradition is preserved to the present day in ancient monasteries like those of Mount Athos that cultivate inner silence so that the practitioner may hear the voice of God. That is, the way to reach God and unite with God is to create space within us, an "inner desert" so to speak, free of egotistical passions, and within that silence, God's voice will echo into the depths of our hearts. The full-time practitioners of this inner silence are the ascetics from whose ranks came most of the leading saints and the great theologians of Eastern Christianity. These holy elders provided the foundations of its healing tradition as well as its mystical theology.

As I learned from Father Maximos and other elders, the hallmark of Eastern Orthodox mystical spirituality is what I have called The Three-Fold Way (Markides 2001, pp. 212–24). The holy elders teach that the re-establishment of the shattered unity between human beings and God proceeds in three identifiable stages: Catharsis (the purification of the soul), Fotisis (the enlightenment of the soul) and Theosis (union with God). Below, I will summarize these three stages. I am struck by their universality. They can be considered the necessary and fundamental path that all human beings must traverse before they re-unite with God, the ultimate healing of the Self and the soul's final destination.

The premise upon which The Three-Fold Way stands is the belief that human beings, since time immemorial, have fallen from Grace. They have shattered their connection with God and live their lives in a state of exile from their true homeland. This is the meaning of "original sin" as understood by the mystical holy elders of Eastern Christianity. A key pre-condition for union with God, as I mentioned, is that the individual undergoes deep metanoia which will lead to the process of catharsis and purification of the soul from egotistical passions. The story of Genesis in the Old Testament and the Parable of the Prodigal Son in the New Testament allude to this fundamental existential truth about human origins and destiny. In the Parable, the prodigal son left the palace of the loving Father and cut himself off from his heavenly, spiritual roots. He eventually squandered his divine inheritance by indulging in the various passions and temptations of the material world. The Prodigal's entire human nature was distorted and the passions that were given as properties of the soul to celebrate the Creator were now employed for the satisfaction of egotism. For example, the capacity of the soul for anger, given to the soul as the power to resist temptation and sin, became a source of discord among human beings both individually and collectively for the satisfaction of lowly desires. Similarly pride in one's divine lineage becomes pride over one's possessions, craving for attention and fame, power over others and so on. I must admit that I found this interpretation of the parable compelling.

At a certain point the Prodigal son is exhausted from his miserable existence (which is life cut off from God) and begins to yearn for the Palace. This is the beginning of the return journey. The Prodigal, after great difficulties and tribulations, eventually returns, and the Father embraces him and orders a feast to celebrate the return of His lost son. I realized that this was meant to be an allusion to the story of every human being who yearns for a connection with God and begins the process of metanoia and catharsis. The Palace, this Inner Kingdom, is always part of us but we do not recognize it because it is covered up by poor habits, inattention, and materialistic desires. The Prodigal Son never stops being a prince even while living among the pigs (notice the similarity of the Prodigal Son story with Plato's parable of the Cave).

The Christian elders teach that the process of healing and the restoration of the soul requires arduous spiritual struggle and effort. This is a point also made by modern religious thinkers. It is a point often lost on a culture that values instant gratification. The Ecclesia, based on its accumulated experiences resulting from the lives and teachings of its saints and holy elders, provides a methodology for how to heal the soul, how to free ourselves from egotistical desires and reestablish our connection to God. This methodology is called askisis which literally means exercise. The full-time practitioners of askisis are ascetics, whose practices and discoveries can help those of us who live in the world to proceed on our journey of re-union with God. It is this askisis that the American Athonite monks taught David in order to help him heal himself from the vast abyss that he created separating him from God's Grace as a result of his earlier life.

Among the set of practices that form askisis are regular participation in the sacraments of the Ecclesia like confession and communion, charitable action in the world, fasting, ceaseless prayer, systematic study of sacred texts and the life of saints, cultivation of deep humility, communal worship and so on. Charity, when given freely and unselfconsciously, is important in all its facets (material and non-material giving and caring for the other) as a way of forgetting our own self-absorption and our tendency to imprison our hearts within the things of this world. Similarly, fasting trains the soul to master the lower passions. The logic behind it is that, unless you learn gradually to overcome small temptations, such as avoidance of certain foods, you will not develop the power to resist greater temptations that unavoidably assault our everyday existence. Confession too, through the spiritual guidance of an experienced elder is essential so that we not only address our sinful actions but we can most importantly become conscious and thus monitor our logismoi, the negative thought-forms that we constantly generate in our minds, which deposit layer upon layer of separation between us and God. We are called to replace these logismoi with systematic and ceaseless remembrance and contemplation of God through prayer. A most important practice is the incessant repetition of short prayers, foremost of which is the Noera Prosefche, or the Jesus Prayer ("Lord Jesus Christ, Son of God Have Mercy on Me"). The practitioner is asked to repeat this prayer as much as possible. It can be recited even while engaging in worldly activities like waiting at a bus stop or washing dishes.

The purpose of this practice is to minimize the creation of negative thought-forms and replace them with the memory of God as a vehicle for re-capturing the paradisiacal stage—which can be attained, by the way, in one's present life. For the holy elders, of course, the Jesus Prayer is an invocation of the Holy Name that in conjunction with reciting long-established prayers like the Psalms, reading about the lives of saints, and attending regular communal services, eventually will bear fruit in the life of the practitioner. There are variants to the Jesus Prayer, like that of Saint Gregory Palamas who used to pray "Lord Enlighten my Darkness", over and over.

At a certain point, for the soul that engages in askisis and the systematic catharsis from worldly passions, Fotisis will follow. At this stage, when the soul has undergone its purification and after attaining depths of humility, Divine Providence offers the soul extraordinary gifts such as contemplating the "Uncreated Light" (God's light), prophetic vision, healing abilities such as those mentioned earlier, phenomena of levitation and bi-location and the like. These gifts are deeply buried within human nature, and as a rule become manifest after the purification of the soul. Therefore, what we call "paranormal" phenomena are in reality very normal at this second stage. These are the gifts that are reported in the lives of saints who serve as models for us of what we may be.

The most prized gift of the Spirit, as far as the saints are concerned superseding all other gifts, is the vision of the Uncreated Light, the mystical contemplation of God's presence in the world that floods the soul with exquisite joy. The following is an example of such an experience as narrated by Elder Joseph from the Vatopaedi monastery of Mount Athos:

> "I remember clearly that as soon as I began to mention in my prayer several times the name of Christ my heart filled with love. Suddenly it increased so much that I was no longer praying but I was in a state of wonder about this overflowing of love. I wanted to embrace and kiss all human beings and the entire creation and at the same time I was thinking so humbly . . . .I felt the presence of our Christ but I could not see him. I wanted to fall down to His immaculate feet and ask Him how does He set fire to the hearts of people and yet remain hidden from them. I was then given to understand that Christ is inside every human being. I said, my Lord let me be in this state forever and I need nothing else. This state lasted for some time and when I came back to my original condition I couldn't wait until I went to my gerontas (elder) to tell him all about it . . . ."

He further had this to say on the matter:

> "When the mind of the person has been cleansed, purified and enlightened . . . . it is given, in addition to its own light, the light of Divine Grace so that it remains permanently within him. Then it snatches him and exposes him to visions and perceptions true to its own nature. However, such a person has the capacity, if he so wishes, to ask through prayer. Then Grace is energized and what he asks is given simply because he asks. But I believe the truly devout avoid such requests except in extraordinary circumstances." (Joseph 1984; Markides 1995, pp. 302–3)

As Elder Joseph states, those who are offered such gifts of the Spirit accept them in utter humility, and they must never be a source for self-promotion and self-aggrandizement. In fact, such gifts may also be strong temptations that can often lead to a spiritual fall. That is why great saints do their utmost to hide them and use them only sparingly and only to help fellow human beings in their spiritual, psychological and medical needs. It is for this reason also that the desert fathers have been called nyptic, meaning vigilant. They were constantly fully conscious and on guard against such temptations. Therefore, from the point of view of the holy elders of Orthodoxy any healing ability that one may be endowed with should not be flaunted for the sake of impressing an audience as happens so often today among certain "New Age" circles. I remember the strong reaction of Elder Paisios when I naively asked him about his reputed abilities to heal people. He emphatically denied such "rumors", stating that all he does is pray for people, and that whatever healing takes place is the result of God's Grace and Providence. Yet these rumors crossed the Atlantic, reaching me in Maine when I first heard of him and of his reputed friendship with wild animals like bears and poisonous snakes. In Orthodox spirituality, the God-realized individual who has reached paradise in this life re-establishes a harmonious relationship with nature that was a characteristic of life before the Fall. Hence the legends of saints who lived among wild beasts without fear of being harmed.

Finally, the third stage in the spiritual development of the self is the attainment of Theosis, the ultimate destination of the human soul and its restoration into the oneness of God. It is the ultimate healing of the soul. Like the previous stage of Fotisis it is totally in the hands of Providence. Human beings cannot re-unite with God strictly on their own accord. Our will must be engaged only at the first stage, the stage of Catharsis. The other two stages follow naturally as God's rewards, as it were, for our struggles to purify our hearts. Therefore, attempts to get to those "Gifts" directly (for example trying to develop one's psychic powers per se) without at the same time struggling to free the soul from egotism, may be the equivalent of "stealing from God", leading to what has been called "black magic".

All of the great sages have pointed out that the oneness with God, at Theosis is beyond all human description or comprehension. I should also point out that in Christian spirituality, the soul upon its return home maintains autonomy within the oneness of God. The self does not get diluted into the All. What is annihilated is the sum total of our egotistical passions and desires, not our uniqueness as persons created in the image of God for eternity. This is a big difference, with some notions stipulating that the final end of spiritual development is the obliteration of personhood, a form of spiritual nihilism. The God-realized human being will retain his or her uniqueness within God while continuing from the paradisiacal side to work for the salvation of others. It is also important to repeat that Theosis is not a stage that one can reach only after one is dead but while one is still alive and active in this world. The paradisiacal stage, the ultimate healing of the human person, is possible from this side of the divide. Our paradise or our hell can start from this life.

Before ending this section, a caveat is perhaps needed here. It would be a mistake to assume that the Athonite elders, abbots, and monastics that I have encountered over the years and written about are perfect souls. They are not infallible. Like all human beings, they make mistakes, and often grave and, yes, appalling mistakes. They do so as a result of the limitations of their formal education and the social and cultural constraints they find themselves in. In this respect it is important to remember that this has been the case with the greatest of saints of the Christian tradition, past and present. Are we, for example, to reject the wisdom of St. Paul because of what has been attributed to him as forms of misogyny and homophobia? Or are we to discredit the entire corpus of St. John Chrysostom because of his alleged antisemitism? Many "cultured despisers" of religion (to borrow Friedrich Schleiermacher's graphic phrase) focused on whatever shortcomings they could uncover and debunk, and discredit wholesale the entire enterprise of monastic life and teachings. It is important, therefore, not to over-idealize monastic communities and expect the behavior of its members to be of the quality, literally speaking, of the angelic orders! Otherwise we may be massively disappointed and in the process deprive ourselves of the benefit of whatever accumulated wisdom is preserved in these institutions over the centuries.

1. Summary and Conclusions

I have tried to show in this paper that in the monasteries of Eastern Orthodoxy, perhaps more so than in any other part of the Christian world, a healing mystical tradition has been preserved (the Three-fold Way) that we assumed was only prevalent in religions like Hinduism, Tibetan Buddhism and native shamanism. Many westerners, disenchanted with the prevailing rationalism of mainstream culture, both in terms of its religious and scientific expression, have turned towards the far east for an experiential and miraculous pathway to Reality, while all the time one has existed right within Christianity.

I have also tried to show that the increasing interest among modern individuals in "paranormal" and miraculous phenomena (angels, prophetic visions, out-of-body travel, near-death experiences, extraordinary healings, etc.), dismissed by doctrinaire skeptics as non-phenomena, have been the sin qua non of the life of Eastern Orthodox saints and a hallmark of Eastern Christianity. Therefore, the miracle, mystical culture of Eastern Christianity might be of interest not only to mainstream Christians of all denominations, but also to an increasing number of westerners who have been attracted to the mystical religions of the East and their New Age variants, a trend that has become so much a part of our cultural and religious landscape today.

Potentially, the Three-fold Way of Eastern Orthodoxy can contribute to the development of what transpersonal theorists call "the eye of contemplation", namely the cultivation of the intuitive, spiritual side of human beings that has been repressed over the last few centuries because of the triumph of rationalism and scientific materialism. This has led to what sociologist Max Weber called the "disenchantment of the world" and theologian Philip Sherrard lamented as "the desecration of the world."(Sherrard 1998) The spiritual methodologies that have been preserved in ancient monasteries of the Christian East may play a role in overcoming positivism, reductionism, relativism and determinism, ideologies that have dominated our higher culture during the last three hundred years. It will be remembered that it is the mystical side of Orthodoxy that led literary masters like Tolstoy and Dostoevsky to be frequent patrons at the famous monastery of Optina, destroyed by the Bolsheviks during the aftermath of the Russian Revolution. It is there that they nurtured their spiritual view of reality, and it is there that Dostoevsky met the elder that he fictionalized in his Brothers Karamazov as "Father Zosima".

The question comes to mind, of course, whether Eastern Orthodoxy as it presents itself today to the rest of the world is ready to play a historical part in the "re-enchantment" or the "re-sacralization" of the world. I posed that question to Kallistos Ware (retired Lecturer of Eastern Orthodox Studies at the University of Oxford and an Orthodox bishop himself) in a recent interview (Markides 2005, pp. 148–77). His answer was unambiguously in the negative, as I would have expected from anyone who understands the state of affairs of the Eastern Church. What are the problems, then, that seem to be obstacles that prevent Orthodoxy from making a contribution to an emerging, modern culture? Here is a short summary.

The eastern part of Christianity, because of historical reasons (triumph of Islam and communist takeover), remained cut off from the cultural and historical forces that shaped the modern age. This isolation from western cultural and intellectual developments (such as the Enlightenment) has served as a double-edged sword. On one hand it helped preserve the Three-fold Way. On the other hand, Eastern Christianity has shown serious deficits and gaps in its ability to deal creatively with the intellectual challenges of a world that is rapidly becoming global and culturally diverse. Therefore, the temptation is strong to nurture an insular fundamentalism, a tendency not only to be indifferent to an understanding of other religions, but to monopolize God, as it were, by demonizing other religions as nothing but heresies. Another difficulty is the tendency of some theologians to nurture hostility towards the West as if they are still living during the time of the Fourth Crusade, when Constantinople was ransacked by the holy warriors of the West, paving the way for the Ottoman takeover of Byzantium. Such xenophobic attitudes are painfully pronounced among several segments of the ecclesiastical establishment of the Christian East. I have time and again been amazed by the extremely reactionary political, religious and cultural utterances of some members of the higher clergy, including Athonite monks. With an inability to understand the modern world and its pluralistic texture and a concomitant wholesale rejection of its cultural values (equality of women, diversity as good rather than demonic), they make it difficult for westerners to discover for themselves the hidden spiritual and healing treasures found in the monastic tradition that I have presented in this paper. Westerners with a thirst for spiritual healing and experience will simply look elsewhere: in the ashrams of India, in Zen meditation monasteries, in native American sweat lodges. These traditions are outside of the cultural baggage that has plagued the troubled histories of the Abrahamic religions. But I remain positive and hopeful. There are many enlightened ones: theologians, monks, patriarchs, and bishops who, being inspired by the mystical teachings of the holy elders, are struggling against such narrowness of vision and quietly working for an open dialogue, understanding and cooperation among the religions. May their efforts bear fruit for the good of Orthodoxy and the World. For I do believe that the mystical pathways of Eastern Christianity can contribute immensely not only to the healing of individual souls, but to the healing of our troubled world, stranded as it is in the quick sands of materialism. We have come to this point by falsely assuming that ultimate reality is the reality of our sensate, observable universe, an ultimately nihilistic outlook on life. The saints and holy elders of Eastern Christianity might help us find our way out from our present predicament.

Conflicts of Interest: The author declares no conflict of interest.

References

No Author. 1976. New York Times Book Review. *New York Time*, January 18.

Brown, Courntney. 2005. *Remote Viewing: The Science and Theory of Nonphysical Perception*. Atlanta: Farsight Press.

Dossey, Larry. 2014. *One Mine: How Our Individual Mind Is Part of a Greater Consciousness and Why It Matters*. New York: Hay House.

Fontana, David. 2003. *Psychology, Religion, and Spirituality*. Oxford: Blackwell.

Frank, Jerome. 1974. *Persuasion and Healing*. New York: Schocken Books.

Harner, Michael. 1982. *The Way of the Shaman: A Guide to Power and Haling*. New York: Bantam.

Joseph, Monk. 1984. *Geron Ioseph Oh Hesychastses*. Daphne: Agion Oros. (In Greek)

Lossky, Vladimir. 1997. *The Mystical Theology of the Eastern Church*. Yonkers: St. Vladimirs Seminary Press.

Markides, Kyriacos C. 1990. *The Magus of Strovolos: The Extraordinary World of a Spiritual Healer*. New York: Penguin; Abingdon-on-Thames: Routledge and Kegan Paul. First Published in 1985.

Markides, Kyriacos C. 1987. *Homage to the Sun: The Wisdom of the Magus of Strovolos*. New York: Penguin/Arkana.

Markides, Kyriacos C. 1990. *Fire in the Heart: Healers, Sages, and Mystics*. New York: Penguin/Arkana.

Markides, Kyriacos C. 1995. *Riding with the Lion: In Search of Mystical Christianity*. New York: Viking.

Markides, Kyriacos C. 2001. *The Mountain of Silence: A Search for Orthodox Spirituality*. New York: Doubleday.

Markides, Kyriacos C. 2005. *Gifts of the Desert: The Forgotten Path of Christian Spirituality*. New York: Doubleday.

Markides, Kyriacos C. 2012. *Inner River: A Pilgrimage to the Heart of Christian Spirituality*. New York: Doubleday.

Meyendorff, John. 1974. *St. Gregory Palamas and Orthodox Spirituality*. Yonkers: St. Vladimirs Seminary Press.

Penfield, Wilder. 1975. *The Mystery of the Mind*. Princeton: Princeton University Press.

Plested, Marcus. 2012. *Orthodox Readings of Aquinas*. Oxford: OUP.

Radin, Dean. 1997. *The Conscious Universe: The Scientific Truth of Psychic Phenomena*. New York: Harper Collins.

Sogyal, Rinpoche. 2012. *The Tibetan Book of Living and Dying*. New York: Harper Collins.

Schulz, Mona Lisa. 2005. *The New Feminine Brain: How Women Can Develop their Inner Strengths, Genius and Intuition*. New York: Free Press.

Sherrard, Philip. 1998. *Christianity: Lineaments of a Sacred Tradition*. Brookline: Holy Cross Orthodox Press.

Smith, Huston. 2002. *Why Religion Matters*. San Francisco: Harper.

Sorokin, Pitirim A. 1947. *Society, Culture and Personality*. New York: Harper.

Stark, Rodney. 2006. *The Victory of Reason: How Christianity Led to Freedom, Capitalism, and Western Success*. New York: Random House.

Stark, Rodney. 2014. *How the West Won: The Neglected Story of the Triumph of Modernity*. Wilmington: Intercollegiate Studies Institute Press.

Ware, Kallistos. 1995. *The Orthodox Way*. Yonkers: St. Vladimirs Seminary Press.

Wilber, Ken. 1998. *The Marriage of Sense and Soul: Integrating Science and Religion*. New York: Random House.

Wilson, Colin. 1988. *Beyond the Occult*. New York: Carroll & Graf.

Yogananda, Paramahansa. 1987. *Autobiography of a Yogi*. Los Angeles: Self-Realization Fellowship.

religions

MDPI

Article

Death and Dying in Orthodox Liturgy

Nicholas Denysenko

Department of Theological Studies, Loyola Marymount University, 1 Loyola Marymount University Dr,
Los Angeles, CA 90045, USA; ndenysen@lmu.edu; Tel.: +1-310-568-6235

Academic Editor: John A. Jillions
Received: 16 November 2016; Accepted: 8 February 2017; Published: 15 February 2017

Abstract: The Orthodox Church is known for its liturgical aesthetics. The rich liturgical cycle consists of several liturgical offices celebrated throughout the year, complete with icons, chant, polyphony, and powerful ritual gestures. The Divine Liturgy is the external symbol of the typical Orthodox liturgy. The liturgical celebration profoundly shapes the inner and outer lives of the liturgical participants, as liturgy is a constant and repetitive rehearsal of dying and rising to new life. This article examines the most salient patterns and instances of dying and rising to new life in Orthodox liturgy and concludes with a reflection on how engaging this process might have a greater impact on the daily lives of Orthodox Christians today.

Keywords: Baptism; death; rising; Communion; repentance

The Orthodox Church projects many images to the public. In Western society, Orthodoxy is known for its ethnic dimension, especially when parishes host festivals with native foods, music, and dancing and invite the public's participation. The public sneaks a glimpse into Orthodoxy at performances featuring world-renowned composers such as Rachmaninoff and Pärt and local art exhibits displaying galleries of icons. The music and iconography belong to Orthodoxy's liturgical tradition, which continues to retain select aspects of the structure and aesthetical performative style of its Byzantine and Russian imperial past. These public images of Orthodoxy do not communicate the fullness of its inner and outer liturgical life, however. Deeper and regular participation in the ordinary weekly worship of Orthodoxy, the Sunday Divine Liturgy, discloses the Orthodox Church as a community of faithful that participates in Christ's death in preparation for eternal life.

In this essay, I argue that Orthodox liturgy initiates the faithful into a process of death in Christ and dying to themselves, preparing them for eternal life. Baptism establishes this process of death and dying, and the pattern is repeated in the regular celebration of the Divine Liturgy, and complemented by participation in other liturgical offices. I begin by showing how Baptism makes death and dying normative for the Orthodox Christian. Then, I explore the Divine Liturgy to show how death and dying to sin are necessary to receive the gift of communion in the Holy Spirit, which is a foretaste of life shared with the Triune God. The analysis of the Divine Liturgy includes consultation of preparation for Holy Communion and the prayers recited after Communion, and I will draw from these to demonstrate how the pattern of death and dying appears throughout the Orthodox liturgical tradition. This analysis applies to both the inner and outer lives of Orthodox Christians, and this essay concludes with a reflection on the challenge of applying the discipline of liturgical death and dying to the challenges of relationships Orthodox Christians confront in daily life.

1. Orthodox Liturgy: Baptism as Death in Christ in Preparation for Eternal Life

The initial participation in Christ's death and dying to sin begins with Baptism in Orthodox liturgy. It might seem absurd to begin with the obvious, since the primary theological motif underpinning Baptism is the paschal mystery of death and resurrection. The primary reason for beginning with Baptism is the inauguration of the ritual pattern of death and dying and rising to new life. It is this pattern of dying to sin with the anticipation of rising to new life that appears in all other Orthodox liturgical services and is repeated most profoundly in the Eucharist. Baptism is particularly helpful for connecting participation in Christ's death with the practices of dying to sin and rising to new life in ordinary Christian daily life.

Patterns of Death in Baptism

The rite of Baptism contains numerous allusions to death. The most prevalent references to death occur in the ritual texts and gestures that cast out powers opposed to God from all places of the ritual celebration. A series of exorcisms take place at the beginning of the rite, followed by the candidate's renunciation of Satan. These ritual components establish the beginning of putting to death the covenant with the evil one in order to rise to life in a new covenant with Christ. The next major apotropaic action occurs in the blessing of baptismal waters, when the celebrant makes the sign of the cross in the water with his hand (three times) and breathing upon the water, casting out God's enemies:

> Let all adverse powers be crushed beneath the singing of your most precious Cross! (3x)
> We pray You, o Lord, let every airy and invisible specter withdraw itself from us, and let
> not a demon of darkness conceal himself in this water; neither let an evil spirit, bringing
> obscurity of purpose and rebellious thoughts, descend into it with him (her) that is about
> to be baptized [1].

The purpose of cleansing the water in this fashion is to make the font a place where the covenant with Christ and the Holy Trinity can commence, without any of God's adversaries laying claim to the one receiving Baptism. After performing the apotropaic rites of casting out dark powers, the presider calls upon God to make the water a place where life begins anew:

> But do you, o Master of All, declare this water to be the water of redemption, water of
> sanctification, a cleansing of flesh and spirit, a loosing of bonds, a forgiveness of sins,
> an illumination of soul, a laver of regeneration, a renewal of the spirit, a gift of sonship,
> a garment of incorruption, a fountain of life. For You have said, o Lord: 'wash, and be
> clean; put away evil from your souls' [1].

The fountain of water becomes a place of transformation ([2], p. 50). The rite denotes the transformation of the water itself, as it becomes God's instrument of redeeming, cleaning, renewing, and illuminating the one receiving Baptism. The most important motif to take from the symbiosis of ritual and text in the baptismal blessing of waters is the inseparability of death and new life. In Baptism, God recreates those receiving the mystery into new human beings who are God's children, but the process of recreating is impossible without death; the entire human participant needs to be made new, and this process can begin only when the candidate partakes of Christ's death and then puts sin to death. The text also refers to the water as a garment of incorruption. The new human being's recreation is preserved by the very water that has been a divine instrument of recreation, and, in practical terms, this is possible only through the community's memory of Baptism, celebrated annually at the blessing of Theophany waters on January 6 [3].

The blessing of the oil that follows the blessing of waters is the next preparatory rite, calling upon God to bless the oil through the descent of the Holy Spirit so that the oil would become:

> An anointing of incorruption, a shield of righteousness, a renewal of soul and body,
> and averting of every operation of the devil, to the removal of all evils from them that are
> anointed with it in faith, or are partakers of it [1].

The presider pours the oil into the water in the sign of the cross three times while the assembly sings 'Alleluia', and then the presider takes some of the oil and anoints the one receiving Baptism with it on the forehead, breast, between the shoulders, and on the ears. The prebaptismal blessing and anointing with oil is preparatory for the Baptism to occur in the font, but, despite its secondary ranking in the ritual performance, it bears the same function as the blessing of waters; to protect the one receiving Baptism from adversarial powers who might struggle with God for dominion over the newly-born Christian ([2], p. 52; [4], p. 107). As with the blessing of water, the oil contributes to the process of new birth, which again requires some action of death, in this case the 'removal of all evils' from the one being baptized.

The prayer recited by the presider over the oil is rooted in an anamnesis of the covenant God created with humanity through the great flood and the renewal of humanity in Noah's ark:

> Sovereign Lord and Master, God of our Fathers, Who did send to them in the Ark of Noah a dove bearing a twig of olive in its beak as a sign of reconciliation and salvation from the Flood, and through these things prefigured the Mystery of Grace [1].

In terms of liturgical celebration, the anamnesis establishes the epiclesis, wherein the Church petitions God to send the Spirit and bless the oil ([5], pp. 46–50). The anamnesis itself functions as the community's reminder that God gave humanity the olive branch as a sign of the recreation of humanity. The olive branch is a token of the new peace between God and humanity following the death of sin in the waters of the flood. In the present, the Church manufactures the oil used to renew the covenant between God and humanity through the olive trees. The use of olive oil as a secondary material instrument of God's recreation of humanity is significant here because it represents the repetition of the pattern established in the blessing of waters as death to sin and evil, leading to recreation and renewal in the new covenant. Therefore, the use of oil is itself a symbol of this process of death in Christ and rising in new life, following the pattern established by the blessing of waters. One should also note that the power borne by the sanctified water and oil is not temporary. I would argue that the power of these elements is permanent because they convey the power of the eternal God, since the ritual texts demand divine intervention and presence in the instruments through which God acts.

The death in Christ and the rising to new life of the one to be baptized moves from preparation to realization when the candidate is immersed into the source of water three times, in the name of the Trinity, with the assistance of the presider. The intonation of Psalm 31 repeats these motifs already established by the preparatory rituals, as the psalm rejoices in the blessings received by those 'whose iniquities are forgiven and whose sins are covered'. The Baptism through immersion in the water results in the death of sin.

The anointing with Chrism occurs at this point in Baptism [6]. Readers should note that there is no separation of Chrismation from Baptism in the Orthodox rite, but the anointing with Chrism occurs as part of the normal sequence of ritual events following Baptism.[1] The rite of Baptism continues with the prayer of Chrismation, which repeats the same themes in conformity with the ritual and theological patterns we have established. The Church prays that anointing with Chrism will deliver the following blessings to the one receiving Baptism:

> Bestow upon him (her) also the seal of your omnipotent and adorable Holy Spirit, and the Communion of the Holy Body and Most Precious Blood of Your Christ; keep him (her) in your sanctification; confirm him (her) in the Orthodox Faith; deliver him (her) from the evil one and all his devices; preserve his (her) soul, through your saving fear, in purity and righteousness, that in every work and word, being acceptable before You, he (she) may become a child and heir of your heavenly kingdom [1].

The anointing with Chrism follows, with the sign of the cross being made on the forehead, eyes, nostrils, mouth, ears, breast, hands, and feet, symbolizing a whole-body anointing but also

---

[1] A methodological note here: the rite of Baptism does not include the prayer for the consecration of the Chrism, which does not observe the same pattern established here, since the prebaptismal oil and water were blessed in the same service. In Orthodoxy, Chrism is prepared by the patriarch or primate of a local church on Holy Thursday, as needed. The head of the local Church distributes the consecrated Chrism to eparchial bishops, who then share it with parish priests for Baptisms.

ritually connecting the Christian's everyday life of thinking and animated human action with the Holy Spirit [1].[2] The anointing with Chrism seals in the gifts bestowed at Baptism; the Christian is expected to continue to die to the temptations of the evil one in continuity with the death to evil inaugurated at Baptism. The prayer of Chrismation also explicates the destiny of the recreated child of God; she is to become a child and heir of God's kingdom. The gifts bestowed upon the baptized at the anointing with Chrism thus continue what was already given at Baptism. What is new in Chrismation is the permanence of the gift; the whole-body anointing denotes God's capacitating action of sustaining the gifts already established at Baptism by adding a new layer to the recreated human being, who is now also a temple of the Holy Spirit ([6], pp. 21–22). Also noteworthy in the text for the prayer of Chrismation is the notion that Chrismation is not a final act of God, leaving the new Christian to their own will; the prayers position Chrismation as the next step of Baptism, preparing the Christian to receive Holy Communion at the Divine Liturgy ([6], p. 22). Anointing with Chrism grants the Christian the sustaining power of the Spirit to animate them to grow in Christ; God will also provide the nourishment of Christ's Body and Blood in the Eucharist, which will enable the Christian to continue to die to the temptations of the evil one in anticipation of the fulfillment of the new life that was inaugurated by Baptism and Chrismation, as we shall see when we explore death, dying, and new life in the Divine Liturgy below.

The remainder of the rite of Baptism continues to build on the foundation established by the blessing of baptismal waters and oil and the anointing with Chrism. Attentive scholars might inquire about the traditional significance attributed to the conferring of the white garment to the new Christian (immediately following Chrismation), not to mention the singing of the hymn 'As many as have been baptized into Christ have put on Christ: Alleluia' (Galatians 3:27) and circumambulation of the table; the public recitation of the Epistle (Romans 6:3–11), which communicates the traditional paschal motif associated with Baptism of late antiquity; the Gospel; tonsure; and the churching of the new Christian. All of these significant ritual components continue the pattern of death in Christ, dying to sin, and rising to new life inaugurated by the preparatory rites of Baptism.

The final liturgical component contributing to the motif of death in Christ and dying to sin in the rite of Baptism is the prayer said by the presider prior to the blessing of the waters [1]. As the deacon intones the litany for Baptism, which emphasizes the blessing of the waters, the presider offers a prayer of apology, asking for God's forgiveness of sins, to make the presider worthy of leading the liturgical rite of Baptism. The prayer emphasizes God's purification of the presider with the powerful language of penitential mortification:

> Neither turn away your face from me, but overlook my offenses in this hour, O You that overlook the sins of men that they repent. Wash away the defilement of my body and the stain of my soul. Sanctify me wholly by Your all-effectual, invisible might, and by your spiritual right hand, lest, by preaching liberty to others, and offering this in the perfect faith of your unspeakable love for humankind, I may be condemned as a servant of sin [1].

The apologetic prayers of the presiding clergy are secondary to the primary rites we have treated earlier, but they are significant when considering the entirety of the liturgical context. The apologetic prayers refer to the gravitas of divine activity and blessing and require the participating clergy to die to their own distractions and their own selves so that their liturgical service is one of cooperation with divine activity and not distraction from it. In other words, a special kind of death to self in the moment is required of the presider, a liturgical asceticism that ensures the clergy will not be obstacles to the Church's prayer that God 'form the image of...Christ' in the baptismal candidate.

---

2   I have limited this discussion to the anointing with Chrism in order to show how the process of dying in Christ and rising to new life occurs primarily in the sacraments of initiation. Orthodox Christianity also observes the tradition of anointing the sick with oil, which is likewise relevant to the process of dying in Christ. See [7] for more details.

2. Eucharist: Remembrance of Death in Preparation for Eternal Life

The regular, weekly celebration of the Eucharist (Divine Liturgy) is the primary liturgical event for the typical Orthodox parish.[3] Through the course of the Liturgy, participants engage the practices of death in Christ and dying to sin in preparation for new life. In this sense, the Eucharist is the regular engagement of the process of dying to sin and rising to new life that was initially established at Baptism and fortified at Chrismation. In this section, we will focus primarily on the remembrance of and participation in Christ's death as the primary way the Eucharist promotes death and dying to sin as a process, and we will also refer to complementary liturgical components echoing death and dying as preparation for new life in the pre- and post-Communion prayers appointed to each participant. The structure of the Liturgy begins with the preparatory rites (prothesis), followed by the liturgy of the Word, the offertory, the anaphora, Holy Communion, and post-Communion. While the anaphora is the most significant component expressing the remembrance of Christ's death, we will observe the order of the Liturgy and begin with the prothesis.

The prothesis is the rite of preparation, in which the priest (and deacon) prepares the material elements for the offering of the liturgy. Fundamentally, the prothesis is a simple and necessary rite of preparing and arranging the bread, wine, and water used for the liturgy. The bread is placed on a special plate (diskos) and the wine is poured into an ornate cup with some cold water. In the early medieval period of Byzantine liturgical history, the prothesis rite endured a transformation ([8], pp. 16–34; [9], pp. 197–228). The deacons used to collect the breads and wine donated by the faithful and select the ones to be used for the liturgy ([8], p. 17). In the early medieval period, after the deacons had arranged all of the material elements, the patriarch would come and say one concluding prayer of preparation ([10], pp. 49–50), but during the middle to later Byzantine period, the preparation evolved into a detailed rite, in which every action of preparation represented some aspect of the life of Christ, from his birth through to his resurrection, possibly in response to the triumph of Orthodoxy and the multiplication of icons decorating Church interiors ([11], pp. 58–59). Stelyios Muksuris's detailed theological analysis of the rite shows that the placement of the particles on the diskos eventually depicted the ecclesiology of the Orthodox Church, while retaining its communication of the life of Christ ([12], pp. 155–59). The Churches observing the Byzantine rite today prepare the elements in memory of Christ's birth, death, and resurrection from the dead.

The remembrance of Christ's death is particularly poignant in the very first steps taken to prepare the bread for the Eucharist, when the priest pierces the bread with a spear, cutting the four sides to lift out the lamb to be used for Communion from the larger portion of the bread ([13], pp. 15–16). The lamb is the largest square part of the bread marked by a seal with the words "IC XC NI KA" (Jesus Christ the victor). The priest's words coinciding with each piercing of the bread denote the performance of a ritual sacrifice, illustrated by Table 1:

Table 1. Rituals and Texts in Preparing the Lamb.

Ritual Action	Text Accompanying Ritual Action
Piercing and cutting on the right side of the bread	'As a sheep led to the slaughter'
Piercing and cutting on the left side of the bread	'or as a blameless lamb before its shearers is dumb, so He opens not his mouth'
Piercing and cutting on the top of the bread	'In his humiliation his judgment was taken away'
Piercing and cutting on the lower part of the bread	'For his life is taken up from the earth'
Piercing the bread on the bottom right, cutting, and lifting	'For his life is taken up from the earth'
Cutting the lamb crosswise, but taking care not to break the seal	'Sacrificed is the lamb of God, who takes away the sin of the world, for the life of the world and its salvation'
Turns the bread over, and pierces under the right side, underneath the seal	'One of the soldiers pierced His side with a spear, and at once there came out blood and water. He who saw it has borne witness, and his witness is true.'

---

[3] The Orthodox Church permits the celebration of the Divine Liturgy on most days of the year, with the exception of weekdays of the forty-day Lenten fast and Good Friday. For parish communities, the Sunday Divine Liturgy is the primary regular experience of the Eucharist.

At this point in the rite, the priest (or deacon) pours the blessed wine and water into the cup. The rite continues with the priest removing particles from other breads and placing them on the diskos in order, which extends the Eucharistic memorializing to include all the orders of the Church, and is concluded by the ritual covering of the gifts, a final prayer, and a dismissal ([13], pp. 17–25).

We owe a debt of thanks to the historians who have explained how this functional rite of preparing a plate of bread and a cup of wine mixed with water evolved into an elaborate remembrance of Christ's sacrificial death. There is no doubt that the rite is one of pictorial historicism, elongating the preparation of the bread into a series of particular incisions and cuts that refer to the Old Testament figures of Christ as the lamb of God and the New Testament witness of blood and water emerging from his side when the soldier pierced him with a spear. Orthodoxy has received a patristic mystagogical interpretation of this rite to understand that the incisions into the bread are not a real sacrifice of Christ occurring anew but the Church's response to Christ's command to remember his death.[4] The preparatory rite collects the entire memory of this death into an anticipation of the offering of the sacrifice to come at the liturgy, as the repetition of remembrance of Christ's death increases its weight in the Liturgy and contributes to the liturgy's exhortation to the people to participate in it ([12], pp. 195–211).

A second remembrance of Christ's death occurs during the Great Entrance, when the gifts are brought from the appointed table in the sanctuary to be ceremonially placed on the altar ([8], pp. 242–50). As with the prothesis rite, the Great Entrance is essentially a functional rite of moving the plate and cup for the offering and Holy Communion to the altar table. The placement of the gifts on the altar table came to symbolize Christ's death and burial in many local Christian centers as early as the fourth century ([8], pp. 35–38). The entrance as a ritual memorial of Christ's burial remains a part of the contemporary Orthodox liturgy, evinced by the Troparia recited by the presider when the gifts are placed on the table:

(1) The noble Joseph, when he had taken down Thy most pure body from the tree, wrapped it in fine linen and anointed it with spices, and placed it in a new tomb; (2) In the tomb with the body and in hell with the soul as God; in paradise with the thief, and on the throne with the Father and the Spirit, wast Thou, o boundless Christ, filling all things; (3) Bearing life and more fruitful than paradise, brighter than any royal chamber: Thy tomb, o Christ, is the fountain of our resurrection ([13], p. 127).

Robert Taft's scholarship shows that the placement of the gifts on the table had come to symbolize the liturgy as an iconic depiction of Christ's death and resurrection, with the altar functioning as the tomb. ([8], pp. 245–46). In this case, the hymns recited during the placement of the gifts refer to the burial of Christ's body while anticipating his resurrection from the dead to be shared with the faithful.

Another element symbolizes the process of dying to sin on the part of the people at this point in the liturgy; namely, the Cherubikon, the well-known hymn chanted as the clergy perform the rituals of preparation to perform the entrance and deposition of the gifts:

Let us who mystically represent the Cherubim and sing the thrice-holy hymn to the life-creating Trinity, now lay aside all earthly cares. That we may receive the king of all who comes invisibly upborne by the angelic hosts. Alleluia, alleluia, alleluia ([13], p. 122).

This well-known hymn is sung as often as needed to accompany the procession of gifts from the sanctuary back to the altar. The hymn's brief reference to 'laying aside all earthy cares' is a final call to attentiveness and effort on the part of the faithful, whose full attention is required as the Church prepares to present its offering to God. The hymn is similar to the prayer of apology recited by the presider at Baptism, as it calls the whole assembly, clergy and laity, to die to selfish concerns in

---

[4]   The pattern of interpreting the ritual actions as historical remembrances of events in Jesus' life occurred in mystagogical treatises on the Divine Liturgy in theologians such as Theodore of Mopsuestia, Germanos of Constantinople, and Symeon of Thessalonike, among others.

preparation for participation in Christ's death memorialized and ritualized.[5] The Great Entrance of the Orthodox liturgy thus functions as a remembrance of death in the interpretation of ceremonially placing the gifts on the altar as a representation of taking Jesus down from the cross and burying him in the tomb. The assembly is called to actively witness the memory of Christ's death, which leads to the ritual act of dying to one's self in order to devote full attention to the primary action of offering in the anaphora.

3. The Anaphora as Remembrance of Death and Resurrection

The anaphora communicates the process of death in Christ and dying to sin more poignantly than any other part of the liturgy. The anaphora emphasizes the transformation of the liturgical participant and the destiny of the communicant, which makes death and dying an essential part of the process but not its goal. The anaphora of St. John Chrysostom is used most frequently in the Orthodox liturgy; its text is brief, and it does not contain many references to the cross. The so-called 'post-Sanctus' portion of the prayer leads into the Institution Narrative and refers to the last supper that occurred 'in the night in which he was given up, or rather gave himself up for the life of the world'. Immediately prior to the elevation of the gifts (by the deacon, or in his absence, the priest or bishop), the presider recites the so-called anamnesis:

> Remembering this saving commandment and all those things which have come to pass for us: the cross, the tomb, the resurrection on the third day, the ascension into heaven and the second and glorious coming ([13], p. 67).

The anamnesis invokes the memory of the entirety of the paschal mystery; it is not only death, but an offering presented in thanksgiving for all of God's action 'for us'. This brief section of the anaphora depicts the actual process in which the participants are engaging; death, burial, and resurrection, all with the hope of ascension to share life with God. Following the ritual actions of consecration, the anaphora continues by iterating the blessing God gives to the participants: purification of soul, remission of sins, communion of the Holy Spirit, and fulfillment of the kingdom of heaven ([13], p. 69). Participation in the Eucharist results in the remission of sins and communion of the Holy Spirit (eternal life lived with God). In other words, the Eucharist repeats the same process of dying and rising to new life in and with God established at Baptism, as these gifts, which are essentially baptismal, are given again and again at the celebration of the Eucharist.

The emphasis on the necessity of living the process of dying and rising to new life is evinced by the next and last part of the anaphora. The prayer connects the Eucharistic offering to 'those who have fallen asleep in the faith', with every imaginable type of person remembered at this point in the liturgy ([13], p. 69). The action of remembrance refers to those who have already been through the process of dying and rising again, as those who are 'asleep' are now alive in Christ, acknowledged through the assembly's act of making memory ([14], pp. 34–37). The Orthodox liturgy's emphasis on the gift of eternal life is communicated by the ritual actions of fracture, commixture, and zeon. The fraction is again functional, the breaking of the Lord's body into the number of pieces required for distribution to all communicants at that particular liturgy. After the fraction, the presider places the lamb into the cup and says 'the fullness of the Holy Spirit'. Another reference to the descent of the Spirit on the cup occurs when the deacon pours the zeon (hot water) into the cup, making the contents of the cup a warm mixture of consecrated water, wine, and bread ([13], p. 79).

In his magisterial study of the Divine Liturgy, Robert Taft summarizes the theological significance of the Byzantine precommunion rites:

---

5   The Cherubikon is sung while the presider recites the prayer of apology, 'No one is worthy', preparing those who officiate at the altar to engage their own process of dying to self in preparation for offering the Eucharist.

Whereas the consecrated bread and wine is a twofold sign of Christ's sacrificial body and blood, the commingling, symbolizing the union of these two species, images the glorified humanity of the Risen Christ and our participation, via communion, in his risen life...the desire to keep the chalice warm right up until communion to signify that we receive the Body and Blood of the living, Risen Christ, eventually led to delaying the infusion of hot water until before the Great Entrance and ultimately until just before communion ([15], pp. 516–17).

The structure, text, and ritual performance of the Orthodox Divine Liturgy call upon the participants to remember Christ's sacrificial death and resurrection and participate in it. The act of remembering leads to participation in anticipation of the ultimate gift offered by God; eternal life to be lived with God, which can occur after death. The particular remembrance of those who have 'fallen asleep' is in itself an engagement of our process for the participating faithful, as their memory of the dead conveys an acceptance of the inevitability of dying in this life, with the hope of receiving the same gift granted to the saints; eternal life in Christ, in the communion of the Holy Spirit. Certainly, the Orthodox liturgy emphasizes the whole point of the paschal mystery and the resurrection; eternal life with God. Death is not the goal of liturgy; it is a requirement for eternal life, which is why it is repeatedly rehearsed.

4. Intense Rehearsal of Dying: Pre- and Post-Communion Prayers

If the assembly engages the process of dying to sin during the course of the actual Divine Liturgy, this activity is much more intense in the rites the faithful are expected to perform in preparation for the liturgy and in thanksgiving after its conclusion. The prayers said in preparation for Communion are generally available to the laity across the Orthodox world; liturgical books for lay use tend to include the preparatory prayers along with the prayers of thanksgiving. The laity's actual use of the preparatory prayers varies. Those who desire intense and rigorous preparation for Communion will prepare by saying the entire office of preparation for Holy Communion, beginning with the Canon and including all of the prayers. Some kind of fast will accompany the preparation. At minimum, one is to fast from all food and drink from midnight before the liturgy, though some fast for a few days prior to the liturgy and also receive the mystery of penance. This particular fasting practice coheres with the recent instruction of the Holy and Great Council of the Orthodox Church from June 2016, which met in Crete and decreed that 'fasting from foods at midnight' is required for 'frequent participation in Holy Communion' [16]. While the laity has some flexibility in the details of the process for preparation, it is customary to include recitation of the pre-Communion prayers [16].

The prayers in preparation for Holy Communion are a crucial part of the process of dying to sin because of the communicants' consistent and fervent prayers that God would remove inclinations to sin and sin itself. The preparatory prayers ask God to grant that participation in Communion would eradicate passions and deliverance from enemies and afflictions ([17], pp. 29–44). For example, in the Third Ode, the first Troparion asks God to purify the communicant with these words:

Grant me, O Christ, the tears to cleanse the defilement of my heart, so that in good conscience, faith, and fear, I may approach the communion of your divine gifts ([17], p. 29).

The second Troparion on the Third Ode requests that communion might result in eternal life and communion of the Holy Spirit, along with 'estrangement from passion and affliction' ([17], p. 29). There are several references to communion removing passion, exemplified by the second Troparion on the Sixth Ode:

O Christ, grant that I may be rid of my passions and grow in your grace, May I be strengthened and confirmed in life by the communion of Your holy mysteries ([17], p. 32).

The point of Communion is the eradication of sin; the third Troparion on the ninth ode uses the imagery of Communion as fire:

> O my savior, may your body and precious blood be for me like fire and light, consuming
> the substance of sins, burning the weeds of my passions, and wholly enlightening me to
> worship Your divinity ([17], p. 34).

The disposition of the communicant in preparation for Communion is one of fear and trembling, words that occur repetitively throughout the canon. One is to be fearful lest receiving the gift of Communion would result in the worst kind of death: 'I tremble as I take this fire lest I be consumed as wax and grass' ([17], p. 33). The notion of fear and trembling before the indescribable gift of God in Communion illuminates the preparation for Communion as a type of death, as dying to passions and withstanding the assaults of enemies is absolutely necessary before receiving Communion. In other words, the hard work of dying to sinful acts prevents a much worse death, the one of condemnation that results in permanent alienation and separation from God. The inevitable fear of condemnation results in the image of a paradox; God's love granted through Communion is utterly incomparable with the defilement of human sin. The strong language of defilement, despair, and the embellishment of personal failure and unworthiness is extremely heavy, which led the editors of the translation used here to attempt to clarify what is actually meant by the language:

> Parts of these prayers are very direct and uncompromising in their description of human
> sinfulness. The purpose of such expressions is not to debase us, but rather to confront
> aspects of our life, which we frequently try to avoid. If we are to be healed and seek the
> Father's perfection, we must be honest with ourselves ([17], p. 29).

The necessity for an editorial preface explaining the language of the prayers yields two observations. Embracing self-honesty and confronting passions with the hope of personal transformation results in a regular process of practicing death. In this sense, the canon in preparation for Communion coheres strongly with our hypothesis on Orthodox liturgy as an engagement of the process of death in Christ, dying to sin, and rising to new life. The editorial preface also illuminates the possibility that one might misinterpret the intent of the prayers. The weight placed on blaming one's self can be confused for self-deprecation, so pastoral guidance on the true meaning of an honest confession of sin is advisable for communicants to experience the loving embrace of God's reception of penitent sinners. The pre-Communion prayers encourage communicants to engage in a process of dying to passions and the temptations of enemies with God's assistance.

The prayers appointed for preparation for Communion elaborate the themes established by the canon. The communicant is a sinner, unworthy, disobedient, and completely wretched, all images of the self presented in the first prayer of preparation attributed to Saint Basil the Great ([17], p. 37). The prayers juxtapose the fallen character of the communicant with the love and condescension of God. St. Basil's prayer, the first one of this order, remembers the paschal mystery as the event manifesting God's love for humankind:

> Because of your abundant goodness, in these latter days You became flesh and were
> crucified and buried for us thankless and erring people, and by your own blood you
> renewed our nature corrupted by sin ([17], p. 37).

The prayer mentioned that the communicant is 'emboldened' by God's compassion and thus draws near to receive Communion, asking God to grant 'that to my last breath I might partake of your holy gifts uncondemned, looking to the communion of Your Holy Spirit for eternal life', as well as a favorable judgment at God's 'tribunal'([17], p. 38). The third prayer attributed to Saint Symeon Metaphrastes also recalls the paschal mystery and also applies the specific components of Pascha with a type of death in the communicant:[6]

---

[6]   Note that the second prayer attributed to St. John Chrysostom also asks Christ to mortify the passions.

You underwent the life-giving and saving passion: the cross, the nails, the spear, and death itself. Mortify in me the bodily passions that destroy the soul. By your burial you took captive the kingdom of Hades; bury and destroy the devices of evil spirits by purifying my thoughts ([17], p. 39).

The prayers of preparation for Holy Communion require the communicant to adopt an identity of repentance, to be mindful of the depravity of the soul, and to name one's self as a wretch, approaching communion with a petition that Christ would kill the passions and wipe away every aspect of defilement to prepare the communicant for renewing the identity as a partaker of the Holy Spirit. Preparation for Communion involves an expedited process of repentance and transformation, complete with the sacramental theology of Baptism all in one private office recited before the Divine Liturgy.

Communicants are also expected to recite the prayers of thanksgiving after Communion. In some parishes, these prayers are chanted aloud, with the faithful remaining in the Church until their conclusion. The short office begins with a threefold 'Glory to You, o God', followed by approximately six prayers of varying lengths. The first prayer is the longest of these, and all of the prayers thank God for making the sinful communicant worthy of Communion. The primary feature of the prayers after Communion is the petition that God's gift continue the process of repentance. The first prayer after Communion echoes all of the paschal themes we have examined here, applying them to the life of the communicant by interpreting the reception of Communion as a reception of Christ, whose grace assists the communicant in persevering through the process of dying and rising to new life:

O Master, lover of mankind, you died and rose for our sake and favored us with these, your awesome and life-giving Mysteries for the benefit and sanctification of our souls and bodies. Grant that they may be for the healing of my soul and body and for the rout of every adversary, for the enlightenment of the eyes of my heart, for the peace of my spiritual powers, for an undaunted faith, for an unfeigned love, for the fullness of wisdom, for the keeping of Your commandments, for growth in Your divine grace, and for belonging to Your kingdom, in order that, preserved by them in Your holiness, I may always remember Your grace and no longer live for myself, but for You, our Master and Benefactor...Thus, when I depart from this life in the hope of life eternal, may I attain that everlasting rest where the sound of those celebrating never ceases, and where there is no end to the delight of those who behold the ineffable beauty of Your face ([17], pp. 324–25).

This short excerpt from the first prayer after Communion demonstrates that the paschal mystery imparts the activity of the risen Christ, whose grace capacitates the communicant to die to the temptations and sin confronted in this life, with the promise of eternal life granted to those who stay the course. The prayer emphasizes the relationship between receiving God's divine grace, imparted through Communion, and dying to one's self for the purpose of living for God. This phrase shows that participation in the Eucharistic Liturgy continues the process of death in Christ and dying to sin inaugurated at Baptism and expresses the point of the outer life of a Christian; the glorification of God, not one's self. The text of this prayer also presents an important feature of the liturgical process of death and dying; rehearsing death to sin is preparation for the death that ends this life and inaugurates life in God. If one learns how to die and rise to new life in this life, the death of the next life will naturally result in rising to life as one who belongs to God's kingdom ([17], p. 324).

This portion of the paper has developed a thesis arguing that liturgical participation is learning how to die to sin and rise to new life. This process begins with Baptism and is engaged regularly in the Eucharist. Learning how to die depends on the memorial of Christ's death and resurrection and the confidence granted by the saints whose memory testifies to the joyful life in Christ that follows death. The process also appears to require the participants to adopt a lowly stature, which presumably inspires them to desire the gift of Christ and to honestly confront their sins. Brutal self-honesty prepares one to truly want to end the cycle of sin that permeates this life. In principle, this presentation on the inner life of Orthodox liturgy also depicts its outer life, as the liturgical participants are capacitated for authentic transformation into sinless people who are like Christ.

The contemporary Orthodox liturgy continues the tradition of rigorous self-examination established and cultivated during the Byzantine era. Derek Krueger published a study of several liturgical examples from the Byzantine liturgical repository in which the liturgical participants apply the archetypal penitents of the Bible to themselves [18]. Krueger's analysis examines models of shaping the liturgical self from Romanos the Melodist, Eucharistic prayers, the penitential Canon of St. Andrew of Crete, the Lenten Triodion, and the texts of St. Symeon the New Theologian [18]. Krueger summarizes the liturgical experience of the participants as one of participating with the fathers and mothers of the Biblical past:

> The rites and offices of the church offered the forum where Byzantine Christians learned to apply a penitential bible to themselves...Within the space of Byzantine Churches, Orthodox Christians learned the history of their own redemption. But they were more than spectators. Through the hymns of the Church, Byzantine worshippers joined a large cast of biblical characters. They lamented with Adam; repented with David; approached Christ in supplication with the Harlot, the Leper, the Samaritan, and the Hemorrhaging woman; awaited Christ's saving hand like Peter...By historicizing Byzantine concepts of guilt, our inquiry has articulated the cultural construction of self-blame and penance as a method for resolving the potential effects and apparent consequences of sin ([18], p. 218).

Krueger's thorough examination of the formation of penitents through the Byzantine liturgy within the particular Byzantine cultural framework explains why there is so much weight on self-examination in the process of dying to sin. The contemporary services continue this tradition but in new cultural contexts. The point of the process is to be honest about sin; admitting sin is the first step towards awareness of sin and of the need to modify one's patterns of thinking and acting that result in sin. The regular practice of dying in Christ is a way of putting sin to death and rising to new life in Christ. In the Orthodox Church, pastors charged with the responsibility of spiritual direction should emphasize the good resulting from dying to the patterns and actions leading to sin to ensure that faithful do not misunderstand the language of these texts and prayers and come to believe that they are inherently bad or evil.

5. From Liturgy to Daily Life: Do People Rise to New Life?

In the concluding portion of this paper, I will reflect on the challenges of applying the liturgical principle of death in Christ and dying to sin to the ordinary daily life of Orthodox people. The presentation of death and dying in the liturgy is based on a careful examination of the contents of the liturgical offices. The first challenge occurs when we apply reality to the ideal of liturgical engagement. In teaching the meaning of Baptism and Chrismation, a pastor has published material to share with the people, but there is no guarantee that they will read it nor remember particular themes from the rite of Baptism. The prothesis rite is celebrated privately and quietly, and, even if it was offered publicly, it occurs so early, often long before the beginning of the Divine Liturgy, that most people would not participate. The memorial of Christ's death and resurrection is powerful in the anaphora, but most parishes do not read the text aloud for the people to hear, and, even in some places where the prayers are read, it is not comprehensible to the people. The above presentation depicts the fullness of what the liturgy can offer in terms of a rehearsal of dying and death for the purpose of rising to new life; this is why I deliberately use the word 'capacity' throughout, because even the most sensitive and caring pastor can only do so much to grant the people access to the riches of the liturgical celebration.

In terms of engagement, one could persuasively argue that a small percentage of very devoted parishioners is committed to engaging the fullness of the liturgy. These are people who regularly submit lists of the names of beloved dead and living for commemoration at the liturgy, who attend regularly and receive liturgical catechesis with enthusiasm and interest. These are people whose liturgy books are worn and who know how to find the prayers in preparation for Holy Communion. They are also to be found among those who linger after Church for the prayers of thanksgiving after Communion. Only a small cohort of the devoted faithful would be able to follow the paschal passages from the liturgy, commit them to memory, and attempt to apply them to the transformation of their own souls and hearts.

A larger group of people has some sense of what is happening in the liturgy. This larger group attends with some frequency and is attuned to the primary features of Sunday worship. They cannot identify the prothesis or anaphora, and they are more likely to read the bulletin than a pew prayer book with Communion prayers, but they will reflect upon Christ's sacrifice on the cross, they will faithfully request prayers for their beloved dead and living, and they will come forward for Communion when the deacon commands them to 'draw near'.

Pastors have complained about the tepid attitude of people to liturgy since the beginning of Christianity. It is an eternal phenomenon affecting all Christian churches, and the persistence of this reality has resulted in a consistent gap between the capacity of liturgy to transform people and the reality of the people's commitment to liturgical engagement. If Orthodox Church leaders would be honest about their ability to change this paradigm, they might be content with a slight increase in the numbers of people who are wholly devoted to the Church and those who attend with some frequency. Expecting the masses of people whose names are officially inscribed in Orthodox parish membership books to become regular and devoted participants is delusional.

In addition to the realities of people's commitment to liturgical participation, one must also consider the degree, or lack thereof, in the people's ability to consciously recognize that the liturgy is teaching them to engage the process of death in Christ and dying to sin in preparation for the next life. The Orthodox liturgy is organized in such a way that the most minute component related to the Divine Liturgy is essentially a microcosm of the liturgy itself. For example, saying the prayers of preparation for Communion is engaging the process of dying to sin in preparation for new life. The same process occurs in the Divine Liturgy, and one reflects upon it afterwards with the prayers of thanksgiving. The Liturgy itself repeats the opportunity to engage this process throughout its structures. The need to inscribe the process of death and dying upon each layer of liturgical structure and component demonstrates just how easy it is to avoid the process, to gloss over it, and to ignore it. In some way, each liturgical office presents a memorial of the paschal mystery and invites participation, with rising to new life and permitting God to recreate the participants always being the primary goal. The appearance of this process of dying and rising to new life on the periphery of liturgy, in places such as the private prayers of the faithful Orthodox Christian, attests to its potential significance in contributing to the outer life of the Christian.

There are natural points of intersection between the primary features of liturgy that promote death in Christ and dying to sin amongst faithful Orthodox Christians who participate in the Church's liturgical life with varying degrees of frequency. These points of intersection are memorials for the dead and the solemnities of the liturgical year, especially Lent and Pascha. Holy Week offers an opportunity for both devoted Orthodox Christians and the masses of people to attend the offices of Good Friday. Even minimal participation opens the door for the pastor to connect the liturgical process of death in Christ and rising to new life with the ordinary daily life of the people. Like the Divine Liturgy, Good Friday is a memorial of the paschal mystery, only much more intense because it is appointed to a particular day on the calendar. It is on these occasions that the critical masses of people who participate in liturgy for any number of reasons might consider the invitation to practice dying and rising with Christ. For those attending the solemnities with extended family or at the invitation of a more devoted participant, the people of the Church themselves become the models of dying and rising with Christ. For example, a grandmother who has been faithful to her family for generations despite tribulations and more attractive alternatives is modelling the process of death in Christ and dying to sin for her extended family. The same is true for the sick person who is enduring tribulation and carrying a burdensome cross, not to mention the caretaker who gives freely of herself to serve one who is unable to function on their own.

In summary, the Orthodox liturgical legacy of dying in Christ and rising to new life is alive and well for all faithful people, since God transforms those who have the courage to 'draw near' to God. The people who respond affirmatively to the invitation to participate become the teachers who model the value of dying to sin to rise to new life.

Conflicts of Interest: The author declares no conflict of interest.

References

1. "The Service of Holy Baptism." *Greek Orthodox Archdiocese of America.* Available online: http://www.goarch.org/chapel/liturgical_texts/baptism (accessed on 10 February 2017).
2. Alexander Schmemann. *Of Water and the Spirit: A Liturgical Study of Baptism.* Crestwood: St. Vladimir's Seminary Press, 1974.
3. Nicholas Denysenko. *The Blessing of Waters and Epiphany: The Eastern Liturgical Tradition.* Farnham and Burlington: Ashgate, 2012.
4. Maxwell Johnson. *The Rites of Christian Initiation: Their Evolution and Interpretation.* Collegeville: The Liturgical Press, 1999.
5. Kevin Irwin. *Context and Text; Method in Liturgical Theology.* Collegeville: The Liturgical Press, 1994.
6. Nicholas Denysenko. *Chrismation: A Primer for Catholics.* Collegeville: The Liturgical Press, 2014.
7. Paul Meyendorff. *The Anointing of the Sick.* Orthodox Liturgy Series Book One. Crestwood: St. Vladimir's Seminary Press, 2009.
8. Robert Taft. *A History of the Liturgy of St. John Chrysostom: The Great Entrance,* 4th ed. Orientalia Christiana Analecta. Rome: Pontifical Oriental Institute, 2004, vol. 2.
9. Thomas Pott. *Byzantine Liturgical Reform: A Study of Liturgical Change in the Byzantine Tradition.* Orthodox Liturgy Series. Edited and Translated by Paul Meyendorff. Crestwood: St. Vladimir's Seminary Press, 2010.
10. Robert Taft. "The Liturgy of the Great Church: An Initial Synthesis of Structure and Interpretation on the Eve of Iconoclasm." *Dumbarton Oaks Papers* 34 (1980–1981): 45–75. [CrossRef]
11. Hans-Joachim Schulz. *The Byzantine Liturgy: Symbolic Structure and Faith Expression.* Translated by Matthew J. O'Connell. New York: Pueblo Publishing Company, 1984.
12. Stelyios Muksuris. *Economia and Eschatology: Liturgical Mystagogy in the Byzantine Prothesis Rite.* Brookline: Holy Cross Orthodox Press, 2013.
13. *Service Books of the Orthodox Church. The Divine Liturgy,* 3rd ed. South Canaan: St. Tikhon's Seminary Press, 2013.
14. Nicholas Denysenko. "Retrieving a Theology of Belonging: Eucharist and Church in Post-Modernity, Part 2." *Worship* 89 (2015): 21–43.
15. Robert Taft. *A History of the Liturgy of St. John Chrysostom: The Precommunion Rites.* Orientalia Christiana Analecta. Rome: Pontifical Oriental Institute, 2000, vol. 5.
16. Holy and Great Council of the Orthodox Church. "The Importance of Fasting and Its Observance Today." Available online: https://www.holycouncil.org/-/fasting (accessed on 10 February 2017).
17. Peter Galadza, ed. *The Divine Liturgy: An Anthology for Worship.* Ottawa: Metropolitan Andrey Sheptytsky Institute of Eastern Christian Studies, 2004.
18. Derek Krueger. *Liturgical Subjects: Christian Ritual, Biblical Narrative, and the Formation of the Self in Byzantium.* Philadelphia: University of Pennsylvania Press, 2014.

religions

Article

The Problem of Church's Defensiveness and Reductionism in Fr. Alexander Schmemann's Ecclesiology (Based on His Journals)

Boris Knorre

Faculty of Humanities, National Research University Higher School of Economics, Moscow 101000, Russia; knorre@hse.ru; Tel.: +7-926-482-7131

Received: 1 November 2017; Accepted: 17 December 2017; Published: 21 December 2017

Abstract: This article analyzes Schmemann's ecclesiology in the context of his attempt to give an assessment of the Church's attitude to life; as well as the problem of defensiveness in Orthodoxy; reductionism of ecclesial culture; "rejection" of the world and traditionalistic isolation. The author focuses upon the socio-cultural interpretation given by Schmemann to such important categories of the ecclesial language as "piety," "humility," "churchliness," "spirituality," etc.; showing that in real life these categories express the isolation and stereotypification of Orthodoxy. In the context of "lived" religion, these categories deliver a protective and reductionist message, justifying a kind of anthropological pessimism, "religion of guilt" and psychological self-closure of a person. The theologian juxtaposes two religious traditions: one based on the defensiveness and the other based on a sense of joy; the feeling of God's presence and affinity to the Kingdom of Heaven. According to the author, the accents put by Schmemann in his ecclesiology can promote the formation of ethics of laity and a more adequate attitude towards the world in the 21st century Orthodoxy.

Keywords: Orthodoxy; Russian Church tradition; ecclesiastic culture; defensiveness; Orthodox piety; cultural attitudes; behavioral preferences

---

Theologians as well as ecclesiastical journalists have said much about protopresbyter Alexander Schmemann's ecclesiological legacy and its relevance for the present times, so there is no need to reiterate their arguments here. Notably, Fr. Alexander is a rarity among Orthodoxy due to his deep-seated sensitivity to developments in the modern world. In his works he pays specific attention to the Church's vision of the world (Agadjanian 2016, pp. 255, 262, 271–72). Within this framework, he insistently asks how Church mentality affects behavioral stereotypes in this particular milieu and analyzes how loyalty to Orthodoxy shapes believer's lives. In fact, he raises the question how to bear witness to one's faith and thus how to attest to the truth of Orthodox Christianity and the Church.

Schmemann articulates these issues most naturally and explicitly in his *Journals* (composed from a number of diary notebooks that document the last ten years of his life, from 1973 until 1983). The genre of diary allows the writer to talk freely and to express various and contradictory ideas that would be difficult to present in their natural variety in an analytical essay. A key feature of the genre is that the writer feels entitled to question an idea even while trying to explicate it. In the case of Schmemann, his *Journals* present the greatest range of his thoughts by affording him the freedom of speech rarely permitted in an essay, which normally is constructed around and substantiating just one specific idea.

We shall here consider Schmemann's ecclesiology from the perspective of social theology, and partly also that of social psychology. Anthropological issues with which Schmemann engages in his *Journals* are vital for our evaluation of contemporary issues, as well as for understanding whether specific ecclesiastical conflicts and socio-cultural paradoxes are systemic or accidental.

Let us look at some particular paradoxes in the culture of the churchly social environment that Fr. Alexander elaborates on. Quotations are taken from the English translations by the theologian's widow Juliana Schmemann (who died in January 2017) whenever such a translation exists and adequately renders Schmemann's Russian text. It should be noted, however, that in translation many concepts have been modified, particularly the term *tserkovnost'* which is often translated as "life of the Church", while in cases where Schmemann appealed to negative connotations of key concepts of the churchly culture, Mrs. Schmemann rendered them as "pseudo"-concepts. That is to say, she did not always dare to convey the highly critical attitude toward the Church's social environment and culture that had been present in the original version of Fr. Schmemann's diaries.

1. Subculturization and Reductionism in the Church

Let us note, that the key question Schmemann asks himself along his spiritual way, is a problem of "institutional conservatism", which often realizes itself as "defensiveness" of the Church, that is expressed in the priority of limitative attitudes upon motivating ones. This priority often presupposes not approval of the lay–activity forms, not encouraging certain innovations which are usually welcome in the so called "secular world." Schmemann keeps remarking the fact that the preoccupation with "guarding" the Church, like a "recurrence of the Old Ritual", leads to negativity essentially prevailing in churchly life over positive affirmation, which should have informed life within the Church. He characterizes defensive attitude as "the position of the Russian Church in Exile and of the Old Believers. To keep, to guard, to protect the Church not only from evil, but from the world as such, from the contemporary world. No checking, no verification—everything, every stikhera is equally important" (Schmemann 2000, p. 144).[1]

Here Schmemann actually echoes Maria Skobtsova, who wrote that the Old Believers were "the extreme expression of this stagnant, splendid, immovable, protective spirit," and that "it kept in place, away from life's surges, a kind of a fixed form in the development of piety." (Skobtsova 1998).

Notably, Schmemann uses the term "Old Belief" here in its socio-cultural, rather than historical meaning—as a synonym of defensiveness. He is forever puzzled as to why the Church's attempts to defend itself all too often lead to a primitive denial of culture, isolationism and escapism. Why for Orthodoxy "to escape or to deny is stronger than to affirm"? (Schmemann 2000, p. 29).

In expressing these and similar criticisms, Fr. Schmemann does not adopt any kind of modernist standpoint. On the contrary, he censures those willing to "surrender to the world" (Schmemann 2005, p. 108). His critique of secularism and the rationalizing western lifestyle is a special theme in his legacy (Shishkov 2015). Thus Fr. Schmemann's negative assessment of the defensive socio-cultural attitude of the Church does not presuppose the Church's adaptation to modern culture:

> Christianity's intimate, indispensable bond with culture does not necessitate that Christianity ought to be made "cultural" and thus attractive and acceptable for a "cultured" person. (Schmemann 2005, p. 110)

Rather he maintains the opposite: it is the Church's calling to affect culture by changing and elevating it.

> It is Christianity's call to keep blowing culture up from within and to make it face the Last one: One who is above it, but who, simultaneously, also "performs" it, for at its ultimate depth culture is, in fact, a question man addresses to "the Last one". (Schmemann 2005, p. 111)

That is, although condemning various forms of defensiveness in churchly life, Fr. Alexander does not deny the Church the right to employ defensive mechanisms against worldly influences or to be selective about "worldly novelties." For Schmemann, however, the ability to withstand "the spirit

---

[1] Normally we cite the English edition—the translation of Schmemann's *Journals* made by Juliana Schmemann, a widow of the theologian. In case the passages by Schmemann's *Journals* are missed in English edition we give our own translation of the Russian edition which is much more complete than the English one.

of the world" (I Cor. 2.12) did not mean a primitive overall rejection of the world as something one ought to step away from in disgust. He stated that the popular mode of guarding the Church, which prescribes that the religious distance themselves from the world and from modernity, was a dead-end track (he even suggested that this method be called *"estranged Orthodoxy"*).

As an example of Orthodoxy's rejection of culture Schmemann cited ecclesiastics' proclamations against theatre and literature, "impossible in how primitive they are". Schmemann believed the Christians' vocation is to transform culture rather than reject it. "It is culture (not biology, physiology or 'nature') that constitutes the world judged, condemned and, in the end, transformed by Christianity. Christianity is above nature, but it cannot be under or outside of it" (Schmemann 2005, p. 110).

As the theologian wrote,

> Historical forms of Christianity, including "Orthodoxy", are attested to in the cultures they created or inspired. Every given period's culture is a mirror, in which Christians should have seen themselves and the degree of their faithfulness to the "one thing needful" for "the victory that overcometh the world … " But usually, they do not even look into that mirror, believing it to be "lewd" and "irreligious". (Schmemann 2005, p. 109)

According to Schmemann, when the aspiration to limit the impact of the "world" turns into "unconditional rejection", the Church acts like a barbarian. "For it becomes more and more negative and throws away everything it simply does not comprehend and 'could not care less about'" (Schmemann 2005, p. 111).

In fact, Schmemann shows that, by adopting a position of denial and estrangement (or detachment), and by refusing "to blast culture from within," Orthodoxy turns into a subculture that shapes the habitual way for the Church to look at itself, rather than the world.

2. In the System of Cultural References: A Phenomenon of Orthodox Piety and Its Interpretation through Synonyms

A general question Schmemann asks in his deliberations is what the Church offers in place of the cultural values of the secular world. What advantages does the former have over the latter? The theologian points out that, by turning away from culture and *refusing to influence it*, Orthodoxy presents its own system of references and its own, in a sense, alternative cultural values. This refers primarily to a mindset and behavior known as "piety," which serves as a marker of belonging to the Church.

A few words need to be said about the concept of piety. In and of itself, it is a rather broad notion, which, before the New-Testament Christian tradition, existed also in the Old Testament and Judaism, where it was used to mean "the fear of God". The same concept was also known to the Hellenistic tradition (греч. εὐσέβεια), where it denoted "reverence, fear, loyalty" in relation to parents or pagan deities (Igumnov 2002).[2] Both the Old and the New Testament traditions share their understanding of "piety" as "a form of religious worship focused on strict observation of religious and moral commandments and norms".

In the Christian tradition, the idea of "piety" builds specifically on the Greek term (ʹεὐσέβειαʹ), which in the writings of Church fathers and Christian hermits acquires connotations of a mindset and a lifestyle based on man's filial yearning for God and a desire to correlate one's every deed with God's will[3] in the firm belief that God's eyes are on us throughout our life.

Today, the Russian Church tends to interpret "piety" mostly as "an internal arrangement of the spirit founded on fearing God and complying with religious and moral commandments" (Igumnov 2002). Also important for Russian theology is the understanding of "piety" as "a principle

---

[2]   See also a dictionary article "La piété" in (Vocabulaire de Theologie Biblique 1970) (La Piété 1970).
[3]   See in more details: (Ershova 2005).

of man's religious attitude to God", "built mainly around experiencing God's holiness and glory—His absolute inapproachability and unfathomable proximity revealed in the blessed natural force of churchly life" (Igumnov 2006).

Such an understanding of "piety" finds a matching dimension in the sphere of practical morals: to the theologian, hegumen Platon (Igumnov), piety is "a path of active and contemplative life" filled with multiple and varied Christian virtues. These are a "constant repentance, ... reassessment of one's way in life, admission of one's errors, contrition of spirit, immersion into the depths of humility, rejection of haughty ambitions and exclusive privileges, the beginnings of unselfishness and equanimity," and, lastly, "a growing recognition of the importance and value of other people's interests." In the oft quoted in the Russian churchly milieu words of Anthony the Great, "piety" has to do with an aspiration "not to be jealous, but chaste, gentle, as generous as possible, sociable, not too given to arguing, and to do all that pleases God".

"Piety" thus also entails openness to self-imposed limitations of all sorts and forbearance in the face of whatever sufferings one may encounter. A distinctive feature of "piety" in the Russian ecclesiastic tradition is kenoticism, which was peculiar to Russian Church culture from the times of Ancient Rus'. It is expressed in striving to obtain the "likeness" of Christ through self-belittling, underlining the role of suffering and martyrdom. Kenoticism has been described by Georgiy Fedotov (Fedotov 1975, pp. 99–112).

To a certain extent, at least in the Russian tradition, "piety" seems to be a feat of sorts, a combination of virtues, just as a life of a Christian person in itself is an act of courage. Yet, in contrast to, say, martyrdom—the act of valour few people are capable of, "piety" is both accessible and prescribed to all members of the Church. There is even a notion of *"podvizhnik blagochestiya"* [champion of piety]—a person who did nothing special during his lifetime, but proved to be a faithful and obedient member of the Church, a mild, gentle soul living to God's truth in spite of any obstacles and temptations.

In the Russian church, biographic descriptions of such "champions of piety" have become a special, very popular genre of edifying didactic literature. However, there are also scientific analytical works by different scholars, who analyze 'piety' and pious practices of Russian Church tradition in framework of studying history and phenomenology of sainthood. There is a great amount of such a literature now, so we do not list it. A good historical review of this literature through the end of XIX—beginning of XXI is given in (Semenenko-Basin 2011, pp. 70–123). However, for understanding Schmemann's assessments of piety is important to appeal to the works of Georgiy Fedotov (Fedotov 1975, 2000), a founder of special research tradition. Among the most recent works on hagiography or hagiology one can see also: (Loyevskaya 2005; Lurie 2009; Pliguzov and Yanin 1989; Ziolkowski 2014; Giambelluca 2007).

However, in the context of hagiographic studies, "piety" is seen mainly in a certain 'ideal', imaginary and 'perfect' point. That is, I think, one can find rather the Church's ideals concerning pious behavior, than the real behavioral manifestations of piety in life, rather the examples what piety should be, than what it actually is. These imagological representations of piety were *volens-nolens* elaborated on the basis of hagiographical life stories of saints and spiritually-edifying teachings of ecclesiastical writers.

Formed in this way, the Church's idea of piety, partly adopted by Russian culture, in certain aspects does not coincide with the real picture of behavior of Church members. In this article we consider those semantic connotations of piety, which Alexander Schmemann noted in his observation of real human behavior, motivated by Church's norms. We are focusing on how people, according to Schmemann evidence, interpret the norms of piety in the XX—and in the beginning of the XXI century, and how people actually display (or failed to display) them beyond the lofty declarative statements.

3. "Piety" in Contemporary Church Life

In the contemporary ecclesiastical system of values, "piety" has become a sort of moral-behavioral category—a kind of an "overarching virtue" unifying various behavioral puzzles. "Piety" can characterize both individual acts and a person's life as a whole. In fact, this category bespeaks the peculiar nature of Orthodox religiosity in that it connotes spiritual strength, spiritual growth, and loyalty to the Church. The notion of churchliness (*tserkovnost'*), which has become synonymous with "piety," as well as with "*dukhovnost'*" [spirituality] is a category that functions as a marker of belonging to churchly culture (or, rather, subculture). Actually, "piety" sometimes even means the same as "Orthodoxy" in its theological sense. It is, therefore, no accident that ecclesiastical didactic literature equates "piety" with "churchliness," and Schmemann, too, often uses these two categories simultaneously and interchangeably.

We must admit that the ethical evaluation of "piety" on the part of Schmemann is very critical. Despite the significance of this concept for the Church ascetical language, Schmemann mentions "piety" mainly in the negative sense, as "imposing limitations on human consciousness" (Schmemann 2005, p. 79), "replacing faith" (Schmemann 2005, p. 95), and even more so, "weakening the Eucharistic awareness in the Church and supplanting the Eucharist." He speaks of a certain sentimentality typical of piety; of "piety" turning into a kind of outward form whose only purpose is to declare "churchliness." In the ecclesial environment, a lack of tangible piety may give rise to censure: Schmemann refers to cases when, for example, seminary students scolded others for their "insufficient piety" (Schmemann 2005, p. 306), or when priests did the same addressing their parishioners (Schmemann 2005, p. 479).

Basically, in a critical assessment of piety in the ecclesial social environment, Schmemann is by no means alone. Metropolitan Anthony (Bloom) in his various articles and pastoral conferences and talks also very often uses the concept of "piety" in a negative connotation. For example, one can speak about the need to «remove from prayer "a raid of piety"» (Bloom 2014), that "very pious people" find it difficult to pray with all the depth of their souls, contrasts "the outward pious speeches" with a true appeal to God with the whole being. (Bloom 2014). Speaking out against imitation and stylization in Orthodoxy, he warns: "Do not repeat endlessly certain prayers or insist on some specific praying practices, just speak to God!" (Bloom 2014).

Alexander Schmemann points out that the earlier noted "unconditional rejection" of the world and the Orthodoxy's strife for isolation depredates the Church's own values, such as piety and churchliness, in the real life of the Orthodox believers. "Piety" taken in the external form the theologian watched in no way contributes to meaningfulness, but, on the contrary, promotes primitivism, proving to be a sort of mask that a person puts on, immersing in the ecclesiastical societal environment. This is how Schmemann writes about it:

> Being in church should be liberating. But in the Church's contemporary tonality, church life does not liberate ... Instead of teaching man to look at the world through the Church's vision, instead of transforming man's view of himself and his life, one feels obliged—in order to be "spiritual"—to clothe oneself in an impersonal, soiled "garment of piety". Instead of at least knowing that there is joy, light, meaning, eternity, man becomes irritated, narrow-minded, intolerant and often simply mean. He does not even repent of it because it all comes from "churchliness" ... (Schmemann 2000, p. 33)

Mother Maria Skobtsova also mentions this primitivization and avoidance of meaningfulness in relation to the ritualist type of piety. She notes that the commitment of "pious atmosphere" in the church, which is characteristic of the ritualist type of piety, allows one to adopt indifferent attitude to the worship.

> The lengthy recitations by the Psaltis immerses him into a particular atmosphere of piety, bringing on a specific rhythm to his spiritual life. This is what he really wants, he is not so interested in the content. < ... > If you tell him that you don't understand something, either in essence or because the Psaltis is reading too rapidly, he will answer that it isn't necessary to understand, it is only necessary to achieve a particular atmosphere of piety during which occasional words come through clearly which are understandable and necessary for you.

While in worship, within the ritualist type of piety, reductionism is expressed in blocking off a meaningful understanding of the text, in the non-religious communicative space such reductionism manifests itself in the fact that in communication people get accustomed to using special declarative forms, a special "churchly stylistic". Moreover, in the contemporary post-Soviet Russia, there is even a notion of churchly decorum, according to which one is judged to be more or less "churchly" or "pious". Special books on churchly manners and communication rules exist, for instance, "*Chto nado znat'o tserkovnom etikete*" [What you need to know about Church etiquette] by hieromonk Aristarkh Lokhanov and the *Church protocol* by bishop Mark Golovkov (Lokhanov 1999; Golovkov 2007).

The so-called "humble appearance" has become a standard element of decorum in contemporary churchly social milieu (with the exception of hierarchs and ecclesiastical superiors). In many parishes, though not in all, appearances are often used as a signifier of "piety" and "churchliness". Hieromonk Aristarkh (Lokhanov) gives the following criterion to identify a churchly person: "Very often one's gaze—a mild, humble, downcast gaze—bespeaks good upbringing, in our case, a churchly person" (Lokhanov 1999).

As Ivan Zabaev notes (Zabaev 2007, p. 20), "Orthodox actors easily detect humility through its outward representation, through a pose and facial expression, through an absence of objection in response to any critical remark." That means that in these circles it is perfectly acceptable to determine "piety," "churchliness," "spirituality," and other such qualities through outward appearances.

In the language of sociological theory, what we are dealing with in this case is a habitus, firmly embedded in the churchly milieu; or in other words, a system of acquired behavioral patterns. This system is quite complex. It includes, on the one hand, a shared notion of the Orthodox person as someone who looks humble; on the other, an idea of what this humility must look like across the repertoire of respective attributes: posture, mimics, gait, voice, etc. *Humility* must be declared even in business correspondence, especially when addressing ecclesiastical superiors: "I consider it my filial duty to humbly inform His Eminence about the following … ".[4]

Notably, believers themselves may see this behavior as completely natural, authentic, and the only appropriate mode. But this, in Pierre Bourdieu's view, constitutes the essence of any habitus. After all, Bourdieu states, agents are never free, but the illusion of freedom (lack of coercion) is not so complete as in the case when they are following the schemes of their habitus, i.e., the objective structures, the product of which itself is a habitus: in this case, the agents feel the compulsion no more than the weight of the air (Bourdieu 1977, pp. 79–80; see also Shmatko 1998, pp. 60–70). In other words, declarative forms become second nature to the people of churchly subculture: they get so used to them, that they end up taking them for granted.

Especially early on in the process of religious revival in Russia, believers looked markedly different from anyone else. They had their eyes ostentatiously lowered, their back stooped in an attempt to outwardly reflect their humility and pious mindset. The problem of such "despondency" was even discussed in Orthodox mass media; for example, an article in the Orthodox popular magazine "Delovoy khristianin" (Pal'cheva et al. 2007) had the characteristic title: "Why do some Orthodox look like dead fish?".

Let's note that under Putin's rule, the overwhelming popularity of this image began to wane, because a moderate national revival, changes in social-economic climate in Russia as well as changes in social attitudes influence the moods and aesthetical preferences in the Church's social milieu. On the one hand, the rehabilitation of some historical pre-revolution traditions in certain parishes took place, for example, the centers of "*Slavyano-goritskaya bor'ba*" [Slavic-hill wrestling] (Filatov 2005) as well as the centers of Russian national dances (Filatov 2009). On the other hand, alongside the process of partial rehabilitation of the soviet culture, the elements of soviet 'monumental style' have been reproduced in the Church's official ceremonial (Volkova 2009).

---

4   Such a form of address is typical for Russian Orthodox Church senior officials, see also (Golovkov 2007).

A special phenomenon of Russian Orthodoxy in the 2000-ies, however, happened to be a certain "militant piety" (Rock 2002) as well as cultural-symbolic forms of "Church-military aesthetic" (Briskina-Müller 2015; Knorre 2015, 2016). The changes of religiosity in the framework Post-Soviet Orthodoxy in zeros were quite various, including the emergence of different forms of so-called "user-friendly" Orthodoxy. As long as it is not the main topic of our article, we just draw the reader's attention to the literature focused on it: (Filatov and Lunkin 2006; Kormina 2010; Köllner 2013).

However, alongside the all aforementioned forms of the Church aesthetics and piety, the "humble style" has remained an integral part of ecclesial subculture, at least in places where people consistently turn to the Church's legacy of asceticism (Knorre 2011, pp. 317–40) and where the "strict ritualist" type of religiosity was peculiar to the Church parish life (in the wording by Mother Maria Skobtsova (Skobtsova 1998)).

A failure to comply with the humble style may cause rebuke in Church milieu and even bring about some sort of punishment from a priest in case the offender is in some way subordinate to him. For example, a parishioner from one of the Nizhniy Novgorod churches (Hanna, 35 y.o.) shares the following episode from her life during her studies in the Nizhniy Novgorod school of theology: "In the Church college, they used to wake me up at night and send to clean all toilets ... Or do kitchen duty for a week for I didn't look humble enough".[5]

4. Category of "Spirituality" and Specific Character of Spiritual Guidance in the Church

One of the topics that was most frequently raised by Schmemann is comprehending the concept of "spirituality," "spiritual'" in Orthodoxy, not as ontological dimensions of human life, but as a certain quality, understood in a narrow reduced sense and style conditioned by ecclesial context. Fr Alexander listed this "spirituality" among the modern Orthodox fetishes, such as "Byzantinism," "Russism," "historicism" and equated it to pseudo spirituality, so, it was not accidentally that he put it in quotation marks, stressing that he was referring to the concept of "spirituality" in its distorted understanding he always had to deal with. He confesses to himself, how he has been tired of it.

> I realize how spiritually tired I am of all this "Orthodoxism" of all the fuss with Byzantium, Russia, way of life, spirituality, church affairs, piety, of all these rattles ... It all literally obscures Christ, pushes Him into the background. (Schmemann 2000, p. 146)

Let us note that it corresponds to Mariya Skobtsova's *"The Synodal type of religious life"*, which, according to her words, "promoted other values along with spiritual ones, namely those of the State, the way of life and of tradition" (Skobtsova 1998). Michael Plekon states, that historical and legal obsession of the Church for Schmemann served to be one of disappointing reductions of the Church. (Plekon 2016).

"Spiritual life", "spiritual talk", "spiritual literature"—all these are concepts that Schmemann put on a par with "piety", noting that they serve along with piety as a marker of belonging to a subculture and are associated with the retreat of the socio-ecclesial community inside itself. And in pastoral practice, in the domain of "spiritual eldership" (almost synonymous with the modern Russian "spiritual guidance") the concept of "spiritual", among other things, is very closely intertwined with the concepts of "spiritual authority" and the guidance of souls, as the practice of eldership, assuming personal guidance on human life, expresses very often an authoritarian model of personal interactions. As a result, "eldership" (starchestvo) proves to be "pseudo eldership", i.e., it is not a value but an anti-value.

> The system itself pushes to pseudo-eldership, making every priest a "confessor" and a little "starets". The Orthodox Church has almost no monks who would not have deemed it their

---

sacred duty to write already in two years the treatises on Jesus prayer, on spirituality and asceticism, to teach "mental doing", etc. There are also no priests, who would not have believed themselves capable of solving all problems in five minutes, and direct to the right path . . . (Schmemann 2005, p. 35)

Metropolitan Anthony (Bloom) expresses similar thoughts on the frequent abuse by priests of their pastoral authority over the flock, saying that

"Unfortunately, this happens all too often, in all different countries: a young priest, by virtue of his priesthood—not because he is spiritually experienced, not because God had led him to it—begins to direct his spiritual children and command them: Don't do this; do that; read this or that spiritual literature; go to church; make prostrations . . . As a result, his victims become caricatures of spiritual life, doing everything that the ascetics of piety did. However, the ascetics of piety did all this out of their spiritual experience, and not because they were trained animals". (Bloom 2012)

The use of the wording "trained animals" points to the fact that Metropolitan Anthony (Bloom), similar to Schmemann, feels there is a problem of imitation, stylization in the ecclesial life, which comes in the place of authenticity.

According to hegumen Peter (Meshcherinov), abuse by priests of their pastoral authority makes possible the situation when "a spiritual father becomes a head of one's family instead of the husband," or when a confessor is influencing the process of performing official duties by his "spiritual child." (Meshcherinov 2005).

The Russian Orthodox Church's leadership is not unaware of these issues. 28 December 1998 at the session of the Holy Synod a special decision on this problem was accepted (Zasedanie 1999). Patriarch Alexiy II referred several times to the problem of *"mladostarchestvo,"* and publicly stated on the facts of abuse of spiritual power by priests, particularly in matters of family relations (Alexiy 1999, 2004).

Metropolitan Anthony (Bloom) formulated the appropriate approach to spiritual guidance in a way one can use to distinguish healthy spiritual guidance from its distortions:

Cultivating them [spiritual children] means treating them and working with them as a gardener would with flowers or other plants. He has to know the soil, the nature of the plant, the climactic or other conditions they are set in, and only then can he help. And help is all he can do, because one or another plant can only grow into what it should be by nature. We should never break a person in order to make him like ourselves. One religious writer in the West said: A spiritual child can only be brought to his own self, and the road in his life can be very long. If you read the lives of the saints you will see how great elders were able to do this, how they were able to be themselves, but also see in another person his exclusive, inimitable qualities, and to give that person—and another, or a third person—the opportunity to also be himself and not a replica of an elder; or in the worse case, a cookie-cutter repeat. (Bloom 2012)

While pondering what caused the parishioners' heightened attention to their own "spiritual life," Schmemann sees here not only a feature specific for the ecclesial milieu, but a fruit of individualism and narcissism, which are peculiar to modern Western culture as such. The theologian advances the thesis that Christians, as customers of organizations, started seeing the main task of the Church as "attending to their spiritual needs" and sought "therapeutics" from the Church. According to Fr. Schmemann, personal confession and "spiritual guidance" became the instruments to support this approach, and for that reason he considers them to be useless, while many domestic problems and concerns discussed in confession might be "eliminated" through a genuine sermon:

I might be terribly wrong, but somehow I have seen no slightest benefit around me and in the Church—from this spiritual guidance. On the contrary, I have always seen more harm:

self-centered indulgence, subtle spiritual pride (on both sides), some kind of reduction of faith to oneself and one's own problems ... < ... > Personally, I would abolish private confession, except for the cases where a person has committed an obvious and particular sin and confesses it, and not their sentiments, doubt, discouragement and temptations. (Schmemann 2005, pp. 34–35)

In one of his articles, the protopresbyter notes that the parishioners, succumbing to the individualistic orientation of Western culture and the desire to seek one's own "self" and "spiritual path", expect therapeutic effect from the Church, and that the priests indulged them in this by offering "spiritual direction" and their own methods of problem solving. That is, Schmemann discerns the phenomenon of self-centeredness not only in ecclesial community as such, but also in the way ancient church traditions, in his view, are being overlapped by phenomena that belong to Western individualistic culture. All this, according to Schmemann, is the exact opposite of the true contemplative sense of Christianity. He perceives the savoring of triumph of one's own decency and pious sentimentality as "abolition of the cross of Christ", its replacement by "professional religiosity".

In contrast to this "professional religiosity", the theologian finds examples of true Christianity in the Arab East, writing how impressed he was by three monasteries he saw during a trip to Egypt.

But then today I had an extraordinary day: a visit in the desert to three monasteries with an uninterrupted tradition from Anthony the Great, Makarios, etc. In one of them is the sarcophagus of Ephrem of Syria. And the most amazing, of course, is how very much alive it all is: Real monks! In my whole life, I have seen only imitations, only playing at monastic life, false, stylized; and mostly unrestrained idle talk about monasticism and spirituality. And here are *they*, in *a real* desert. A real, heroic feat. (Schmemann 2000, p. 189)

5. The Problem of Neurotization. A View through the Lens of Fromm's "Escape from Freedom"

"Piety," Schmemann notes, "is soaked through with religious egocentrism" (Schmemann 2005, p. 359). "The narrowing of man's conscience through piety ... leads to a rather dull, gray digging into one's self" (Schmemann 2005, p. 79, emphasis added). However, an individual's egocentrism does not exist all by itself. To Fr. Alexander's mind, it intertwines with the egocentrism typical of the churchly social environment as a whole, and even with the egocentrism of the Church herself (sic!), with her withdrawal from the world and her rejection of her mission towards all humankind.

In this connection, Schmemann speaks negatively about various church activities. For instance, churchly periodicals are no more than "a pious conversation of pious people about their piety" (Schmemann 2005, p. 460). That is to say, ecclesiastical mass media also boost Orthodoxy's tendency to withdraw and to reduce Christianity to piety, to circle it in its own (Schmemann 2005).

Among other things, Schmemann interprets the phenomenon of encapsulation he observes in churchly life as a sign of neurotic fear and lack of confidence in the face of the world and freedom. The churchly subculture offers a welcome refuge to anyone wishing to escape freedom. The word "escape" is key in this context:

"People escaped—to the Fathers, to the Typikon, to Catholicism, to Hellenism, to spirituality, to a strictly defined way of life, anywhere. Fundamentally, one escaped. To escape or to deny is stronger than to affirm. It is easier to cling to the old calendar to the letter of the law, to fear and angry defense". (Schmemann 2000, p. 29)

"Religion was born from fear, they say, and this is basically true," notes the theologian (Schmemann 2005, p. 243). That is, the empiric evidence of churchly life leads him to believe that "religion ... is almost always born from a lack rather than surplus, from a fear of life rather than gratitude for it" (Schmemann 2000, p. 35) (emphasis added). In his words, "there is a lot more fear in the world than before, there is even religious fear, only it is not at all the fear of God" (Schmemann 2005, p. 152). And this fear is often accompanied by triumphalism and narcissism.

The Orthodoxy is filled through and through with idolatry ... , < ... > but also with fear, triumphalism, narcissism ... < ... > It speaks a kind of artificial language, completely unrelated to reality; it has neither love, nor freedom, and in some sense, the Karlovchane [adherents of "Karlovcian Church"[6]] express it most adequately. Whatever the "Orthodox" talk about, they always speak in a falsely high-spirited tone, and at the same time irresponsibly in terms of "semantics". (Schmemann 2005, p. 376)

Upon reading such statements, one might feel that the defensive settings of churchly cultural space observed by Schmemann reflect a deep psychological conflict—a heavy load of various defense mechanisms, a lack of balance between conventional norms of human identification and a genuine internal self-identification, between the declared norms and a real ability to live up to them.

Schmemann does not ever mention Erich Fromm, but Fromm's descriptions (Fromm 1969, pp. 21–36, 54) are very similar to the problems individuals are facing in a society devoid of a rigid social structure ("primary ties") which with one hand grants him freedom of personal self-expression, and with the other dooms him to insecurity, anxiety and, at times, to a sense of powerlessness.

"Although society was thus structuralized and gave man security, yet it kept him in bondage". To the degree to which the individual, figuratively speaking, has not yet completely severed the umbilical cord which fastens him to the outside world, he lacks freedom; but these ties give him security and a feeling of belonging and of being rooted somewhere (Fromm 1969, p. 21). Freedom from the bondage of structured society, of "primary ties" is bound to create a deep feeling of insecurity, powerlessness, doubt, aloneness, and anxiety. These feelings must be alleviated if the individual is to function successfully. (Fromm 1969, p. 54)

Fromm's thoughts on "Escape from Freedom" apply even more to the aforementioned abuse of spiritual authority, the specifics of the type of spiritual guidance called "mladostarchestvo". Fromm's view can also be applied to the sometimes blind consent for parishioners in following the arbitrary directions of "mladostartsy". Without such a free consent, without free subordination (submissiveness) the practices of spiritual guidance of "*mladostarchestvo*" would be impossible, so not only the clergy is responsible for it.

"Escaping from freedom", according to Fromm, "is the tendency to give up the independence of one's own individual self and to fuse one's self with somebody or something outside of oneself in order to acquire the strength which the individual self is lacking" (Fromm 1969, p. 140). Fromm argued that this striving to submit to authority happens when individuals feel that they are not aware of their own needs, goals, and desires. They also have difficulties in articulating their personal identities. As a result of these conditions, such people are inclined not only to submit themselves to the forces of powerful authorities but also to experience "feelings of inferiority, powerlessness, individual insignificance. . . . these persons show a tendency to belittle themselves, to make themselves weak, and not to master things" (p. 141). Escape from Freedom can be carried out by means of submission to authority, any proven tradition that a priest may represent, in other words, the confessor can act as a person called "magic helper" in psychoanalytic literature (Schmemann 2005, p. 150).

We can see here a realization of such a model when people strive to be included in practices of spiritual guidance in accordance with the type of *mladostarchestvo* as one of the forms of managing their psychological freedom and their lives. This phenomenon evidences that many people accept the church as an institution because it affords them opportunities to get rid of the burden of self-determination and personal choice in the socially and ideologically unstructured world. By subordinating his or her

---

6   "Karlovcian Church"—non-official title of Russian Orthodox Church Outside of Russia (ROCOR). It has been adopted to ROCOR, because its Synod of bishops was established in Serbian town of Sremski Karlovci, where Russian Orthodox hierarchs met on 13 September 1922.

will to a confessor, a "starets", whom parishioners usually tend to absolutize, such a person gets an opportunity to throw off the said burden of freedom, to "escape" from it.

This issue is particularly relevant to the ecclesial life in Russia, where, in the words of hegumen Peter (Meshcherinov)[7], the attitude to mystify phenomena is thriving, where the confessor's importance in the guidance of his flock's life is strongly exaggerated. Hegumen Peter points out a phenomenon, where a churched person seeks to shift personal responsibility onto the confessor, and thus be free of the need to make decisions him- or herself.

Accordingly, this scenario of joining the Church is not so much a coming to Christ, or not a "coming to" at all, as it is a "flight from", with subsequent fear of experiencing anything new. To use Schmemann's words, this is a "recurrence of the Old Ritual" (Schmemann 2000, p. 144), where the term "the Old Ritual" is used as a socio-cultural term, synonymous with "defensiveness".

Schmemann admits, however, that he is not yet ready to offer a clear, concisely formulated way out of this situation. The Orthodoxy's neurasthenia comes through also in the fact that, even upon having realized the need to replace a defensive paradigm, one finds it hard to offer a specific remedy as clearly defined as that of the "defenders".

> A relative success of any "old ritual"—among the "converts," for example,—lies in the fact that they offer a ready formula: accept and obey. I know, with my whole being, that this formula is wrong ... What do we offer when we say; here is the wonderful design of God for the world, for man, for life. Go and live by it! But how? Little by little, Orthodoxy becomes neurotic, people are rushing around searching for answers, and there are no answers, or rather, the answer is so general that people do not know how to apply it to their lives. (Schmemann 2000, p. 144)

6. "Religion of Joy" vs. "Religion of Guilt": Reference to Heavenly Kingdom

While reading this article, a reader may have a legitimate question as to whether the author of the *Journals* sees the true spiritual life, a true communion with God, and not declarative and simulative ones? Studying the (Schmemann 2000), one can easily see that Fr. Alexander's criterion of genuine communion with God and genuine religious experience is the ability to rejoice. It is the joy as a state, accompanying the true communion with God that is an indicator of genuine ideas, opposing the connotations that Schmemann criticized so much in his *Journals*. Any religious virtues and states acquire their true meaning, if joy accompanies them.

> Joy is absolutely essential because it is without any doubt the fruit of God's presence. One cannot know that God exists and not rejoice. Only in relation to joy are the fear of God and humility correct, genuine, fruitful. Outside of joy, they become demonic, the deepest distortion of any religious experience. (Schmemann 2000, p. 129)

The ability to take pleasure in being as the divine gift that, according to Schmemann, allows acquiring the religious experience, which is not opposed to life, but on the contrary, reveals it. It is absolutely logical to Schmemann that it is impossible to feel the living God and all His perfection without rejoicing, as in his view, joy is a kind of key dominant of Christianity.

> I think God will forgive everything except lack of joy, when we forget that God created the world and saved it. Joy is not one of the "components" of Christianity, it's tonality of Christianity that penetrates everything—faith and vision. (Schmemann 2000, p. 137)

---

[7] Hegumen Peter (Meshcherinov) is one of the famous pastors in today's Russia. A writer and journalist, raised in the middle of the two thousands the issue of substitutions in the life of the Church, in particular, the distortions in spiritual and pastoral guidance.

According to Schmemann, the feeling of joy is connected with yet another very important capability—directedness not towards oneself, but towards the others, attention to others. That is, the joy of which Schmemann writes, helps to overcome the very narcissism and self-centeredness that the theologian sees in the socio-cultural precepts of the ecclesial subculture. It is in the tonality of joy that a person sees another person, but in the absence of joy, on the contrary, he is self-absorbed, "enslaved to his own self." In this relation, Fr. Alexander notes: " . . . the directedness towards other people, other things—God, man, world—and not religiosity," meaning by religiosity one of those code subcultural constructs of the socio-ecclesial milieu, which we mentioned earlier.

It should be noted, however, that the nature of happiness, of which Schmemann speaks, is not confined to the glamour optimism, expressed in such concept as "fun." Christian joy of communion with God is quite compatible with the sorrow over one's imperfection.

"The knowledge of the fallen world does not kill joy, which emanates in this world, always constantly, as a bright sorrow" (Schmemann 2000, p. 137). In one of the texts of his *Journals* father Alexander speaks about "joyful, humble, sad melody of the Lenten, 'Lord, have mercy!'", designating that bright-sorrow feeling, which Orthodox people have while listening to the chanting of the canon by Saint Andrew of Crete (Schmemann 2000, p. 9). And there is nothing contradictory in this feeling for Schmemann, because it is associated with the transition to another "dimension," a different reality, to which the worship should lead. Contradictions, in contrast, begin where there is no joy.

> Without joy, piety and prayer are without grace, since their power is in joy. Religion has become the synonym of a seriousness not compatible with joy. So it is weak. People want answers, peace, meaning from religion, and the meaning is joy. That is the answer, including in it all answers. (Schmemann 2000, p. 140)

That is, according to Schmemann, in modern Orthodoxy, the religion of joy is often replaced by its opposite pole—a phenomenon that can be qualified as a "religion of guilt". "Religion of fear. Religion of pseudo-humility. Religion of guilt: They are all temptations, traps—very strong indeed, not only in the world, but inside the Church. Somehow 'religious' people often look on joy with suspicion,"—the theologian writes (Schmemann 2005, p. 297). Let's note that Georgiy Fedotov in his work "The Russian Religious Mind" argued, that a fear was an integral part of the atmosphere amidst monks in Ancient Rus', however, he drew his attention to the fact that in Byzantine tradition fear in the face of God often transformed into the fear in the face of earthly people hierarchy. And it seemed to be an obvious distortion of Gospel ethical principles. (Fedotov 1975).

One can see an explanation of the notion "religion of guilt" in (Hankiss 2001). Let's say that in the Western science the issue of religiously stipulated emotions of guilt was discussed quite widely, as well as considering different functions of "guilt" as a regulator in religious groups and as an element in ethical religious codexes (Sheldon 2006; Albertsen et al. 2006). There are different works analyzing emotions of guilt within Catholicism and Protestantism (Luyten et al. 1998; Walinga et al. 2005; Martinez-Pilkington 2007; Stotts 2016). However, this issue was still not so much analyzed with regard to Orthodoxy (see, Knorre 2011, 2017; Lorgus and Krasnikova 2010).

And the "religion of guilt" cannot give man freedom, cannot release him from slavery to sin, worldly things, temptations, and therefore cannot reunite with God. "The fear of sin does not save from sin. Joy in the Lord saves. A feeling of guilt or moralism does not liberate from the world and its temptations. Joy is the foundation of freedom, where we are called to stand" (Schmemann 2000, p. 126).

It should be noted that Schmemann indicates that, depending on the presence or absence of joy, such an ethical ecclesial category as "humility" produces a genuine or, on the contrary, a distorted sense. Genuine "humility," according to Schmemann, is not based on focusing on one's own sinfulness and imperfection, but on the tonality of joy, since joy is associated with turning to God as the source, taking interest in one's neighbor, which means overcoming egocentrism and obsession with one's self.

> All of creation rejoices in you, o full of grace," here the point is in rejoicing about the other, in admiration of the other, and it means—in "ontological" humility, which alone

makes possible this rejoicing, this admiration, while such religiosity lacks this directedness towards the other—to God, man and the world. (Schmemann 2005, p. 360)

Schmemann believes that freedom to which Christianity calls man is "first and foremost the freedom from enslavement primarily to one's own self," expressed in the feelings, "in the directedness of heart and mind". "For only in freedom illuminates "the joy of ... ," the admiration, only within it all becomes clear and the integrity lost in the original sin is being restored (Schmemann 2005, p. 360).

That is, the directedness towards the neighbor, as well as joy, are the qualities that define the actual content of such most important ethical quality for Christianity as humility, which, as it turns out, can be of two types—the one associated with the egocentric focus on one's self, the other—with directedness to the neighbor:

> ... humility is deemed a fruit of person's knowledge of his own shortcomings and unworthiness, while it is the most divine of all the properties of God. We are made humble not because we contemplate ourselves (this always leads to pride in one form or another, for the false humility is simply a kind of pride, perhaps—the most irreparable of all), but only if we contemplate God and His humility. (Schmemann 2005, p. 13)

Here, perhaps, Fr. Alexander comes to the key point—the directedness towards God, contemplation of God, the capability that he also names "correlation" (Schmemann uses the words "correlation" and "reference"), to emphasize that we are talking about the correlation of "terrestrial" reality with the "heavenly" one. This is why Schmemann pays so much attention to the criticism of self-centeredness in his deliberations in (Schmemann 2000) entries—self-centeredness, retreat inside oneself—the most serious obstacle to conversion to God, to correlation. Accordingly, it is understandable why the theologian is so critical of the principles and precepts of the ecclesial culture that indulge this egocentrism.

I would suggest that it is the reference of all in this world to the Kingdom of God—the main idea for Schmemann, if one can ever speak about the main idea in relation to his work. This idea dominates the entire array of the *Journals*, and, of course, to Schmemann is it the very truth that he is ready to juxtapose to narrow-minded religiosity and church reductionism.

> This correlation is a tie, not an "idea"; an experience. It is the experience of the world and life literally in the light of the Kingdom of God, revealed through everything that makes up the world: colors, sounds, movements, time, space—concrete, not abstract. When this light, which is only in the heart, only inside us, falls on the world and on life, then all is illuminated, and the world becomes a joyful sign, symbol, expectancy. (Schmemann 2000, pp. 20, 52)

In other words, the worldview of a man who comprehended this correlation is the feeling of a different depth in the ordinary things, the divine reflection in all creation, a touch of authenticity to the "substratum of life," joy and gratitude. The experience of correlation reveals a different reality to the person, and the service, according to Schmemann, is intended to bring people into this reality, creating a special "dimension" to perform the sacraments. The Church itself exists only "to make this dimension really manifest," and without this feature, Fr. Alexander argues, all of the Church's teaching does not mean anything.

Michael Plekon writes in his cognominal article that a pivotal idea of Schmemann's outlook was "Liturgy of Life." Plekon draws the reader's attention to the theological affinity in such a mystical understanding between Schmemann and Mariya Skobtsova. He notes that "Schmemann never loses sight of liturgy continuing in life, what Mother Maria Skobtsova called 'liturgy outside the church walls'" (Plekon 2016). Like Mother Maria, Father Alexander "envisioned a transforming, a reintegration of liturgy and life, of faith and everyday activity that is subversive of the strategies of the church growth movement and of every other market-driven tactic for expansion of membership and revenue" (Plekon 2016).

Plekon also justly states that for Schmemann "sacrament is hardly just a religious ritual but the transformation of each person, of humankind and of all creation by Christ, through the Spirit, to the glory of the Father. The rule of prayer *is* the rule of faith." (Plekon 2016) while citing F. Alexander: 'In the world of the incarnation, nothing 'neutral' remains, nothing can be taken away from the Son of Man'" (Schmemann 1979, p. 216).

> The Church is a point of view of reference, so that we know, to what everything is related, what reveals the truth about everything, what is the content of our life. As soon as the Church becomes one of the components of the world (Church, government, culture, ethics, *et tutti quanti*) as soon as the Church ceases to be a point of reference, which means to reveal and to judge by this revelation, to convert and transform, it becomes itself an idol". (Schmemann 2000, p. 167)

The Church for Schmemann is not only a community of coreligionists, but a "fragment of eternity" in the non-eternal world, which has its "unique vocation—to be love, truth, faith and mission—all of these fulfilled in the Eucharist; even simpler, *to be* the Body of Christ (Schmemann 2000, p. 25). The theologian compares Church with "a home".

> It is "the home each of us leaves to go to work and to which one returns with joy in order to find life, to which everyone brings back the fruits of his labor and where everything is transformed into a feast, into freedom and fulfillment, the presence. Only this presence can give meaning and value to everything in life, can refer everything to that experience and make it full". (Schmemann 2000, p. 25)

7. Ascetics Based on Anthropological Pessimistic Views

Taking a look at the modern Russian ecclesial community milieu, one can see that all of the above questions relating to defensiveness of tradition, reductionism, replacement of spiritual freedom by stylization of the primitively understood piety, neuroticism and narcissism, and the impact of the culture of guilt on the Church ethics are still relevant for it, and even to the greater extent. Of course, it is necessary to bear in mind that as the Orthodox factor is gaining strength in Russian politics and the ROC is being involved as an influential actor in the ideological and political space of Russia, sub-cultural attitudes are often discarded or at least minimized. At a time when Orthodoxy becomes the majority religion, certain roughening and decay of the rules formed by tradition is inevitable. However, the elements of tradition, albeit in a diffuse form, can be perceived as an element of Russian culture, as a basis of certain stereotypes, i.e., can be translated into the culture of the society, mainly related to this religion. After all, in those communities who want to follow all the rules of the Church, to live "according to ecclesial rules," the substitutions, which Fr. Alexander Schmemann pointed out, are being revealed.

What Schmemann writes of "piety," "churched life," and "spirituality" manifests itself sometimes even more prominently in the Russian socio-ecclesial community. Schmemann's words on the rejection of Orthodox culture, cited in the beginning, are being confirmed today. Today we can find very similar "recitations [by clergymen] against the theater and literature that are impossible in their primitivism" (Schmemann 2005, p. 67), of which the theologian wrote. For example, in Orthodox monasteries in Russia today sometimes it is forbidden to read fiction, as is vividly described in "*Ispoved' byvshey poslushnitsy*", the newly published personal description of the monastic experience by Maria Kikot in the genre of confession (Kikot 2017, p. 17). There are also church officials of the ROC who speak against some of the classic Russian literary works. At a time when the Orthodox factor is gaining strength in Russian politics, the obscurant of ROC representatives can be spread out far beyond the Orthodox milieu itself. In particular, in 2015 a member of the Patriarchal Commission on family matters, protection of motherhood and childhood, archpriest Artemy Vladimirov proposed to withdraw from the school program some works by Russian classic writers—Anton Chekhov, Alexander Kuprin and

Ivan Bunin based solely on the fact that there is "glorified free love". "These literature images are a time bomb for our children,"—states Vladimirov (Roshchenya and Vladimirov 2016)[8].

Modern literature is also attacked and exposed by the clergy or church laymen, for example a lot of protests are spoken against fantasy novels written by British author J. K. Rowling which chronicle the life of a young wizard, Harry Potter, as it is written in (Moslenta 2016). The groups of churched Orthodox believers also often protest against theatrical performances and rock musicians' touring.[9] In particular, the rock Opera "Jesus Christ superstar" performed in November 2016 in Omsk was even thwarted by. See (Majorova 2016).

A no less striking expression of the simulated piety is the requirement to comply with formalities, declamatory forms of humility and piety, and what is more striking—to comply with declamatory forms of guilt. A very eloquent testimony to this is again *Ispoved' byvshey poslushnitsy* by Maria Kikot' where the ex-novice tells about the practices in the monastery when every nun or sister should declare their guilt, wrongness irrespective of the real situation (Kikot 2017, pp. 5, 6, 65–67). What she describes absolutely corresponds with the notion of a "religion of guilt" used by Schmemann. According to Maria Kikot's testimony in the Orthodox monasteries where she has lived, *nun-sisters or novices* "constantly live in tension, feeling deeply guilty for not meeting the standards in some kinds of their doings" (Kikot 2017, p. 67).

And indeed, a certain peculiar sense of guilt as a priori given a permanent state of consciousness was inherent in many monastic, but partly also parish communities, who were trying to revive Typicon piety by books in the post-Soviet period. Some theologians offer the awareness of guilt, a sense of being guilty as an integral element of asceticism, which allows us to introduce such a concept as "asceticism of guilt". In modern Russian Orthodoxy one can really distinguish a certain focus on the "presumption of guilt", and a certain "culture of guilt" is deeply ingrained in Russian spiritual tradition, both at the ecclesial, institutional, and cultural level, for example, at the level of classical literature. This "culture of guilt' is present as a kind of set of being a priori "guilty" which is imposed on any person, regardless of whether they did something wrong in their lives or not. So, one of the modern Russian theologians, Archpriest Vladislav Sveshnikov, the author of the book *"Essays on Christian ethics"*, by which students of theological schools currently study moral theology, emphasizes that, as part of ecclesial tradition, the moment of being wrong is rightly incriminated to a person who even just enters a conscious age. Archpriest Vladislav Sveshnikov notes that it is not by chance that a person just entering the "age of reason" is told: "Repent! Even if a person is only seven or eight years old. Repent!—it means, admit your guilt. Guilty means wrong. And so, gradually, half-consciously, a person entering the ways of the rightful life receives an experience of his or her own wrongness" (Sveshnikov 2000, pp. 179–80).

This permanent socio-cultural set is paired with a different imperative—constant soul-searching, focus on one's imperfections, wrongness, i.e., with the retreat inside oneself. For example, Archpriest Vladislav Sveshnikov stresses:

> It is necessary to recollect more often your meanness and baseness, and the imperfection of the human nature, in general. The more clearly and constantly you see your own sinfulness, the more obviously you acknowledge its inevitability, the more serious is the work of repentance, the natural and the first fruit of which happens to be humiliation. (Sveshnikov 2000, p. 179)

---

8   See: in details also the News published in Gazeta.Ru: "V Russkoy Pravoslavnoy Tserkvi predlagajut iskljuchit' iz shkol'noj programmy rasskazy Chehova i Kuprina" [ROC offers to exclude from the school curriculum the stories by Chekhov and Kuprin]. Available online: https://www.gazeta.ru/culture/news/2016/03/14/n_8367569.shtml (accessed on 14 March 2016); See also: http://www.pravmir.ru/protoierey-artemiy-vladimirov-shkola-ne-mozhet-byit-domom-tolerantnosti-i-terpimosti/ (accessed on 4 April 2016).

9   See «Karyakina protiv Enteo—Bez nazvanija» [Karjakina protiv Enteo—without title] (Audiorecord, December 2015), https://vk.com/search?c%5Bperformer%5D=1&c%5Bq%5D=Карякина%20против%20Энтео&c%5Bsection%5D=audio.

Note that the desire to "often remember one's meanness and baseness", focusing on wrongdoings is termed "getting stuck" in the language of psychology. In the book "Essays on Christian ethics" it is proposed as a means to maintain a constant feeling of guilt, and through the prism of this mindset the ethical and behavioral categories of "humility" and "repentance" shall be read. And that means that the other of the above categories—"piety", "churched life", "spirituality" cannot be seen in isolation from this kind of "asceticism of guilt" (Knorre 2011).

That is, we see the definition of the concept of religious ethical qualities that is opposite to the vision that Schmemann offered as authentic. We see the worst-case scenario imminent in the absence of joy and self-centeredness. This phenomenon is very systematic and engrained in Russian Orthodoxy. Hegumen Peter (Meshcherinov), a resident of St. Daniel Monastery, notes that the ascetic tradition of crying over one's sins and self-flagellation (for the record, it is typical of the monastics, and not of laymen) gained extensive application in the post-Soviet Orthodoxy.

> It boils down to this: I am a nonentity, a miserable sinner, everything in me is evil and sin, I am worthy of eternal torment, the last judgment, hell, death; however, there is a chance to avoid all this. This chance is just to always feel a worthless, wicked, ugly, and unworthy creature capable of nothing but sin (this is called "humility") and repent, repent, repent, all of my life. The goal of the spiritual life then becomes solely the persuasion of oneself in one's sinfulness and total self-reproach, because we are absolutely unworthy of other things. (Meshcherinov 2006)

As you can see, Fr Alexander Schmemann was right, discerning the phenomenon of the "religion of guilt" in relation to Orthodoxy. One can see that the "religion of guilt" permeates Russian Orthodoxy probably stronger than in American Orthodoxy, as Fr. Schmemann saw it. It should be noted that the ascetic tradition of crying over sins and self-flagellation is typical for monastics rather than laymen, but in Russian Orthodoxy no separate "ethics for the laity" have been developed, and therefore it is the monastic ethic that work in the lay social context too. There is real evidence to this on the part of the ecclesial milieu. For example, one of the active parishioners of the Church of the Holy Martyr Tatiana, Natalia Kholmogorova frankly admits: "I have learned to look at myself as guilty, but have learned to look at others as even more guilty and take pleasure in it" (Kholmogorova 2007). In fact, what we have in practice, may be called indoctrination of guilt (Knorre 2011, p. 37).

The sense of guilt is inherent not solely in the Russian ecclesial tradition but also in the secular one, which is reflected in particular in the Russian literature. For example, in Gogol's reflections on the "Selected Passages from Correspondence with Friends" it is stated that there are no innocent or guilty, only God is righteous. Gogol stresses that this idea is innate to the Russian people. Gogol cites as evidence to this idea a passage from "The Captain's Daughter" by Pushkin, where the commander's wife, who sent a Lieutenant to settle a dispute between a policeman and a woman who had fought in the bath over a wooden tub, punished them both (Gogol 2009, pp. 164–65). The imperative to consider all the people guilty in their own way and who deserve to be punished, is not just a kind of ideological phenomenon, but is also a prerequisite for implementing the corresponding model in the real social life. In "Resurrection," Leo Tolstoy shows that by virtue of a prevailing social consensus the repressive formalist state system is being maintained, which already implements the culture of blame in state paperwork through the judicial machine, whereby each man, even without having committed any particular crimes, can be convicted. That is, the "presumption of guilt" is realized far beyond the socio-ecclesial milieu as such. But this is a topic for a separate study, for a separate article and not even one.

8. Conclusions

Delving into Schmemann's reasoning, one can see the arguments proving the existence of two ecclesial and ascetic paradigms within Orthodoxy having unconditional socio-cultural significance. One of them approves the "religion of guilt" making the tradition of defensiveness, reductionism, suppression of feelings an end in itself, it can be called the "oppressive" or "deprivation" paradigm (Knorre 2011). The second paradigm, laying the emphasis on the joy of communion with God, a living sense of beauty of the world as God's creation, respectively inspires a person to comprehend this world, direct efforts and apply capabilities to its beautification—it can be called the "empowerment paradigm" in the language of socio-cultural studies.

On the part of church analysts, Hegumen Peter (Meshcherinov) speaks nowadays about distinguishing these two paradigms. He also draws attention to the paradigm in the Church which focuses on human unworthiness and failure in this life to accept the grace of God because of sin and the passionate state of "fallen nature" of man, that is, a complex of guilt, fear for noncompliance with God's requirements is imposed on mankind (Meshcherinov 2006). It can be correlated with what we call the "deprivation" paradigm (Knorre 2011). However, hegumen Peter (Meshcherinov) singles out also the paradigm which sets as priority of spiritual life the contact with God, the vibrant, unceasing, and joyful sense of faith, a willingness to fulfill the will of God with reverence and awareness of "son-like dependence from God". (Meshcherinov 2006).

It turns out that for today Schmemann is not the only one to point to the "religion of guilt" as an integral large-scale phenomenon, using for its designation such synonyms as "religion of fear," "religion of pseudo guilt," "religion of pseudo humility." Wondering about this "religion of guilt," Fr. Alexander, however, cannot find the answer to the question about its origin: "Where, how, when has this tonality of Christianity become distorted, dull—or rather, where, how, why have Christians become deaf to joy? How, when and why, instead of freeing suffering people, did Church begin to sadistically intimidate and frighten them?" (Schmemann 2000, p. 129).

In other words, we see that Schmemann has exposed a whole layer, a large-scale phenomenon—a sort of "religion within a religion", "Orthodoxy inside Orthodoxy", which can also be called "counter-Orthodoxy"—a parallel Orthodoxy, or a parallel pattern of religiosity, using the term offered by professor Per-Arne Bodin (Bodin 2009). Using the concept of Sergei Fudel, the Soviet era religious writer, "professional religiosity" referred to by Schmemann correlates with such a term as "dark lookalike of the Church" (Fudel 2012). We can say that Schmemann and Fudel wrote about the same order phenomena, and what Fudel designates as the "Church's lookalike", Schmemann calls "fake", "surrogate".

Given the current context that urges the Orthodox tradition to establish its modus of interaction with the world, Schmemann's Journals are priceless reflections for social theology, for generating the church's position regarding the secular reality. The questions raised by the theologian can help modern Orthodox believers (and perhaps not only Orthodox) become cognizant of their position and strategy in relation to the changing realities of our time and life.

Given that the Orthodox Church has only recently started focusing on social theology, understanding of social problems and political theology, Schmemann's deliberations on church culture, reductionism, guardianship and defensiveness of tradition, and on the other hand, the "correlation", "reference" as the cultural mission of the Church, seem to be more than relevant.

In Orthodoxy, especially in Russia, the monastic ethics currently prevails, while laymen's ethics is yet to be developed. In that regard, it seems that the above ecclesiological ideas of Schmemann are more relevant than ever, and can substantially facilitate the search for forms of existence of Orthodoxy in the III millennium world.

Acknowledgments: In this study are used the data of the research supported by European Community Mobility Programme Erasmus Mundus Action 2, Strand 1 (EMA2)—AURORA20121593 conducted by the author. Support from the Basic Research Program of the National Research University Higher School of Economics is gratefully acknowledged. The author is particularly grateful to Madina Kochieva for her constructive suggestions, discussions and encouragement.

Conflicts of Interest: The author declares no conflict of interest.

References

Agadjanian, Alexander. 2016. Pravoslavniy vzglyad na sovremenniy mir. Kontext, istoriya i smysl sobornogo dokumenta o missii Tserkvi [Orthodox Vision of the Modern World. Context, History and Meaning of the Synodal Document on Church Mission]. *Gosudarstvo, Religiya, Tserkov' v Rossii i Za Rubezhom* 34: 255–79.

Albertsen, Elizbeth, Lynn O'Connor, and Jack Berry. 2006. Religion and interpersonal guilt: Variations across ethnicity and spirituality. *Mental Health, Religion & Culture* 9: 67–84.

Alexiy, II. 1999. Podlinniy starets berezhno otnositsya k kazhdomu cheloveku [A true elder carefully treats each person]. *Tserkov' i Vremya* 2: 7–16.

Alexiy, II. 2004. Doklad Svyateyshego Patriarkha Moskovskogo i vseya Rusi Alexiya II na Eparkhial'nom sobranii goroda Moskvy 15 dekabrya 2004 goda [The report of his Holiness Patriarch of Moscow and all Russia Alexiy II to the Diocesan Assembly of the city of Moscow 15 December 2004]. Available online: http://patriarh-i-narod.ru/slovo-patriarha/doklady-na-eparkhialnyh-sobraniyah-patriarha-alexiya-ii/142-vystuplenie-na-eparkhialnom-sobranii-2004-g (accessed on 20 November 2017).

Bloom, Anthony. 2012. Spirituality and the Role of Spiritual Father. Available online: http://orthochristian.com/54517.html (accessed on 11 November 2017).

Bloom, Anthony. 2014. Mozhet li eshe molit'sya sovremenniy chelovek? [Can a modern man still pray?]. Available online: http://litresp.ru/chitat/ru/Б/blum-antonij/mozhet-li-eschyo-molitjsya-sovremennij-chelovek#sec_6 (accessed on 20 November 2017).

Bodin, Per-Arne. 2009. *Language, Canonisation and Holy Foolishness. Studies in Post-Soviet Russian Culture and the Orthodox Tradition*. Stockholm: Stockholm University Press.

Bourdieu, Pierre. 1977. *Outline of a Theory of Practice Context*. Cambridge: Cambridge University Press.

Briskina-Müller, Anna. 2015. Power and Victory as Central Categories of the Russian Orthodox Public Discourse Today. Paper present at the Conference Political Orthodoxy and Totalitarianism in a Post-Communist Era, Helsinki, Finland, May 28–31.

Ershova, Anna. 2005. Blagochestie pokaznoe i podlinnoe [Ostentatious piety and genuine]. *Pravoslavnaya Aentsiklopedia "Azbuka Very"*. Available online: http://azbyka.ru/dictionary/02/blagochestie-all.shtml (accessed on 3 October 2017).

Fedotov, Georgiy. 1975. *The Russian Religious Mind*. Belmont: Nordland, vol. I, pp. 99–102.

Fedotov, Georgiy. 2000. Svyatye Drevney Rusi [The Saints of Ancient Rus]. In *Sobranie Sochineniy v 12-ti Tomakh [The Complete Works Collection in 12 Volumes]*. Edited by Georgiy Fedotov. Moscow: Martis, vol. VIII.

Filatov, Sergey. 2005. Russkaya pravoslavnaya tserkov' v poiskakh kul'turno-aesteticheskogo ideala. [The Russian Orthodox Church in search of cultural, aesthetic and national ideal]. In *Aesthetics as a Religiuos Factor in Eastern and Western Christianity (Eastern Christian Studies 6)*. Edited by Wil van den Bercken and Jonathan Sutton. Leuven, Paris, Dudley and Walpole: Peeters.

Filatov, Sergey. 2009. Tantsuyushee pravoslavie. Volgodskiy opyt [Dancing Orthodoxy. Vologda experience]. *Russian Review*. Available online: http://www.keston.org.uk/_russianreview/edition37/01-dancing-orthodoxy--filatov.html (accessed on 22 November 2017).

Filatov, Sergei, and Roman Lunkin. 2006. Statistics on Religion in Russia: The Reality behind the Figures. *Religion, State & Society* 34: 33–49.

Fromm, Erich. 1969. *Escape from Freedom*. New York: Henry Holt and Company. First published 1941.

Fudel, Sergey. 2012. O Tyomnom Dvoynike Tserkvi. [About the dark lookalike of the Church]. *Pravmir.Ru*. Available online: http://www.pravmir.ru/o-temnom-dvojnike-cerkvi/ (accessed on 3 October 2017).

Giambelluca, Kossova A. 2007. *Alle Origini Della Santita Russa: Studi e Testi*. Milano: San Paolo Edizioni.

Gogol, Nikolai. 2009. *Selected Passages from Correspondence with Friends*. Translated by J. Zeldin. Nashville: Vanderbilt University Press.

Golovkov, Mark. 2007. *Tserkovniy Protocol [Church Protocol]*. Moscow: Izdatel'skiy sovet Russkoy pravoslavnoy tserkvi.

Hankiss, Elemér. 2001. *Fears and Symbols: An Introduction to the Study of Western Civilization*. Budapest: Central European University Press, pp. 157–79.

Igumnov, Platon. 2002. Blagochestie [Piety]. *Pravoslavnaya Aentsiklopedia* 5: 334–38.

Igumnov, Platon. 2006. *Pravoslavnoe Nravstvennoye Bogoslovie. [Orthodox Moral Theology]*. Sergiev-Posad: Holy Trinty Sergiev Lavra. Available online: http://azbyka.ru/otechnik/bogoslovie/pravoslavnoe-nravstvennoe-bogoslovie-igumnov/7_10 (accessed on 3 October 2017).

Kholmogorova, Nataliya. 2007. Confessiones. Livejournal. Available online: http://nataly-hill.livejournal.com/ 661078.html#cutid1 (accessed on 10 October 2017).

Kikot, Mariya. 2017. *Ispoved' Byvshey Poslushnitsy. [Confessions of an Ex-Novitiate]*. Moscow: AeKSMO.

Knorre, Boris. 2011. Kategorii viny i smireniya v sisteme tsennostey tserkovno-prikhodskoy subkul'tury [Categories of guilt and humility in the value system of Church-parish subculture]. In *Prikhod i Obshina v Sovremennom Pravoslavii. Kornevaya Sistema Rossiyskoy Religioznosti*. Edited by Alexander Agadjanyan and Kati Rousselet. Moscow: Ves' mir, pp. 317–40.

Knorre, Boris. 2015. *'Bogoslovie Voyny' v Postsovetskom Rossiyskom Pravoslavii ['Theology of War' in the Post-Soviet Russian Orthodoxy]*. Stranitsy: Bogoslovie, kul'tura, obrazovanie, vol. 19, pp. 559–78.

Knorre, Boris. 2016. The Culture of War and Militarization within Political Orthodoxy in the Post-soviet Region. *Transcultural Studies* 12: 15–38.

Knorre, Boris. 2017. Mekhanizmy formirovaniya i rol' chuvstv viny i styda v tserkovnoy sotsio-srede [The mechanisms of making guilt and shame. Their role in the Church social environment]. Paper present at the XVIII April International Academic Conference on Economic and Social Development, Higher School of Economics, Moscow, Russia, April 11–14.

Köllner, Tobias. 2013. Businessmen, Priests and Parishes. Religious Individualization and Privatization in Russia. *Archives de Sciences de Sociales des Religions* 162: 37–52. [CrossRef]

Kormina, Jeanne. 2010. Avtobusniki: Russian Orthodox Pilgrims' Longing for Authenticity. In *Eastern Christians in Anthropological Perspective*. Edited by Chris Hann and Hermann Golz. Berkeley: University of California Press, pp. 267–86.

La Piété. 1970. *Vocabulaire de Theologie Biblique*, 2-me ed. Paris: Editions Du Serf.

Lokhanov, Aristarkh. 1999. *Chto Nado Znat' o Tserkovnom Aetikete [What You Need to Know about Church Etiquette]*. Moscow: Novaya Kniga.

Lorgus, Andrey, and Ol'ga Krasnikova. 2010. Vina i grekh [Guilt and Sin]. *Konsul'tativnaya Psikhologiya i Psikhoterapiya* 3: 165–75.

Loyevskaya, Margarita. 2005. Russkaya Agiographiya v Kul'turno-Istoricheskom Kontexte Perekhodnykh Epokh. [Russian hagiography in the Cultural-Historical Context of Transition Periods]. Ph.D. Thesis, Moscow State University after the name of M.V.Lomonosov, Moscow, Russia.

Lurie, Vasiliy. 2009. *Vvedenie v Kriticheskuyu Agiographiyu [Introduction to the Critical Hagiography]*. Sanct-Petersburg: Axioma.

Luyten, Patrick, Jozef Corveleyn, and Johnny Fontaine. 1998. The relationship between religiosity and mental health: Distinguishing between shame and guilt. *Mental Health, Religion & Culture* 1: 165–84.

Majorova, Julia. 2016. Kak Sryvali Operu "Iisus Hristos—Superzvezda" [The Procedure of Thwarting Opera "Jesus Christ Superstar"]. Available online: https://life.ru/t/культура/940757/ kak_sryvali_opieru_iisus_khristos_-_supierzviezda (accessed on 3 October 2017).

Martinez-Pilkington, Amber. 2007. Shame and Guilt: The Psychology of Sacramental Confession. *The Humanistic Psychologist* 35: 203–18. [CrossRef]

Meshcherinov, Peter. 2005. O dukhovnichestve [About practices of spiritual guidance]. Available online: http://www.pravmir.ru/o-duhovnichestve/ (accessed on 14 November 2017).

Meshcherinov, Peter. 2006. Muchenie lyubvi ili . . . (Razmyshleniya nad knigoy arkhimandrite Lazarya Abashidze) [Suffering of Love or . . . (Reflections on the Book by Archimandrite Lazar' Abashidze 'Suffering of love')]. *Kievskaya Rus*. Available online: http://kiev-orthodox.org/site/churchlife/1262/ (accessed on 3 October 2017).

Moslenta. 2016. Pravoslavnye Aktivisty Obnaruzhili v Potteriane "Myagkiy Satanizm" [Orthodox Activists Found in Harry Potter "Soft Satanism"]. *Moslenta*. Available online: http://moslenta.ru/news/2016/12/08/potter/ (accessed on 8 December 2016).

Pal'cheva, Anna, Alisa Orlova, and Svetlana Gadzhinskaya. 2007. Delovoy khristianin [Business Christian]. *Neskuchniy Sad* 7: 65–69.

Plekon, Michael. 2016. The Liturgy of Life: Alexander Schmemann. *Religions* 7: 127. Available online: http://www.mdpi.com/2077-1444/7/11/127/htm#B31-religions-07-00127 (accessed on 17 November 2017). [CrossRef]

Pliguzov, Andrey, and Valentin Yanin. 1989. Posleslovie [The Epilogue]. In *Drevnerusskie Zhitiya Svyatykh kak Istoricheskiy Istochnik [Ancient Russian Hagiographies as a Historical Source]*. Edited by Vasiliy Kyuchevskiy. Moscow: Nauka, pp. 1–19.

Rock, Stella. 2002. Militant piety: Fundamentalist tendencies in the Russian orthodox brotherhood movement. *Religion in Eastern Europe* 22: 1–17.

Roshchenya, Dariya, and Artemiy Vladimirov. 2016. Protoierey Artemiy Vladimirov: Shkola ne mozhet byt' domom tolerantnosti i terpimosti [The school cannot be a house of tolerance]. *Pravmir.Ru*. Available online: http://www.pravmir.ru/protoierey-artemiy-vladimirov-shkola-ne-mozhet-byit-domom-tolerantnosti-i-terpimosti/ (accessed on 8 December 2016).

Schmemann, Alexander. 1979. *Church, World, Mission*. Crestwood: St. Vladimir's Seminary Press.

Schmemann, Alexander. 2000. *The Journals of Alexander Schmemann 1973–1983*. Crestwood: St. Vladimir's Seminary Press.

Schmemann, Alexander. 2005. *Dnevniki 1973–1983 [Diaries 1973–1983]*. Moscow: Russkiy put'.

Semenenko-Basin, Iliya. 2011. *Personifikatsiya Svyatosti v Russkoy Pravoslavnoy Kul'ture XX Veka. [The Personification of Sanctity in the Russian Orthodox Culture of the XX Century]*. Moscow: Russian State University for the Humanities.

Sheldon, Kennon. 2006. Catholic Guilt? Comparing Catholics' and Protestants' Religious Motivations. *International Journal for the Psychology of Religion* 16: 209–23. [CrossRef]

Shishkov, Andrey. 2015. Osmyslenie sekulyarizatsii v bogoslovii prot. Alexandra Shmemana [Reflection of secularization in the theological thought of Archpriest Alexander Schmemann]. Paper present at the Conference Chelovek v Krizisnom Obshestve XX–XXI vv: Khristianskaya Refleksiya, Biblical Theological Institute after the name of St. Apostle Andrew, Moscow, Russia, May 20.

Shmatko, Natal'ja. 1998. 'Gabitus' v strukture sociologicheskoj teorii. *Zhurnal Sociologii i Social'noj Antropologii* 2: 60–70.

Skobtsova, Mariya. 1998. Types of Religious Lives. Translated from Russian by Fr. Alvian Smirensky. Available online: http://www.rocorstudies.org/2017/03/31/types-of-religious-lives/ (accessed on 8 November 2017).

Stotts, Jonathan. 2016. The Confessional, the Couch, and the Community: Analyzing the Sacrament of Penance in Theological, Psychological, and Cultural Perspectives. Ph.D. Dissertation, Faculty of the Graduate School, Vanderbilt University, Nashville, TN, USA, August.

Sveshnikov, Vladislav. 2000. *Ocherki Khristianskoy Aetiki [Essays on the Christian Ethics]*. Moscow: Palomnik.

Volkova, Elena. 2009. Religiya i Khudozhestvennaya kul'tura: Khudoy mir luchshe dobroy ssory [Religion and Artistic Culture: Better a Bad Peace than a Good Fight]. In *Dvadtsat' Let Religioznoy Svobody v Rossii*. Moscow: ROSSPAeN.

Walinga, Pieter, Josef Corveleyn, and Joke van Saane. 2005. Guilt and Religion: The Influence of Orthodox Protestant and Orthodox Catholic Conceptions of Guilt on Guilt-Experience. *Archiv für Religionspsychologie/Archive for the Psychology of Religion* 27: 113–35. [CrossRef]

Zabaev, Ivan. 2007. Osnovnye kategorii khozyaystvennoy aetiki sovremennogo russkogo pravoslaviya [Basic categories of economic ethics in modern Russian Orthodoxy]. *Sotsialnaya Realnost* 9: 5–26.

Zasedanie, Sinoda. 1999. Zasedanie Svyashennogo Sinoda 28–29 Dekabrya 1998 g. [Session of the Holy Synod on 28–29 December 1998]. *Mospat.Ru*. November 2. Available online: https://mospat.ru/archive/sr291281/ (accessed on 28 November 2017).

Ziolkowski, Margaret. 2014. *Hagiography and Modern Russian Literature*. Princeton: Princeton University Press.

![religions logo] *religions*

MDPI

Article

The Liturgy of Life: Alexander Schmemann

Michael Plekon

Sociology/Anthropology, Religion and Culture, Baruch College of the City University of New York, Box 04-260, 55 Lexington Avenue, New York, NY 10010, USA; mjplekon@aol.com; Tel.: +1-845-380-6343

Academic Editor: John Jillions
Received: 26 August 2016; Accepted: 20 October 2016; Published: 31 October 2016

Abstract: The émigré Russian priest and theologian Alexander Schmemann (1921–1983) spent most of his career as a faculty member and dean of St. Vladimir's Orthodox Seminary in Crestwood, New York, not far from New York City. For over 30 years, in lectures, teaching and numerous publications, he presented the distinctive vision of the Eastern Church, mostly unknown to Western Christians, in which the church's liturgy was the primary source not only of its theology but of all other aspects of its life. I offer an overview of his work, with analysis and criticism and an assessment of his continuing significance.

Keywords: Alexander Schmemann; Eastern Orthodox Christianity; theology; liturgy

---

> ... the true sense of worship is to be found not in the symbolic, but in the real fulfillment of the Church: the new life, given in Christ, and that this eternal transformation of the Church into the Body of Christ, her ascension, in Christ and with Christ into the eschatological fullness of the Kingdom, is the very source of all Christian action in the world, the possibility to "do as he does" ... not a system of astounding symbols, but the possibility to introduce into the world that consuming and transfiguring fire for which the Lord pined—"and wished that it were already kindled" ... [1]

1. Transcending Borders

Now, over 30 years after his death, is it still the case that Alexander Schmemann is listened to as a significant voice for Orthodox Christianity? As with most writers in the Eastern Church, he always had his critics, but during his lifetime he was largely respected, even revered for his powerful, relevant thinking on the connection of faith and action, liturgy and life. While a figure such as Archbishop Iakovos of the Greek Archdiocese is perhaps the best known Orthodox cleric for his accompanying Dr. Martin Luther King, Jr. and others on the Selma march and his most public presence, Schmemann's influence has been pervasive and wide. That the majority of Orthodox churches in North America use English as the language of worship, that most Orthodox Christians receive communion frequently, many every Sunday, that the services of Lent and Holy Week are fully celebrated and well attended, even that baptism has been restored to a communal/parish celebration in many places, and faith is linked to everyday life—all of these and more were what Schmemann wrote and spoke about during his long career as dean of St. Vladimir's Seminary in Crestwood, New York. He lectured all across the country, and his work was ecumenical—he lectured at Catholic and Protestant seminaries and churches.

In addition to the significant works he published in his lifetime, we now have a in various languages and versions selections his journals. A massive volume of his Russian language talks for Radio Liberty, broadcast to Eastern Europe over decades, has appeared in Russia along with translations of his many talks [2,3]. While it is impossible to ignore his liturgical theological contributions, the focus here is on his vision of faith integrated into everyday life.

Born in Tallin, Estonia, in 1921, his family emigrated to Paris, where he attended both a Russian *gimnaziya* and French *lycee*, eventually the University of Paris and St. Sergius Theological Institute. Among his teachers and colleagues at St. Sergius were Nicholas Afansiev, Kyprian Kern, Anton Kartashev, Basil Zenkovsky and, perhaps the strongest influence on him, the great theologian Sergius Bulgakov. The influence of Bulgakov is evident even in journal entries that are critical as well as in an article that Schmemann later wrote about him and in a remark made toward the end of his own life [2,4]. When asked which of all the intellectuals had the most impact on him, the instantaneous reply was Bulgakov. Married in 1943, he was ordained priest in 1946 and began teaching at St. Sergius. In post-WWII Paris he was exposed to and shaped by the *ressourcement*, the "return-to-the-sources", namely the scriptures, liturgy and writings of early church teachers. Kern and Afanasiev would later establish the liturgical week of study and prayer at St. Sergius, still being held over 60 years later.

Thus, in his earliest publications as well as in his doctoral thesis, one can read the names of not only the emigre scholars who shaped his thinking but of many from the Western churches associated with the "return-to-the-sources": Baumstark, Congar, Brilioth, Botte, Bouyer, Daniélou, Dalmais, Cullman, Rousseau and Dix, among others [4,5]. While devoted to Russian literature and culture, Schmemann resisted complete identification with things Russian. There was a sense of frustration with an essentially ethnic definition of Orthodoxy that eventually led him, as well as John Meyendorff and others, to America. Schmemann came with his family in 1951 and began what would be a long career as a professor and dean of St. Vladimir's Theological Seminary. Here he and Meyendorff, who came a few years later, worked for an indigenous, non-ethnic Orthodox Church in America. After much effort, against much resistance both internationally and at home, the Russian Church granted autocephaly or ecclesiastical autonomy to the former Russian Metropolia in America in 1970. When the seminary moved to suburban Crestwood, NY, in 1962, Schmemann was appointed its dean and he remained in that office until his death on December 13, 1983, the feastday of St. Herman of Alaska. His posthumously published journals, from the last decade of his life, have proved to be a rich account of his personality and thinking [5–7].

Schmemann's principal gift was his vision of "liturgical theology", liturgy as the heart and as the primary theology of the church. Inspired by his teachers, he argued that the church's identity and life could best be seen in the assembling for the Eucharist, assembling for liturgy being the best expression of the church and the life of mission leading from this [8–11]. In this he was influenced both by Bulgakov's eschatological thinking on the church and by Afanasiev's "eucharistic ecclesiology" [12–15]. Yet, in his pursuit of the life of the kingdom of God in church and the liturgy, Schmemann never abandoned the world of literature and politics, of culture, society and historical process [16]. Above all, his keen understanding of the world, his ease in its midst, whether Paris or New York City, his intense delight in the good things of this life were profoundly grounded in the triadic poles of his theology and, indeed, of his own faith and holiness: creation, the fall and redemption.

To listen to Schmemann is to be wonderfully startled by the wealth of his humane learning and thinking. Though his work as a liturgical historian is well known, his work in other areas is impressive, such as his commentary on the history of doctrine, monasticism, schism, and beyond ecclesial subjects, the history of contemporary political movements [17]. Schmemann's assessment of modernity, the society, culture and politics of America and Europe raises more questions than it answers [18–23]. He provided a critical perspective on American society and the place of religion in it. He recognized the social pressure that kept religion influential well into the 1960s but saw, as well, the growing cultural diversity and secularism that would make for great changes. Insightful as some of his America-watching was, his ear was deaf to the civil rights, anti-war, anti-poverty and women's movements. He and his family benefitted greatly from the opportunities of American society, in particular the educational system. Yet his journals show little interest in the expansion of these opportunities or the continuing force of race and sexism. His own conservatism seemed also to gradually diminish his interest in ecumenical work and seemed to distance him further from the mainstream of American life. His colleague John Meyendorff's columns for the church periodical show greater awareness and interest in the intense changes in American life in the 1960s–1980s. Despite something of a retreat into liturgical and ecclesial matters, however, even there one finds great insight ([10], pp. 89–100; [24], pp. 187–89; [25]).

2. Teacher of Tradition

But all that said, Schmemann displayed a remarkably humane and worldly sense of the spiritual life. He was, above all, a teacher. Tapes and the texts transcribed from them and from the thousands of "Sunday Talks" he recorded over the years for Radio Liberty capture his warm, direct speaking [26]. These talks, on the Creed, on the feasts of the liturgical year and on literature and numerous other topics, intended for listeners in the USSR (Soviet Russia) with little knowledge of the faith, are among the most eloquent, humane and beautiful of his writings [3].

Those who knew him recall his pastoral gifts as confessor and counselor. At his funeral, his colleague and friend, Veselin Kesich, eloquently summed up his witness throughout his life and particularly in his terminal illness:

> He was a free man in Christ; he was a man full of joy . . . He taught us a lesson on how, in suffering, the power of the eternal God may be revealed. He taught us a lesson about power in weakness. My dear friends, to teach this particular lesson—power in weakness—is *the* fundamental lesson: that is the Gospel. The Gospel is nothing else but power in weakness. The One who was sacrificed in weakness was raised by the power of God ([27], pp. 41–42).

Schmemann was far from being sentimental. His piety was vibrant, not the antiquarian, stereotypic, formal sort. He served the church vigorously and practically in a number of positions. Not only did he teach at St. Vladimir's Seminary for over 30 years, serving as dean in the last 20, but he was also theological advisor to the synod of bishops and, as noted, was one of the principal architects of the autocephalous status granted to the OCA (Orthodox Church in America) in 1970. He worked as theologian with the Standing Conference of Orthodox Bishops in America (SCOBA), with various domestic and international inter-Orthodox groups for theological education and youth work such as Syndesmos, and the Orthodox Theological Society. He promoted *St. Vladimir's Theological Quarterly*, helped create the seminary's annual summer institute for liturgical and pastoral theology, modeled on the "liturgical weeks" of St. Sergius Institute. The mission of St. Vladimir's Seminary Press, the preeminent English language publisher of Orthodox theology, owes much to his ideals of learning for the whole Church and for the world [28].

Yet it is necessary to say that he met with often bitter resistance and rejection in his own lifetime, from the hierarchy, clergy and laity of his church. In addition, since his death I would say his work has been either politely ignored or contradicted, often diplomatically, without express reference to his name. While his name is still officially honored, his vision is very much in eclipse. While a few of his liturgical renewal efforts have held on, such as frequent, even weekly reception of communion, much of the rest of his efforts are rejected by present practice and rationale. His effort to return baptism to communal celebration, his arguing for saying the prayers of the liturgy aloud and reverently, and his critical ideas on specific rites such as those of burial are not practiced or even discussed as they now are cast as innovations. Especially in his last years, he was extremely critical of what he saw as increasing sectarianism and a rise in clericalism, both rooted in for him, a pseudo-traditionalism among many Orthodox laity and clergy. These now have become strong tendencies across Orthodoxy internationally. The Pentecost 2016 Pan-Orthodox Council in Crete gave many indications of the strength of sectarian fundamentalism rather than open churchliness. The opposition to recognizing marriage between Orthodox and non-Orthodox Christian partners, as well as the extreme resistance to calling other, non-Orthodox communities "churches", since this detracted from Orthodoxy's monopoly on the reality of "church", were the two principal examples, among others [29]. Schmemann's own church body, the Orthodox Church in America, was rocked in the last decade by internal scandal—financial abuse, mismanagement, denial and cover up—yet with no acceptance of responsibility by the leadership or sanctions, the principal perpetrators allowed to retire or disappear to less conspicuous positions. His death and that of his colleague, John Meyendorff, have left a vacuum in the intellectual and spiritual leadership of the Orthodox churches in America. Missing, above all, is the spirit of freedom, joy and love for the world which so characterized both teachers and all of the others profiled in this volume.

Schmemann was also an active intellectual outside Orthodoxy. He lectured at Catholic, Presbyterian and Episcopal seminaries and cathedrals. He contributed articles to an international array of journals and scholarly collections. He was a signer of the 1975 Hartford Statement, originated by Peter Berger and Richard John Neuhaus, highly critical of tendencies with the American mainstream churches and culture, a discerning view of the "culture wars" and erosion of Christian tradition to come. He prepared an insightful essay for the collection that interpreted the statement's intent [30]. It is striking to hear what Schmemann said at the close of this essay in the context of regressive sectarian and traditionalist tendencies today.

> I know that are those Orthodox who affirm and preach that the Orthodox can and must live in the West without any "reference" to the Western culture except that of a total negation, to live in fact as if the West did not exist, for it is totally corrupt, heretical, and sick beyond repair. To achieve this, one must create artificial islands of Greek or Russian or any other Orthodox culture, shut all doors and windows, and cultivate the certitide of belonging to the sacred remnant. What these "super-Orthodox" do not know, of course, is that their attitude reflects precisely the ultimate surrender to that West which they abhor: that in their ideology Orthodoxy is being transformed for the first time into that which it has never been—a *sect*, which is by definition the refusal of the *catholic* vocation of the Church. And there are those who maintain, as I have tried to say, a peaceful coexistence of Orthodoxy with a culture which, in reality, claims the whole man: his soul, his life, and his religion. Both attitudes are ultimately self-destructive ... ([30], pp. 136–37).

In a life filled with both academic and ecclesiastical obligations, Schmemann was nevertheless able to produce a substantial body of writing. His earliest published essays, in Russian Orthodox journals in the late 1940s and early 1950s, already take up such issues as the centrality of Pascha—the feast of the resurrection—the liturgy as the heart of the church, and the church as more than institutional structures, dogmatic and canonical formulations, and national (ethnic) associations ([28], pp. 11–13). His earliest English language articles, from the mid-1950s, begin with the festal cycle of the liturgical year, and emphasize the Church's eucharistic nature [9,11,17,31–35]. Kern and Afanasiev, in particular, influenced him with their indictment of the loss of eucharistic centrality amid accumulated piety, devotional acts, individualism and ecclesial pragmatism [12–14,36]. These two teachers of his were not the only ones to shape his thinking. Despite his tendency to mentioning them and Sergius Bulgakov only rarely in his own writings, the imprint of these three was distinctive throughout his work. Within a few years, Schmemann would be expanding his teachers' judgment not only of this liturgical decline, but of the ecclesial crisis [21–23]. Schmemann may not have always cited them or even agreed with all of their points of view, but he did express much of the same, open and outgoing sense of church characteristic of the faculty of St. Sergius Institute and the larger "Paris School" [37].

3. World as Sacrament, Liturgy as Life

Schmemann was a most discerning critic, but he consistently affirmed the Church's essentials. The finest expressions of these are his volumes on the principal sacraments [9,38,39]. One finds in them what was also expressed in what has been the best known, most widely read of his books, *For the Life of the World*. The recent fiftieth anniversary of the talks Schmemann gave at the National Student Christian Federation assembly in 1963 inspired a historical reassessment of the significance of his perspectives in American church life, as William Mills has shown [40,41]. The liturgy is presented, not as one more thing the Church does, not just her enactment of historical, colorful, symbolic rites, but as the very presence of God among his people and their ascent to the Kingdom of Heaven. In Schmemann's vision, as Aidan Kavanagh argues, the classical principal holds, *(ut) legem credendi lex statuat supplicandi*—"the rule of prayer establishes that of belief" [42–44]. All of time is sanctified in the liturgy. All of human activity is transformed. Every moment in life is one of God's saving and bringing us back: from our burial and resurrection in Baptism, to marriage, the anointing of the sick, and burial. All the material things we need—bread, wine, oil, water, words, touch—are directed back to what they were created to be—good in God's sight and, in the case of humankind, his very image and likeness. The consequence of this life of God and with God in liturgy is made explicit. Time becomes the very "sacrament of the world to come", the eschatological icon of God's saving and reclaiming of his fallen creation ([9], p. 65). From this follows the mission of the Church, to be witnesses of these things, proclaiming the Gospel to all. Schmemann constantly emphasized the *paschal* or resurrectional nature of the church, the liturgy and of Christian living, intensely experienced by numerous holy women and men even into our era, such as Seraphim of Sarov, Maria Skobtsova and Elisabeth Behr-Sigel, among others [45–48]. The utterly "catholic", that is ecumenical and universal, even cosmic vision is fundamental to him.

The liturgy, especially the Eucharist, as the procession, the journey of the people of God into the Kingdom, is pursued carefully [9,25,39]. The missionary thrust of the liturgy, indeed the missionary rationale of the Church, runs through all of his writing. Frank Senn and Gordon Lathrop both echo Schmemann in his examination of the Church's primary and traditional mode of evangelization: the liturgy [49–55].

Schmemann unfolds an expansive, catholic understanding of the liturgy through contemplation of each sacramental element of the eucharistic celebration [39]. In the Eucharist, the Church is assembled by the Holy Spirit to enter and ascend to the Kingdom. This occurs in the whole action of the assembly: by reading, singing, preaching and hearing the Word, by praying for all, by offering in unity the bread, cup and themselves in thanksgiving and remembrance, and by being joined to the Lord and each other in communion in the body and blood of Christ, his life in, with and for the life of the world. Schmemann never loses sight of liturgy then continuing in life, what Mother Maria Skobtsova called "liturgy outside the church walls" ([47], pp. 80–83). In almost every piece of his writing he specifies the connections among liturgy, faith and life for church, world and mission. These connections lay in the three "moments" of salvation history he consistently stressed.

> First, God has created the world; ... To claim that we are God's creation is to affirm that God's voice is constantly speaking within us and saying to us, "And God saw everything that he had made, and behold, it was very good." (Gen 1:31) The Fathers state that even the devil is good by nature and evil only through misuse of his free will. Then there is a second element, inseparable from the first: this world is fallen—fallen in its entirety; it has become the Kingdom of the prince of this world. The Puritan world view, so prevalent within the American society in which I live, assumes that tomato juice is always good and that alcohol is always bad; in effect tomato juice is not fallen. Similarly the television advertisements tell us, "Milk is natural"; in other words, it is not fallen. But in reality tomato juice and milk are equally part of the fallen world, along with everything else. All is created good; all is fallen; and finally—this is our third "fundamental acclamation"—all is redeemed. It is redeemed through the incarnation, the cross, the resurrection and ascension of Christ, and through the gift of the Spirit at Pentecost. Such is the intuition that we receive from God with gratitude and joy: our vision of the world as created, fallen, redeemed. Here is our theological agenda, our key to all the problems which today trouble the world ([10], pp. 98–99).

Seriousness, passion, yet good humor, and, above all, joy pervade this theological vision. In addition there is discernment, too, for perhaps the most prevalent heresy of our day about humanity is described and dismissed here in the earthly terms of liquor, milk and tomato juice! In other places in his writings, Schmemann uses standard American images of wealth, power, and pleasure: skyscrapers, huge shopping centers, big cars, steaks, cocktails and romance. Schmemann's effort, as he often put it, using Johannine language, was to "discern the spirits" of the time and culture, to learn whether they were of God. This sharp scrutiny of the ethos of both the church and the world was always accompanied by the basic vision of creation, fall and redemption. Put another way, he saw the world as sacrament.

> ... in the first chapter of Genesis, we find a clear statement of this sacramental character in the world. God made the world, and then man; and he gave the world to men to eat and drink. The world was God's gift to us, existing not for its own sake but in order to be transformed, to become life, and so to be offered back as man's gift to God ... But sin came, breaking this unity: this was no mere issue of broken rules alone, but rather the loss of a vision, the abandonment of a sacrament. Fallen men saw the world as one thing, secular and profane, and religion as something entirely separate, private, remote and "spiritual". The sacramental sense of the world was lost. Man forgot the priesthood which was the purpose and meaning of his life. He came to see himself as a dying organism in a cold, alien universe ... And so the Eucharist is not simply a way of discharging our duty of thanks to God, although it is that as well. It is not merely one possible relationship to God. It is rather the only possible holding together—in one moment, in one act—of the *whole* truth about God and man. It is the sacrament of the world sinful and suffering, the sky darkened, the tortured Man dying: but it is also the sacrament of the change, His transfiguration, His rising, His Kingdom. In one sense we look back, giving thanks for the simple goodness of God's original gift to us. In another sense we look forward, eschatologically, to the ultimate repair and transfiguration of that gift, to its last consummation in Christ ([31], pp. 223, 225).

Sacrament is hardly just a religious ritual but the transformation of each person, of humankind and of all creation by Christ, through the Spirit, to the glory of the Father. The rule of prayer *is* the rule of faith. The continuous death of fallen humankind is continuously trampled down by the death and rising of Christ. No corner of life is neglected, no aspect of humanity is spared. Everything is touched by Christ: "In the world of the incarnation, nothing 'neutral' remains, nothing can be taken away from the Son of Man" ([31], p. 216).

4. Against the World, for the World

In his evaluation of American society and culture, Schmemann spoke of "secularism," but with a distinctive understanding ([22], pp. 172–75, 183–85; [23], pp. 173–74; [31], pp. 67–84). In a way, he anticipated what most sociologists would later admit they had erred in diagnosing, namely that secularization did not mean the end of religion [56]. For him by no means was secular culture without religion, and only rarely could real anti-religious sentiments be found. On the contrary, America is both diverse and secular and awash with religiosity. But here is where Schmemann is critical of "religion", particularly religion that conforms to the values, ethos and life of Americans. It must meet their needs, console, encourage and generally support what its consumers demand or expect. The purposeful, enlightened religion he criticizes is politically and socially useful. Yet it has little to do with the Gospel or Torah, given its shallowness and functionality. Today, I am certain Schmemann would have recognized that despite the "religious nones" lack of membership in churches or adherence to traditional religious teachings, they nevertheless had a spiritual dimension, the "upper storey" of Solzhenitsyn.

Schmemann also catalogues a variety of "reductions" of the parish, the local community of faith. Some of this criticism is dated, coming from a time decades ago, of much larger, more active congregations. By now, as the 21st century moves into its third decade, the landscape is dramatically different, one of shrinking and disappearing congregations. It is not possible to ask him to comment on a set of circumstances he did not experience or know. That said, he still has valuable things to say. Schmemann objected to the parish primarily defined as a constant fund-raising association, perhaps with strong ethnic or class roots. He surely had in mind the then still very ethnic character of most Eastern Church parishes. He was skeptical about "Sunday" Christianity, an hour or so that inspires, even "entertains" the parish clientele and attracts new members, as well as the priest essentially as administrator-executive and a therapeutic professional. As cutting as some of his attacks on parish life are, I myself believe some are dated and no longer accurate, while others remain discerning. Even though he was never really a parish priest himself in all his years of ministry, he did work within the parish community of St. Vladimir's Seminary chapel ([22], pp. 164–69, 174–75; [23], pp. 171–73, 177–86). His journals indicate not just his work in confession but also in pastoral counseling. His attitude toward both ministry and the ministry is totally free of legalism, clericalism and theological triviality. As with so much else, his humane and open spirit pervades what he says about the personal problems and sufferings of those who sought him out. Standing out is his recognition of the always personal character of Christian faith. Christianity is not equivalent to individual salvation. Thinking that it is has reduced faith to a kind of cosmic insurance policy one pays premiums on throughout life, investing on the "next life". But if paradise is not here in each moment, then the entire project of Christianity is a fraud.

> ... the salvation of the world is announced and *entrusted to each person*, is made a personal vocation and responsibility and ultimately depends on each person ... The whole world is given—in a unique way—to each person and thus in each person it is "saved" or "perishes." Thus in every Saint the world is *saved* and it is fully saved in the one totally fulfilled Person: Jesus Christ ([23], p. 178).

5. Martyria: The Personal Struggle

It is not surprising at all that Schmemann's responses to the very real problems of the church ran provocatively counter to prevailing churchly wisdom, both in his day and now. I would argue that he sounds a great deal like another critic of not only church life and the clergy but of the economic and political systems of power in our world. I mean here the bishop of Rome, Francis. When Schmemann thought of the "churching" of life as he did the renaissance of faith, in the Paris in which he grew up and was educated, it was not having more services or longer ones, not about hanging up more icons and lighting candles before them. Like Mother Maria, he envisioned a transforming, a reintegration of liturgy and life, of faith and everyday activity that is subversive of the strategies of the church growth movement and of every other market-driven tactic for expansion of membership and revenue ([22], p. 178).

Rather than promoting ecclesiastical and ritual pomp, he rather lampooned the "vaudeville" of ecclesiastical headcovering and the lack of connection between so many clerics and ordinary life and people ([5], pp. 284–85). He called for the restoration of real pastoral identity and behavior by bishops and priests. The love for the "holy things" in which we have communion with God and each other should translate into love for our communities, for our neighbors ([22], pp. 175–80; [23], pp. 186–93). He makes it clear that the clergy have been not just the victims but the principal perpetrators of the many "reductions" in the life of the Church. The real encounter with the crisis is not in some church-wide restoration of rules or diocesan program of fundraising, membership growth or revival of patristic literature. The "churching" of which he speaks is a personal encounter with Christ, a personal acceptance of the Gospel and a personal confrontation with oneself, one's neighbors (even in the Church) and with the world. Schmemann notes that his use of the term *martyria* is hardly a rhetorical flourish.

> For if one takes Christianity seriously, be it only for one minute, one knows with certitude that *martyria*, or what the Gospel describes as the narrow way is an absolutely essential and inescapable part of Christian life. And it is a narrow way precisely because it is always a conflict with the "ways of life" of "this world." From the very beginning to become and to be a Christian meant these two things: first, a *liberation* from the world, i.e. from any "reduction" of man, and as such has always been the significance of the Christian rites of initiation. A man is set free in Christ because Christ is beyond and above all "cultures,"

all reductions. The liberation means thus a real possibility to see this world in Christ and to choose a Christian "way of life." In the second place, Christianity has always meant an *opposition* to and a fight with this world—a fight, let me stress it again, which is primarily, if not exclusively, a *personal* fight, i.e., an internal one—with the "old man" in myself, with my own "reduction" of myself to "this world." There is no Christian life without *martyria* and without *asceticism*, this latter term meaning nothing else, fundamentally, but a life of concentrated effort and fight ([23], pp. 179–80).

6. Church: Mission, For the Life of the World

It is perhaps startling to hear such conviction about personal conversion and transformation at the heart of Christian life. Yet Schmemann's perspective was rooted in lived faith and was counter to, even subversive of, hardened, legalistic ideas from his own Orthodox tradition. He was, despite his own political conservatism, a spiritual revolutionary precisely because he was so radical, so aware of authentic tradition and its lived experience. Here one sees the imprint of his teachers. He relentlessly affirmed the conciliar nature of the Church in the face of clerical domination, and struggles about power ([31], pp. 169–70). Over against models of representative democracy and clericalist autocracy, he put forward the icon of ecclesial life, namely the unity-in-diversity and personal distinctions of the Trinity. The Father, Son and Holy Spirit reveal the unity of persons living in obedient, submissive and sacrificial love—of the Son to the Father and to humankind, of the Father to the Son and of the Spirit towards the world. So clericalism, indeed, any other "reduction" of the church's life—legalism, fundamentalism, and the like—is illegitimate and destructive. Both clergy and laity are capable of such anti-ecclesial reductions ([31], pp. 164, 170–78). The clergy can be reduced to elected, hired functionaries or can reduce themselves to religious tyrants. Neither is their true office of pastoral ministry to the flock. Laity can be reduced to fund raisers, administrators, social activists or passive dues-paying members of a voluntary organization, or to a merely political constituency that acts on majority vote. In none of these reductions is the people of God affirmed, the chosen race the royal priesthood and holy nation called out of darkness into God's marvelous light (I Pet 2:9).

Schmemann leans on the 19th century lay Russian theologian Khomiakov on the tendency to reify the church into some *thing*, externalize it as authority, a reality other and thus *alien* to us ([31], pp. 182–85). Perhaps because of the Russian heritage of theological personalism, perhaps also because of the context in postwar Paris of personalism in philosophical and religious thought, Schmemann insisted that there had to be a personal encounter and experience of God and of the kingdom; otherwise, the liturgy and the rest of church and spiritual life would end up as superstition or legalism. Here, he was much in sync with the visions of "churching" life that characterized the Russian Christian Student Movement of which he was part throughout his life, that which inspired Mother Maria and others we have encountered here. His understanding of the personal encounter was expressed as *martyria* and asceticism, personal conversion and transformation and struggle, participation in a communion both human and divine. This is what the liturgy seeks to proclaim and effect ([31], pp. 209–16).

The church is the sacrament of the Kingdom, the "fullness" of God here and now, the "pascha" or passage, through Baptism and the Eucharist, into the Kingdom ([31], p. 212). At the same time, church is "increase and growth in faith and love, knowledge and *koinonia*" ([31], p. 213). So, church is also a "human response to the divine gift, its acceptance and appropriation by man and humanity ([31], p. 212)". As such, the church must always be *simultaneously* "God-centered" and "man or world centered ([31], p. 213)". The church reduces, distorts itself if it becomes only one or the other. It is especially telling, given his concern for liturgy, Schmemann's harsh criticism of its being the object of historical or legal obsession. He wrote an open letter to his bishop about this as well as discussing it in numerous lectures and articles. His journal revealed, years after his death, his awareness of just such obsessions with ritual, clerical dress and appearance and many other efforts to repristinate other times as places in place of living faith. What he wrote over 30 years ago, primarily about the Orthodox Church, is still penetrating, provocative and necessary for the churches, East and West, in America today.

> The Church, the sacrament of Christ, is not a "religious" society of converts, an organization to satisfy the "religious" needs of man. It is *new life* and redeems therefore the whole life, the total being of man. And this whole life of man is precisely the world in which and by which he lives. Through man the Church saves and redeems the world. One can say that "this world" is saved and redeemed every time a man responds to the divine gift, accepts it and lives by it. This does not transform the world into the Kingdom or the society into the Church. The ontological abyss between the *old* and the *new* remains unchanged and cannot be filled in this "aeon." The Kingdom is yet *to come*, and the church is not *in* this world. And yet this Kingdom to come is already present, and the Church is fulfilled *in* this world. They are present not only as "proclamation" but in their very reality, and through the divine *agape*, which is their fruit, they *perform* all the time the same sacramental transformation of the *old* into the *new*, they make possible real action, real "doing" in this world ([31], p. 216).

Schmemann's personal witness and struggle were to "church" life; that is, to connect what one confessed, celebrated, received and prayed to what one did, how one lived. This was the vision of the émigré church and theological school and its teachers in Paris from which he came. Throughout his writings it is important to note that water and bread and wine and oil are not somehow magically endowed with power by a ritual blessing. Rather, the celebration and use of them revealed their inherent purpose—to cleanse, to feed and sustain, to heal. This also held true for everything said in the scriptures, in the prayers and hymns of the services. Often in his journal Schmemann lamented bad translations. But he also spoke of texts that really could no longer be effectively translated and used, much to the disdain of liturgical purists. He ridiculed the exaggerated regard of devotees of "mystical" texts and figures and their unusual, out-of-the-ordinary ways of life, dress and thinking. For this healthy criticism of religious extremism, he was labeled "anti-monastic" and "modernist" by neo-traditional opponents. A noted cleric from the Russian Church Outside Russia, Michael Pomazansky, attacked him for daring to use historical methods in researching and analyzing liturgical texts. Such was secular, non-believing behavior, unfit for texts revered for coming directly for the apostles! In talks about the funeral service he decried the fact that the resurrection was almost absent from the texts and the manner of celebrating, and that the terrors and suffering of the dying and the grieving took up more space than the mercy of God and promise of resurrection life [57].

For him, because of the incarnation, the coming of Christ into human flesh and blood, into time and space, into the creation, then "nothing 'neutral' remains, nothing can be taken from the Son of Man", nothing can be separated or protected or distinguished from God. In a curious, seemingly paradoxical way, everything is of God, of the Kingdom, perhaps one could say, "religious" or many would say today "spiritual", in the deepest, most authentic sense. When Schmemann spoke of the "world as sacrament", this was not mere theological lyricism. He was a man for whom the world was holy, beautiful and worthwhile in itself, even if there was the fall. The liturgical prayers did not produce holy water, holy oil, holy bread and wine, but rather sought to recognize what was nourishing, healing, good in these creatures of God and of our making as well ([9], pp. 14–18, 33–36, 42–43).

In the books and taped talks he left behind there are lively miniatures, small "sacramental" scenes, icons of everyday life. Traveling home on the commuter train, he wonders about all the lives being lived behind the lighted windows of houses he sees from his seat. There is the picture of love revealed in the elderly Parisian couple, sitting silently, hand-in-hand on a park bench in the sunlight of an autumn afternoon ([9], p. 90).

Then there the signs of success and happiness so much sought after—promotion and raise, the luxury car, fine dining, enviable spouse and children and home—all vanishing in the hospital room, on the bed of sickness. There is the comedy that is close to tragedy—religious fanatics interrogating a host on what is in a soup or cake that might be uneatable in the Lenten fast. There are hilarious descriptions of "wannabe" monastics and mystics poring over the *Philokalia* and debating prayer rules, prostrations, and ascetic practices, meticulously pious individuals tracing enormous signs of the cross upon themselves … for all around to see. There are the many idealistic but stressed and extreme seminary students and parish members who unload on him in confession and in pastoral conversation. Schmemann notes the comic yet tragic scene at an international conference on the Eucharist where no one except the celebrating clergy received communion. He recalls the elderly parishioner's question after the joyous services of Easter night: "But what if all this really happened, Father?" He once told a suffering, troubled friend that God was as real and as near as the blades of grass upon which they were sitting in a field [58]; and if God were not that real and that close, he said further, then God was of no use. He was able to befriend the wealthy, intelligent, perennial "seeker", who saw no contradiction in being, at one and the same time, a Christian, Muslim and Buddhist.

Here was a theologian whose reading embraced e.e. cummings, Gide, Julien Green, Léautard, who revered the classics of his beloved Russian literature but who devoured as well biographies, the writings of critics of religion, the daily *New York Times*, numerous periodicals. Nothing truly human was alien to him and this humanity pervaded his theology. At the end of his essay "The World as Sacrament", he summed up his vision and it still is a strong statement of the relationship of faith and life, one that the church, especially the Orthodox Church, needs to reclaim.

> Sacrament is movement, transition, passage, Pascha: Christ knows the way and guides us, going before. The world, condemned in its old nature, revealed as life eternal in its new nature, is still the same world, God's good work. Christ came to save it, not to allow us means of thankful escape before it was discarded as rubbish. Thoughts of the "life to come" can be misleading. In a sense, we have no other world to live in but this, although the mode of our occupying it, our whole relationship to space and time … will be very different when we are risen again in Christ … Our lives are congested and noisy. It is easy to think of the church and the sacraments as competing for our attention with the other world of daily life, leading us off into some other life—secret, rarified, remote. We might do better to think of that practical daily world as something incomprehensible and unmanageable unless and until we can approach it sacramentally through Christ. Nature and the world are otherwise beyond our grasp; time also, time that carries all things away in a meaningless flux, causing men to despair unless they see in it the pattern of God's action … we should concentrate upon this world lovingly because it is full of God, because by way of the Eucharist we find Him everywhere … ([25]; [31], pp. 226–27; [59]).

Conflicts of Interest: The author declares no conflict of interest.

References

1. Alexander Schmemann. *Foreword to the Russian Edition of Introduction to Liturgical Theology.* Translated by Alexis Vinogradov. Paris: YMCA Press, 1961.
2. Alexander Schmemann. "Trois Images." *Le Messager Orthodoxe I* 57 (1972): 2–20.
3. Protopresbyter Alexander Schmemann, and Besedi na Radio. *Svoboda.* Edited by Helen Dorman. Moscow: St. Tikhon's Humanities University, 2009.
4. Alexander Schmemann. *Introduction to Liturgical Theology.* Translated by Ashleigh E. Moorhouse. Crestwood: St. Vladimir's Seminary Press, 1966.
5. Alexander Schmemann. *The Journals of Father Alexander Schmemann 1973–1983.* Edited and Translated by Juliana Schmemann. Crestwood: St. Vladimir's Seminary Press, 2000.
6. Alexander Schmemann. *Dnievniki (1973–1983).* Moscow: Russkii Put', 2005.
7. Alexander Schmemann. *Journal (1973–1983).* Translated by Anne Davidenkoff, Anne Kichilov and René Marichal. Edited by Nikita Struve. Paris: Éditions des Syrtes, 2009.
8. Aidan Kavanagh. *On Liturgical Theology.* New York: Pueblo, 1984.
9. Alexander Schmemann. *For the Life of the World.* Crestwood: St. Vladimir's Seminary Press, 1973.

10. Alexander Schmemann. *Liturgy and Tradition*. Edited by Thomas Fisch. Crestwood: St. Vladimir's Seminary Press, 1990.
11. Alexander Schmemann. "Liturgical Theology: Its Task and Method." *St. Vladimir's Theological Quarterly* 1 (1957): 16–27.
12. Nicholas Afanasiev. *Trapeza Gospodnia, (The Lord's Supper)*. Paris: YMCA Press, 1952.
13. Nicholas Afanasiev. "The Church Which Presides in Love." In *The Primacy of Peter*. Edited by John Meyerdorff. Crestwood: St. Vladimir's Seminary Press, 1992, pp. 91–143.
14. Nicholas Afanasiev. *The Church of the Holy Spirit*. Translated by Vitaly Permiakov. Edited by Michael Plekon. Notre Dame: University of Notre Dame Press, 2007.
15. Aidan Nichols. *Theology in the Russian Diaspora: Church, Fathers and Eucharist in Nikolai Afanas'ev (1893–1966)*. Cambridge: Cambridge University Press, 1989.
16. Alexander Schmemann. "'On Solzhenitsyn,' 'A Lucid Love,' and 'Reflections on the Gulag Archipelago'." In *Aleksandr Solzhenitsyn: Critical Essays*. Edited by John B. Dunlop, Richard Haugh and Alexis Klinoff. New York: Collier, 1979, pp. 28–40, 382–92, 515–26.
17. Alexander Schmemann. *The Historical Road of Eastern Orthodoxy*. Translated by Lydia Kesich. Crestwood: St. Vladimir's Seminary Press, 1977.
18. Peter L. Berger. *A Rumor of Angels*. New York: Anchor-Doubleday, 1990.
19. Peter L. Berger. *The Heretical Imperative*. New York: Anchor-Doubleday, 1979.
20. Peter L. Berger. *A Far Glory*. New York: Free Press, 1992.
21. Alexander Schmemann. "Problems of Orthodoxy in America: The Canonical Problem." *St. Vladimir's Theological Quarterly* 8 (1964): 67–85.
22. Alexander Schmemann. "Problems of Orthodoxy in America: The Liturgical Problem." *St. Vladimir's Theological Quarterly* 8 (1964): 164–85.
23. Alexander Schmemann. "Problems of Orthodoxy in America: The Spiritual Problem." *St. Vladimir's Theological Quarterly* 9 (1965): 171–93.
24. Bruce Morrill. "Review. The Journals of Father Alexander Schmemann (1973–1983)." *Worship* 76 (2002): 187–89.
25. Michael Plekon. "'The world as sacrament': The world in Fr. Alexander Schmemann's vision." *Logos* 50 (2009): 429–39.
26. Alexander Schmemann. *The Celebration of Faith*. 3 Vols. Translated by John A. Jillions. Crestwood: St. Vladimir's Seminary Press, 1974, 1991, 1994.
27. Veselin Kesich. "Freedom and Joy." *St. Vladimir's Theological Quarterly* 28 (1984): 41–42.
28. Paul Garrett. "Schmemann bibliography." *St. Vladimir's Theological Quarterly* 28 (1984): 11–26.
29. Paul Gavriyuk. "Historic Orthodox Council Meets Despite Absence of Four Churches." 2016. Available online: http://americamagazine.org/issue/historic-orthodox-council-meets-despite-absence-four-churches (accessed on 24 October 2016).
30. Alexander Schmemann. "That East and West Yet May Meet." In *Against the World, For the World*. Edited by Peter L. Berger and Richard John Neuhaus. New York: Seabury, 1976, pp. 126–37.
31. Alexander Schmemann. *Church, World, Mission*. Crestwood: St. Vladimir's Seminary Press, 1979, pp. 7–24, 193–208.
32. Alexander Schmemann. "Pentecost, the Feast of the Church." *St. Vladimir's Theological Quarterly* 1 (1953): 38–42.
33. Alexander Schmemann. "The Eucharist and the Doctrine of the Church." *St. Vladimir's Theological Quarterly* 2 (1954): 7–12.
34. Alexander Schmemann. "The Mystery of Easter." *St. Vladimir's Theological Quarterly* 2 (1954): 16–22.
35. Alexander Schmemann. "The Sacrament of Baptism." *The Word* 1 (1957): 36–40.
36. Kyprian Kern. *Evkharistia*. Paris: YMCA Press, 1947.
37. Antoine Arjakovsky. *The Way: Religious Thinkers of the Russian Emigration in Paris and Their Journal 1925–1940*. Translated by Jerry Ryan. Edited by John A. Jillions and Michael Plekon. Notre Dame: University of Notre Dame Press, 2013.
38. Alexander Schmemann. *Of Water and the Spirit*. Crestwood: St. Vladimir's Seminary Press, 1974.
39. Alexander Schmemann. *The Eucharist: Sacrament of the Kingdom*. Translated by Paul Kachur. Crestwood: St. Vladimir's Seminary Press, 1988.

40. William C. Mills. "Alexander Schmemann's For the Life of the World: A Retrospective." *Logos* 54 (2013): 199–228.
41. William C. Mills. *Church, World and Kingdom*. Chicago: Hillenbrand, 2012.
42. Aidan Kavanagh. *Elements of Rite*. New York: Pueblo, 1994.
43. Robert F. Taft. "The Liturgical Enterprise Twenty-Five Years after Alexander Schmemann (1921–1983): The Man and His Heritage." *St. Vladimir's Theological Quarterly* 53 (2009): 163–64.
44. André Lossky, Cyrille Sollugub, and Daniel Struve, eds. *La joie du Royaume*. Paris: YMCA Press, 2012.
45. Saint Herman. *Little Russian Philokalia, Volume I: St. Seraphim of Sarov*. Platina: St. Herman Press, 1991.
46. Sergei Hackel. *Pearl of Great Price: The Life of Maria Skobtsova*. Crestwood: St. Vladimir's Seminary Press, 1980.
47. Maria Skobtsova. *Mother Maria Skobtsova: Essential Writings*. Translated by Richard Pevear and Larissa Volonkhonsky. Maryknoll: Orbis, 2003.
48. Olga Lossky. *Towards the Endless Day: A Life of Elisabeth Behr-Sigel (1907–2005)*. Translated by Jerry Ryan. Edited by Michael Plekon. Notre Dame: University of Notre Dame Press, 2010.
49. Frank Senn. *The Witness of the Worshipping Community*. Mahwah: Paulist Press, 1993.
50. Frank Senn. *Christian Liturgy: Catholic and Evangelical*. Philadelphia: Fortress, 1997.
51. Frank Senn. *Embodied Liturgy*. Philadelphia: Fortress, 2016.
52. David W. Fagerberg. *Theologia Prima*. Chicago: Hillenbrand, 2007.
53. Gordon W. Lathrop. *Holy Things*. Philadelphia: Fortress Press, 1998.
54. Gordon W. Lathrop. *Holy People*. Philadelphia: Fortress Press, 2006.
55. Gordon W. Lathrop. *Holy Ground*. Philadelphia: Fortress Press, 2009.
56. Peter L. Berger. *The Many Altars of Modernity*. Berlin and Boston: DeGruyter, 2014.
57. Alexander Schmemann. *The Liturgy of Death*. Edited by Alexis Vinogradov. Crestwood: St. Vladimir's Seminary Press, 2016.
58. Michael Plekon. *Uncommon Prayer*. Notre Dame: University of Notre Dame Press, 2016.
59. Michael Plekon. *The World as Sacrament*. Collegeville: Liturgical Press, 2017.

MDPI AG

St. Alban-Anlage 66

4052 Basel, Switzerland

Tel. +41 61 683 77 34

Fax +41 61 302 89 18

http://www.mdpi.com

Religions Editorial Office

E-mail: religions@mdpi.com

http://www.mdpi.com/journal/religions

www.ingramcontent.com/pod-product-compliance
Lightning Source LLC
Chambersburg PA
CBHW051314020426
42333CB00028B/3332